THE

DECADENT

IMAGINATION

THE
DECADENT
IMAGINATION
1880-1900

JEAN PIERROT

Translated by
Derek Coltman

The University of Chicago Press
CHICAGO AND LONDON

JEAN PIERROT is professor in the Faculty of Letters of the Université de Rouen. He is the author of several scholarly articles and two previous books: *Edition commenteé du Lorenzaccio d'Alfred de Musset* and *Enthologie thématique sur le rêve de Milton aux Surréalistes.*

THE UNIVERSITY OF CHICAGO PRESS, CHICAGO 60637
THE UNIVERSITY OF CHICAGO PRESS, LTD., LONDON

LIBRARY OF CONGRESS CATALOGING IN PUBLICATION DATA

Pierrot, Jean.
The decadent imagination, 1880–1900.

Originally presented as the 2nd part of the author's
thesis (doctoral—University of Paris IV, 1974) under
title: Marveilleux et fantastique.
Includes bibliographical references and index.
1. French literature—19th century—History and
criticism. 2. Decadence (Literary movement) I. Title.
PQ298.P5   1981   840'.9'008   81-4828
ISBN 0-226-66822-3   AACR2

CONTENTS

CONTENTS

PREFACE

This Publication Originally Formed the Second Part of a Thesis, written for my doctorate under the supervision of Mme M.-J. Durry, and presented to the University of Paris IV on 27 April 1974.

In that thesis, entitled *Merveilleux et fantastique: Une Histoire de l'imaginaire dans la prose française du Romantisme à la Décadence (1830–1900),* and reproduced in offset by the thesis reproduction department of the University of Lille III in 1975, I attempted to indicate and isolate the presence and development, during the course of the nineteenth century, of a number of imaginative currents and tendencies, sometimes linked with the "tale of mystery and imagination" yet differing from it in both technique and coloration. I concentrated particularly on the use of mythical and legendary themes, dream narratives, texts devoted to the effects of drugs on the imagination, which remained fashionable throughout the century, and lastly on what, influenced by the work of Gaston Bachelard, I termed "elemental reverie," which consists in the free play of the imagination upon the great natural kingdoms, or upon nature's primordial elements.

I felt that I was able to show how these imaginative currents, preceding and paving the way for surrealism, achieved their full flowering at the end of the century in what I have termed the decadent imagination, in order to distinguish it from the symbolist movement, with which it has many affinities while failing to coincide with it exactly. This then led me on to attempt a further task—that of describing the vision of the world and the esthetic that underlay the creativity of so many artists of that time, painters as well as writers—and to use pictorial as well as literary examples in my analyses.

That this period, certainly one of the richest and most full of ferment in the history of French artistic creation, despite producing few indisputable masterpieces, deserves more sustained attention than has been accorded it hitherto is confirmed by a number of recent events: for example the recent exhibitions in Paris devoted to symbolist painting (*Le Symbolisme*

en Europe, Grand Palais, May–July 1976), and to Puvis de Chavannes
(Grand Palais, November 1976 –February 1977.) The publication of this
book therefore represents an attempt to make a modest contribution to a
better understanding of the literature and art of this period.

PART I FOUNDATIONS OF THE DECADENT IMAGINATION

1 THE DECADENT ERA

FROM THE VIEWPOINT OF FRENCH POLITICAL HISTORY, THE LAST TWENTY years of the nineteenth century constitute a fairly clearly defined period and form a coherent whole. After the double trauma of the Franco-Prussian War and the Paris Commune, these two decades saw the definitive establishment of the Republic and the republican institutions in France, together with the promulgation of a whole battery of laws that progressively brought the new political ideal further and further into the realm of reality. From now on, and for a relatively long period, the nation was to enjoy a certain stability, apart from occasional hiccups such as the financial crises of 1884, the unrest linked with Boulangism in 1888–89, or the Panama scandal. Later, however, during the final years of the century, with the Dreyfus affair, that stability was jeopardized by a major crisis that shook the national consensus and set Catholics against anticlericals, *revanchards* against pacifists, partisans of law and order against partisans of truth and justice, conservative right against liberal left. The results of this deep rift, a rift that the high society jinks and goings-on of the Belle Epoque as the century ended may have masked but did not cure, continued to be felt in a more or less subterranean way until the outbreak of war in 1914.

If we turn from the realm of politics to that of literature and the other arts, however, the panorama becomes much less clear-cut. In poetry, the first decade after the proclamation of the new republic was dominated by the figure of Victor Hugo. After his return from exile right up until his death in 1885, his preeminence was scarcely even contested, while at the same time those poets then already dubbed the Parnassians—Leconte de Lisle, Coppée, Banville, Dierx, and a few more—were also rapidly rising to fame and could claim before long to be the dominant school. The masters of the generation after theirs, on the other hand, were still being paid scarcely any attention at all: Mallarmé, although he had lived in Paris since 1871, published very little and remained totally unknown to the

3

reading public in general; Verlaine, after his two years of prison in Belgium, was to spend several months in England, and even after his return to France did not make contact with Parisian literary circles again until 1882. As for Rimbaud, whose two major works, *Les Illuminations* and *Une Saison en enfer*, would not be published until 1886, he had already deserted literature for good in about 1875 and later left Europe altogether, so that the majority of those who might have met him during his brief visits to Paris in 1870 and 1871 were to suppose him dead.

In the field of prose fiction, the main phenomenon during those same years, from 1870 to 1880, was the rise of naturalism. In 1871, Zola began publication of his Rougon-Macquart series, which was to continue appearing until 1893, and, gradually, along with Flaubert and the Goncourt brothers, he was to become the center of a growing constellation of younger novelists, so that by 1877 it had become possible for such gatherings as the famous Trapp dinner to take place.[1] Huysmans, born in 1848, published his first novel, *Marthe: Histoire d'une fille*, in 1876; the same year *La République des Lettres* began its publication of Léon Hennique's *Les Hauts Faits de M. de Ponthault;* while Henri Céard and Maupassant were already writing their first works. The naturalist movement, which claimed to be a reaction against the insipid novels published under the imprint of the *Revue des Deux Mondes* and written by such authors as Octave Feuillet and Victor Cherbuliez, reached its peak in 1880, with the publication of the *Soirées de Médan* and the press campaign mounted by Zola to promulgate his theories and ideas.

After 1880, however, everything was to be thrown back into the melting pot. At the very moment when they had achieved such success with an ever vaster public, both the Parnassian and the naturalist movements were to encounter violent opposition from newcomers on the scene, while also being weakened by growing internal divergences. As far as naturalism was concerned, for example, by 1881 Huysmans had already begun writing *A Rebours*, and its appearance in 1884 not only began his break with Zola but also constituted the manifesto of a new esthetic; Maupassant, though continuing to publish numerous novellas and stories in a variety of periodicals, was already turning in an increasingly different direction from the naturalists, as his later novels clearly show; while with *Un Caractère*, published in 1887, Léon Hennique had already begun turning his attention to various phenomena brought to the fore by the rise of spiritualism. This fragmentation of the naturalist movement was to be made abruptly apparent after the publication of *La Terre*—a further instalment of the Rougon-Macquart saga—by the appearance in 1887 of a violent manifesto against Zola signed by five of his erstwhile disciples. Meanwhile, in the field of poetry, the decade between 1880 and 1890 was characterized by the emergence of a whole series of new trends, the history of which has been well documented and which have come to be denoted by the general term symbolism.[2]

Symbolism or Decadence?

The generally adopted view of developments in French poetry during the late nineteenth century is that the emergence of symbolism proper some time in 1885 or 1886—and specifically with the publication of the famous literary manifesto by Moréas in *Le Figaro,* and the polemic it provoked[3]—was preceded and prepared by a seven or eight-year transitional decadent period, the distinguishing features of which faded away once the symbolist doctrine had been definitively formulated.[4] This limited view of decadence as merely an early and gestatory stage of symbolism is put forward and developed, in particular, by Guy Michaud. His classic interpretation presents decadence as a merely negative reaction to naturalism and Parnassianism, in contrast to the positive stance taken by symbolism.[5] As symbolism took over from decadence, Michaud says, the expression of sadness and melancholy was succeeded by that of joy in life,[6] vague emotionalism was replaced by the intellectual rigor of a coherent doctrine,[7] and Verlaine was correspondingly ousted by Mallarmé as the preponderant influence. Finally, the introversion of a self imprisoned within its own closed world was succeeded by the discovery of a higher reality at once impersonal and general in character.[8]

Such a point of view seems to me far too restrictive, and on two counts. First, even on the level of poetic development alone, the decadent trend during the last twenty years of the century was much less transitory and much less negative than such a hypothesis might suggest. The shift from decadence into symbolism that is seen as occurring round about 1886 was undoubtedly much less perceptible and much less radical in reality than is generally claimed. It is true that Mallarmé did begin in that year to have a stronger influence over a certain number of young poets, such as René Ghil, Moréas, Henri de Régnier, and Vielé-Griffin, and also that certain others, proclaiming themselves direct disciples of Verlaine and advocating an expression of man's inmost nature, did stand somewhat aloof from the rest; but the fact remains that there was never, properly speaking, to be a "school of Mallarmé." Amid the welter of short-lived magazines and manifestoes of those years, disagreements were to proliferate with amazing rapidity, and the transition from a negating pessimism, allied with skepticism and sadness, to an optimism based upon adhesion to a clear and coherent metaphysical doctrine remained an exceptional phenomenon, even among the most assiduous visitors to Mallarmé's "Tuesdays" in the rue de Rome. The term symbolism, although it did serve as a rallying point for a certain number of writers in the 1880s, and even more so in the '90s, also remained a vague word, as the difficulties experienced by those who have tried to present a precise definition of it make abundantly clear.[9] The gospel of "correspondences," the importance of music, the use of free verse, a constant concern with technical detail, philosophical idealism, a predilection for the world of dream and legends, and, lastly, an abundance of works with double meanings, these are trends that all coexisted without ever really combining to form a single very coherent doctrine, or certainly not one that was shared by all. The very confusion surrounding the word idealism, to which we shall have occasion to return, fed a great many misunderstandings, since it covered such different trends: transcendental idealism that denied man any possibility of knowing the external world, thus imprisoning him in the cage of solipsism; belief that the world possesses an inherent rationality expressible by language; and the confused reveries or suspect practices of those engaged in various forms of occultism.

Moreover, although there were undoubtedly certain writers who, in reaction against the inevitably pejorative overtones of the adjective "decadent" with which the national press was labeling everyone indiscriminately at the time, did prefer from 1886 onward to use the term symbolist, any entente that may have existed among them was certainly very short-lived. René Ghil, whose *Traité du verbe* was honored with an important preface by Mallarmé when it appeared in 1886, was soon to plunge into the cul de sac of pure verbal juggling, a mechanical application of the theory of correspondences quite alien to the metaphysical ambitions of the master. Only a few short months after the *Pèlerin passioné* banquet, which has been regarded as the apogee of the symbolist movement.[10] Moréas, in whose honor the banquet was given, broke with the symbolist movement in order to found his own "Roman School." Further signs of dissension continued to become apparent during the ensuing years, such as Retté's attack on Mallarmé in 1894, the founding of naturalism in 1895, and numerous other new movements that also came into being at that time, in either the capital or the provinces.[11] Mallarmé himself never set out the metaphysical ideas underlying his poetic ideal in any clear-cut and systematic way, in either his articles or his prefaces, any more than he presumably did orally during his Tuesday salons. We know that he had a repugnance for dogmatism, and the allusive nature of his conversation would scarcely have permitted any clear-cut logical conclusions. If one needs proof of the fact that there was no one among his contemporaries, even among the most assiduous of the faithful—with the possible exception of Valéry—who was ever able to arrive at a complete and total vision of his ideas, than one need only observe the errors and gaps to be found in the commentaries of Téodor de Wyzewa, who was not only one of the period's most intelligent critics but also a great admirer of Mallarmé.[12]

Moreover, where poetry is concerned, it is certainly untrue to claim that all specifically decadent inspiration vanished with the appearance, during 1885 and 1886, of the term symbolism, and with the growing preponderance of Mallarmé's influence over that of Verlaine. In the verse collections published by Mallarmé's close disciples up until 1895—for instance Henri de Régnier, Stuart Merrill, and Vielé-Griffin—the nature of the poetic inspiration changes only slightly, almost imperceptibly: the emotional tone remains in general fairly melancholy, and decadent imagery, based on dreams and legends, is still predominant. The transition from sadness to a certain ardor and joy in life does not occur until relatively late, and then in the work of poets outside the inner circle of Mallarmé's most faithful disciples, such as Saint-Pol-Roux's *Les Reposoirs de la procession* of 1893, Verhaeren's *Les Campagnes hallucinées* of 1893 and *Les Villes tentaculaires* of 1895, poems by Retté or Francis Jammes, or Paul Fort's *Ballades*. Moreover, two of the most significant works deriving from the decadent poetic esthetic did not appear until 1889: Retté's *Les Cloches dans la nuit,* and Maeterlinck's *Serres chaudes.* Even Guy Michaud himself recognizes that poets such as Albert Samain, for example, went on developing decadent themes right up until the last years of the century.[13] So that although Mallarmé's influence did indeed lead the trend toward a poetic theory based on a more coherent and ambitious metaphysical foundation, although, from 1890 onward, the majority of avant-garde writers did in fact prefer to be called symbolists rather than decadents, the fact remains that right up until the end of the century, until the resurgence of a love for life and the reconciliation with the modern world that were to characterize the next era, the decadent sensibility continued to imbue the entire poetic movement in France.

Above all, however, it would be committing a serious error to regard the decadent movement as being merely a poetic period. In fact, decadence constitutes the common denominator of all the literary trends that emerged during the last two decades of the nineteenth century. Far from being limited just to poetry, decadence exercised possibly its widest and most durable influence in the field of prose writing, a fact that has led certain critics to regard it as a movement in the field of prose parallel to that which was to come to its full flowering in poetry as symbolism. Certainly, after the naturalist thrust between 1870 and 1880, decadence did leave its imprint on a large proportion of the fiction being produced, and was at the source of a whole spate of novellas and tales published during the nineties in such periodicals as *L'Echo de Paris* and *Le Journal*. In the field of the novel proper, the year 1884 alone saw the appearance, for example, not merely of *A Rebours*, which was subsequently to be regarded as the gospel of the new esthetic, but also of two works as significant as *Le Crépuscule des dieux* by Elémir Bourges, and *Le Vice suprême* by Joséphin Péladan. The last fifteen years of the century also brought a rich harvest of stories from authors such as Rachilde, Jean Lorrain, Rémy de Gourmont, Marcel Schwob, Dujardin, Georges Rodenbach, and Bernard Lazare.

It would also be an error to draw the boundaries between the various literary currents vying for attention during these years too sharply. Even between the naturalists and the symbolists, on the surface apparently so far apart, there were also very real affinities. Although their end points were diametrically opposite, since the former delighted in the minute description of life's seamier aspects and concentrated their attention on the degradation of people in the humblest social categories, whereas the latter retreated into an inner paradise furnished with the utmost luxury and refinement, oddly enough their starting points were basically one and the same: a fundamentally pessimistic conception of life. In order to illustrate the way in which the two coexisted, and until a fairly late date, in a state of relative symbiosis, one needs only to instance the contents of various literary magazines appearing during the last quarter of the century in whose pages the two schools quite evidently cohabited quite happily. One of the most celebrated of these periodicals was *La République des Lettres*, edited by Catulle Mendès, which appeared from December 1875 until June 1877. *La République* in fact published poems by Parnassian writers such as Leconte de Lisle, Heredia, Bouchor, Dierx, and Banville, pieces by Flaubert, Zola's *L'Assommoir*, works by younger naturalists such as Maupassant, Huysmans, and Hennique, poems by Anatole France, Paul Bourget, and Emile Goudeau, a number of stories by Villiers de l'Isle-Adam, and a number of works by Poe. The same eclecticism is to be found in the *Revue littéraire et artistique* which, between 1879 and 1882, despite a general bias in favor of the Parnassians, also defended the naturalists, published texts by Huysmans, articles by Gabriel Sarrazin on Rossetti and Swinburne, pieces by Wagner, and, again, one of Poe's tales.

Lastly, no periodical of the 1880s was more successful in collating the various avant-garde literary currents of the time within its pages than the *Revue indépendante*, which succeeded in grouping the epoch's most important writers together in issues whose literary quality was to remain unequaled—unless by the *Mercure de France* after 1890—up until the end of the century. For a number of years it was the true crossroads of modern

French literature, and it would be impossible to exaggerate its importance.[14] Like *La République des Lettres*, it kept open house to the most varied of schools and trends. Within its pages one finds texts by Goncourt and Zola, poems by Mallarmé,[15] who was also its dramatic critic throughout 1887, and stories by Villiers de l'Isle-Adam.[16] Huysmans is represented by *En Rade*,[17] as well as a variety of essays and art reviews, dealing in particular with the salons of 1884 and 1887, and Laforgue by his *Chroniques parisiennes*, written during the months just before his death, and also by *Pan et la Syrinx*, one of his *Moralités légendaires*.[18] In addition, one also finds texts on Wagner,[19] a fragment of De Quincey's *Suspiria de Profundis* in translation,[20] an important article by Gabriel Sarrazin on the Pre-Raphaelites,[21] extracts from Francis Poictevin's *Paysages*,[22] and, finally, in serial form, Edouard Dujardin's novel *Les Lauriers sont coupés*, often regarded as the very first example of the stream of consciousness technique.[23] Its chief literary critic, moreover, was the brilliant Téodor de Wyzewa. Endowed with an encyclopedic culture, and invariably well informed about all the latest developments in the field of poetry, we find him writing many articles on Mallarmé, expressing a lively admiration for the work of Villiers de l'Isle-Adam, and also commenting on the appearance of the Russian novel on the French scene. Reading his pieces today, one finds in them a detailed and faithful reflection of the literary scene of his day and also certain essential and recurring themes of the decadent esthetic.

The Decadent Esthetic

I call decadence an esthetic because the trends I have just outlined, whose foundations had been laid, as we saw, during the previous period, were not confined to literature. They also bore fruit in the work of contemporary painters such as Gustave Moreau and Odilon Redon, left their mark on the "symbolist" painters of the nineties, whether French like Maurice Denis and the Nabis or Belgian like Khnopff and Ensor, and finally led to the renewal of European art constituted first by Art Nouveau and then by expressionism. In the context of the history of the imagination, the decadent esthetic thus constitutes a major stage in the continuous development that had its source in romantic "fancy" and led eventually to the equivocal wonderland of surrealism. It can also be seen to be an accentuation of the tendencies we have already discerned in writers such as Baudelaire, Flaubert, or Gautier in the preceding period.

It is based, firstly, on a somewhat pessimistic conception of human existence, seen as subject to the pitiless necessities of a physical, physiological, and social determinism that holds man in thrall to the laws of heredity, the species to those of evolution, and the exceptional individual to the law of the majority decreed by democracy. Religious faith has ceased to be anything other than a nostalgic memory; love is merely an unconscious subjection to an instinct aimed solely at the survival of the species. Nature, far from being the attentive and responsive witness conceived by the romantics, is an unfeeling and pitiless mechanism. The best thing for us to do therefore, surrounded by such anguish and sadness, though not without a certain feeling of guilt, is to attempt to escape from that nature, to reject the biological laws of our species as far as is possible, and to hold ourselves aloof from society. Influenced by this conception of life, artists were to shut themselves away inside their inner worlds, straining to perceive the slightest tremor from their secret depths, often terrified by the strange or monstrous feelings that could suddenly erupt into the light of day; and in this anguished quest many were to discover, even before Freud, the realities of the unconscious. They were to seek for escape from the boredom and banality of everyday life through exquisite refinements of sensation. Convinced that the material universe is nothing but an appearance, and that our consciousness can never apprehend anything but its own ideas or representations, they were to make of imagination a kind of higher power by means of which the world's reality could be transformed. They were to create secret, inner paradises for themselves, peopled with creatures of legend, where they could cultivate the dream. They were to reinforce the work of the imagination either by stimulating it with skillful simulacra that deceived the senses with agreeable illusions, or else by using drugs that modified its action. Contemptuous of contemporary reality, they were to turn their gaze backward toward certain favored and prestigious past eras, such as that of the Roman decadence or legendary Byzantium, or else, attempting a sort of flight into the future, they were to proclaim their allegiance to the most spectacular aspects of modernity, such as the new face of the industrial city, or machinery. By throwing themselves heart and soul into this desperate quest for the new, the rare, the strange, the refined, the quintessential in everything, or for the exceptional—terms that recur constantly in the writing of the time—they were to come eventually to feel that they had pushed literature to its furthest limits, that they had dethroned life and put art in its place, thereby, for a while at least, rendering it bearable, despite the risk to their physical, nervous, and mental health. In retrospect, we know that the decadent era proper was to produce few indisputable masterpieces, and a majority of mediocre works that are sometimes difficult even to read today, as a result of their excessively specialized vocabulary. Nevertheless, by dissociating art once and for all from the goal that had always been assigned it—the faithful imitation of nature regarded as the supreme norm—the decadent period does constitute an essential line of cleavage between the classical esthetic and the modern esthetic.

In working out this esthetic, and in making their contemporaries conscious of these new trends, two writers in particular played an essential part: Paul Bourget and Oscar Wilde.

Theoreticians of Decadence: Paul Bourget

Between 1873, when he first came to Paris, and the moment, after the success of *Cruelle Enigme*— published in the *Nouvelle Revue* of 1 October 1884—when he finally turned to exploiting a type of novel dependent solely upon psychological analysis within the narrow confines of fashionable society (a genre that was to become his specialty and make him one of the most adulated authors of his day), Paul Bourget played an immeasureable literary role.[24] The proliferation of his connections in the most varied literary circles, the storehouse of knowledge he had acquired by his extensive reading, and the acuity of his critical intelligence were to make him the most faithful sounding board we have of contemporary esthetic sensibility. It was a sensibility of which he in fact might be called the midwife, and whose most important dogmas he was frequently the first to formulate. As early as 1876, he was the first to revive the heritage handed down by Baudelaire and relaunch the very term decadence, when he wrote: "We accept, without humility as without pride, this terrible word decadence."[25]

His education completed, and having made his way to Paris, Bourget for several years earned his living by teaching in a private school. It was not long, however, before he found his way into the capital's literary circles, where his career soon began to excite interest. After working for a short while for the *Revue des Deux Mondes*, he achieved critical acclaim with a collection of poems, *La Vie inquiète*, published in 1875. Then, in 1878, came *Edel*, a novel in verse, mostly autobiographical in content, and the first appearance in print of the decadent hero. In it, Bourget analyzes a consciousness at once avid for sensual refinements, afflicted by angst and sadness, and searching for a way of escape from a reality that offers nothing to fulfil the needs of either the intelligence or the heart. In one passage, for example, in which the influence of Baudelaire reaches almost caricatural proportions, Bourget evokes the spiritual fate of modern poets:

> Frenzied, haunted by guilty desires,
> Spurred on by that harsh and dismal rider Spleen,
> Driving themselves on in desperation
>   to refine their hearts,
> Searching for a new ideal, finding the strange,
> Imagining that man forever sleeps, forever eats,
> Upon the brink of vice, or worse,
> Of madness.[26]

It was at this stage that he was taken up by the Parnassians. Banville and Leconte de Lisle invited him to their homes, he became a friend of Coppée, Sully-Prudhomme, and Heredia, and four of his poems appeared in the third issue of *Le Parnasse contemporain* in 1876. Simultaneously, however, he also became a close friend of Barbey d'Aurevilly, whom he met that same year and with whom he often spent his evenings. It was to Barbey that he was to owe his sense of the artist's aristocratic vocation, his tendency toward both literary and personal dandyism, and perhaps, though his expressed opinions at this time were those of a nonbeliever, the first seeds of his future spiritual development. At the same time he was also contributing to a number of literary magazines, such as *Le Réveil littéraire et artistique, Le Siècle littéraire, La Vie littéraire,* and *La République des Lettres.* It was as a result of his connection with the last of these publications, renowned as we noted earlier for its eclecticism, that he came into contact with the naturalists. He became friendly with Maupassant, and in late 1876 met Zola, of whose works he wrote sympathetic reviews and whose ideas he championed in a long series of articles that continued up until late 1881. He even began to draft a novella of his own at this period dealing with the harsh life of seamen from a naturalist viewpoint.[27] He also enjoyed visiting the Goncourt studio at Auteuil. Indeed, after Fromentin's death, Edmond de Goncourt was to add Bourget's name to his will for a time as one of the prospective members of the Goncourt Academy.

In 1880, he found a platform worthy of his critical gifts and ambition in the daily *Le Parlement,* which for three years provided him with space in its columns for twice-weekly articles, while he also contributed spasmodically to *La Vie moderne* and *Le Gaulois.* It was at this period too that he published in Juliette Adam's *Nouvelle Revue* the long pieces that were to provide the material for his two collections, *Essais de psychologie contemporaine,* and to make him one of the most talked about critics of the day.[28] The years between 1879 and 1883 were thus a period of intense activity for him. It has been calculated that he wrote and published during that time more than four hundred articles, read and wrote in-depth reviews of more than three hundred books, and saw something like a hundred plays.[29]

During those years, which established him as a brilliant and respected critic, and during which he managed to assure himself of sufficient income from his writing to devote himself entirely to literature (in 1879 he gave up the teaching profession for good), he also kept up with the latest advances in psychology and psychiatry, read and thought deeply about the work of Taine and Ribot, and, as a consequence of the latter's book on him, underwent the influence of Schopenhauer. Moreover, having signed a contract with Hachette guaranteeing publication of any material that might arise from his projected travels in England, Scotland, and Ireland, and probably also impelled by a lively curiosity about British society, which undoubtedly attracted the dandy that occasionally surfaced in his character, he spent several periods of varying duration on the other side of the Channel.[30] In the resulting travel diary, later published episodically by the *Nouvelle Revue* and eventually, in 1889,[31] in book form, he shows himself at once avid for acquaintance with foreign customs and landscapes, acutely aware of the latest developments in industrial civilization and urban life of which England was still the symbol at that time, dazzled by the life style of her upper classes, and passionate in his admiration of her literature. Indeed, following the method of Taine, he undertook visits to the Lake District and Oxford largely as a kind of pilgrimage to the places where the great English romantic writers had lived. While there he immersed himself in the works of Wordsworth, Coleridge, and especially Thomas De Quincey. It was there, too, that he discovered the Pre-Raphaelites, whose influence on French decadent literature is indisputable.

In his *Essais de psychologie contemporaine*, and in various other works he published at about the same time, we find the essential themes of the decadent sensibility and esthetic formulated with great clarity.[32] In this first collection of essays, which deal in depth with the five great recent or contemporary French writers that Bourget regarded as most representative of French thought at that time, and as being those whose influence was deepest, his principal underlying concern was to arrive at a diagnosis, from the viewpoint of social psychology, of the ills then afflicting the soul of modern man.

The first of these themes is clearly that of pessimism, a pessimism that Bourget saw as arising from awareness of a fundamental disharmony between the reality of the world and man's desires, a disharmony that the advances brought about by civilization can only aggravate: "When the human being is extremely civilized," he writes with reference to

Baudelaire, "he requires that things shall exist in accordance with the dictates of his own heart, a coincidence made all the rarer by the fact that his heart is curiously refined, thus producing irremediable unhappiness" (*Essais*, p. 14). This same idea reappears a few months later in a passage from the essay on Flaubert: "The man who dreams up a setting of fascinating and complicated events for his personal destiny has every chance of finding the reality of things in disharmony with those dreams, above all if he was born into an aging civilization where a more general distribution of welfare is accompanied by a certain banality in private and public lifestyles" (p. 127).

This disharmony stems first and foremost from the physical and nervous exhaustion that is the price being paid for centuries of past civilization: the human species, like any individual organism, has reached the age of decline, particularly in those countries where civilization has a long history. "Emma Bovary and Frédéric," he says of two of Flaubert's creations, "are the product of a tired civilization, whereas they would have attained their full vigor had they been born into a younger world.... That at least is what we think of them, what we think of ourselves when, suffering from the throes of exhaustion, that too painful price we pay for the benefits of the modern world, we take to yearning for those long-gone ages of untamed energy or deep faith" (p. 144).

This physical exhaustion of the advanced nations apart, however, the disharmony Bourget perceives is also a result of the exercise of thought itself, which he regards to some extent as an accidental and monstrous excrescence in the life of the species. For not only does reflection, by anticipating pleasure, empty that pleasure of all its substance and turn all experience into ineluctable disillusion,[33] but at the same time, made hyperactive by the conditions of the modern world, the brain exhausts the organism. Thus Flaubert's characters provide "the symbol ... of all those epochs when abuse of the brain is the great sickness" (p. 149) and reveal "the disintegration produced in men's souls by this daily more frantic exaggeration of the life of consciousness" (p. 150). Thus, our great capital cities provide us with the spectacle of a humanity annihilated by the "poison" of thought: "Modern man, as we see him coming and going on the Paris boulevards, carries within his less-robust limbs, in the too-expressive features of his face, in the excessive acuity of his gaze, the only too evident signs of thinner blood, diminished muscular energy, and an exaggerated disposition to pathological nervosity" (p. 152).

Added to this disharmony between self and world, there is also the baleful influence of science, which simultaneously depoeticizes reality and destroys the consoling certainties of religious belief. The first of these points forms the subject of a dialogue Bourget wrote during this same period, and published under the title *Science et poésie*. Set in Cannes, first inside a florist's shop then outside on the Croisette, it consists of an imaginary conversation between two young men, the Marquis Norbert de N—, a man of action, a soldier, and an athlete, and Pierre V—, a young esthete of delicate physique and refined sensibility. "I am not unaware," one of them remarks, "that science contains within it an irremediable fund of pessimism, and that the ultimate fate of our generation's immense hopes will be bankruptcy—a bankruptcy by now already recognized as certain by those who have gauged the abyss that gapes behind that word: the Unknowable. The experimental method contains, by very definition, an assured principle of despair, for, by condemning itself to the acquisition of facts alone it thereby condemns itself also to an ultimate phenomenalism, which is the same as saying to nihilism."[34] What science reveals is a universe governed entirely by an absolute determinism, thereby destroying our sense of mystery without ever being able to offer us anything but relative certainties in exchange. Meanwhile, Bourget observes in the *Essais*, the disappearance of religious belief brought about by this same science leaves man with "a feeling of emptiness in the face of this world" that nothing can fill (p. 20).

This being so, modern man is inevitably doomed to sadness and despair. In the second chapter of his essay on Baudelaire, entitled "Le Pessimisme de Baudelaire," Bourget offers a survey of European civilization as a whole and then puts forward his general theory of the pessimism to be observed in modern man, a pessimism that with the Slavs takes the form of nihilism, among German speakers is illustrated in the work of Schopenhauer, and among the French manifests itself as those "solitary and bizarre neuroses" exemplified most significantly in the works of Baudelaire and Flaubert (*Essais*, p. 15).

Convinced of the inevitability of this chronic unhappiness, Bourget goes on, artists will seek to escape from the reality causing it by any means available. In the case of Baudelaire those means include a systematic preference for the strange and rare,[35] the search for new sensations in a "mystical, licentious, and analytic attitude to love" (*Essais*, p. 4), the use of Catholicism for purely esthetic purposes ("faith will depart, but mysticism, even when expelled from the intelligence, will linger on in the sensations" [pp. 8–9]), and, lastly, a systematic concentration on the artificial. In Flaubert's case, "the flight from, and hatred of, the modern world are expressed in terms of the bizarrest archeological fantasies" (p. 121), and the aim of his art is to depict not so much reality as mental images, dreams, or hallucinations.[36]

Bourget's originality does not spring solely from the critical intelligence so evident in these analyses, from the precision with which he diagnoses the main trends governing contemporary sensibility, or from the wide-ranging faculty for synthesis he displays. The most remarkable thing is that, while accepting the view that decadence does constitute a grave spiritual crisis, he also asserts, unlike most traditional critics, that it possesses a positive literary influence. This diametrically opposite viewpoint, this resolve to accept decadence, to shoulder the burden it represents, and to make it into the very essence of literary modernity, is made very evident in the third section of his Baudelaire essay, actually entitled "The Theory of Decadence," which can justifiably be regarded as the first true manifesto of the decadent esthetic. For even though, in Bourget's eyes, decadence must inevitably entail disastrous consequences on the collective or national level, since it heralds the approaching dissolution of any state in which it appears, on the other hand, by exacerbating the individuality of that state's artists it provokes a flowering of great works: "Although the citizens of a decadent period are inferior as builders of national greatness, are they not also very superior as artists of the inner soul?" (*Essais,* p. 27). He therefore concludes by inviting his contemporaries to follow the example of Baudelaire: "Let us therefore delight in the singularities of our ideals and forms, and pay the price of imprisonment in a solitude without visitors" (p. 29).

Oscar Wilde

It might seem strange, in an investigation into the development of French esthetic sensibility during the last two decades of the nineteenth century, to refer to the personality and work of an Anglo-Irish writer, Oscar Wilde. Detailed consideration, however, will show that such reference is both historically and esthetically justified. First it must be pointed out that it was Wilde, during the last decade of the century, who most clearly formulated the esthetic foundations of the two parallel currents, decadence in France and the Aesthetic School in Britain. The latter owed its existence very largely to his influence, and an analysis of his ideas and theories is absolutely necessary for any clarification of the profound essence, intentions, and meaning of the French movement as well. Moreover, as a consequence of the relations he always maintained with French writers, the striking way in which he expressed his ideas, and the well-orchestrated publicity with which all his visits to Paris were surrounded, he succeeded, between 1890 and 1895, in exerting a considerable personal influence within the heart of the French literary world itself. There can be no doubt that during his visit to the French capital in 1891 he acted as a catalyst of the avant-garde just as Bourget had done a few years earlier.

It must also be remembered that French literature has the right to number Wilde among its contributors, since he was in fact deeply imbued with French culture. If we examine the various influences he underwent during the formation of his literary personality, we find first and foremost a solid background of classical culture, based on Greek literature, and built up during his years at the Portora Royal School in Dublin, at Trinity College, Dublin (from 1871 to 1874), then at Oxford (from 1874 to 1879). It was to this early literary training that he owed his taste for pure beauty and an ideal of paganism later reinforced by the influences of Gautier and Walter Pater. Then came the London years and his entry into English literary life. If we examine the choices he made at that time, as expressed in his writings and letters, choices which contributed to the assertion of his own personality, we find that the periods of English literature he seems to have preferred are, on the one hand, medieval and Renaissance literature, the study of which flattered his taste for high culture, and, on the other hand, the Elizabethans, including Shakespeare, whom he appreciated for their contempt for humdrum probability, their predilection for violence, and their striking blend of comedy and tragedy. Among the romantics his favorites were Keats for his love of Greek beauty, Coleridge for the power of his imagination, and De Quincey. Indeed, one of Wilde's own essays, *Pen, Pencil and Poison*, is merely an extension of De Quincey's famous essay *On Murder Considered as One of the Fine Arts*. Extremely critical of Dickens and all the realist novelists, he was also clearly much influenced by the Pre-Raphaelites, albeit by Pater more than by Swinburne and Rossetti, and also, in the esthetic field, by Ruskin.[37] However, during this period, which one might term that of his second education, it is indisputable that these home-grown influences were supplemented with an impregnation by nineteenth-century French literature. The intensity of this influence can be disputed,[38] but that it was a major one cannot, as has been made even more evident by the recent publication of a complete edition of his letters.

We find, moreover, that his most lively expressions of admiration were reserved for those nineteenth-century writers who were to prove the masters of the decadents: Gautier,[39] Baudelaire,[40] Poe,[41] and above all Flaubert, of whom he explicitly declares himself a disciple in this letter written in 1888: "To learn how to write English prose I have studied the prose of France. I am charmed to know that *you* recognize it: that shows I have succeeded. . . . Yes! Flaubert is my master, and when I get on with my translation of the *Tentation* I shall be Flaubert II, *Roi par grâce de Dieu*."[42] It is clear from the many critical articles of his that appeared in London periodicals during the period 1885 to 1895 that he had taken on the task of introducing French literature to Britain and championing its cause with the British reading public. So much so that he was soon acknowledged as ringleader of the group of young, francophile writers that was to launch the Aesthetic School during the 1890s. Wilde himself made no attempt to conceal his preference for French writers,[43] and the sentence passed on him in 1895 was the product, in fact, not merely of Victorian puritanism but also of a chauvinist reaction to what were seen as excessive French influences on the nation's literature. On 6 April 1897, a few days before his release from prison, in a letter to Robert Ross listing certain books he wished salvaged from his personal library, broken up as a result of the sale of his belongings forced on him by his debts, the forerunners of the decadent movement figure very largely.[44] Last, let us remember that it was in France, which he came increasingly to regard as his true spiritual home, that he spent the last years of his life.

It now remains to consider whether his esthetic ideas did in fact gain any hold in France, and whether they were disseminated to any significant extent in decadent literary circles. At first sight it would seem doubtful, when one considers that the majority of his works, and his criticism in particular, were not translated until after his death.[45] That does not allow, however, for the direct influence he could have exerted during his visits to Paris, visits to which his love for shocking people and his talent for publicity succeeded in drawing the maximum possible attention. As early as 1883, at a time when he had published very little and was still almost unknown in London, he traveled to Paris for the first time and spent several weeks there.[46] The first thing he did after unpacking was to send copies of his first volume of poetry, published in 1881, to a number of the best-known French writers of the day, and thereby succeeded in becoming acquainted with some of them. Before long he received invitations from both the Goncourts and Daudet, became friendly with a number of younger writers such as Moréas and Jean Lorrain, and visited Gustave Moreau, whose work made a great impression on him. From then on he was accepted by all the principal Parisian literary groups and was to remain in constant contact with them. The following year, during a brief stopover in Paris in the course of his honeymoon, he gave a dinner at his hotel in honor of his French friends, and we know, for instance, that Bourget in particular was one of those who attended it.[47] For the next few years, caught in the whirlwind of London high society, and tied down by family problems and frequent financial difficulties, it is true that he found no opportunity of returning to Paris. Yet he still followed literary developments in France very closely and remained in touch with his French friends, some of whom, like Gabriel Sarrazin, a specialist in English literature, frequently called on him during their London visits.[48]

Meanwhile, the French public was also being kept well informed about the latest developments in English literature.[49] In 1887 there appeared a French translation of Vernon Lee's novel *Miss Brown,* which is a satire on the British Aesthetic School. Reviewing this translation in the *Revue des Deux Mondes,* the critic Théodore Bentzon describes the circles to which the heroine was introduced as follows:

> Increasingly weary, she moves through the fogs of Aesthetic London, asked to tea by this lady, taken to visit the studio of that painter, drenched with Wagnerian music by long-haired German pianists, condemned to listen to "lectures" that shock her to the core with their accounts of the crudest of Shakespeare's predecessors, whom a rooted prejudice in favor of everything archaic places above even Shakespeare himself. Never the slightest question of good or evil. In the name of art everything has become legitimate. Such is the morality professed by those very aesthetes most incapable in real life of the slightest reprehensible action. Strange conversations about Baudelaire's view of God or *Mademoiselle de Maupin* take place in drawing rooms decorated with peacock feathers and old blue and white china, where chasubles spirited away from Gothic sacristies hang spread-eagled on the walls cheek by jowl with Japanese dragons.[50]

That excerpt, gathering together as it does many of the essential elements of decadent fashions, reveals the profound kinship that existed between the Aesthetic School in Britain and the decadent movement in France, a kinship that largely accounts for the ease with which Wilde's ideas were disseminated in decadent circles over here.

This dissemination was certainly furthered by Wilde's next visit to Paris in 1891. By then a well-known writer, author of the two collections of stories *The Happy Prince* and *A House of Pomegranates,* the novel *The Picture of Dorian Gray,* and the volume entitled *Intentions,* which gathers together his most important theoretical essays, he was to cause a sensation in the Parisian literary world. He revived his former association with writers such as Jean Lorrain, and met newcomers like Pierre Louys, whom he was to see again in London the following year, and Gide, who was fascinated by Wilde's personality and, as we know, deeply influenced by him. He was to be seen in the fashionable cafés, where his equivocal behavior and appearance created a great deal of outrage, took part in literary life generally, and was for some weeks the capital's most fashionable figure. There are numerous later accounts describing the impact this visit had.[51] From this point on he was to be regarded by Parisian writers of the younger school as one of their own. It is worth remembering that the most indignant reactions to his sentence were to come, not from London, but from the French capital, and that the performance of *Salomé* on 11 February 1896 was one of the great events of the Paris theater season.

It may be objected that Wilde's stay in Paris, whatever the publicity attending it, does not necessarily guarantee any dissemination of his ideas. But that is to ignore the fact that Wilde was essentially a conversationalist, that the majority of his ideas were always tried out first in the course of his oral improvisations, and that the most important of the essays in *Intentions* still retain even in print their original dialogue form. So we have very good reason to believe, arriving as he did with that volume almost still hot from the press, that much of his time in Paris was spent promulgating its essential ideas, in the course of those spellbinding conversations that bewitched so many young writers.

Moreover, there was also very good reason why those young writers should have found Wilde's ideas both striking and memorable. Not only were they usually couched in typically paradoxical and exaggerated terms, but they also echoed the listeners' own preoccupations, and were in fact the crystallization of some of the French decadent movement's own essential themes.

Wilde's originality lay, in fact, as we have already seen, in pushing the postulates of the decadent esthetic to their logical extreme, and in organizing the esthetic heritage left by the masters of the previous generation, particularly Gautier, Baudelaire, and Poe, into a relatively coherent synthesis. Bolder and more lucid than the majority of the French decadents, unhampered by the polemical turmoil forever on the boil in Parisian literary circles, he was, in fact, on the evidence of his articles and the four essays of *Intentions,* now so unjustly neglected, the prime theoretician of French decadence.

With Wilde, as with most of the French decadents, the metaphysical basis of these theories seems to have been a more or less conscious form of transcendental idealism. This is apparent in the first essay of *Intentions,* where he maintains, for example, that "things are because we see them,"[52] and even more overtly in *De Profundis* later on, when he writes that "time and space, succession and extension, are merely accidental conditions of thought.... Things also, in their essence, are what we choose to make them. A thing is according to the mode in which one looks at it."[53]

The essential esthetic idea that animated Wilde was a radical antinaturalism. The first pages of *Intentions* are given over to a violent diatribe against nature, which is described as incapable of providing any true beauty:

> Enjoy Nature! I am glad to say that I have entirely lost that
> faculty. People tell us that Art makes us love Nature more

than we loved her before; that it reveals her secrets to us; and that after a careful study of Corot and Constable we see things in her that had escaped our observation. My own experience is that the more we study Art, the less we care for Nature. What Art really reveals to us is Nature's lack of design, her curious crudities, her extraordinary monotony, her absolutely unfinished condition. Nature has good intentions, of course, but, as Aristotle once said, she cannot carry them out. When I look at a landscape I cannot help seeing all its defects. It is fortunate for us, however, that Nature is so imperfect, as otherwise we should have had no art at all. Art is our spirited protest, our gallant attempt to teach Nature her proper place. [Pp. 290–91]

It follows from this that art must repudiate the doctrine of the imitation of nature, that foundation stone of the classical esthetic, and move as far as possible away from reality. Thus a landscape cannot be a source of inspiration: "If we take Nature to mean natural simple instinct as opposed to self-conscious culture, the work produced under this influence is always old-fashioned, antiquated and out of date" (pp. 300–301). Thus Wilde condemns absolutely the realist trends that had characterized nineteenth-century literature, attacks the great English novelists and the French naturalists for debasing art by reducing it to a mere attempt at reproducing everyday reality, asserts that "if nothing can be done to check, or at least to modify, our monstrous worship of facts, Art will become sterile and Beauty will pass away from the land" (pp. 294–95), and concludes by maintaining that "as a method realism is a complete failure" (p. 303).

As he saw it, the traditionally established relationship between nature and art had to be reversed. Indeed, pushing this thesis to its ultimate conclusion, Wilde even expresses the paradox that, far from imitating nature, true Art serves as its model. This conviction can be found expressed in a letter written in December 1891 to the editor of *The Speaker*, in which he defends the illustrations to his *House of Pomegranates*:

> What the gilt notes suggest, what imitative parallel may be found to them in that chaos that is termed Nature, is a matter of no importance. . . . A thing in Nature becomes much lovelier if it reminds us of a thing in Art, but a thing in Art gains no real beauty by reminding us of a thing in Nature. The primary aesthetic impression of a work of art borrows nothing from recognition or resemblance.[54]

In the same vein, we also find him asserting that "Life imitates Art far more than Art imitates Life" (*Intentions*, p. 307), and that "Nature, no less than Life, is an imitation of Art" (p. 311). As proof of this he instances the prevailing type of beauty to be found among English women at that time, a look modeled on the heroines of Rossetti or Burne-Jones, and maintains that "a great artist invents a type and Life tries to copy it, to reproduce it in a popular form like an enterprising publisher." The great artist is the man who transforms our vision of reality:

> The nineteenth century, as we know it, is largely an invention of Balzac.... From where if not from the Impressionists do we get those wonderful brown fogs that come creeping down our streets, blurring the gas-lamps and changing houses into monstrous shadows? The extraordinary change that has taken place in the climate of London during the last ten years is entirely due to this particular school of art. [Pp. 309, 312]

Just as art must be independent of nature, so it must be liberated from all moral preoccupations. Following Gautier and Baudelaire, Wilde denounces the subjection of the esthetic to the ethical. In a letter of 1890, for example, he writes: "An artist, Sir, has no ethical sympathies at all. Virtue and wickedness are to him simply what the colours on his palette are to the painter."[55] And the second essay of *Intentions*, entitled *Pen, Pencil and Poison*, is devoted entirely to illustrating this notion of art's autonomy in the person of Thomas Griffith Wainewright, an early-nineteenth-century artist who, by virtue of his culture and artistic predilections, deserves according to Wilde to be regarded as a forerunner of the decadents, and who was sentenced to death for poisoning several people close to him. Wilde then goes on to oppose the classical identification of art with morality by asserting that a great artist can perfectly well be a great criminal as well: "The fact of a man being a poisoner is nothing against his prose. The domestic virtues are not the true basis of art.... There is no essential incongruity between crime and culture" (*Intentions*, p. 339). He then follows Baudelaire in affirming the esthetic fecundity of evil.[56]

Art, once freed from the imitation of nature and from all moral considerations, will then be able to create its own domain, invent new forms, imbue them with life, and use them to enrich the domain of reality. Art is therefore essentially fiction, which Wilde provocatively refers to as "Lying," as opposed to the flat truthfulness of imitative and realist art, and his defense of this lying forms the theoretical backbone of the first essay in *Intentions*. Scorning the gifts of observation so dear to the realist writers, he sings the praises of imagination, which for him, as for Baudelaire, is the "queen of the faculties." Thus we find him confessing in a letter of 1886 to his "love of the impossible," and in 1891 he was to write to Edmond de Goncourt—in French—"Although the basis of my esthetic is the philosophy of unreality" (*Letters*, p. 303). That is why the essay "The Decline of Lying" culminates in a ringing appeal for the renewal of imagination:

> Out of the sea will rise Behemoth and Leviathan, and sail around the high-pooped galleys, as they do on the delightful maps of those ages when books on geography were actually readable. Dragons will wander about the waste places, and the phoenix will soar from her nest of fire into the air. We shall lay our hands upon the basilisk, and see the jewel in the toad's head. Champing his gilded oats, the Hippogriff will stand in our stalls, and over our heads wilh float the Blue Bird singing of beautiful and impossible things, of things that are lovely and that never happen, of things that are not and that should be. But before this comes to pass we must cultivate the lost art of Lying. [*Intentions*, p. 319]

A similar assertion of the sovereign powers of the imagination and the rights of absolute invention is to be found in a letter to the *St. James's Gazette* replying to an article in which the characters in *The Picture of Dorian Gray* had been criticized for being "mere catchpenny revelations of the non-existent." To this charge, Wilde replied:

> Quite so. If they existed they would not be worth writing about. The function of the artist is to invent, not to chronicle. There are no such people. If there were I would not write about them. Life by its realism is always spoiling the subject-matter of art. The supreme pleasure in literature is to realise the non-existent. [*Letters*, p. 258]

This attitude was also to lead Wilde to advocate a stylized, abstract, decorative approach in the plastic arts. In "The Decline of Lying," Vivian's article contains the following passage:

> Art begins with abstract decoration with purely imaginative and pleasurable work dealing with what is unreal and non-existent. This is the first stage. Then Life becomes fascinated with this new wonder, and asks to be admitted into the charmed circle. Art takes life as part of her rough material, recreates it, and refashions it in fresh forms, is absolutely indifferent to fact, invents, imagines, dreams, and keeps between herself and reality the impenetrable barrier of beautiful style, of decorative or ideal treatment. [*Intentions*, p. 301]

The essential notion then becomes that of style, a deliberate distortion applied by the artist to the materials that life provides and the only method by which reality can be given an esthetic dimension.[57] In short, Wilde provides an esthetic justification not merely of the developments in the decorative arts that were to characterize turn-of-the-century art, but also of twentieth-century nonfigurative art.

In the field of literature, Wilde championed, and sought to exemplify in his own works, a kind of writing dominated by imagination and a sense of wonder.[58] In *Intentions,* he advocates a literature of the fairy tale, and celebrates Shakespeare as the creator of wonder-filled fables: "him who made Prospero the Magician, and gave him Caliban and Ariel as his servants, who heard the Tritons blowing their horns round the coral reefs of the Enchanted Isle, and the fairies singing to each other in a wood near Athens, who led the phantom kings in dim procession across the misty Scottish heath, and hid Hecate in a cave with the weird sisters" (p. 306). In certain of his letters he even sketched out a theory of the short story or tale that could be applied to the products of French practitioners of the genre during the 1890s. In a letter of 1888, for instance, he describes his own tales as dreams in prose, intended for readers who have retained their youthful faculties of wonderment and joy (*Letters,* p. 219). And in another letter, written the same year, he claims that they are manifestoes, written in reaction to the realist trend of so much recent literature (p. 221).

Even such a brief survey of Wilde's critical and theoretical writings thus provides ample justification for asserting that his influence on the formation of the modern esthetic was a major one. By making constant use of paradox, and the liberty it confers, he was able to take Baudelaire's basic intuitions to their extremes, thus placing himself at the crossroads between the classical esthetic, based upon the imitation of nature and the supremacy of reason, and the modern esthetic, which is founded upon the artificial and the power of imagination. Possibly he failed to be absolutely modern, in that he never accepted the essential themes of modernity or recognized the new forms of beauty introduced by industrial and urban civilization; yet even in that respect he was very much like the majority of French decadents.

Forerunners of Decadence: Baudelaire

As I have already tried to show, the essential elements of the French decadents' vision of the world were already present, embryonically, in the work of earlier writers, particularly Baudelaire, Poe, De Quincey, Flaubert and Gautier. And unsurprisingly, it was for these figures, the men who had exerted the deepest influence on them, that writers of the rising generation expressed their greatest admiration. In order to conclude this historical panorama of the fin-de-siècle era, it is therefore necessary to review the literary fortunes of these forerunners during the decadent period, and to attempt some assessment of their standing and the extent to which they were understood and appreciated.

Among writers working in the immediately preceding period, the figure who most influenced the decadents was clearly Baudelaire. After his death in 1867, and during the first years of the Third Republic, Baudelaire's influence appears on the surface to have been weak, insofar as the poets who openly declared themselves to be his immediate disciples—Mallarmé, Verlaine, and Rimbaud—remained somewhat in the background, while the Parnassians occupied the center of the literary stage. But the legend that had surrounded the great poet's personality in his lifetime had nevertheless survived his disappearance from the scene and continued to inspire a great many critical works, as is quite clear from A. E. Carter's list of all the critical references to Baudelaire between his death and 1917.[59] Apart from the edition of the complete works published by Michel Lévy immediately after Baudelaire's death, which appeared over the period 1868 to 1870 and included Gautier's famous assessment of *Les Fleurs du mal,* more accurate accounts of the writer's life, together with excerpts from his letters, were published in a collection brought out in 1872.[60]

After 1880, the picture is very different. With the rise of the new generation that regarded Baudelaire as its most important teacher and guide, he was to return very swiftly to a position of preeminence. In an article already alluded to, published in the 15 November 1881 number of *La Nouvelle Revue,* Bourget acclaimed Baudelaire as the most significant representative of the modern sensibility, the writer whose work had most actively molded the modern soul. Then came Verlaine's article in the famous *Poètes maudits* series, published in *Lutèce* in 1883, then brought out in book form the following year. It was also in 1884 that Huysmans, who had already written about Baudelaire in the most laudatory terms in his preface to Théodore Hannon's *Rimes de joie* published in Belgium in 1881, expressed the very liveliest admiration for him in *A Rebours.* Indeed, Des Esseintes, the central character of that novel, when decorating his house, went so far as to place a canon book on the mantelpiece of his library upon which three of the master's poems—*La Mort des amants, L'Ennemi,* and *Anywhere out of the World*—were reproduced in full.[61] Moreover Huysmans also devoted several pages of encomium to him in chapter 12 of the same work, in which we are given a survey of Des Esseintes's favorite modern authors. Huysmans's hero expresses an "unlimited" admiration for the poet, glorifies him for having opened up hitherto unexplored regions of the human soul, for having "revealed the morbid psychology of the mind when it has reached the October of its sensations," for having concentrated attention upon the spiritual anguish of "spleen" and his desperate attempts to escape from it by deviant expressions of love or the use of drugs (*A Rebours,* p. 183).

From that point on, the new generation of writers, those who began to occupy the center of the stage in about 1884, were to swear by Baudelaire alone. From the end of 1882 to July 1883, when he returned to his own country, Maurice Rollinat became the darling of the literary salons by singing the master's poems to his own piano accompaniments, and publishing his own collection of verse, *Névroses,* in which all the macabre and depressive themes of *Les Fleurs du mal* were only too recognizable in caricature form.[62] In an article that appeared in March 1883, it is precisely the ever-growing influence of Baudelaire that Barrès singles out to explain the extraordinary vogue enjoyed by this ultimately rather mediocre poet:

> This swift rise to fame ought not to amaze us. Baudelaire
> had forged ahead too quickly. His contemporaries, unable
> to keep up, had let him disappear from sight. The next gener-
> ation then caught up with him; yet, either because the speed
> of its own progress had left it breathless or because the scent
> of those evil flowers gave rise to apprehension, it failed to
> pick up that admirable but somber posy. But Baudelaire's
> flowers had impregnated the air all the same; and there were
> those who dared to pluck themselves a boutonnière or two,
> and little by little they became a part of everyone's intelli-
> gence until, today, they are not only cherished by many
> minds among us but tolerated by all.[63]

In the little magazine *Les Taches d'Encre* he had just started, Barrès also devoted two articles to Baudelaire in which he expressed the view that through his frenzied quest for sensation he was the ancestor of all decadent writing.[64] And Barrès's friend Stanislas de Guaïta, like Barrès freshly arrived in the capital from their native Lorraine, and destined to become one of the leading figures of fin-de-siècle occultism, dedicated a poem to their great predecessor which appeared in the *Revue indépendante* in 1881.[65]

All those who have left accounts of the developments taking place in literature at that time agree in recognizing the growing place that Baudelaire occupied in the minds of the younger literary generation. "The new generation," the critic Louis Desprez observed in 1884, "knows *Les Fleurs du mal* by heart; it is intoxicated with Baudelaire;"[66] and in an article for *La Revue contemporaine* the following year Théodore de Banville wrote: "The poet's work has spread through the reading public with unprecedented explosive force, and now counts among the most popular works of the century."[67] Brunetière himself, the augur of the *Revue des Deux Mondes,* the inflexible guardian of tradition, was eventually reduced to acknowledging—and lamenting—the phenomenon: "Baudelaire, his legend, his ridiculous affectations of dandyism, his paradoxes, his *Fleurs du mal,* have exerted for the last twenty years, and still exert today, a great and disastrous influence on the younger generation in literature. . . . Along with Stendhal, Baudelaire is one of the idols of the age."[68]

Nor was Brunetière mistaken. By the time Eugène Crepet was publishing the volume of *Oeuvres posthumes* that contained not merely the first serious biography of the great poet but also a series of his hitherto unpublished texts, and particularly the private notebooks so necessary to any understanding of Baudelaire's true personality,[69] the young writers of the day were unanimously acclaiming him as their principal intercessor. René Ghil, for example, was calling him the "first, the magical Master,"[70] while Anatole Baju was writing in the introduction to his pamphlet *L'Ecole décadent:* "This literary movement dates further back than today, however: Baudelaire could be called its true precursor. We find in *Les Fleurs du mal* the seeds of all the beauties we admire, and above all the idea that presided over the conception of the decadent school."[71] Later still, in one of the articles in his *Livre des masques,* Rémy de Gourmont was to observe that "all today's literature, and above all what is termed symbolist literature, is Baudelairian."[72] In a work entitled *Les Artistes littéraires,* published in 1889, Maurice Spronck devoted a fairly long and extremely well-documented chapter to an analysis of Baudelaire's work that undoubtedly constitutes one of the most intelligent and comprehensive studies of its kind produced during the last third of the century. After first noting the profound originality of Baudelaire's temperament, tastes, and ideas, Spronck goes on, quite rightly, to stress the esthetic importance of his subject's theory of the artificial, and to draw attention, after Bourget and before so many modern critics, to his sadism and "love of evil for evil's sake."[73] What the decadent writers prized above all else in Baudelaire's work were in fact those very elements that had so shocked his contemporaries: primacy of sensation, taste for the bizarre and horrible, cultivation of the artificial, and abandonment of the self to melancholy ("spleen") and sensuality.

Edgar Allan Poe

The literary fortunes of Edgar Allan Poe, as we noted earlier, were to remain linked in France with those of Baudelaire, his principal translator, thanks largely to the famous article by Gautier, which by stressing the similarity between their talents made them inseparable in the eyes of posterity. During the last three decades of the nineteenth century, even apart from the posthumous edition of Baudelaire's complete works between 1868 and 1870, which included all the Poe translations, various collections of the American author's tales also appeared separately under the titles *Histoires extraordinaires*[74] and *Nouvelles Histoires extraordinaires.*[75] From 1880 onward, Poe's hitherto untranslated work also began to appear in a series of new translations. In 1882, for example, there came a collection entitled *Contes grotesques,* translated by Emile Hennequin, one of the new generation's most outstanding critics and a friend of Huysmans and Odilon Redon, and containing both a biography of Poe and excerpts from his *Marginalia.*[76] Three further collections then followed: the first, translated by Ernest Guillemot, appeared in 1884 and contained a selection of tales supplemented by passages from *Marginalia* and *Eureka;*[77] the second, translated by W. L. Hughes, came in 1885;[78] the third, translated by F. Rabbe, in 1887.[79] That same year also brought a new translation of *The Adventures of Arthur Gordon Pym.*[80] Thus, over a period of a very few years almost all of Poe's prose works were republished, and the fact that the market was able to sustain so many new translations is alone sufficient indication of the new upsurge of his fame linked with the rise of the new literary school in France.

Moreover Poe's success in France was by now no longer limited to the tales, as had been the case under the Second Empire. In the years from 1870 to 1880, thanks to the efforts of Mallarmé, quite a number of his poems also appeared in French translation in a variety of periodicals. In 1872, eight poems were printed in *La Renaissance littéraire et artistique,* followed by a further series of translations in *La République des Lettres* during 1876 and 1877. During the same period, two further translations were published in small limited editions, that of *The Raven* by Mallarmé[81] and that of *The Bells* by Emile Blemont.[82] It is true that these particular translations, given their mode of publication, could have reached only a very small public; yet they do constitute evidence of the efforts being made by Baudelaire's most devoted disciples, such as Mallarmé and Villiers de l'Isle-Adam, to foster admiration for the great American writer in France. It was also at this time that Mallarmé was working on his *Tombeau d'Edgar Poe,* which eventually formed part of a collective memorial volume published in Baltimore to commemorate the erection of a monument to the poet's memory.[83] The *Tombeau* was later reprinted by Verlaine, in 1883, in *Les Poètes maudits.*[84] The way had thus been prepared for the two collections of Poe's poems in French translation that were to appear, almost simultaneously, ten or so years later, that by Mallarmé[85] and that by Gabriel Mourey.[86]

Evidence of critical interest in Poe's work also becomes much more widespread during these years. In 1883 came Barbey d'Aurevilly's review of Hennequin's collection of tales.[87] In 1884, in *A Rebours,* apart from a reference to *The Adventures of Arthur Gordon Pym,* Huysmans also inserted a laudatory reference to "that profound and strange Edgar Poe, in whom, since he [Des Esseintes] had begun rereading him, his delight was never in danger of waning" (pp. 49, 235–36). The following year brought a major article by Hennequin in *La Revue contemporaine,*[88] and during the last years of the century there were several major critical works devoted wholly to Poe, among them one by Téodor de Wyzewa[89] and another by Camille Mauclair.[90]

These various studies display an increasingly profound understanding of the American author's personality and work. Not only had a number of critics begun to react against the legends that had surrounded Poe in the previous period, such as that depicting him as an inveterate alcoholic and a kind of madman, or that, deriving from Baudelaire, of his having been a genius crushed by the hostility of his fellow citizens, but emphasis was increasingly being placed not just upon his talents as a teller of tales but also, and perhaps primarily—as a result of the waning of the fashion for things supernatural—upon his verse and his esthetic theories.

As far as the poet's life and personality are concerned, those critics most strongly influenced by recent psychopathological theories and predisposed, as we shall see, to identify genius with madness, naturally adduced Poe's life, especially in the grossly tendentious version of it presented by his first biographer, Griswold, as irrefutable proof of their theories. Thus in Charles Richet's preface to a translation of Cesare Lombroso's *Man of Genius* we find the following judgment:

> In the work of Edgar Poe, for example, do we not find the element of fantasy, invention, original creation, assimilation of extraordinary ideas, completely dominating the critical aspect? Moreover Poe was somewhat given to dipsomania, even to alcoholism. Although it is true that his works are those of a genius—and they are absolutely remarkable—one might nevertheless take them very easily for the divagations of a maniac, so close is the resemblance.[91]

This opinion was to be expressed even more forcefully in an article by Arvède Barine published in 1897,[92] and also, early in the next century, in a study by Emile Lauvrière.[93] Wyzewa, on the other hand, making use of the extracts from Poe's correspondence that had recently been published in the United States, took violent issue with Griswold and the image he had presented of the poet, who was in reality, he claimed, "an excellent man, a noble and upright soul, industrious, modest, deeply faithful in his emotional attachments, and bearing with admirable resignation the unhappy fate that weighed upon him."[94] Echoing Mallarmé, Wyzewa was also somewhat critical of Baudelaire for having elevated Poe's life to the status of a myth. Some years later, Mauclair was to express similar reservations with regard to such an overdramatized interpretation:

> It is only right to dissociate ourselves totally from Baudelaire's judgment, however lucidly expressed, and to repudiate the error in his evaluation that led him to regard Edgar Poe's drunkenness and neurosis as the inevitable price of his noblest gifts, as faults for which the works were a more than adequate excuse. The assertion of moral suicide, of systematic exaltation of the imagination by alcohol, is a seductive and ingenious justification in which one recognizes Baudelaire's own predilection for tragic fiction, but one that is categorically contradicted by Poe's entire intellectual existence.[95]

In the work of Poe the teller of tales, it was not so much the macabre effects achieved that the younger critics responded to as the technical perfection displayed. Thus Hennequin stresses the extreme rigor of Poe's construction, points out that "the spell cast by each of Poe's works is immediate," and defines him as "a mathematician of the supernatural, [an] imperturbably logical mind on the frontiers of the rational."[96] Hughes, for his part, comments on the conjunction of poet and mathematician to be observed in the works: "He describes his dreams with the eloquence of a seer. Nothing could be more improbable than *The Descent into the Maelstrom*, yet the reader feels himself drawn irresistibly along, utterly convinced by the realism of the narrative. What we find in Poe are two qualities rarely combined in the same individual: a tremendous power of imagination linked with an analytical mind of mathematical precision."[97]

Above all, however, these later critics stress, as Baudelaire had done, the originality of the psychological analyses, and Poe's recreation of a whole series of emotions and feeling existing at the fringe of normal psychic life. Hennequin praises him as the analyst of "those twilit states of mind in which the anemic brain is incapable of anything more than slow churnings and dying thoughts" observes that he "excels in capturing the rudimentary states of damaged or sleeping minds, the extreme vertigo, the spiritual nausea of a man dying of hunger, the ghostly remnants of thought in a brain swooning with horror, the slow, reptilian movements of a brain emerging from catalepsy."[98] Mauclair defines Poe's art in a way that clearly reveals the change that was taking place at that time with regard to the fantastic element in literature: it is now seen as deriving not from the supernatural but rather from a new dimension revealed in the heart of reality:

> Far from deriving his fantastic effects from an arbitrary distortion of real life, he calls them into being by means of a deeper and more directly applied study of the reality whose known aspects his intuition is able to pierce and go beyond. His imagination consists, not in creating a chimerical world far removed from our own, but in penetrating that world and extracting the strangeness inherent in it by means of the most unexpected psychological investigations. When we finish reading one of Poe's tales, we have not forgotten the visible universe in order to wander for a moment in a land of dreams; we have acquired a new motive for dreaming from a more attentive contemplation of what lies all around us. We have in some way increased our idealism by means of processes provided by materialism itself.... [His imagination] is an instinctive contact with the general laws of the universe; it is the action of pure reason intervening in the observations of practical reason. And by that very fact it stands opposed to all distortion of the real: if it appears to contradict apparent truth, it is only in order to replace it with an inner truth. It is not by summoning us to an assembly of unusual and purely fictitious forms and circumstances that Edgar Poe astonishes us, but by showing us that the smallest fact of everyday life, when we are able to see it with his eyes, is incomparably fertile in subjects for amazement. He does not lead us out of the world, he takes us by the hand and draws us further into it, in order to show us mysterious wellsprings we did not know were there.... The fantastic in Poe is psychic in essence.[99]

Like Hennequin, Mauclair also emphasizes the profundity of Poe's psychological analyses, beneath which he also perceived metaphysical concepts founded on the central idea of perversity. "In every case," he writes, "a mysterious principle, a solvent originating beyond the visible universe, causes the disintegration of the beings he presents, and destroys their mental powers by arming those powers against themselves."[100] For Mauclair, this principle lies at the source of all the malfunctions of personality that it is Poe's essential purpose to describe.

Above all, however, these critics attempted to direct the main thrust of their analyses away from the tales to Poe's verse, or to his philosophical and esthetic works. In the preface to the *Oeuvres choisies* he edited in 1885, Hughes claims that the principal merits of Poe's works, taken as a whole, are to be found in his verse.[101] The previous year, Guillemot had defined his selection of Poe's works as "a collection whose exclusive intention is to present a specimen of the author's poetic and philosophic genius."[102] In 1889, Charles Morice was to base his admiration less upon "the infallible construction of his tales," than upon his "feeling for the poetic consciousness."[103] Mauclair went further still. He claimed to regard Poe principally as a thinker, an "ideologue," as the very title of his article in fact proclaims. In his view, "[Poe] the man of letters took pains to conceal Poe the thinker with a brilliant display of coquetry." In other words, the thinker was merely making use of the tales as a way to illustrate his psychological and metaphysical intuitions: "It must be said: Poe is not a teller of fantastic tales; or, if he is, it is only in order to achieve a much vaster result. . . . We should regard him above all as a philosopher, and treat his talent for expressing terror, admirable though it is, almost with indifference, as something secondary and incidental."[104] And even though this conception of Poe must ultimately be regarded as no more than an intelligent misinterpretation, it does provide a very clear insight into the change of approach to Poe's work that characterized the writers and critics of the decadent period.

Certainly it can come as no surprise that his work, like Baudelaire's, came to enjoy an ever-increasing prestige as the century moved toward its close. "It is already a commonplace," Charles Morice writes, "that Edgar Poe, only so recently discovered in France, has now found the true homeland of his fame here."[105] In a later article, published in 1912 as part of an issue of *La Vie* in honor of Odilon Redon, Gabriel Sarrazin was to evoke that painter's work in these terms: "It was like nothing else being exhibited at the time, yet could be placed by the eye-catching affinities it possessed with the inspiration of Edgar Poe and Baudelaire, two poets about whom we were all constantly talking."[106]

As for Poe's influence on literature in general during the last twenty years of the century, it would take an entire book to list its principal manifestations, and accounts of this phenomenon have already been attempted by a number of authors.[107] We know that Baudelaire's earliest disciples, Mallarmé, Verlaine, and Villiers de l'Isle-Adam, were all deeply imbued with Poe's work, and I have already mentioned the efforts Mallarmé made between 1870 and 1880—and indeed right up until his death—to acquaint the French reading public better with the verse of the man he regarded as his "great master."[108] There is no doubt, moreover, that Poe's influence was just as intense on writers of later literary generations. Léon Lemonnier devoted a whole series of chapters to Poe's work in relation to a number of French writers, including Rollinat, Samain, Rodenbach, and Gustave Kahn. He also quoted from a letter that Maeterlinck wrote to him in 1928 as follows: "Edgar Poe exerted a great, lasting, and profound influence upon me, as indeed he did upon all those of my generation. It is to him that I owe the blossoming of an inner sense of mystery, and a passion for all that lies beyond life."[109]

We also know that Poe's influence, exerted via that of Mallarmé and mingled with it, was a predominant element in the intellectual growth of Valéry, and later in the construction of his poetic theories. Here, for example, is a quotation from a letter to Gide, written in 1891: "My mind is irradiated and as it were scattered, and my reading these days is still such books as De Quincey's *Confessions*, [Flaubert's] *L'Education sentimentale*, and above all and always, and without being able to tear myself away from that dizzying and as it were mathematical opium: Poe! Poe!"[110] In addition, any detailed study of the work of short story writers such as Jean Lorrain, Marcel Schwob, Rachilde, and many others, will always reveal that same influence at work on almost every page. If one wished to establish a distinction between the "symbolists" and the "decadents" from this particular point of view, then one might say that the former, guided by Mallarmé, were most receptive to Poe's ideas on creativity, the poetic consciousness, and the theory of effect, so that the work of Valéry, from this point of view, is that most representative of Poe's influence in the deepest sense, whereas the "decadents" proper were primarily imitators of Poe's taste for the morbid, his macabre effects, his interest in dreams, and his descriptions of abnormal nervous phenomena.

De Quincey

After the publication of Baudelaire's *Les Paradis artificiels* in 1860, Thomas De Quincey's literary fortunes in France, as in the case of Poe, were very much linked to his. Thanks to Baudelaire's account of De Quincey's work in his *Un Mangeur d'opium*, the English writer's fame, which had in fact persisted in a clandestine fashion throughout the romantic era, was abruptly restored to its full glory. After Baudelaire's death, we may presume that the memory of *The Confessions of an English Opium Eater* was kept alive within the group formed by his friends and most fervent disciples. In the section of his long article on *Les Fleurs du mal* devoted to *Les Paradis artificiels*,[111] for example, Gautier was analyzing De Quincey's work as well as Baudelaire's. And there is also good reason to suppose that Villiers de l'Isle-Adam continued to express admiration for De Quincey's work at this time: two chapters of *Claire Lenoir*, published in 1867, have headings drawn from *The Confessions*.[112] Moreover, the memory of Musset's translation of the *Confessions* had not been completely lost: in 1872, in his bibliography of the romantic era, Asselineau mentions this work, originally brought out in 1828, and gives a brief description of it. Then, in 1878, under the aegis of the *Moniteur du Bibliophile*, there was even a new edition of the Musset translation with a new introduction.

Then, from about 1880 onward, probably as a result of Baudelaire's growing influence among those who were later to form the decadent school, a number of signs indicate that a rediscovery of De Quincey's work was taking place, doubtless instigated to a large extent by the publication of Edmond de Goncourt's *La Faustin* in 1881 and 1882.[113] There is a passage in Goncourt's novel, an account of the private life and career of an actress, in which the author has a copy of *The Confessions of an English Opium Eater* fall by chance into his heroine's hands, and one day when she is bored and despondent she opens it:

> In the bad times of your life, has it ever occurred to you, in order to escape from the long, inimical hours of a tedious day, to absent yourself from existence for a while by reading some work of unbridled, insane, crazed imagination, and to do so moreover in the slightly hallucinatory environment of a bed surrounded by shadowy darkness? Well, that was the expedient hit upon by La Faustin.... The pages of that little book transported her into a strange world, a world filled with landscapes of terrifying grandeur, with gaping chasms of unmeasurable depth, with infinite expanses of rushing water, with the glare of flaming planets, with the architectural phantasmagorias of a Piranesi, with an endless procession of myriads of human creatures eternally winding past.... And in these supernatural landscapes, the entire past returned, unordered and at random; the whole history of humanity, but shattered, shaken as it were in a kaleidoscope, tumbled endlessly around her in abrupt and magical tableaux, constantly riven and dissolved by further changes, further transpositions of both background and time.[114]

Goncourt then devotes several paragraphs to brief accounts of the most famous episodes in De Quincey's work. At about the same time, possibly as a result of reading *La Faustin*, Bourget also seems to have been gripped by a passion for the *Confessions* and an intense curiosity about their author. The visit he made to England during the summer of 1882, which provided him with the material for an article in *La Nouvelle Revue* later that year,[115] was very much a pilgrimage in quest of De Quincey. The account he wrote of his visit to the Lake District, where so many of the great English romantics had lived, includes studies of some of the others, but De Quincey emerges as very much his favorite among them. He uses a rereading of the *Confessions*, undertaken in his hotel one day when it was raining too hard to go out, as a peg upon which to hang an account of De Quincey's personality and of his own admiration for the English writer's powers of imagination and sense of mystery:

> He was a visionary by nature, convinced as Shakespeare was that we are such stuff as dreams are made on, and, like Carlyle, that there is an ineffable, a divine mystery of splendor, astonishment, and awe concealed in the being of every man and every thing. De Quincey also said that he could not live without mystery, and his eccentric and solitary existence had increased in him that inborn power to discern, behind the world's visible phenomena, the secret and fearful causes of which those phenomena are merely the efflorescence. [*Etudes anglaises*, pp. 141–42]

Having given a brief account of the principal events of De Quincey's life as recounted in the *Confessions*, Bourget then goes on to recall some of the most famous visionary episodes in the work. Above all, Bourget reveals both his own personal beliefs and the underlying trends of his age when he draws conclusions from his meditation on De Quincey's work that are very much in line with the theory of transcendental idealism:

> Hurled abruptly into this measureless universe that assaults us with so many confused impressions, what do we know of it, other than the idea we form of it? The idea, that is to say a floating image that in the darkness of our mind continually takes the place of absent reality.... And so we move through life, each imprisoned in a personal circle of phantoms and always cut off from an ungraspable reality by the abysses that the demons of Time and Space make gape implacably between our desire and the objects of our desire. [*Etudes anglaises*, pp. 149–50]

Since reality is unknowable, since the universe is nothing more to us than an accumulation of representations, let us dare to modify those representations by our own decisions, whereupon the use of drugs will immediately appear, from such a viewpoint, as one of the most effective means to achieve escape from that dilemma:

> When one's brain has been molded in a particular metaphysical way, how is one not to wonder if it would not be better, since this universe is nothing but an invincible and unverifiable appearance, to come to terms with that fact once for all, and courageously augment one's inner power to feed off illusion and to live upon mere appearances?...

> Opium and hashish, and, to a lesser degree, that cruder
> opium of the West, strong drink, are one way of unlocking
> the door to a more intense, more systematic, and more
> opulent dream world. [*Etudes anglaises,* pp. 150–51]

The memory of the great English visionary is moreover present throughout this travel diary, like a watermark, whether in a visionary evocation of Manchester, De Quincey's home town (p. 117), in a reworking of the prostitute with a heart of gold theme, inspired by the figure of little Ann (pp. 144–45), or in the frequent expressions of social conscience, in which De Quincey's influence is doubtless reinforced by that of Baudelaire's *Poèmes en prose* (pp. 117, 171–73). Even during Bourget's later visits to England, which took him to Oxford in May and June of 1883 (p. 184), then to London in 1884 (p. 184), the memory of De Quincey was still with him. It would seem, then, that the anglomania Bourget displayed at this period of his life was compounded partly of a fascination with the work of the celebrated opium eater and partly of a more general interest in the British way of life, and that the two were closely linked in his own mind. Moreover this admiration for De Quincey is also to be found expressed in other works that Bourget completed at about the same time. For instance, in his review of Villiers de l'Isle-Adam's play *La Révolte,* printed in the *Parlement* of February 1883, he likens Villiers's work to that of De Quincey and also that of Poe.[116] Similarly, in his preface to Barbey d'Aurevilly's *Memoranda,* dated May 1883, he identifies the exaltation caused by drugs with that produced by literature.[117] And there is yet another reference to De Quincey in his review of *La Légende du Parnasse contemporain* by Catulle Mendès of 1884.[118]

There can thus be no doubt that during the years 1880 to 1885 De Quincey's work and personality were objects of great admiration and curiosity on Bourget's part. From the idealist viewpoint he was to adopt from then on, the use of drugs was regarded as one of the possible means of escaping from reality in order to transfigure it, and the attitude and writings of De Quincey seemed to him to be exemplary guides on that new path. This being so, and given his great influence in literary circles, we may also suppose that Bourget played a considerable role in the rediscovery of De Quincey in France at this time. And that this rediscovery continued to make steady headway during the next few years is indicated by a considerable body of evidence. Huysmans, for instance, did not miss the opportunity of introducing this newly fashionable writer into *A Rebours,* and at one point Des Esseintes's hallucinations are quite clearly inspired by the famous Consul Romanus episode from the *Confessions* (p. 116). In that same year, 1884, in a review of the annual Salon for *La Revue indépendante,* he compared the impression produced by Whistler's paintings to De Quincey's opium-induced hallucinations.[119] The following year, in Edouard Rod's *La Course à la mort*, we find an allusion to Oxford Street and little Ann.[120] In 1886, a novel by Paul Bonnetain appeared under the title *L'Opium* and bearing the famous phrase from the *Confessions* "O Just, subtile and mighty opium" as its epigraph.

The progress of this De Quincey vogue can also be discerned in the efforts made by Wyzewa between 1886 and 1888 to celebrate the qualities of the great opium eater's work and make it more widely known. In an article for the December 1886 number of *La Revue indépendante*, seeking to define the poetic qualities of Villiers de l'Isle-Adam's prose, he compared it with De Quincey's.[121] In that very same number of the magazine, moreover, there appeared a translation of another of De Quincey's dream texts, *The Daughter of Lebanon*. Two years later, in the same periodical, Wyzewa published an article entirely devoted to the English author. "By the strangest of fates," he remarks in the course of it, "in France today Thomas De Quincey is at once famous and unknown"; he then goes on to analyze the stages of his discovery in France and, having defined the qualities of his prose, acclaims him as the inventor, before Baudelaire, of prose poetry.[122]

These efforts were to result, during the last years of the nineteenth century and the early years of the twentieth, in a series of new translations that were to give the French reading public an opportunity to become acquainted with De Quincey's works more directly. In 1890, for instance, there appeared the first authentic translation of the *Confessions*, preceded by a preface in which the translator, having first covered the historical development of opium consumption in nineteenth-century Europe, then briefly described the drug's effects, offered a series of personal reflections on dream literature, and concluded by pondering the question whether drugs can really aid artistic creation.[123] Then, the following year, there came the translation of a minor work by De Quincey on Joan of Arc. In a somewhat lengthy preface, the translator, Gérard de Contades, a former diplomat and undoubtedly very knowledgeable in the field of English literature, provided an appreciation of De Quincey's talent in general and celebrated his visionary qualities in particular.[124] In 1899 came *The Last Days of Immanuel Kant*, translated by Marcel Schwob;[125] in 1901 *On Murder Considered as One of the Fine Arts*, translated by André Fontainas;[126] and lastly, in 1903, *Autobiographical Memories of the Opium Eater* translated by Albert Savine. In his preface to the last of these the translator, a former publisher of and specialist in foreign literature, confirms the vogue that De Quincey was then enjoying when he observes that "there has been a great deal of interest in Thomas de Quincey here in France during the past few years."[127] Moreover, the English writer's influence was also clearly evident in a number of fictional works published at this time, such as Schwob's *Livre de Monelle* and Jarry's *Les Jours et les nuits*. In short, the diffusion of De Quincey's work at that time, together with the power of his imagination and the unequaled beauty of his prose, undoubtedly helped to direct the contemporary imagination in France toward the world of dreams and the use of drugs.

Flaubert

Flaubert, the Flaubert of *Salammbô, La Tentation de saint Antoine*, and *Trois Contes*, was likewise a great influence, and provided the decadent imagination with a great many of the themes from which it was to draw its inspiration. First and foremost, the decadents found in his work what was perhaps their most favored theme of all, that of the femme fatale, whose cold and lascivious beauty lures men to their doom: the mysterious Queen of Sheba or the magical Ennoia in *La Tentation;* Salammbô eternally haunting Matho's dreams, an oblivious spectator at his execution, for which she was responsible; and lastly, in *Hérodias*, the princess Salomé, innately and innocently perverse, demanding and receiving the Baptist's head from Herod the tetrarch as the price of her dance. This image of woman as an idol, at once mysterious, inaccessible, and cruel, accorded too well with the antifeminism so widely disseminated by the teachings of Schopenhauer—a subject we shall return to—not to become one of the most significant symbolic figures of the whole decadent era. Moreover, this female figure moved and had her being in an oriental and barbaric antiquity, against a background of sumptuous and convoluted palaces constructed on a titanic scale, surrounded by an unparalleled opulence of raiment and jewels. This meant that the theme of the femme fatale was indelibly associated with a rising fashion for a certain kind of exoticism in which we find mingled, in varying proportions, a concern for exact historical reconstitution, as in *Salammbô*, and a desire for escape into the nowhere land of dreams.

Flaubert's imagination was also characterized by a strain of sadism, apparent in the extremely detailed descriptions found throughout *Salammbô* of scenes of carnage or prolonged torture associated with rape. Lastly, with *La Tentation*, there was the theme of abandonment to the delirium of hallucinations, the vertigo produced by confrontation with the extraordinary accumulation of doctrines, beliefs, and absurdities piled up over the centuries by mythic or religious thought, the fascination experienced when faced with the figures of so many gods, seers, and monsters eternally engendered by a mankind tortured by its own anxiety at the mystery of existence and life's ultimate purposes. In the maelstrom of *La*

Tentation, Flaubert's grand attempt to create a synthesis of all the thought of all ancient civilizations, the reader's consciousness was deluged and saturated with an imaginative conglomeration of unprecedented richness.

This torrent of thoughts, myths, and dreams was probably only partially perceived and assimilated by Flaubert's contemporaries; for although *Salammbô* achieved enormous success, the majority of the critics and the public recoiled from *La Tentation* with distaste. Yet after the writer's death, in 1880, it was precisely this aspect of his work that was to receive an ever-increasing acclaim, right up until the first years of the next century. Albert Samain, recalling his early days as a writer in his *Carnets intimes,* was to rank Flaubert among the masters whose influence was most powerful at that time: "Coming to 1880, we find three directors of souls: Baudelaire, Verlaine, and Mallarmé. . . . All three had taken a strong hold upon the esthetic imagination of that period, which was dominated in the field of prose by the Flaubert of *La Tentation de saint Antoine* and, some way behind him, Villiers de l'Isle-Adam."[128] Similarly, Gustave Kahn was to write in his book of reminiscences published in 1902: "The Symbolists had read Baudelaire and Flaubert a great deal."[129] In his manifesto of 1886, Moréas was to place *La Tentation* among the greatest works of world literature, alongside *Hamlet,* The *Vita Nuova,* and the second part of *Faust.* On the occasion of the fiftieth anniversary of symbolism, in 1936, Edmond Jaloux, who had himself been an active participant in the last years of the symbolist era, was also to assert that "*La Tentation de saint Antoine* is one of the books that had the greatest influence on symbolism."[130]

The proofs of this passionate preoccupation with Flaubert's work among late-nineteenth-century literary circles are legion. First, let us remember Bourget's article on Flaubert first printed in *La Nouvelle Revue,* then reprinted in his *Essais.* In it we find Bourget the critic laying much less stress on the depiction of everyday life to be found in *Madame Bovary* or *L'Education sentimentale* than on what he called Flaubert's "romanticism," and on his "nihilism," his rejection of the world he lived in and his passionate desire for escape into past civilizations. In chapter 9 of *A Rebours,* Des Esseintes has a woman ventriloquist recite the "admirable prose" of the dialogue between the Sphinx and the Chimaera, while in chapter 14 Huysmans devotes two paragraphs to summing up the fascination that the great writer held for his central character:

> Flaubert gave him gigantic and solemn tableaux, grandiose rituals through whose barbaric and splendid settings there circled delicate and quivering creatures, mysterious and haughty women, their souls steeped in suffering beneath the perfection of their beauty, and in whose depths he could

discern appalling signs of ruin, insane aspirations, ravaged as they already were by the menacing mediocrity of pleasures that might be to come.

The great artist's whole temperament exploded in those incomparable pages of *La Tentation de saint Antoine* and *Salammbô* in which, far from our cramped little lives, he conjured up the Asiatic brilliance of long-gone ages, their ejaculations, and their mystical founderings, their crazed idleness, their sudden ferocities provoked by the burden of boredom that flows in such abundance from opulence and prayer, even before they have been exhausted. [*A Rebours,* pp. 224–25]

The desire to escape the boredom of everyday life, reconstitution of paradise by means of art alone in the distant realms of long-past eras characterized by titanic and barbaric architecture, an attraction mingled with dread for the woman-idol, a fascination with subtly refined pleasures and forbidden delights, the dizzying pull of sadism and cruelty, those were indeed the essential constituents that the fin-de-siècle spirit was to owe to Flaubert.

At much the same time, Emile Hennequin—who after his premature death was described by Jules Huret in the introduction to his *Enquête sur l'évolution littéraire* as "unanimously acknowledged as the most considerable of the younger writers"[131]—wrote a long article about Flaubert that was to be published later in his *Etudes de critique scientifique.* In both the verse and prose writings of Jean Lorrain, whose first collection of poems, *Le Sang des dieux,* appeared in 1882, the influence of the Parnassians is clearly combined with that of Flaubert.[132] Lastly, in 1887 the Théâtre du Chat Noir mounted a *Tentation de saint Antoine,* apparently a kind of spectatular masque in two acts and forty scenes, devised by Henri Rivière, a former naval officer who had published a number of fantastic stories and had connections in decadent literary circles.

The interest in this aspect of Flaubert's work was to continue throughout the 1890s. In the first part of his *Thulé des brumes,* entitled "Fumées nocturnes" and first published in the December 1889 issue of *La Wallonie,* Adolphe Retté evokes the figure of Salammbô;[133] in 1893, Marcel Schwob wrote a preface for a new edition of *La Légende de Julien l'Hospitalier* in which he relates the theme of Flaubert's story to that of a number of other legends occurring in world folklore.[134] It was also at this time, during his visit to Paris, that Wilde wrote his *Salomé,* with a little help from some of his friends, such as Pierre Louys, over details of French grammar. In his collection of stories entitled *Monada,* published in 1894, Gabriel Mourey, using one of his characters as a mouthpiece, ranked *La Tentation* among the "masterpieces of dazzling splendor," alongside part 2 of *Faust,* and *Axël.*[135] In Marseilles, among the little coterie of young writers centered on the magazine *Méditerranée,* admiration for Flaubert in the years 1896 and 1897 was unanimous. Later still, during the first years of the twentieth century, in the salon frequented by the friends of Gilbert de Voisins, "hovering above everything were the shades of Baudelaire and the Flaubert of the *Tentation de saint Antoine* and the *Trois Contes.*"[136]

Flaubert's influence was also very much in evidence, moreover, in the work of two of the period's most original painters, Gustave Moreau and Odilon Redon, who in turn were to inspire many writers. The result was that during the last two decades of the nineteenth century a number of Flaubert's themes, and particularly the figure of Salome, acted as a catalyst, as it were, for a kind of osmosis between literature and the plastic arts. It was the legend of Salome, for example, that inspired two of Moreau's most famous paintings, *Salomé* and *Apparition,* the first of which depicts the princess dancing before the tetrarch, and the second a sort of hallucination in which Salome gazes at the head of John the Baptist, severed a moment before as the price of her dance, hovering in the air before her, surrounded by a halo, and fixing her with its eyes. In the ten or so pages devoted to Moreau in *A Rebours* Huysmans describes these two paintings in detail, evokes their backgrounds, which he describes as "that extraordinary palace so vague and grandiose in style," and interprets Salome as the symbol of "indestructible lust, goddess of immortal Hysteria, a Beauty accursed... first cause of all sins and all crimes" (pp. 83–91). Moreover this theme is one we find Jean Lorrain borrowing from Huysmans on several occasions, for example in a passage of his *Sensations et souvenirs,* then later, in 1901, in *Monsieur de Phocas.* Concluding the first of these two passages, Lorrain draws an explicit parallel between Flaubert and Moreau:

> This art of Gustave Moreau's... makes us think, despite ourselves, of the art of another visionary, Gustave Flaubert, the Flaubert who conjured up those refulgent nightmares in his *La Tentation* and that awe-inspiring dream of Carthaginian power.... Like Gustave Moreau, Gustave Flaubert was obsessed by ancient myths. Like the painter of the Sphinx, he was preoccupied above all with their cruel and sinister side.... And then, Flaubert and Moreau, writer and painter alike, did they not both conjure up for us that figure so dear to guilty lovers, Salome the drinker of blood, the poisonous flower at the tetrarch's feast, Salome and her mother, the bane of prophets, the adulterous princess...?[137]

Redon too, probably under the direct influence of Moreau,[138] depicted Salome in his charcoal drawing also entitled *Apparition,* which dates from the period between 1876 and 1879. However, the influence of Flaubert was to be even more pronounced in his work. In 1882, fired with enthusiasm for Redon's first exhibition of charcoal drawings in the *Gaulois* salons, Emile Hennequin made contact with the artist and introduced him to Flaubert's *La Tentation,* a move that led directly to the three famous series of Flaubert-inspired lithographs, the two *Tentations* of 1888 and 1896, and the album entitled *A Gustave Flaubert* of 1889.[139] These three sequences, which together contain forty-two lithographs in all, or almost a quarter of Redon's work in the medium, are startling proof of the fascination that Flaubert's work held for so many artists of the time. Furthermore, Redon's work was to provide abundant material for the pens of Hennequin, Huysmans, and Lorrain.[140]

Thus, whether directly or indirectly, through the work of painters like Moreau or Redon, the imaginative themes developed in certain of Flaubert's works were to be disseminated throughout French literary and artistic circles in general, and to make a very deep impression upon the entire decadent sensibility. From this Flaubert vogue, which became mingled with that of Parnassian exoticism and the fashion for far eastern art that originated in about 1870 with writers or art critics such as the Goncourts or Philippe Burty, there was to stem a whole stream of tales, novels, or novellas that all created a double artistic displacement, of time as well as space, by using more or less mythical settings located somewhere in the east at a time when its ancient civilizations were coming to an end and Christianity was looming on the horizon.

Theophile Gautier

The last of the previous generation of writers to capture the particular attention of decadent artists and writers was Théophile Gautier, and, more specifically, Gautier the theoretician of the famous *notice* on *Les Fleurs du mal* and the *Progrès de la poésie* of 1869, as well as Gautier the author of *Mademoiselle de Maupin.* After the series of tributes that followed his death, in 1872, it is true that Gautier's memory seems to have faded rather quickly. Neither the Parnassians, nor those destined to be leaders of the symbolist movement, appear to have felt any great enthusiasm for his verse works, despite isolated exceptions such as the sonnet that Mallarmé wrote in memory of him. Moreover his prose works, admittedly both diffuse and excessively prolix, if we take into account the vast quantity of critical articles and theater reviews he regularly contributed to *La Presse* and, later on, to *Le Moniteur,* had by no means all appeared in book form, so that they remained difficult of access. However, during the fifteen years after his death a few faithful disciples did make an effort to keep the memory of their master alive, and to celebrate the achievements of his work. In 1879, for example, Emile Bergerat published the first important critical work devoted to Gautier, and the preface was contributed by Edmond de Goncourt.[141] And even before the poet's death, the Vicomte Spoelberch de Lovenjoul had already started work on his monumental Gautier bibliography, which finally appeared in 1887.[142] Moreover, in the introduction to it he makes no secret of his great admiration for Gautier, and praises the power and precision of his descriptive writing, his total mastery of the language, and the breadth of his culture.

Although a large part of Gautier's work was no longer in print during the decadent period, the definitive edition of *Mademoiselle de Maupin,* on the other hand, first published by the house of Charpentier in 1851, was reprinted thirteen times between then and 1877, when a new edition appeared, and by 1883 that in turn had been reprinted nine times. By that time, moreover, Gautier had acquired a passionate disciple across the Channel in the person of Swinburne, and we may justifiably presume that the English poet, who was in constant touch with a number of French writers throughout his life, played some part in keeping the French master's reputation alive.[143] One has the impression that a literary polemic was developing during this period between two opposing trends in French literary criticism, one side viewing Gautier's work as a dead letter, the other continuing to assert its merits. We may perceive an echo of this dispute in the review Brunetière wrote of Lovenjoul's Gautier bibliography, where he distinguishes very clearly between the thunderous appreciations of Bergerat and Lovenjoul himself and the evaluations offered by other, more hostile critics, such as Faguet—in a chapter of his *Etudes littéraires sur le XIXe siècle* of 1886—and Scherer. While refusing to become embroiled in this dispute, Brunetière does nevertheless acknowledge that Gautier's work contains sufficient merits to keep it alive: "very real and quite rare poetic qualities," and esthetic ideas that "are not only clearer than many have wished to admit [but] also profounder." Lastly, and most importantly, he acknowledges the extent of Gautier's influence.[144]

Another indication of the renewed interest in Gautier is undoubtedly provided by the long and very detailed study of him by Maurice Spronck in his book *Les Artistes littéraires* mentioned earlier. Having first alluded to the conflicting opinions then prevalent as to Gautier's literary standing,

Spronck then offers a detailed analysis of d'Albert, the central character of *Mademoiselle de Maupin,* in whom he discerns one of the first expressions of the decadent sensibility. First and foremost, d'Albert suffers from a too precociously acquired experience of things and people, as well as from the corrosive influence of a self-critical dual personality:

> He was painfully burdened with an excessively acute experience of everything around him; even in childhood he had too easily acquired, by a sort of divination, an exact knowledge of life and humanity that made him unable to enjoy any pleasure unthinkingly. . . . The acuity of his critical sense, his detestable and all-dissolving critical turn of mind enveloped him so tightly that he could feel neither sensation nor emotion.[145]

Thus Spronck sees Gautier as a precursor of the pessimism so prevalent in the decadent era:

> Faced with his ruined loves, beliefs, and hopes, man is possessed by a furious passion for self-destruction, a desire to kill off his own individual thoughts, to sink himself without a trace in a sleep without dreams: and Théophile Gautier, long before Schopenhauer, long before the introduction of Buddhist doctrines into France, aspired to nihilism, to the dark Nirvana of Sakya-Muni and his disciples, to that absolute lethargy in which the being loses all capacity to suffer because it has lost all possibility of feeling.[146]

Thus we find yet one more illuminating example of the continuity existing between the romantic *mal du siècle* and the decadent sensibility.

These, then, were the principal authors whose memory and influence were to inspire French avant-garde writers during the last twenty years of the nineteenth century. Constantly read and consulted, celebrated as the great initiators, they were the figures who helped to mold the specific world vision, the metaphysical, moral, and esthetic concepts that form the background of that period's sensibility and imaginative orientation. And it is this intellectual underpinning to which we must now turn our attention.

2 THE SPIRITUAL HORIZON

THE WAY IN WHICH THE HUMAN MIND BEHAVES WITH REGARD TO ITS power of imagination, the greater or lesser trust it places in fiction and dreams, are always closely related to its general attitude with respect to reality and life, since it is the case that imagination usually plays an equilibrating and compensatory role in human existence. Any attempt to draw up a summary of the principal paths taken by imagination in French literature during the late nineteenth century must therefore be prefaced by a description of the world view generally prevalent at that time, and an examination of the period's fundamental convictions in the metaphysical, moral, and esthetic fields. If successive generations of writers at the end of the century hurled themselves so recklessly, with an often despairing and pathetic ardor, into the creation of compensatory worlds, then the reason must lie first and foremost in their fundamental dissatisfaction with reality. And the last twenty years of the nineteenth century did indeed see the steady rise of a wave of melancholy even more intense than that which had characterized the minds and works of the romantic era. It was the final resurgence of romanticism, its death throes, or, to borrow the term that Mario Praz employed in the title of his classic work, its agony. This is why it is important at this point to examine the general spirit that animated literary circles during these two decades, which were also called the age of pessimism, and to investigate the principal causes and forms of that pessimism.

The Decadent Sensibility: Pessimism

That the whole of French literary production at the end of the nineteenth century was impregnated with an atmosphere of pessimism is beyond dispute. Both the partisans and the opponents of the decadent movement were agreed in recognizing the extent of the phenomenon, which was moreover by no means confined to France, but

45

affected the whole of European literature. Evidence abounds in innumerable books and articles written at that time by such diverse writers as Ernest Caro, the Englishman James Sully, Emile Hennequin, and Brunetière; and the findings of these various observers all appear to point in the same direction. "Never has the question of evil and that of life's value been argued with such passion as in our own time," Caro claims in the preface to his work. "Is it true that the world is ill-begotten, that there is a radical, absolute, insuperable evil inherent in nature and mankind, that existence is a misfortune and that nothingness is better than being?" Pessimism, he also observes, "is a popular sickness that is spreading its subtle contagion in a certain number of minds and disordering them."[1] Some years later, in the course of an article on Schopenhauer—whose influence coincided with this fashion and, as we shall see, provided it with a doctrinal justification—the philosopher Burdeau notes, not without irony, that "one can observe a kind of dilettantism of weltschmertz, a certain metaphysical distaste for life, a platonic renunciation of the illusions of love, worn like a cosmetic by faces radiant with youth and vitality."[2]

"Literature seems determined that it shall be called Pessimism," Wyzewa observes for his part. "It gives us pessimist novels, pessimist plays, pessimist poems, pessimist criticism."[3] And Bourget, in the 1885 preface to his *Nouveaux Essais,* wrote that "the existence of pessimism in the soul of youth today is now recognized even by those who find this spirit of negation or depression most repugnant."[4]

What were the motive forces that governed this tide of melancholy now flowing through French literature for the second time in a century? The first, without doubt, was a specific belief, shared by most minds of the day, concerning the physical and biological state of modern man. The underlying melancholy of the decadent era stemmed first and foremost from a pseudomedical theme, that of the degeneration of the race. Even before the German journalist Max Nordau published his vast tome on this theme,[5] the idea of a general degeneration of the European races was already widespread. This belief had its origin in Darwinian theories concerning the evolution of species: like all animal species, man must follow the same path as that of each individual organism, from youth, through maturity, to old age. The peoples of Europe, inheritors of centuries of evolution, were therefore threatened with inevitable senility, and their civilization doomed to imminent death at the hands of peoples who had remained in a state closer to that of nature. Hovering over this entire era, therefore, we find the myth of a Twilight of the West, of a wholesale destruction of civilization similar to that which submerged Rome, then Byzantium, beneath the incoming waves of barbarian hordes. Indeed, even mankind in its entirety could very well vanish from the earth it if was true, as modern astronomers were then claiming, that every planet, too, had its own inevitable and circumscribed destiny, and that a cosmic catastrophe, involving collision with a comet, for instance, could not be excluded. Seen from this point of view, the moon, such a frequent presence in the literature of the time, could symbolize the astral corpse that the earth was sooner or later doomed to become. For the decadent sensibility, earth's satellite had ceased to be Chateaubriand's pale vestal; even sailing through dark and starry splendor it had become a macabre Damoclean reminder forever hanging over mankind's head. Moreover, since the species was condemned to annihilation, the meaning of the whole human adventure had become even more obscure. And if we add the fact that these astronomical data were also being vulgarized in works such as those of Camille Flammarion, and that certain philosophers, like Hartmann, were coldly envisaging the disappearance of the human race as a beneficial event, or even urging humanity to hasten its own end, it is not hard to see why ideas of this kind were able to exert such a dismal influence upon the contemporary imagination.

To these biological and astronomical justifications for such fatalism we must add the influence of contemporary theories concerning heredity, often posited on the basis of an inflexible belief that the defects acquired by any given generation must necessarily be handed on in perpetuity through all succeeding generations. This notion, a modern dress version of fate that provides the foundation for Zola's entire Rougon-Macquart series, was accepted all the more readily because it provided a sort of a posteriori justification for the Christian notion of original sin, the visiting of Adam and Eve's first error upon all mankind.[6] These themes, that of cosmic catastrophe or that of implacable heredity, recur constantly in the work of Laforgue, as in his *Hamlet,* for instance, when he writes "besides, everything is heredity,"[7] or in his *Chanson du petit hypertrophique* or his *Marche funèbre pour la mort de la Terre.*[8] Among other examples, further evidence of this widespread belief in the approaching dissolution of European civilization is to be found in Péladan's *Le Vice suprême* of 1884, in which he writes: "At those moments in history when a civilization is coming to an end the central fact is a spiritual nausea and, among the upper classes particularly, a weariness with existence."[9]

At the individual rather than the collective level, the idea then gaining ground was that modern man lives in a constant state of imbalance summed up in the new term neurosis; since the human machine was now worn out, man could keep going only by living on his nerves. In addition, recent psychiatric research had helped to remove the previously accepted boundaries between mental health and mental illness by revealing the very varied forms the latter can take, some of them quite capable of coexisting with an appearance of perfectly normal behavior.[10] Just as consumption had become fashionable in the romantic era, so it was now the vogue to present oneself as suffering from some nervous complaint, and even to cultivate one's malady. "My taste, if you wish, is depraved," Zola wrote as early as 1866, "I love literary ragouts that have been well spiced, decadent works in which a sort of nervous hypersensitivity has replaced the well-fleshed and blooming health of the classical periods. I am of my age."[11] Bourget, diagnosing this sickness of the age, wrote of "that state of continual and exacerbated agitation to which science has given the vague label of "nervous diathesis."[12] *Névroses* ("Neuroses") was the title Maurice Rollinat chose for his collection of Baudelairean poems published in 1883; and no less significant was the one he used for his famous pastiche collection of 1885: *Déliquescences. A Rebours,* published the previous year, not only provided the most complete condensation of all the decadents' esthetic themes, but also contained a clinical description of the progress of a nervous disease. In a review of it, Barbey d'Aurevilly was to define the central character's personality in these terms:

> Des Esseintes is no longer an organic being in the same way as Obermann, René, Adolphe, those heroes of human, passionate, and guilty novels. He is a mechanism breaking down. Nothing more.... In writing his hero's autobiography [Huysmans] has not just given us the confessions of a particular depraved and solitary personality, but he has at the same time written the nosography of a society destroyed by the rot of materialism.... Make no mistake! For a Decadent of this power to appear, and for a book such as M. Huysmans's to take root inside a human skull, we must truly have become what we in fact are—a race at its last gasp.[13]

This pessimism was reinforced on the political level by the emotional repercussions of France's defeat at the hands of Prussia in 1870, after a brief but catastrophic war which resulted in loss of territory, payment of a considerable indemnity, and lasting humiliation. Toward the end of the century French nationalism did begin to revive, and the idea of revenge gradually infiltrated ever broader sections of the population, but in the interim it was possible for many Frenchmen to believe that the dream of France's greatness was ended forever, that in the face of a unified and victorious Germany and a solid Victorian Britain, prodigiously enriched by its industrial economy and mistress of an immense empire, France was never again to carry any weight in world, or even European, affairs. It began to be said that a people could simply vanish—was history not filled with examples?—and that a nation could disintegrate, could cease to exist as an entity, its former territory irrevocably fragmented. Perhaps the defeat of 1870 was merely the first portent of a more general catastrophe, one in which the French state would be annihilated totally and forever. Responsibility for the defeat was undoubtedly laid largely at the door of the Second Empire it had destroyed; but the feeling remained that France, precisely because of the high level of civilization it had attained, had now become a particularly fragile organism, under threat of destruction by unspecified barbarian forces somewhere to the east. The memory of that defeat, which was the unspoken background to all French political thought in those days, also contributed to a predisposition among French thinkers to melancholy and disillusion.[14]

Finally, quite apart from prevalent ideas regarding the degeneration of the race and the accumulation of hereditary defects, the findings of positivist science were contributing still further reasons for pessimism, since they seemed to entail a view of the world as being totally determined by a series of laws at once ineluctable and blind, in other words, devoid of all poetry. This was in fact the burden of Bourget's essay *Science et poésie* referred to earlier. The advances of science entailed a reciprocal loss of religious belief and its consoling illusions. Maurice Spronck wrote:

> Unfortunately, and despite the efforts made earlier in the century to resuscitate dogmas already entering upon their death throes, Christianity seems to be a religion now advancing only under the momentum of its earlier acceleration, and losing further impetus with every day that passes. To any impartial judge of these things, its moral role in the history of humanity appears to be played out, and the hour is possibly not far off when the teachings of the dreamer of Nazareth will become irrevocably part of the past, along with the theogonies of the Greeks, the Celts, and the Scandinavians, upon whose ruins the Christian doctrine raised its dominion. No one can affect such inevitable developments: our poets, temperaments of ardent and delicate sensibility, contemplate them and draw attention to them, their hearts filled with terror. All, one after the other, take their turn to weep over the dying god, anguished at the knowledge that they will soon find themselves face to face with the void.[15]

The Tragedy of Art

To these general causes underlying the growth of pessimism in the population as a whole, however, we must also add certain other causes with a specific application to the situation of the artist. To begin with, it is a necessity of his profession that the artist continually search out new elements in reality, and to do so he must constantly probe ever deeper into his own sensations, discovering and experimenting with new ones, a process that can sometimes amount to a terrible kind of penal servitude, for example in the case of Rimbaud.[16] In 1881, Bourget defined Baudelaire as "a mind breaking down and analyzing its own sensations."[17] The following year, Rodenbach was to restate the same notion when he wrote in his *Notes sur le pessimisme:* "Never has the human mind been so complicated, so hypersensitized, so goaded by every conceivable curiosity with regard to its own sensations. Abuse of the brain, that is the great sickness. And the modern mind, overtaxed in this way, reaches a point where it agonizes over details, labors over the refinement of the most subtle anxieties."[18] In 1885, commenting on a work by Villiers de l'Isle-Adam, Henri Laujol expressed a similar view:

> This book needs readers such as Edgar Poe's sickly Usher, exquisite beings undermined by an incurable neurosis, whose senses, confused by the very power of their own acuity, succeed eventually in sniffing sounds and hearing scents. Nor are they uncommon today, those who have so abused their powers of sensation and dried up the wellsprings of pleasure in themselves! I have heard an exquisite dilettante say that the last act of *Tristan und Isolde* is "bliss in the spinal cord." This extremely modern remark sums up very well the perverted and sensual delights that certain gourmets now seek for in art. One does not read the *Tales of Mystery and Imagination* and *Les Fleurs du mal* with impunity. It is not without risk that one breathes the rarefied air of those gardens "from which the vegetable kingdom has been banished," magical hothouses warm with poisoned fragrances, artificial paradises saturated with dubious and unsettling scents.[19]

This frenzied quest for new sensations soon exhausts the possibilities provided by the senses, however, and persisting in it quickly turns the artist into a sick man. His hypersensitized nervous system on the verge of breakdown, he soon sinks into depression or "spleen" as the reality he has inventoried from top to bottom gradually, inexorably, ceases to hold any charm for him, and the preconditions of happiness become ever more rarefied. It was this process that Bourget had diagnosed, as we saw earlier, in both Baudelaire and Flaubert.

By vocation, and compelled by the very acuity of his critical intelligence, the artist is also led to dissect every possible emotion, those he experiences himself as well as those of others, in order to discover their hidden causes and mechanisms. Victim of a fatal duality inherent in his personality, he destroys all spontaneity in himself, so that he is doomed to be constantly torn between the two sides of his own nature, one experiencing with great intensity, and even pain, all the impressions life has to offer, the other, lucid and disillusioned, coldly observing and judging them. This affliction specific to the writer was often deplored during the decadent period, and particularly by Emile Hennequin in his article, mentioned earlier, "Le Pessimisme des écrivains," and by Maupassant in several passages of his *Sur l'eau*. Both remark that artists tend to fall victim to the hyperacuity of their sensations: "What usually drives them into hypochondria," Hennequin observes,

> is an abnormal exaggeration of their sensibilities. The very essence of the artistic temperament is to possess a vivid perception of all the spectacles presented by the world about us, which normally elude obtuse and healthy minds to a large extent. The artist is like a stretched string, a sheet of sensitized paper, or a chemical reagent, he is bound to react sharply to all sounds, all sights, all smells, to a sunbeam striking a wall, the screech of an oar in its oarlock, the delicious trail of fragrance left by a delicately complexioned stranger in her wake.... Hence the habitual pessimism of most modern French writers, from Chateaubriand to Gautier, from Flaubert to M. Huysmans, from M. Zola to the Goncourts, who have themselves written a number of significant reflections on this subject.[20]

Maupassant defines the originality of the artistic temperament in these terms:

> The artist's mind is so constructed that the repercussions set off within it by external stimuli are much sharper, much more natural, as it were, than the first shock of contact.... His specific and morbid sensibility turns him, moreover, into a being flayed alive, for whom almost all sensations have become painful. I can recall those black days when my heart was so lacerated by things glimpsed only for the merest second that the memories of those visions still live on in me now like open wounds.[21]

Having developed these personal variations on Baudelaire's *Le Confiteor de l'artiste*, however, both writers also go on to deplore the deadly consequences of this schizoid state, the existence of that "impassive and too perspicacious onlooker who destroys all spontaneous activity within them by constant censorship,"[22] the "second sight that is simultaneously the strength and the whole wretchedness of writers."[23] And we find Maupassant describing the workings and effects of this dual personality in detail:

> In the writer all simple emotion has ceased to exist. Every-
> thing he sees, his joys, his pleasures, his suffering, his de-
> spair, instantly become subjects for observation. Hearts,
> faces, gestures, intonations are all analyzed, endlessly and
> despite everything. As soon as he has seen whatever he has
> seen, he must know the why and wherefore of it. Not a
> single impulse, or cry, or kiss of his is ever unequivocal. . . .
> An actor and a spectator of himself and others, he is never
> just an actor, as those good and simple folk are who live life
> unaware. Everything around him is transparent glass,
> hearts, actions, concealed intentions, and he suffers from a
> strange affliction, a sort of dual personality, that makes him
> into a terrifyingly contrived and complicated creature in a
> state of constant vibration. [*Sur l'eau,* pp. 106, 109]

This being so, the artist becomes an unbalanced being in whom an
excessive delicacy of the sensibility and the nerves, plus a hypertrophied
critical intelligence, takes its revenge by destroying the faculty of will and
the desire to act. This impotence of the will is aggravated by the very
breadth of his culture: when he turns his gaze back to the past, to the
successive civilizations of which he has become the depository, when he
observes the infinite diversity of customs and beliefs that mankind has
successively adopted and then rejected, the incessant contradictions of
dogmas and religions, then the modern artist experiences the same anguish as that which lacerated Flaubert's St. Anthony, and the naive faith
of former ages is succeeded by an inevitable and profound skepticism. In
Bourget's eyes, the chief promoter of this skepticism was Renan, aided by
recent developments in the history of religion and the increasing familiarity of Europeans with Eastern cultures. In essence a relativism taken to its
furthest extreme, such skepticism resulted, in practical terms, in two
specific contemporary trends that Bourget then goes on to analyze. First,
dilettantism, which consists in a refusal, and an incapacity, to take up any
definitive moral or esthetic stance, a sort of Don Juanism of the intellect. Second, cosmopolitanism, which makes the artist into a being
forever deprived of roots, incapable of integrating himself into any national collectivity. The modern artist, by the very fact that his reading or
esthetic experiences are so far-ranging and disparate, is afflicted by indifference, is transformed into a being aware of universal futility, convinced of the inevitable death of all civilizations and all religions, forced to
contemplate the ideas that keep the common run of mankind
functioning—and constantly at each other's throats—with an ironic or
bitter skepticism. Some years later, when the tide of nationalist feeling
had begun to run more strongly again in France, these same tendencies

were to elicit vociferous attacks from those writers who had become the high priests of national energy or champions of established values, such as Barrès or, again, Bourget. For the moment, however, the decadent artist felt himself isolated, cut off from the society around him; he shrank from contact with his fellow men, and, out of aristocratic disdain for vulgar ambition, shut himself away, retired to his own inner world, which he made into a paradise of art dedicated to esthetic contemplation. Often, indeed, like the Bourget of *Science et poèsie,* his rejection of the modern world led him to repudiate everything that constituted the ideological foundation of contemporary society: progress, science, democracy, universal suffrage, and the spread of education.

Such a state of isolation, which the artist experienced as a necessity but which, at the same time, he could not but find painful, was to find apparent scientific justification in the work of certain contemporary physiologists and physicians, who displayed a growing tendency to regard artists as abnormal, and to identify genius with mental disease. Although modern man in general was threatened with neurosis, the artist, by the very fact of his exceptional faculties and the kind of life he led, so the argument went, was doomed to be the first and worst afflicted. This notion, widespread in medical circles at the time, was to give rise to two works that both caused a great stir when they appeared. They were *The Man of Genius* by the Italian physician Cesare Lombroso and *Entartung* ("Degeneration") by the German journalist Max Nordau.

The key notion in Lombroso's work is best summed up by a phrase from his own introduction: Genius is a neurosis. And Lombroso does indeed seem to set out from the a priori notion that the development of certain faculties is necessarily paid for by a corresponding atrophy of certain others. Lombroso therefore begins by attempting to establish the influence of a certain number of objective factors, such as climate, heredity, diseases, and the urban environment, on the emergence of men of genius. Then, with the help of copious statistics and erudite references, he lists and examines a large mass of evidence relating to the personal lives of great geniuses of the past, and strives to prove that in every case the genius displayed was closely associated with more or less obvious abnormalities and with pathological or psychological disturbances. At the same time, evidently anxious to discover artistic capacities in mental patients, he devotes another whole chapter of his work to studying the works of art produced by acknowledged madmen (pt. 3, chap. 2). He then proceeds to offer his logical conclusion, which consists in regarding genius as one particular variety of madness. And it is clearly this conviction that is conditioning his account of various trends in contemporary art and literature. The decadents, for example, are in his eyes genuine mental cases, for whom he creates the category "literary and artistic mattoid," the term *mattoid* in his nomenclature denoting a borderline case between the sane and the insane. The French translation of Lombroso's work was preceded by a preface from the pen of Charles Richet, one of the country's most celebrated physiologists at that time, in which, despite several slight demurs, the Italian's thesis is warmly endorsed.[24] Thus the idea that avant-garde artists are a kind of madmen, already commonplace among the lower classes, was provided with a scientific justification in the decadent era by the work and findings of a small section of contemporary medical scientists, a fact that could serve only to widen the divide that had already opened up between writers and society.

A few years later, Lombroso's principal ideas were to be taken up, and exaggerated to the point of caricature, by Max Nordau. Although not a doctor but a journalist, Nordau nevertheless took great pains to lend his thesis an air of scientific plausibility. Not only does its exposition require two large volumes—dedicated, incidentally, to Lombroso—but the first two chapters are entitled "Symptoms" and "Diagnosis," and its author never misses any opportunity to employ the scientific jargon then current among contemporary psychophysiologists and psychiatrists. He likewise undertakes to provide scientific definitions of the objective causes that have produced this state of degeneracy he claims to have discovered: the use of toxic stimulants such as tobacco and alcohol, living in large cities, and the conditions of modern life.

In reality, behind this flashy and superficial scientific facade, the work turns out to be merely a polemic, outrageous and often ridiculous in its exaggerations, against any kind of modern art, all forms of which are branded, indiscriminately and impartially, with the dreadful stigma of degeneracy. Like many of his contemporaries, in attempting to isolate the constituents of the fin-de-siècle zeitgeist Nordau notes the prevalence of an obsession in the minds of the élite with approaching destruction, with a Twilight of the Peoples. He also deplores the profound degradation observable in artistic circles, accuses them of being egotistic, and sees in the psychology of each artist what he regards as proofs of degeneracy: a surrender to impulses and emotivity, a state of intellectual discouragement and impotence, an aversion from any kind of action.

After this general diagnosis, Nordau devotes the remainder of his work to examining the main esthetic trends observable in Europe generally since the beginning of the century. He deals successively with the Pre-Raphaelites, the French symbolists, the ideas and influence of Tolstoy and Wagner, egotism, the "Parnassians and devil-worshipers," the Aesthetes and decadents, and so on. Moreover he sees almost all these trends as echoes of German romanticism, with its reaction against rationalism, its discovery of the unconscious and its irrational forces, its emphasis on emotion and instinct, and its predilection for wild associations of ideas. From this standpoint, the poetic technique of the symbol, as employed by French poets at that time, appears in his eyes to be merely proof of a disordered mind, the result of a preference for imprecise words and chaotic ideas. In the same way, egotism, which for Nordau constitutes one of the prime characteristics of contemporary literature, is to be explained by a breakdown of the perceptual apparatus: the external world does not exist in the consciousness of the emotional degenerate.

These analyses were accompanied, as might be expected, by unflattering assessments of most of the artists concerned. Thus Rossetti is weak-minded, Swinburne a degenerate whose mysticism is characterized as being more perverse and criminal in nature than paradisiac or pious, and Verlaine a dipsomaniac cyclothymic. In Verlaine's case, indeed, while paradoxically admitting that he sometimes achieved results of great beauty, Nordau still did not hesitate to recommend his hospitalization. Nor is he any less severe on Wagner, or on Baudelaire. He also examines the work of the decadents, whom he defines as the school of Baudelaire, including works by Barbey d'Aurevilly, Villiers de l'Isle-Adam, and Barrès; investigates the decadent novel; and devotes ten or so pages to analyzing the ideas of Wilde, whom he regards as the model of the Aesthetes.

Despite its glaringly polemical character, and the evident excesses or gross simplifications that merely sent most of the French writers concerned into gales of laughter—they had already often amused themselves by deliberately leading poor Nordau up the garden path when he was researching his book in Paris earlier—this work does provide a well-documented and complete panorama of all the fashionable artistic trends in Europe at that time, while shedding light on the extent to which artists in general were isolated from the society in which they lived.

Schopenhauer

This pessimism, which existed in a diffused state throughout all the artistic circles of the time, was to find both its doctrinal justification and an added stimulus in the work of a German philosopher who was to enjoy considerable celebrity, and to exert a constantly growing influence, during the century's last two decades: Schopenhauer. His work itself was of course by no means recent—*Die Welt als Wille und Vorstellung* (*The World as Will and Idea*) was published as early as 1819—but even in Germany no real appreciation of it occurred until the ten years before the philosopher's death in 1860. In France, it did not begin to become known, other than by specialists in the field, until after

1880.[25] Indeed, the first French translation of *The World as Will and Idea* did not appear until 1886.[26] Until that date the only translations published had been of extracts or relatively minor works.[27] Nevertheless, the critical studies and commentaries his work had given rise to were sufficiently numerous to give the French public, not a complete view of the German philosopher's thought it is true, but at least a fair enough knowledge of the arguments upon which his pessimist thesis was based.

Starting from the observation that the totality of life's misfortune always far outweighs any happiness that man can achieve, and that any pleasure he can experience is purely negative, since it consists solely in a temporary cessation of suffering, Schopenhauer attributed this fundamental unhappiness of life to a force present in all living species that he termed the Will to Live, or simply Will. It is Will that arouses hopes in man that are disproportionate to his real possibilities for happiness, and thus condemns him to an inevitable and perpetual disenchantment. It is therefore necessary, as he saw it, to liberate oneself as far as possible from this Will to Live, to cease conceiving desires and projecting them onto the world, and to adopt a purely intellectual and disinterested attitude toward that world. Will must be replaced by Idea, a lucid understanding purged of all self-deception. In this way it is possible to achieve a purely contemplative state not far removed from that sought by the Hindu mystics, for whom Schopenhauer felt a great sympathy.

Schopenhauer also devotes a large part of his work to inventorying the various causes of the unhappiness to which men are subjected, and the only answer to which, he asserts, is a total renunciation of all the passions and all the interests that underlie the agitation to which modern man is prey, allied with an attitude of compassion toward those who continue to concern themselves with the illusions of life. He was severe and caustic in his attitude to women, whom he regarded as spiritually inferior to men, and accused of being unconscious but dangerous instruments of the Will to Live and its savage but absurd determination to achieve the survival of the species by all possible means. The only true happiness permitted to man, in his view, was esthetic contemplation, and his philosophy led to a morality based on salvation through art, accessible to that small minority of beings endowed with culture and esthetic sensibility.

Schopenhauer's ideas were later taken further, and expressed in even stronger terms, by one of his disciples, Eduard von Hartmann, whose *Philosophy of the Unconscious* appeared in French translation in 1877.[28] Hartmann, having broadened the concept of Will and renamed it the Unconscious, identified it as the essential factor in the ceaseless and also futile proliferation of life. Subscribing wholly to his teacher's pessimism, he expressed a wish for mankind's early demise, and was of the opinion that the human race, once convinced of the absurdity of existence, would renounce self-reproduction and continued survival of its own accord. That being so, the duty of philosophers and politicians should be to facilitate an acceleration of this inevitable process by every possible means. Thus, while Schopenhauer's philosophy led to the renunciation of the sage, and to the life of the esthete withdrawn into a world of art, Hartmann's much more radical thinking led to a call for the end of the world brought about by voluntary extinction of the human species.

Schopenhauer's and Hartmann's principal ideas soon received wide dissemination in France. After a first article in 1870 by Challemel-Lacour,[29] it fell to Théodule Ribot to become the principal exponent of Schopenhauer's doctrines among French speakers with his book *La Philosophie de Schopenhauer* of 1874. Having first given a brief account of the German philosopher's life, and set out the general principles informing his work, Ribot began by analyzing his theory of knowledge, which had been inspired by that of Kant and was oriented toward transcendental idealism. For Schopenhauer, as for Kant, the subject has no knowledge of the world that is not filtered through man's own mental structure. In other words, he never apprehends reality, the thing in itself, but only his own ideas or representations of reality: "This dependence of the object in relation to the subject constitutes the ideality of the world as representation. Our body itself, insofar as we know it as object, that is to say as occupying space and acting in the world, is no more than a cerebral phenomenon that exists solely in the intuition of our brain."[30] And Schopenhauer's celebrated dictum, "the world is my idea," was quickly to become one of the French decadents' constant leitmotifs, as we shall see. Ribot then went on to investigate the theory of will, to which, it must be said, he attributed a particular meaning ultimately rather far removed from Schopenhauer's own. Finally, Ribot expounded the liberating role that Schopenhauer assigns to creation and esthetic contemplation.

This still somewhat summary account by Ribot was later to be enlarged upon in the works by Ernest Caro and James Sully mentioned above. Caro, whose principal intention was to provide a refutation of pessimism, undertook a detailed analysis of both Schopenhauer's and Hartmann's thought. He rightly lays great stress on the role Schopenhauer attributes to his Will to Live as a force of deception. Caro himself calls it "a cunning force that envelops every living being, especially man, in illusions inimical to his happiness" (*Le Pessimisme au XIXe siècle*, p. 118), and "a blind, unconscious desire to live" (p. 119). He then examines the German thinker's condemnation of the idea of progress (p. 120), elucidates his rejection of sexuality and his antifeminism, and analyzes his "metaphysics of love," which Caro regarded as one of the most original parts of his theory.

Turning to Hartmann, he analyzes in detail the proofs put forward for the statistical superiority of suffering over pleasure. Finally, in his seventh chapter, *Le Bouddhisme moderne,* he studies the role Schopenhauer attributed to esthetic activity, and defines the superior state attained by esthetic contemplation:

> The object no longer exists, it is the idea that exists, the eternal form; and the subject likewise has been raised to a higher plane, has liberated himself: he is free from time, free from Will, free from striving, free from desire, free from pain: he participates in the absolute, in the eternity of the idea, he is dead to himself, he no longer exists other than in the ideal. This being so, of what importance are the conditions and forms of his transitory individuality? Of what importance is it, in this state of absolute disinterest, whether one contemplates a sunset from a prison cell or from a palace? There is no longer any prisoner, no longer any king; there is only pure intuition, a free vision of the ideal, a momentary participation in Plato's idea, in Kant's numen, once one has attained this forgetfulness of one's transitory life, of the role one plays in it, and of the everyday torment thus momentarily suspended! [P. 215]

Such is indeed the state to which most decadent writers, more or less consciously and more or less continuously, were to aspire. Sully, in his book, devotes a chapter each to both Schopenhauer and Hartmann, and concentrates especially on the idea that love, in Schopenhauer, is reduced to sexuality, to an unconscious instinct aimed at the propagation of the species, and that there is no alternative to suffering but boredom.

As translations of Schopenhauer's work began to appear, so commentaries and articles began to flow from the presses in growing numbers.[31] From now on, Schopenhauer was indisputably a writer in vogue, his name definitively associated with the current of contemporary pessimism and modern literary trends. Apart from the obvious literary qualities of his work, the decadents were to find in Schopenhauer many of the ideas dear to their hearts: condemnation of the notion of progress; profound analyses of love and an illumination of the role played by the unconscious; hostility to women viewed as mere instruments of nature; and, lastly, a theory of salvation through esthetic contemplation, which was an extension of the doctrine of art for art's sake and in perfect conformity with the attitude of those soon to be labeled "aesthetes," whose attempted aim was to replace reality with art.

From 1880 onward, proofs of this Schopenhauer vogue abound. Whereas in 1878 Caro was still expressing doubt as to the success of the

German philosopher's teachings in France, only a few years later the evidence of that success was already apparent on all sides. After 1880, for example, we begin to find frequent references to Schopenhauer and his theories in Bourget's articles, and in 1883 his whole column in *Le Parlement* was given over on one occasion to a discussion of the extent of the German philosopher's influence.[32] Maupassant's reaction was similar.[33] In one of the stories he published in 1883, *Auprès d'un mort*, the narrator recounts a chance meeting he had on a journey once with a German who had been one of Schopenhauer's close friends, and had actually been present at his death. And Maupassant makes use of this anecdote to express his admiration for "the immortal thought of the greatest trampler of dreams that ever passed across the face of the earth."[34] A few years later, in *Sur l'eau*, which appeared in 1888 and is in many respects one of the most significant contemporary accounts of the decadent spirit, he was to develop his own variations on the German master's principal themes: the monotony and irremediable boredom of existence; the stupidity of the average man; a denunciation of the notion of progress on account of mankind's incurable barbarism; antinaturalism; and skepticism about democracy. In 1884, in his article for the *Revue des Deux Mondes* mentioned earlier, and written to mark the inauguration of an international committee created to prepare for the centenary of the philosopher's birth, Burdeau records the progress of his influence:

> This moment is all the more propitious for raising a bust to Schopenhauer in that his philosophy, as he himself foresaw, seems to be enjoying that "brief interlude of celebrity between two long stretches of time when it will either be cursed as a paradox or despised as a triviality".... What has become popular in Schopenhauer's work are the pages on ethics, the profound chapter on the metaphysics of love, his acrimonious thrusts at women, and the doctrine of pessimism that occurs throughout all his writings. As in the case of Byron and Byronism earlier, fashion has taken a hand in this.... The name of Schopenhauer is on everyone's lips; he is analyzed by professors of philosophy and quoted in our drawing rooms. The literature dealing with his work, and with his life and character, increases year by year, almost month by month. [Pp. 917–18]

Several weeks after this article came the publication of *A Rebours*, in which Huysmans compares the teachings of the German philosopher with the traditional teachings of the Roman Church as formulated, for example, in *The Imitation of Christ*, and ultimately casts his vote in favor of the former.

Several years later, references either to Schopenhauer or to his theories had become one of the commonplaces of the age, and he had become a major influence far beyond specifically decadent circles. In 1886, Brunetière, who can hardly be accused of favoring the fashionable young writers of the time, felt himself in a position to prophesy that "it may well turn out one day that Schopenhauer, along with Darwin, will have proved to be the man whose ideas have exerted the profoundest influence of all on the last years of this century."[35] In the address to the reader prefacing the first number of *Le Décadent*, which appeared on 10 April 1886, Anatole Baju, its editor and thus, we may presume, the author of this text, lists "Schopenhauerism taken to extremes" as one of the "premonitory symptoms of [contemporary] social evolution." And in 1894 Nordau was to view this success story as confirmation of his theories. Finally, it was also at this time that Rémy de Gourmont discovered in Schopenhauer's transcendentalism one of the bases for his own philosophic idealism.[36]

In short, throughout the last twenty years of the nineteenth century Schopenhauer's literary fortunes in France were to be closely linked with the progress of the decadent esthetic and sensibility. Many writers of that time, indeed the majority, were deeply imbued with his work, which provided them with a philosophic foundation for the profound melancholy and discouragement by which they felt weighed down, and in return they were to guarantee his work an even wider dissemination in France than it probably enjoyed in its country of origin.

A Portrait of the Decadent Hero

Boredom, melancholy, disillusion, discouragement, such were the effects of this pessimism on the decadent sensibility, and also the essential elements in the makeup of the fin-de-siècle hero, of whom certain works, such as Huysmans's *A Rebours* of 1884, Edouard Rod's *La Course à la mort* of 1885, and Rémy de Gourmont's *Sixtine* of 1890, provide convergent descriptions. Des Esseintes's whole existence is poisoned by boredom, despite all the counterirritants he essays one after another. "Despite every attempt he made," the author tells us, "an immense boredom oppressed him,"[37] a boredom one also recognizes in this passage from Maupassant's novella *Suicide:* "Repetition of the same visions ended by filling my heart with weariness and boredom, as though I were a theatergoer walking night after night into the same theater. . . . Everything repeats itself, endlessly, lamentably." This same feeling of life's inexorable monotony was to well up also in *Sur l'eau:*

> Happy those who never experience the sickening disgust
> caused by the same actions endlessly repeated; happy those

who have the strength to begin the same tasks afresh each
day, with the same gestures, around the same furniture,
faced with the same horizon, beneath the same sky, to walk
out through the same streets where they pass the same faces
and the same animals. Happy those who do not perceive
with an immense revulsion that nothing changes, that everything is constant, and constantly more wearisome.[38]

The monotony of an existence perpetually bounded by the same environment, the unchanging banality of nature, the profound triviality of
men, the solitude of the individual eternally imprisoned inside his own
consciousness, the fraudulence of love and those great collective illusions
progress and democracy, these were the wellsprings from which decadent
melancholy constantly replenished itself. It recurs yet again in *La Course
à la mort*, whose hero is afflicted by an inexorable lassitude,[39] sickened by
the routine trivialities of life (p. 97), painfully aware of love's illusions (p.
112), and ultimately convinced of the vanity of everything.[40] It also im-
bues the majority of Laforgue's poems with that sarcastic irony, that
desire for self-destruction through relentless mockery that they display so
constantly. It also leaves its mark on the principal characters of his *Moralités Légendaires:* Hamlet exclaiming, "Ah! how superior my boredom
is!" (p. 50); the tetrarch Emeraude-Archétypas asking Salome to provide
him with some form of distraction because "I'm bored, we are all so
bored!" (p. 165); or Andromeda, confiding in the birds that fly across her
island, "O migrating flocks that pass and do not see me, o waves, you
hordes forever sweeping in to die and bringing nothing for me, how bored
I am!" (p. 218). Anatole Baju, in his book *L'Ecole décadente*, was even to
speak of "a modern spleen."[41] And d'Entragues, the hero of Rémy de
Gourmont's *Sixtine*, confides in the reader: "I'm ashamed to admit it, the
affliction is such a common one, but I am bored. Waking in the morning is
an agony. I believe in nothing and I feel no love."[42] And Gourmont
himself was to observe, in his *Livre des masques* of 1896, referring to the
literature of the day, that "it was the literature of sadness, of anxiety, and
of anguish" (p. 20).

This sadness was much more profound, and more dramatic, however,
than the romantic melancholy of which it constitutes the extreme aggra-
vation. Like Baudelaire's "spleen" it has physical and physiological
foundations. Contemporary observers regarded it as stemming from the
individual or collective pathological disturbances mentioned earlier: the
decline of nations exhausted by the senility of their civilization; the physical instability caused by the ever more artificial conditions of modern life;
and the exacerbation of their nervous sensibilities that led artists to live in
a state of constant mental erethism; an atrophy of the will eventually

resulting in the triumph of uncontrolled association of ideas and anarchic reverie. And it is a fact that most decadent heroes are clearly abulic in character, unable to take any decision, gnawed by doubt, living wholly isolated from society, like Des Esseintes in his retreat at Fontenay. Imprisoned within the narrow circle of their own preoccupations, they yearn constantly for ways of escape not to be found in real life. When they initiate emotional or sexual relationships they are forced before long, like Des Esseintes, to seek for ways of evading impending impotence, to resort to dubious refinements of sensation or the various sexual perversions. Or else, like the hero of *La Course à la mort*, if they do perchance begin to experience some degree of feeling for the object of their advances, however slight, they dare not admit it to her. Or again, like d'Entragues, they allow themselves to be cut out by a more enterprising rival. Every one of their momentary impulses toward action is swiftly balked by the demon of analysis, the fever of intellectual scruple, or the skeptical indifference secreted by their universal satiety. Often, however, they are also genuinely sick men: *A Rebours* is not only a synthesis of all the intellectual themes that constituted the decadent esthetic, but it is also a clinical account of a progressive neurosis, the various phases of which, from simple anemia to various forms of hallucination, are minutely chronicled.

In its most acute forms, this fin-de-siècle sickness leads to morbid obsessions, such as those that inform Rollinat's poems, or those that torture the sensibility of Hughes Viane, the hero of Georges Rodenbach's novel *Bruges-la-morte*. Recently widowed, Viane is at first inconsolable, his life an unending recreation of his dead wife in memory and imagination. Against the melancholy setting of a totally deserted Bruges, a network of stagnant canals and pools, he experiences "the desire to have done with his life, an impatience for the grave";[43] he is pursued by "obsessive thoughts of suicide" (p. 24). For suicide and annihilation are in fact the ultimate desire of the majority of these characters. "We aspired to the NOT TO BE," Rod's hero declares. "We plunged deep together into the sweet waters of nothingness, so deep that no one will ever fathom it" (p. 93). In Maupassant's characters, these morbid tendencies were to manifest themselves in fits of irrational fear and angst which lead them to the very gates of madness, and sometimes beyond. Maupassant was to examine the problem of suicide several times, and expressed his sympathy and pity for those who have the courage to resort to it:

> How I understood them, those poor creatures, hounded by
> ill luck, bereft of their loved ones, awakened from the dream
> of a long-delayed reward, of the illusion of another life
> where God will finally be just after having been so cruel and

> relentless in this one, their eyes opened to the mirage of happiness, all those who have had enough and wish to end this endless tragedy or shameful comedy. Suicide! the strength of those who have no strength left, the hope of those who have ceased to believe.[44]

In a less intense form, this obsession with death that runs through the whole of the decadent era was also to lead to the frequently somewhat overdone element of ghoulishness so often found in stories of the time, such as those by Rachilde or Jean Lorrain.

The decadent spirit thus exemplifies an attitude of total rejection of life, absolute condemnation of existence. "My soul," Villiers de l'Isle-Adam wrote, "is not of these bitter times." This same assertion, already inherent in Mallarmé's *Les Fenêtres,* is encountered time and time again, from the pens of countless writers, throughout the decade between 1880 and 1890. Des Esseintes repeatedly expresses his horror of life and modern society,[45] and we find the hero of *La Course à la mort* exclaiming: "That is life. Oh, how I loathe it in all its manifestation!" (p. 228). It is therefore hardly astonishing that these characters should be driven by a frenzied determination to escape from that life. Des Esseintes feels "an unrelenting desire to escape from the world's vulgarities" (p. 177); requires of the works of art he admires that they shall bring him release from "this trivial life of which he was so weary" (p. 223); and seeks to "escape from the penitentiary of his own time" (p. 224).

Idealism: Villiers de l'Isle-Adam

In order to counterbalance the profound pessimism that possessed them, and to find reasons for living in spite of it, all the decadent writers also expressed allegiance, with varying degrees of lucidity and explicitness, to a philosophic attitude that they themselves described as idealism. This term was used extremely vaguely, however, as Rémy de Gourmont was to observe when, in 1895, he launched an attack on the uses to which it was being put by the press at large and most of the reading public:

> You will find this word lurking in every newpaper. . . . It is used to mean everything and nothing. To these limited and simplistic minds idealism is the opposite of naturalism, so everything is quite simple: it means romance, the stars, progress, hansom cab horses, lighthouses, love, mountains, the common people—the whole of that sentimental mishmash with which our society folk stuff their dainty little sandwiches as they chitter and chatter over the teacups.[46]

Before it became degraded to the status of a mere vague sentimentalism, however, idealism had been adopted by a whole series of writers who had attempted to give the term a more precise connotation, and to base their moral and esthetic conduct on a more or less coherently worked out code.

Among these writers, the first and most representative, as well as the most profoundly influential, was undoubtedly Villiers de l'Isle-Adam.[47] In consequence, I feel it is indispensable to take a fairly detailed look at the phenomenon of idealism as he conceived it, for, although it may have varied as to its form and orientation over his career as a whole, it nevertheless remained a constant and essential constituent factor of all his thought. We find evidence of its presence as early as 1866, in *Morgane*, when he expresses his contempt for the world of appearances and his resolve to regard nothing as real but his inner world, as in these words that Sergius addresses to Lady Hamilton: "Learn, black-masked sorceress, that I scorn the pains of the body . . . and that, strong in the sense of my own eternity, I do not permit what you have decided to call the Real to be anything for me, ever, but that which occurs behind my brow."[48]

In his *Claire Lenoir*, published the following year, he set out his philosophical conceptions, at some length, in fictional form. Of the book's three characters, whose debates during a long evening together occupy an appreciable part of the work, each represents an attitude to the problem of reality. Confronting Tribulat Bonhomet, who symbolizes contemporary positivist science, we have Césaire Lenoir and his wife, Claire, whose divergent attitudes presumably reflect the hesitations and ambivalence of Villiers's own thought at that time. Arraigning the claims of positivism, Villiers begins by denying the reality of the perceptible world. Taking as his example a log that is burning in the fire around which the three are gathered, Césaire observes that this so-called real world is in fact solely composed of constantly changing qualities, and that the real substance of it must always inevitable elude us. It is thus possible to say that the log in question exists solely "between our eyelashes."[49] The "real" universe, with its ceaseless modifications, is nothing but a "phantasmagorical system of creation, disappearance, and transformation" (p. 186). Claire then speaks at length in support of Césaire's ideas and declares that "we are the playthings of a perpetual illusion. . . . And the universe is in a very real sense a dream" (pp. 193–94). Villiers's first concern, then, is to discredit the claim of modern science to be a method of establishing reality.

Having thus contested the reality of the phenomenal world, the first path Villiers seems to have attempted to take out of his dilemma at this period was spiritualism, or spiritism as it is more properly known, in which he hoped to find confirmation of his belief in the presence of a purely spiritual universe (spiritualism in the philosophical sense). Césaire

Lenoir is depicted as an expert in spiritist doctrine and a fervent reader of the great figures of occultism, such as Swedenborg, Raymond Lully, and Eliphas Lévi (pp. 119–28). Césaire himself states his belief in the possibility of direct action on the part of the dead, whose moral personality, he claims, survives for some time at least after physical dissolution. He also reiterates the occultist theory that every human being is a duality, made up not only of a visible and material body but also of an astral body—which Villiers terms the sidereal body (chap. 14)—and which is capable, given certain specific conditions, of leaving the terrestrial world and traveling freely through cosmic space. Villiers became fascinated quite early on by the various spiritist theories that became widely disseminated throughout Parisian society during the Second Empire, and was strongly influenced by *Dogme et rituel de haute magie* by Eliphas Lévi, which he had first encountered in 1866.[50] The influence of these various schools is fairly clearly revealed in his work over a number of years; but after 1875 he was to take an increasingly skeptical attitude toward them, and by 1884, in *Les Expériences du Dr. Crookes*, he was returning a definitive verdict against spiritism, which he had come by then to regard as incompatible with the data of the Roman Church.[51]

This vein of spiritism apart, however, Villiers then goes on, still using Césaire Lenoir as his mouthpiece, to express allegiance to a form of Hegelianism freely interpreted in a spiritualist sense. What he in fact retains from Hegel's own system is in effect a belief that the essence of the real is spiritual in its nature: "The spirit," he states clearly, "forms the basis and the end of the universe" (*Tribulat Bonhomet*, p. 142). And as a consequence of this he also asserts the conformity of reality with the logical structures of the human mind: "It follows that by simply studying the filiations of the idea I shall be studying the constituent laws of things, and my reasoning will coincide, if it is strict, with the very essence of things. . . . The dialectic of nature is the same as that of our brain: its works are its ideas. . . . Things are thoughts clothed in various exteriorities" (pp. 152, 166). From a dialectical viewpoint, therefore, matter need no longer be regarded as anything more than a temporary emanation of mind, the means by which spirit negates itself in order to reach a higher becoming.[52] This in turn means that matter is no more than a creation of the spirit, just as, from a Christian standpoint, the world was wholly created by divine will: "Do the theologians not claim that God is pure spirit, and that he created the world? Matter can therefore EMANATE from spirit." Such is the philosophic justification for an absolute idealism that Villiers claims to be demonstrably compatible with the dogmas of the Roman faith, and that thereby enables him to achieve a conclusive rebuttal of the materialism posited by contemporary science. Moreover, each being, by means of participation in the world of ideas, is capable of escaping from the confines of self by communicating with the universal spirit: "When I raise myself by means of thought to the level of the human spirit, I am the point through which the idea of polyp-humanity is expressing itself at one particular moment."

Despite such attempts on Villiers's part at this stage of his career to retain the possibility of contact with the external world and other consciousnesses at the center of his idealism, from the time of *Claire Lenoir* onward it is undoubtedly true that his idealism began increasingly to take the form of a subjectivism that traps man inside the prison of his own consciousness, and condemns him to total solitude. The external world is never anything more than a projection of each individual consciousness, and, this being so, there is no possible way of distinguishing between hallucination and perception, or, rather, the distinction between them no longer has any rational basis for existence. Indeed, Villiers already asserts this lack of distinction between perception and hallucination on several occasions in *Claire Lenoir:* "If the real is, beyond doubt, what one sees," Césaire observes, "then I do not very well see how the hallucinations of a madman can be denied the status of realities" (p. 132; see also pp. 185–87). In which case, each consciousness must inevitably find itself imprisoned within its own representations, without ever being able to decide whether they do in fact correspond to an objective reality or whether they constitute no more than vain phantasms. This means that, just as all objective knowledge of the world is henceforward ruled out, so any true contact with others, and, in consequence, love, can never be anything more than mere illusion.

This negative aspect of subjective idealism is counterbalanced, however, by belief in the possibility of direct action on the part of thought. If the external world is never composed of anything other than subjective ideas, it follows that every individual consciousness possesses an untrammeled capacity to create a universe in conformity with its own aspirations. Thus, on several occasions, Villiers stresses the quasi-objective reality possessed by ideas, and their ability to act upon the perceived universe in order to transform it. In the very first pages of *Claire Lenoir,* even Tribulat Bonhomet himself, recalling the past events that form the book's main subject matter, recognizes the supremacy of consciousness: "For, even if we accept that the following facts are radically false, just the idea of their mere possibility is quite as terrible as their proven and acknowledged authenticity would be. Besides, once it has been thought, is there anything at all that has not to some extent occurred in this mysterious universe?" (pp. 42–43). And later, during the discussion in which he

counters Tribulat's arguments, Césaire formulates his belief in the power
of ideas even more clearly:

> "If we only knew," he added, "how astonishing and how
> terrible the living force of the idea is in the spheres of faith!
> The power of what has been imagined, of a dream, of a
> vision, sometimes transcends the laws of life. Fear, for
> example, the mere idea generated by superstitious fear,
> without any external motive, can blast a man like some huge
> electric shock. The things a visionary sees are, ultimately,
> material to him, yes, and just as positively so as the sun
> itself, that mysterious lamp which lights this entire phan-
> tasmagorical system of ours . . ." [Pp. 185–86]

Finally, Claire Lenoir defends the orthodox Christian point of view:
through revelation and the exercise of faith, every human being is capable
of reaching reality, of entering into contact with the divine presence
(pp. 167, 173–74).

During the years that followed, although he made gradually decreasing
use of Hegelianism and occultism, then rejected them in favor of an even
more radical subjectivism, before returning to a position very much closer
to orthodox Roman doctrine, Villiers always remained faithful to idealism
as the essential foundation of his world view. In his play *La Révolte*,
written during 1869 and early 1870 and premièred on 6 May 1870, we find
these idealist beliefs in the mouth of his heroine, Elisabeth, who expresses
her contempt for the external world and her belief in the superiority of
thought in no uncertain terms.[53] During the period when he was writing
L'Eve future, which is to say between 1874 and 1879, Villiers's solipsism
became even more pronounced, as did his belief in the power of human
consciousness to create its own reality. As in the earlier *Claire Lenoir* he
begins by asserting the primacy of mind. But now he goes on to draw all
the logical consequences of that absolute solipsism: every consciousness
is indeed ineluctably imprisoned within its own internal world, without
hope of ever knowing anything other than itself, including, first and
foremost, the reality, if any, of the external world. Edison explains this to
Lord Ewald by using a drop of water as an analogy. A microscope can
reveal a whole invisible world in a water drop that is invisible to our
unaided senses, and that tiny world is itself merely an absurdly small part
of all that remains and always will remain hidden within it.[54] The second
consequence of such a radical subjectivism, however, is that every being
has no choice but to live in absolute solitude, and can never hope for any
genuine communication with another. In consequence, love is never
anything but an illusion, a fact that Edison never tires of pointing out to

Lord Ewald in his determination to prove that Evelyn Habal's beauty is no more than a mirage, and that there is no real difference between the automaton Hadaly, whom he, Ewald, must himself endow with a soul, and any real woman:

> As for lovers, as soon as they believe they know one another they stay bound together solely by habit. What they set store by is the sum of their two beings and of their imaginations, with which they have reciprocally imbued one another; they cling to the fantoms they have conceived within themselves, each modeled on the other, yet remain eternal strangers.... I have given you the proof...that in sexual love there is nothing but vanity concealing lies, illusion concealing ignorance, sickness concealing a mirage.
> [*L'Eve future*, pp. 228–29]

Like the image we have of our fellow man, the image of God himself is nothing but a pure projection. Villiers finds himself led, willy-nilly, by the logic of the position he has adopted, to discard Christian orthodoxy in favor of God as an ideal representation, or at least to deny the possibility of any mystical experience that could provide true communication with the deity. The idea of God retains value only because it represents the most sublime idea that man is able to conceive:

> However, in the man who reflects, the idea of God appears only to the degree in which the faith of the looker can evoke it. God, like all thought, exists in man only according to the individual. No one knows where illusion begins or in what reality consists. Further, since God is the most sublime conception possible, and since no conception has reality other than in accordance with the will and the intellectual eyes specific to each being, it follows that to remove the idea of a God from one's thoughts can mean only that one has gratuitously decapitated one's own mind. [*L'Eve future*, p. 43]

The results of this absolute solipsism would therefore lead to total despair, to a state in which each monad is incarcerated in the prison of an infinite solitude, unless, as is the case, Villiers at the same time reaffirmed his determination to draw positive consequences from it: since the external world is constituted for each individual solely by his own mental representations, it is therefore in his power to create his own universe, to replace the random illusions of appearances with willed illusions in conformity with his own desire. In order for these substitute illusions to impose themselves upon the consciousness, all that is needed is to aid the work of the imagination by constructing a subterfuge; such is to be the function of the automaton from which Lord Ewald must create a real human being, and such is the general meaning of *L'Eve future*, specifically written as an illustration of this theory of illusionism.[55] Thus, although imprisoned within the data of his own representation, the human being, provided he trusts to his powers of imagination, is capable of becoming a veritable demiurge, and of creating his own heaven on earth.

An illustration of this faith in the powers of human imagination and will, which enable man to transcend his condition, is to be found in *Vera*, a story later to be reprinted as one of Villiers's *Contes cruels* but first published in 1874, at the very moment when he was presumably just beginning work on *L'Eve future*.[56] Count Athole, the principal character in *Vera*, actually succeeds in bringing his wife back to life, not by the use of some magic spell but by the power of his will alone. By refusing to accept Vera's death, and by continuing to live as if she were still there with him, he gradually succeeds in restoring her ghost to solid existence, or, rather, he shuts himself away so totally in his illusion that it is as though that illusion gradually acquires an ever greater objective solidity and reality for him. Similarly, in *Le Convive des dernières fêtes*, also first published in 1874, the narrator and his companions succeed by pure will power in totally transforming the vulgar opulence of the Maison Dorée, where they are taking supper after an Opéra ball.[57] In *Axël*, probably written over the period 1882–84, the same philosophical positions are restated with even greater force. Once more we find the same negation of the external world's reality;[58] the same belief that each individual consciousness is confined within its own representations;[59] and the same pressing invitation to man to free himself from banal reality by becoming the god of his own universe:

> Truth is no more in itself than a vague concept of the species through which you are passing, and which confers upon Totality the particular forms of its mind. If you wish to possess it, create it! Like all the rest!... The world will never have any meaning for you other than that which you attribute to it.... Since you will not be able to escape from the illusion you make of the universe, choose the most divine.... You are your future creation. You are a God who pretends to forget his omnibeing only in order to make reality of its radiance. What you call the universe is merely the result of that deception, and the secret of it is within you. [P. 203]

Finally, we still find echoes of such affirmations in some of the stories published during the last years of Villiers's life, between 1885 and 1889.[60] *L'Instant de Dieu*, for instance, contains these words, addressed by a priest to a man condemned to death: "My brother, my son, no, I am not saying goodbye to you yet. The earthly miasma of your senses makes you set too much store by this sad sky you see, this fleeting earth that will no longer include you among its shades; these illusions of time and space upon which the gross unreality of this world is woven."[61] Another story, *L'Elu des rêves*, is fundamentally a celebration of the power of illusion. The hero, a poet who was alone able to recognize the old man dying in the next room as a king, and who has been royally rewarded as a result, passes judgment on his two friends, who were unable to see anything in that wretched room other than trivial reality: "In their disdain for that power of imagination which is the only reality for any artist who can command life to conform to it, they preferred to rely on their senses, under the impression that it is possible to see what is."[62]

Variant Forms of Idealism

Largely due to Villiers de l'Isle-Adam's influence, such idealist beliefs were to achieve wide dissemination and continue to develop along the various lines he had laid down, in the work of most writers of the 1885 generation and their immediate successors. Their writings provide clear evidence of a general questioning of the reality of the external world, which is regarded as being merely an illusory appearance. That was the attitude of Barrès, for example, at that time. In an article published in the Dutch magazine *De Nieuwe Gids* in January 1886, for instance, he clearly considers the external world to be no more than a projection of the individual consciousness, and urges the artist to liberate himself from the domination of that world in order to create his own universe:

> The universe in which we live is a dream. There are no things, there are no men. Or rather that is indeed all there, but because the human being must necessarily project himself into appearances.... We project the image of our inner essence upon external nature; then, believing in the existence of that universe, which is merely the reflection of our self, we suffer from its incoherences, even though they are merely our own work.... [The wise man] will renounce this known world, the appearances that surround him with their presence, even after having clothed them with a unity through compassion. And since no man, no thing, or any part of the world exists except through him, he will change his way of creating, and then, above the present universe, construct a new one.[63]

In this questioning of the relation between subjectivity and objectivity, the balance between the self and the world is tilted in favor of consciousness, which becomes the sole reality. An example of this occurs in *Les Hantises,* a collection of stories by Edouard Dujardin published in 1886, in the preface of which we find the following statement: "The idea alone is; the world in which we live is our everyday creation; and sometimes we live other ideas, other worlds."[64] The main character of the story entitled *Le Kabbaliste* professes the same transcendental idealism: "All worlds," he asserts, "are in fact merely representations, appearance, illusions.... Worlds are phantasmagorias.... Whatever world thought conceives, there you will live if your soul retires into it wholly; the world of spirits is a chimerical, dream world that my thought has created; it exists in my thought; therefore it exists, just as the human world does, if my soul takes wing there." (p. 110).

We find a similar belief expressed the following year in *La Revue indépendante* by Téodor de Wyzewa: "The universe is the work of our souls.... Our soul alone lives."[65] In 1889, in the preface to his *Les Grands Initiés,* Schuré was also to assert: "Mind is the only reality. Matter is merely its inferior and changing expression."[66]

In the work of Rémy de Gourmont this subjective idealism takes on a reasoned and systematic form. D'Entragues, the principal character of *Sixtine,* criticizes the naïve faith in reality expressed by naturalist writers:

> Writers of this sort ... are, like most men, like mankind as a whole, or almost, victims of an optical illusion. They imagine that the external world is in constant activity outside them, which is a transcendent piece of idiocy.... The world is the idea I have of it, and that idea is determined by the specific modulations of my own brain.... The material and nonconscious world lives and moves solely within the intelligence that perceives it and recreates it afresh in accordance with its personal forms. [Pp. 76, 136]

Similarly, in his book *L'Idéalisme,* published in 1895, which is a collection of articles printed earlier, Gourmont begins by commenting on the fact that the majority of the literary schools of the day were already converted to the new doctrine:

> At the time of writing, the idealist theory is scarcely disputed by any but a few moldering rags whose antiquated notions it would take a mangle to wring out of them. Even the most obtuse and pigheaded of the naturalists have by now yielded to the weight of intellectual pressure that over the past four years, since the death of Villiers de l'Isle-

Adam, has been brought to bear on a world where thought is being developed into a work of art.[67]

Gourmont then goes on to provide philosophical foundations for what he clearly sees as a major spiritual trend, adduces the transcendentalism of Kant and Schopenhauer in support of his view, and draws some implicit practical conclusions: "The logical conclusions of these aphorisms are quite clear: man knows nothing other than his own intelligence, his self, the only reality, the special and unique world that I contain, carry within me, distort, dissipate, and recreate according to my own personal activity; nothing moves or has its being outside the knowing subject; everything I think is real: the only reality is thought" (*L'Idéalisme*, pp. 12, 13).

The preface to *Le Livre de masques* of the following year, returning to the same ideas, was to acclaim symbolist and decadent writers as the heralds of a new truth rich in exciting spiritual prospects:

> This evangelical and wonderful, liberating and revitalizing truth is the principal of the world's ideality. In relation to man as thinking subject, the world, all that is external to the self, exists only in accordance with the idea of it that the subject constructs for himself. We know nothing but phenomena, we reason only on the basis of appearances; all truth-in-itself evades us; essence is unassailable. This is the doctrine that Schopenhauer has popularized in his extraordinarily clear and simple phrase "The world is my idea." I do not see what is; what is, is what I see.[68]

In his article on Villiers, Gourmont summed up the attitude of the writer he then regarded as his spiritual master thus: "Without going as far as the pure negations of Berkeley, which are nevertheless the logical endpoint of subjective idealism, he accepted both the internal and the external, mind and matter, into his conception of life on an equal footing, albeit with a very clear tendency in each case to give the first term precedence over the second" (*Le Livre des masques*, p. 93).

At this same period, and for some years to come, Adolphe Retté's work was to be based wholly on this same total belief in the world's unreality and the primacy of consciousness. In his *Mémoires de Diogène*, for example, he refers to "this phantasmagoria that many eccentric individuals take for reality."[69]

Once this general postulate that the only true reality for man is his own consciousness had been accepted, however, the younger writers of the day gradually came to adopt slightly divergent attitudes, conditioned by the various practical consequences this fundamental philosophic idealism could entail. As a consequence, we find the literature of the time displaying a variety of trends, sometimes parting company with one another, sometimes intersecting and overlapping, according to the individual personality of each writer.

One line adopted by a number of authors, once the initial identity of perception with hallucination, of objective reality with imaginative experience, had been accepted, was to modify the conditions of representation in accordance with a conscious aim, so as to lend objective life to the imaginary universe existing within them. This meant, in practice, insisting on the unity of all representation, whether apparently derived from the external world or from the self. "Ordinary sensations," d'Entragues declares in *Sixtine*, "are merely true hallucinations. True or false, to me that is of no consequence, a matter of really no concern" (p. 66). Similarly, in the chapter of *Le Livre des masques* devoted to Verhaeren, Gourmont, citing Taine as his authority, demands the right of the artist to endow his purely internal representations with an importance equal to that granted to impressions produced upon him by the so-called real world:

> Sensations, Taine said, are hallucinations that happen to be true. But where does truth begin or end? Who would dare to prescribe its boundaries? The poet, who has no psychological scruples, does not waste his time sorting hallucinations into true or false; for him, they are all true if they are sharp or strong, and in all innocence he relays them all. [P. 35]

This same idea recurs in Alfred Jarry's *Les Jours et les nuits* of 1897, when he justifies the determination of his leading character, Sengle, to abolish the difference between dreaming and waking, and to replace real life with an existence pursued within a purely fictitious universe:

> The result of these reciprocal relations with things, which he had become accustomed to controlling by means of thought (but that is true of us all, and it is by no means certain that there is any difference, even of time, between thought, volition, and act) . . . was that he no longer made the slightest distinction between his thoughts and his acts, or between his dreams and his waking moments; and, perfecting the Leibnitzian definition that perception is a true hallucination, he failed to see why one should not say: a hallucination is a false perception, or, more accurately, a weak one, or best of all, a predicted one (or sometimes remembered, which is the same thing). And he thought above all that nothing exists but hallucinations, or perceptions, and that there are neither nights nor days (despite the title of this book, which is why it was chosen) and that life is a continuum.[70]

If real perception and purely imaginary ideas are not susceptible of differentiation by the individual consciousness, it follows that each individual, being capable of modifying his ideas, becomes capable of creating a universe just as believable as the so-called real one. In consequence, we find all these writers stressing the power of thought, which is seen as capable of imposing its views on the objective world and transforming it at will. As a result, ideas, thoughts, take on a kind of objective and independent existence; the imaginary universe possesses a reality equal to that of the perceptible world; and fictional beings become equal rivals with the beings of everyday life. That is the belief we find expressed by Victor-Emile Michelet, for example, in an article of 1885:

> It is the poet's duty to follow the instinct that urges him on toward the mysterious domains he senses ahead, and to hurl himself, head down, into the world of fantasy. By the very fact that a mind has created it, every imaginary conception is as real as the most everyday object or being. Fairies exist just as much as aldermen, and the symbolic chimaera with its wings spread to heaven has just as much right to existence as a cab horse.[71]

The same writer, in a novella published by the magazine *Psyché* in 1891, after describing a being created purely from fantasy, offers the following reflection:

> It is certainly true that this apparition, destined to have such a decisive influence on my future life, would constitute what the vulgar call a hallucination. But what is a hallucination, if not the projection onto the visible plane of an invisible reality obeying the summons of imagination? My thought creates what it asserts, and are the Platonists not right to regard ideas and images as being alive, immortal offspring of the mind, emanations of the eternal word? Besides, the distinction that is commonly made between reality and unreality seems to me a kind of hair-splitting on the part of intelligences so coarse that I will not deign to dwell on it. Is reality not a subjective creation of the mind that perceives it?[72]

This possibility that thought and imagination have the power to intervene in real life, and to modify it, is precisely what the principal character of *Sixtine* investigates, and eventually establishes to his own satisfaction. He perceives that the chance events of real life, or rather the imperceptible influence of his own will, has enabled him to make real an adventure that began as a dream, to bring reality into conformity with his own desire:

> He had so often intervened by means of dreams in the active
> series, and so shattered its determinism, that such a result
> certainly no longer aroused any childish astonishment in
> him; but this time there was a truly miraculous subordina-
> tion of fact to idea.... Such an experience could not be
> accounted for by presentiment or coincidence, and, besides,
> he had already observed a hundred such experiences before.
> This meant that it was the conception of a possible fact that
> had motivated the occurrence of that fact, modified by the
> intervention of an external will, in his life.... It was thus
> apparent that d'Entragues had reached that threshold of in-
> tellectuality beyond which one can command obedience: the
> order of things, apparently incoercible, was yielding to his
> dream. He now had to master that dream, and exert his will.
> [Pp. 134–37]

Thus, as early as 1890, we already find a first approximation of what the
surrealists, thirty years later, were to term objective chance. A man endowed with sufficient imagination is capable of forcing his dreams to take
on reality, of obliging the objective world to submit to his wishes.

If the development of the oneiric faculties, the progressive invasion of
real life by dreams, the assertion of omnipotence on the part of desire, all
constitute means of demonstrating the primacy of the internal universe
over the external world, it is also possible to activate the powers of
illusion deliberately by creating material simulacra as a means of freeing
the imagination. This is the principle employed by Villiers de l'Isle-Adam
in *L'Eve future*, when, in order to bring about Lord Ewald's moral recovery, Edison replaces a real woman, the perfectly beautiful but
essentially vulgar actress Alicia Clary, with the automaton Hadaly, upon
whom the young man is able to project his own soul, thus transforming
her into the ideal woman that life has not given him the opportunity to
meet. Thanks to Hadaly, "sovereign machine for the creation of visions"
(p. 150), the schism between life and the dream is abolished. Announcing
his intention to create an automaton that will be an exact double of the
living woman, Edison cries: "I shall overcome illusion! I shall capture it.
In this vision I shall force the ideal itself to manifest itself, for the first
time, before your eyes, PALPABLE, AUDIBLE, AND MADE MATE-
RIAL" (p. 215). Thus, thanks to a collaboration between Edison's
technical genius and Lord Ewald's passion, a "voluntary illusion," a
"metaphysical phantasmagoria," is made real and becomes capable of
"the redemption of love" (p. 215). Des Esseintes is also applying this
same principle when he furnishes his diningroom so as to create the illusion of being in the cabin of a ship, uses his bathtub to recreate the
impression of swimming in the sea, or simulates an actual journey to

London by consulting various guidebooks and eating dinner in the English tavern in the rue d'Amsterdam. Once the real-life setting has been modified sufficiently to excite the imagination, the latter is able to take wing and substitute for that real experience, with all its attendant disappointments, an imagined experience that remains unflawed and ideal. The artificial setting or object thus becomes the principal aid of a liberated imagination now able to produce a perfect substitute for real life.

Escape from banal reality and deliberate modification of perceptual data can also be achieved by the use of drugs, since the hallucinations they induce possess the same degree of reality for the user as normal perceptions. Bourget makes this point in his dialogue *Science et poésie* quoted earlier, in which one of the young men claims: "If I have drunk opium, and under the poison's influence time becomes so amplified as to have apparently stopped, then that illusion is in its own right a reality, against which no evidence offered by a clock has any validity. . . . In the same way, the fact that at certain moments the universe appears to me an inexpressible mystery of melancholy or delight is in itself a real fact."[73] From there, moreover, it is not a great step to thinking that artistic creation alone, without adjuncts of any kind, is capable of provoking reactions similar to those produced by hashish or opium: "There is a group of writers," Bourget wrote in 1883, "for whom writing is a mode of living and nothing more. These writers have no other aim but that of keeping the inner wounds of their sensibility alive with their own phrases. That sensibility oppresses them, lacerates them. Their souls find nothing in their surrounding circumstances, or in this reality that is their jail, with which to satisfy their appetite for huge and intense emotions. They demand of words and the sorcery of art what eastern peoples obtain by using hashish, what the Englishman De Quincey procured by pressing that black phial of laudanum to his lips."[74] There, Bourget is already expressing, in embryo, the form of idealism that was to consist in the substitution for real life of constant contact with works of art, an attitude characteristic of the esthete that Wilde was to adopt and make the supreme principle of his morality, and that Rémy de Gourmont was also to subscribe to for a while, as for instance when he says of d'Entragues that "he had put art above everything, and even in the place of life" (*Sixtine*, p. 58).

Idealism can take another direction, however, not toward subjectivism, imagination, or dreams, but toward belief in the existence, above this concrete life, of a universe of ideas, a world of abstract relations of which the perceptible world is no more than the approximate projection and symbol. Such, as we know, was Mallarmé's position. For him, the essence of the real was constituted by language, which endows it with form and meaning, so that the function of the artist, and more specifically of the poet, is to communicate that spiritual essence through words. The concrete universe must be supplanted by a universe of pure notions, the particular flower with the ideal flower, which exists solely in the consciousness. Hence the famous statement in his *Avant-dire* of 1885: "I say: a flower! and up from the oblivion to which my voice is relegating any one outline, musically emerging as something other than all experienced calices, there appears the laughing or the proud idea, that flower absent from all bouquets."[75] Absolute subjectivism was thus to be replaced by an idealism more intellectual in its thrust and based upon the occultist doctrine of correspondences. This opposition between intellectualism on the one hand, and subjectivism on the other, is in fact one of the lines of cleavage that becomes evident, during the last fifteen years of the century, between symbolism and decadence. Certainly this intellectualist strain is to be found in varying degrees, fundamentally as a result of Mallarmé's influence, in the work of several writers of that time. It surfaces at certain moments, for instance, in d'Entragues's musings, as when he declares: "Nothing exists other than through the word, which is as much as to say: the word alone exists" (*Sixtine*, p. 257). The same influence is also strongly evident in Gide's *Traité du Narcisse* of 1891:

> The reverent poet contemplates, and bending, gazing down at symbols, he sinks in silence to the heart of things—and when his visionary eyes have sought out and captured the idea, the inner and harmonious number of his being, which underpins the imperfect form, he seizes it, and then, regardless of the transitory form that fleshed it out in time, he is able to reendow it with eternal form.... For the work of art is a crystal—a partial paradise in which the idea can flower again in all its higher purity.[76]

Camille Mauclair, too, in an article in the September 1892 issue of the *Mercure de France*, wrote: "Every object is absorbed back into its pure idea. The reality of an object, which is to say its sensorial relation to the nervous centers of the conscious being, is merely a mode of apperception and revelation of its idea, or logically, its symbol."[77] Much later, summing up the essence of the message Mallarmé had handed on to his immediate disciples, Dujardin was to write: "The external world existed for Mallarmé solely as the symbol of the world of ideas; it did not exist for the young men we were in 1885–86 except as a conception of the mind. The external world was merely stage scenery, to be set up or struck at the poet's convenience."[78] However, despite the undoubted fervor of the master's close disciples, this interpretation of idealism, by reason of the intellectual rigor it entailed, and because it ran the risk of turning literature into mere illustration of sterilizing abstractions, into bald allegory, could scarcely make any great headway among a generation thirsty, ulti-mately, for refined sensations, emotions, and dreams.

Lastly, Gourmont was to steer idealism along one further path, that of individualism. Since the world is never anything other than my repre-sentation of it, it follows that each individual has a perception of the real universe particular to himself, irreducible to that of any other conscious-ness. That being so, the function of every work of art will be precisely to emphasize that individual factor, to bring out what is specific and irre-placeable in each artist's vision of the world; so that artistic genius will be bound up with the degree of individuality expressed in each work. Having taken that stance, Gourmont was thereafter to regard idealism, sym-bolism, and individualism as identical. On the one hand he spoke of "idealism, of which symbolism is after all only a surrogate," and on the other he asserted that "idealism signifies free and personal development of the intellectual individual in the intellectual series" (*L'Idealisme*, pp. 24, 32). The artist is thus ineluctably alone: "He is sufficient unto himself, and he must be so, since he is as isolated from his fellow men as two planets in the solar system are from one another" (pp 13–14). The artist conscious of his goals must therefore constantly aim by all possible means at accentuating what makes him different, and cultivate his self with a total contempt for all rules and all schools.

Such, then, are the varying meanings that writers in the last decades of the nineteenth century in France attributed to the term idealism, which was clearly one of the period's key words. From the depths of a real existence governed by the pitiless laws of science, oppressed by gnawing boredom, sadness, solitude, and angst, they cried out to it to provide them with both a foundation for their esthetic and revenge against that life. It was in the name of idealism, after a period in which literature had been dominated by the exact reproduction of a monotonous or trivial reality, that they advocated a return to the powers of the imagination, aided by a refinement of sensations, by dreams, by drugs, by legends, or by use of the artificial in various forms.

3 RELIGIOUS UNEASE

Despite the Efforts of the Roman Catholic Hierarchy, and of certain intellectual or literary circles, from the Restoration of Louis XVIII onward, to expunge all traces of the general dechristianization that had accompanied the Revolutionary era, the history of French society in the nineteenth century undeniably reveals a progressive decrease in religious faith and practice. As the century progressed, so the social and political obstacles to religious belief—the gap already existing between the Church and the new social category formed by the workers in large-scale modern industry, and the hostility of the Church to the republican form of government—were reinforced by an increasing number of intellectual obstacles. The development of positivism and the scientific approach, the discoveries and new hypotheses emerging in geology, astronomy, and paleontology, were increasingly undermining the vision of the origin and evolution of the world traditionally derived from the Bible. The scientific conception of a universe governed by strict and immutable laws, perfectly ascertainable by the unaided human mind, was eliminating recourse to revelation and superseding the hypothesis of a mysterious and unpredictable providence governing both the universe and human life. Open war between science and religion had been declared long since; and in that struggle the majority of intellectuals and artists of the day were led to side with the former. Only a few isolated figures continued to offer unconditional support to Roman dogmas, and their very isolation led them to adopt a particularly intransigent attitude, as in the cases of Barbey d'Aurevilly, Ernest Hello, and, later on, Léon Bloy. As a result, these writers, accepting the logical implications of that attitude, were forced to reject all the idols of modern civilization indiscriminately: science, progress, and democracy.

With the advent of the Third Republic, this conflict between the Church and contemporary thought simply became more acute, since the Roman Church, far from becoming more flexible in its attitudes, continued for some time to harden them. On the doctrinal level, Rome had already

79

promulgated a general condemnation of all the modern ideologies, as early as 1864, in the encyclical *Quanta cura* and then the *Syllabus*. The achievement of Italian unity at the expense of the Papal States, and the nationalization of Rome itself, were taken by the papacy as a humiliation, and without doubt helped to provoke the intransigent dogmatic attitude revealed by the proclamation of papal infallibility. In France, the return of the Republic was achieved only by surprise tactics, under cover of the national defeat in 1870, and the majority, if not the totality, of conservative and Roman Catholic circles in fact paid no more than lip service to the new regime at first, while retaining a firm intention of restoring the monarchy, or at least some authoritarian form of state rule, at the earliest opportunity. Then, after 1877, the reinforcement of the republican regime, followed by the introduction of a series of new laws, particularly those relating to public education and union rights, perpetuated this rift between conservative circles and the Republic, which drew its supporters mainly from the left and the intelligentsia.

Whatever the causes, however, there is no doubt that unbelief was very widespread in artistic and literary circles during the 1880s. Most writers belonging to the two broad movements then occupying the foreground of the literary scene, Parnassus and naturalism, either felt nothing but indifference with regard to the dogmas and institutions of the Roman Church or else expressed open hostility to them. The fact that the judgments delivered by the conservative critical establishment, through such mouthpieces as *La Revue des Deux Mondes,* for example, were always based more or less consciously on certain moral presuppositions did nothing to help close the rift between writers and religion. For many of them, there was no longer anything to have faith in. The Church, as they saw it, was in its death throes, and Christian dogmas were regarded as no more than legendary themes, on exactly the same footing as the beliefs and myths supplied by so many other religions similarly rendered obsolete in the course of history, and particularly the religions of the far east, which had been attracting the attention of scholars and writers for some time by then. It was from just such a purely historical and mythical standpoint that Renan, for example, chose to view the Christian faith. So that, although extremely sensitive to the poetic and cultural aspects of the Christian tradition, his interpretation of the life of Christ was a consciously rationalist one that finally led him to view the tradition's founder as a mere prophet. The skepticism produced by increased knowledge of the history of religions led intellectuals in general to integrate the history of Christianity, too, into the evolution of religious belief as a whole, and to regard all religious faith as no more than a kind of consoling error. This general attitude among intellectual circles at that time is confirmed, for instance, by the quotation from Maurice Spronck given earlier; faced with the ineluctable disappearance of all religious belief, the only emotion that remains is one of nostalgia.

Yet the decadent era coincided, as we have seen, with the appearance of a new and profound trend, a tendency to reject the very things that, in the previous period, had accelerated this disillusion with religion, which is to say positivism and the scientific spirit. The resurgence of idealism was an attempt to escape from that vision of the world which held the human being prisoner in a network of implacable laws, which reduced existence to its physiological data, which limited reality strictly to the knowable, the visible, the palpable. Suddenly people were rediscovering the values of sensibility, confronting purely determinist conceptions of consciousness with the notion of the soul, which traditionally had always contained religious connotations. The idealist stance, which on the metaphysical plane led to subjectivism and the loneliness of a self confronted with a world made up solely of changing appearances, and on the emotional plane to indulgence in a narcissistic rejection of life or an increased desire to escape from it, also manifested itself in a kind of diffuse religious sensibility. Faith has gone, artists seemed to be saying, yet we cannot be satisfied with a universe reduced solely to the interplay of purely material and physical forces. Faced with the sterility of the positivist world, they proclaimed their belief in a supernatural universe, even though that belief remained rather vague and imprecise, largely because the intransigence of the Roman Church at first made any return to the relative certainty of traditional dogmas impossible. This is why the last two decades of the century saw the emergence of a whole gamut of trends that often, from the standpoint of Christian orthodoxy, are merely deviant products of a religious sensibility that is drawn toward the supernatural while remaining incapable of finding any solution to its needs in any of the already-existing religions.

Writers of the time were in the habit of referring to these tendencies by a term to which, it must be said, they do not seem to have attached any very precise meaning: mysticism. There is a book by Victor Charbonnel, published in 1896, *Les Mystiques dans la littérature présente*, that analyzes the development of this phenomenon in a particularly lucid, thoughtful way, and I shall often have occasion to refer to it during this account.[1] There were a number of phases in the development of this wave of mysticism during the last decades of the century whose sequence can be schematized as follows: during a first stage, lasting about ten years and coinciding roughly with the eighties, the term mysticism was used to denote a sort of esthetic Roman Catholicism. Certain artists, most of them fundamentally unbelievers, made use, sometimes with deliberately sacrilegious intent, of Roman Catholic themes and the external aspects of religion and religious observances, almost always from a purely esthetic standpoint, even though there is already a diffuse nostalgia for the supernatural already lurking in the background of some of their work. Then, for a period of several years, beginning in 1890, this literary exploitation of religious themes becomes increasingly charged with a more intense coloration, while at the same time a vogue for satanism and a considerable occultist movement emerged. Over this same period it also becomes apparent that curiosity for things religious was taking a more serious turn. A certain uneasiness that was previously merely literary in character begins to take on a moral and more genuinely religious character, and finds expression in a number of works of moral philosophy in which thinkers of the day, although still remaining outside Christian orthodoxy, strove to define the moral foundations of practical life. Finally, though only in the case of a limited number of artists and writers, the most famous of them being Huysmans, this religious unease led to a return to traditional beliefs, a trend that is also apparent in the developments in painting at that time. It is these various currents, which in practice often coexisted before one of them ultimately gave way to another, that I should like to examine chronologically, albeit leaving a study of occultism till the end of the chapter, since its importance merits a more detailed investigation. First, however, it is essential to take a closer look at the connotations of this term mysticism, which was to become one of the period's vogue words.

Mysticism

The word mysticism is one of those most frequently used to denote the characteristics of the new literature. Bourget, in his often-quoted essay on Baudelaire, observed that the general decline in religious belief in France had left the way open for a kind of mysticism confined to the search for new sensations. "Is there not enough [Roman] Catholicism surviving in our century," he wrote, "for a child's soul to become saturated with mystic love of unforgettable intensity? Faith will depart, but mysticism, even when expelled from the intelligence, will remain in the sensations."[2] Several years later, Charles Morice explained this resurgence of mysticism as the result of an inevitable reaction against science's tendency to depoeticize the world: "A short while since, science had struck out the words: beauty, joy, truth, humanity.... Mysticism has recaptured from science, the annexing intruder, not only all that she had stolen but perhaps, too, something that is part of science herself.

The reaction against the insolent and soul-killing negations of scientific literature . . . came about . . . as the result of an unexpected restoration of [Roman] Catholicism in poetry."[3] Similarly, in the literary prospectus he set out in the first issue of *L'Ermitage* in April 1890, Henri Mazel defined the literary period France was then going through in terms of "a religious and sometimes mystical spirit."[4]

Nordau, on the other hand, described mysticism in his famous *Entartung* as one of the major symptoms of degeneration, and interpreted it in terms of mental pathology, an attitude that had been prevalent among materialist psychiatrists since the beginning of the century. Charbonnel, too, in the introduction to his work, remarks on this same tendency, which he views as no more than a superficial fashion: "They dragged it into everything," he observes ironically of mysticism, "into magazines, both old and new; into newspapers; into poetry, the novel, criticism, songs; into the theater, into concerts, into the café-concert, into revues, into specially written tragicomedies, into every genre you can think of" (*Les Mystiques,* p. 7). He also quotes a similar observation made by the famous drama critic Francisque Sarcey, some years earlier, with reference to an Ibsen play he had seen: "There is an unaccountable wind of mysticism blowing through France." In 1892, in his preface to Rémy de Gourmont's *Latin mystique,* Huysmans also displayed great skepticism: "It appears that our young writers are turning mystics, or so the rumor was running in Paris recently, and many journalists, in their wisdom, lost not a second in their haste to inform us of this amazing and heaven-sent transformation."[5] Meanwhile Gourmont himself, in his introduction to the book, was confessing that "mystical literature alone, whether one is a believer or not, can provide any answer to our immense weariness" (p.12).

These pieces of evidence from contemporary witnesses indicate quite clearly that "mysticism" was beyond doubt one of the fashionable literary ingredients of the day. However, the way in which the term was used, or, as is clearly the case, misused, leaves us very little the wiser as to the exact content that writers of the time attributed to it. By 1896, near the beginning of his *Livre des masques,* Gourmont was writing: "Mysticism, that word has taken on so many extraordinarily diverse and even divergent meanings during these past few years that we ought to redefine it, very explicitly, every time we find ourselves about to write it" (pp. 23–24). An attempt must be made, therefore, to identify and isolate the tendencies that the term mysticism was used to cover.

At a first level, the term mysticism denotes a rejection of any purely scientific and rational vision of the world. It expresses a growing desire to free man from the remorseless mechanism of the world posited by positivist science, and to regard him as capable of restoring a deeper and personal meaning to his life. Beyond the still recent discoveries of science, it therefore postulates the existence of an irreducible unknowable, and it is in this unknowable that man's need for mystery and a sense of mystery can take refuge. From this viewpoint, then, mysticism is no more than a synonym for the idealism whose manifestations we have already examined.

However, this philosophical idealism, here oriented in a clearly religious direction, this belief in the existence of a supernatural universe independent of the perceptible world, and doubtless also in an eternal life after death for the human soul, often remains on the plane of simple, and rather vague, postulation. There is no question of allegiance to clear-cut dogmas or believing in any historical and specific revelation, but merely of restoring their rights to certain areas of the human mind and spirit, all those areas in the domains of emotion, sensibility, and imagination that the development of western thought had been tending increasingly to repress during the previous century or so. Certainly it is in the form of a diffuse religious faith, without dogmas and outside any established religion, that this feeling of vague mysticism is found in many writers at the time. "Our modern soul," one critic wrote in a book on Gustave Moreau, "lacks the power to raise itself to heaven through the ravishments of prayer. It feels a need to believe working within it; respects the symbols in which the divine spark once gleamed, yet refuses to bow to the slavery of any dogma, even though it communes with all the mysteries and hurls itself into any and every initiation; adores the spirit of divinity with fervor, without believing firmly in any one God, and, powerless to satisfy its desire for a celestial love, bleeds ceaselessly from the violence of that grief. It is tortured by the regret of its apostasy, yet makes no move to emerge from it."[6] This is very much the same state of mind that Victor Charbonnel described as developing in the late eighties under the combined influences of Renan and Tolstoy: "More than one mind, while stubbornly rejecting the submissions that religious faith demands, still acquired those sages' tolerance and something one might call an intellectual religiosity. Drawn by a mingled feeling of respect and curiosity, they communed in a mysticism without God and a troubled yearning for divinity" (*Les Mystiques,* p. 28).

This kind of mysticism was to crystallize around a notion then returning to fashion, that of the soul. Traditionally, the word *âme* had always possessed a religious resonance, in contrast to words like *esprit* signifying mind in the sense of the intellectual faculties, and *conscience* in the sense of consciousness, which had a more purely psychological and technical ring. What the word "soul" was to denote increasingly for those who employed it during this period, however, was principally a mysterious and "deep" self, as opposed to the immediate certainties provided by the consciousness as it processed the interplay of phenomena, perceptions, and sensations. "Soul" in this sense was the individual, permanent, and perhaps eternal essence, as opposed to a view of human life interpreted by physiologists in terms of simple physiochemical reactions. In Tolstoy's *The Power of Darkness*, a French translation of which appeared in 1887, one of the characters, old Akim, cries out: "One must have a soul," and this affirmation was to serve as something of a rallying cry for all those who were striving at that time to help bring about a resurgence of spirituality. We find it recurring, for instance, not only in the work by Paul Desjardins,[7] but also in Charbonnel's. The latter, indeed, identifies the soul with the emergence into lucid consciousness of the being's deeper impulses:

> And it is thus the soul that is passing through us, that is rising from the depths, as it were, onto the shore of our being. Christians may speak of a divine grace that is renewing and revivifying nature within us. Optimist philosophers will delightedly assert their belief in instincts springing from man's original goodness. Scientists and psychologists will see no more in it than the accumulated advances of a long evolution, and a great conquest on the part of our will to civilization. And the mystics will herald the advent of the "unknown gods" they see in us. At least all of them recognize that there is a soul within us, manifesting its presence, inspiring us, causing us to act.... It is this soul that we must seek for, of which we must become conscious, and by which we must live.[8]

It is the soul, too, as Maeterlinck was to tell his readers repeatedly in *Le Trésor des humbles* of 1896, that enables human beings to engage in a profound dialogue beyond the superficial language of explicit discourse. A key word of the whole fin-de-siècle period, the term soul thus summarizes all the demands of contemporary consciousness: need for the supernatural and nostalgia for faith; desire to rediscover reasons for hope and goals for existence; insistence upon the rights of the sensibility and the imagination.

Esthetic Roman Catholicism

There was a first phase, however, roughly coinciding with the 1880s, as I indicated earlier, during which this "mystical" current took a form that, one must admit, had very little indeed to do with any genuinely religious feeling. It was characterized by the exploitation of certain outward aspects of religion often in an entirely profane way. Already, early in the century, Chateaubriand had attempted to bridge the gap between France's intellectuals and her Roman Catholic artists by drawing attention to the great store of esthetic riches accumulated by the Christian tradition, from its medieval architecture to the solemn rituals of its forms of worship. And it was this esthetic dimension of religion that alone held any interest for the decadent minds of the eighties. They borrowed from Roman Catholicism, not its dogmas or its moral philosophy, but merely certain decorative elements that could be exploited to picturesque effect.

In *A Rebours,* for example, we find Des Esseintes decorating his retreat at Fontenay with religious objects: an antique cope, old stoles, a Flemish dalmatic, Byzantine monstrances used as ornaments, a canon book with poems inscribed in it. Indeed, he even requires his housekeeper to wear a nun's habit while serving at table. Later, Rémy de Gourmont's d'Entragues, a disciple of Des Esseintes, was to assert both his religious unbelief and the fascination he feels, like his illustrious master, for the Latin literature of the Roman decadence. "As for life after death," he says, "I have no such reassuring data on that point . . . for that truly supreme moment, that of our corporeal decomposition, it is possible that the delightful Unconscious still has a good trick or two up its sleeve, who knows? This relative fear no doubt stems from my Christian youth, and I repudiate neither the one nor the other: Roman Catholicism is an aristocracy. . . . Theology always provides me with the most agreeable reading" (*Sixtine,* p. 26). Moreover the setting in which Sixtine receives our hero is undoubtedly religious in inspiration. "She had a somewhat fourteenth-century look about her," Gourmont writes, "imprisoned in her abbess's throne. Her feet, shod in red, rested disdainfully upon a black hassock" (p. 61). In fact, right on until the end of the century, religious subjects were to invade literature in ever-increasing numbers, as Huysmans remarked in 1892, in the course of an attack on what he regarded as "contemptible assaults on the true faith." "Poets relinquished Venus in favor of the Virgin and treated saints as nymphs. For the deities of paganism, so long cherished by the Parnassians, they substituted Mary Magdalen."[9] A particularly telling example of this fashion is to be found in certain Valéry poems written in 1889 and 1890. There is the sonnet called *Le Jeune Prêtre,* for instance, entered by its author in the competition organized by *La Plume* in the last quarter of 1890—together with another, erotic sonnet called *Viol*—which received a commendation and, Jean Hytier informs us, 119 points,[10] and also the unfinished poem *Messe angélique.*[11]

Almost at the same time, Camille Mauclair was commenting on the fact
that religious themes had also invaded the field of painting.

> The Salons bulged with Holy Women at the Sepulchre, Seas
> of Galilee, crucifixions, roads to Emmaus, pardons, and
> benedictions, all executed in the same leached-out tones and
> with the same magic lantern lighting effects. . . . An appalling
> and unending plethora of missals, chasubles, monstrances,
> and lilies. . . . All the external signs of faith were dragged in,
> and only faith itself was left out. . . . The theaters put on
> Passions in verse, or as tableaux vivants. Poems sagged
> beneath the weight of knights errant, palfreys, crenelations,
> and troubadours. The same label was used to cover Liberty
> fabrics, anemia, the Virgin Mary, stained glass, Edgar Poe,
> the Primitives, Sarah Bernhardt (in any role), braided
> hair, . . . slender waists, M. Péladan, waistless dresses, and
> M. Huysman's latest books. Such was the arsenal of mysti-
> cism: a jumble sale stall.[12]

All the critics who took note of this phenomenon at the time agreed in
referring to it as no more than a purely superficial trend, and one perfectly
compatible with a total indifference to religion itself. "Let us beware,"
Barrès wrote in 1884, for example, in the first number of *Taches d'Encre,*
"let us beware of greeting them too eagerly as Christians, these poets.
The liturgy, angels, devils, the whole apparatus of piety, all these are no
more than a decorative setting for the artist who has decided the picturesque is well worth a mass."[13] Moreover the origin of this movement is
clearly visible in the influence of Baudelaire. The surface effect of his
work, as Charbonnel noted in 1897, is in fact that of "a conglomeration of
Epicurean sensuality and ascetic Christianity, of fleshly pleasures and
mystical piety, of debauch and prayer" (*Les Mystiques,* p. 60). After all,
was the Baudelairean attitude to woman not a combination of quasi-
religious worship and a sensual urge toward profanation? "Of woman,"
the same critic observes, "even in the languors of sensual pleasure, he
made an immaculate virgin to whom homage must be paid. He provided
incense burners, monstrances, altars, hosts, and pyxes for the 'hot and
shadowy nymph,' who at the height of sensual ecstasy becomes a Christian divinity. Love was an adoration, or even a Holy Communion" (p.
61). It is true that publication of the poet's *Oeuvres posthumes* by Eugène
Crepet in 1887, together with the discovery of the *Journaux intimes,* must
have made the reading public aware of the authenticity and true force of
Baudelaire's religious feeling; but the conjunction of religion and sensuality in his work was so startling that his more fervent admirers could be
forgiven for regarding his use of religious themes as a purely literary

means of injecting originality into his depiction of sexual love. In the same way, the religious belief that Verlaine began to profess, from *Sagesse* onward, might justifiably have been regarded as a mere condiment by those who became aware of the way in which mystical and erotic collections alternated in his work.

So what the decadents in fact demanded of religion was not just the picturesque element provided by its decorative exterior, but also a means of stimulating a surfeited sensuality. This sensual element in decadent mysticism was denounced, in fact, in 1895, by René Doumic, in his review of Huysmans's *En Route*. And however unjust it was with regard to Huysmans himself, the observations contained in this piece do apply perfectly to the general situation prevailing several years earlier. "*En Route*," Doumic wrote, "is above all a piece of documentary evidence. It provides us with information on the state of certain souls today. . . . What gives M. Huysmans's books their great value is that in studying himself he has revealed the existence of a number of features, and very troubling features, in contemporary sensibility."[14] Doumic goes on to observe that the onset of religious preoccupations in the central character of the book has as its essential consequence the reawakening of a suppressed sensuality:

> Such is the mechanism of conversion in Durtal that just as his declining sensuality needs cerebral stimulation, mysticism intervenes. It operates in the manner of a pharmaceutical adjuvant. . . . A man of letters he has never ceased to be; and he is so in the way in which the Goncourts understand the term when they define literature as "a state of violence." What he is seeking at the moment his lips murmur the sacred name of our Lord are new sensations, strange sensations. [P. 463]

Although Doumic was certainly in error when he cast doubt on the sincerity of Huysmans's conversion, as depicted in the change that overtakes Durtal, and when he stated, quite specifically, that "Christianity doesn't enter into it" (p. 465), his observations do nevertheless apply to the part played by the religious element in one particular section of French literature at that time. There we do indeed find religious feelings acting as a stimulus through a consciousness of sin, to eroticism and sexuality.

Decadent literature and art do, frequently and unmistakably, display a curious and often sacrilegious admixture of religion and eroticism. Among so many works displaying such an admixture, let me cite, for example, the engraving made by Félicien Rops in 1888 entitled *L'Amante du Christ*, which shows a Mary Magdalen stretching up her arms despairingly to the crucified Christ. This erotic use of mysticism led eventually, with the snowballing effect of fashion, to much writing of extremely dubious flavor, as may be judged from this sonnet written by a certain J. Clozel and printed in number 30 of *La Plume*, dated 15 July 1890, under the title *Les Mystiques:*

> It is very strangely I will pay you court.
> In a pale, rose-tinted room, at dusk,
> Lit by an incense burner on a table,
> That leaves the room in shadowy half-light.
> To whisper of our love we will repair
> To a low, deep sofa where we'll sit,
> And very gently I'll undress you. Black,
> A great Christ will stretch his long arms
>   on high
> To bless us both. Then most inscrutably,
> I'll fetch an ancient Bible from the dark
> With clasps of gold and silver filigree.
> And then devoutly, lost in mystic ardors,
> I shall read out the sweet, sweet Song of Songs
> And kiss your breasts—the Bible on your thighs.

All the "mystic" writing of the day does not reach quite that degree of vulgarity, needless to say; but it has to be said that even in works of higher literary quality, such as certain poems by Laurent Tailhade, the novels of Rachilde, or those of Péladan, the presence of this "mysticism" represents little more than a passing fashion. In any case, this mixture of sensuality and religion, with its often sacrilegious atmosphere, certainly came to be one of the most conspicuous ingredients of the decadent imagination.

Satanism

I shall have occasion shortly to draw attention to the almost total disappearance of the demoniac strain in imaginative literature that had enjoyed such popularity in the romantic era. Yet, although the fantastic tales of the decadent period hardly ever make use of satanic intervention to justify the fantastic element that is introduced, it is nevertheless true, even outside the genre of the fantastic tale, that the figure of Satan did briefly come back into fashion at this time. It is also undoubtedly true that the decadent version of Satan was exploited above all for the picturesque element it could provide: what came back into fashion were extremely traditional themes linked with diabolical imagery, and in particular everything relating to the black sabbath or mass. Even so, however, at a less superficial level this reemergence of the devil also undoubtedly reveals an exacerbation of the religion-oriented anxiety that was already beginning to find expression, as we saw earlier, in the 1880s. The decadent consciousness was a suffering consciousness, one that lived its moral and esthetic experience in the mode of guilt. This feeling of guilt, which, together with a preference for antinature to the detriment of nature, permeates the entire decadent sensibility, was to exacerbate the consciousness of evil and sin, of which the devil remains the traditional embodiment. This is why it is not inaccurate to regard the temporary fashion for satanism, which occurred mainly from 1890 onward, as one of the stages in the development of the fin-de-siècle consciousness as a whole, starting as it did from the vague idealism of the early mystical phase and moving progressively toward a more serious consideration of problems in the religious sphere.

As far as the origin of this satanist fashion is concerned, we once again have to take Baudelaire's influence into account. The section of *Les Fleurs du mal* entitled *Révolte* had, after all, exalted an attitude of rejection and revolt against the traditional subjection of man to the divine will, above all in the *Litanies de Satan*. "He took pleasure," Charbonnel writes of Baudelaire, "in the joy of doing evil, and of doing it diabolically. . . . Even in his exaltation of mysticism, which led him to seek the bitter joy of sin in that evil, he was satanic" (*Les Mystiques*, p. 61). Not long afterward came Barbey d'Aurevilly's *Les Diaboliques*, which depicted the devil's influence in an interiorized form, acting not upon the world of perceptible phenomena but directly upon the human consciousness, thereby leading some of those so assailed to choose the path of evil. Nor should we forget that Flaubert, in one episode of *La Tentation de saint Antoine*, described Satan whirling the hermit out into the immensities of the cosmos and showing him the universe.

The foundations of this new fashion for satanism were also laid in part by the work of the painter and engraver Félicien Rops during the eighties. Many of his drawings and engravings contain satanic elements, and none more so—apart from the series of nine illustrations for a new edition of Barbey's *Les Diaboliques* in 1886—than the most famous of all his works, the five plates collectively entitled *Les Sataniques*, which appeared in 1883 and achieved immediate success.[15] Evidence of that success is provided, for example, by the enthusiastic reception they were given by Huysmans and by Péladan, who wrote of Rops: "He has conjured up the devil once more, in this age when belief is dead, even in God, and he shows him triumphing over all ridicule, all laughter."[16] The movement thus launched, the figure of Satan and the themes associated with the black sabbath were to continue appearing frequently, from 1884 onward, in various collections of poems. In *Les Syrtes* by Moréas, for instance, which appeared that year, one of the poems is entitled *Le Démoniaque*, and another, *Accalmie*, depicts a coven setting out for a sabbath. Such imagined scenes, in which the satanist element is given a fantastic and macabre coloration, also occurred in the collections of some young poets, such as Guaïta[17] or Albert Jhouney,[18] who were later to direct their attention in a much more specific way to occultism.

In the field of prose the essential impetus was provided by Huysmans. In 1889, in his collection of art criticism entitled *Certains*, he had published a long essay on the work of Félicien Rops, and in particular the *Sataniques* sequence.[19] Using the engravings as his material, and following a method that was habitual with him, he had conjured up his own, literary, version of the black sabbath by transposing one art into another. It was in 1891, however, with the appearance of *Là-bas*, that the satanist vogue really got under way, impelled by the tremendous success Huysmans's novel achieved. *Là-bas* included, in particular, the famous chapter that caused such outrage at the time in which Durtal, the central character, escorts Mme. Chantelouve, a member of high society, to a black mass. In the previous chapter, during a conversation between Durtal and his friend Des Hermies, Huysmans had expressed his own opinion on satanism: "Worshiping the devil is no more insane than worshiping God. . . . No, the followers of satanism are mystics of a vile and loathsome order, but mystics they are. . . . It is precisely at the moment when positivism is at its high-water mark that mysticism stirs into life and the follies of occultism begin."[20]

The plot of the novel also involves the use of evil spells by practitioners of black magic in Paris against a miracle worker from Lyons, and Huysmans describes in detail the rituals and ceremonies with which the latter attempts to ward off these diabolical attacks. The anecdotal aspect of the book apart, however, what Huysmans was really trying to present was a kind of sociological document. He was trying to establish the survival, in the very heart of contemporary France and its capital, of magical practices and devil-worshiping sects. His spells and counterspells, black and white magic, devil worship, and black masses were situated not in some semilegendary Middle Ages, but squarely in modern times, the era of positivism, science, and general unbelief. *Là-bas* was to excite many echoes, and most particularly in Stanislas de Guaïta's *Le Temple de Satan* published later in the same year. Guaïta, who since his conversion to occultism five years before had set himself up as an expert on all matters relating to arcane knowledge and demonology, had already dealt briefly with satanism in his essay *Au Seuil du mystère* of 1886.[21] In 1891, concerned to correct some of Huysmans's statements, he returned to the subject, and *Le Temple de Satan* was very largely devoted to an evocation of the devil. While denying Satan any individual existence, and criticizing the Church for having yielded throughout the centuries to a kind of manicheism, he provides a long account of the history of witchcraft in France since the Middle Ages, and then, taking a somewhat too evident pleasure in the task, offers his own detailed description of a black sabbath.[22] The result, ultimately, is that his book appears less concerned with replying to Huysmans that with cashing in on Huysmans's success. That was certainly the motive inspiring the journalist Jules Bois, author of a play entitled *Les Noces de Sathan* given at the Théâtre d'Art on 29 and 30 March 1892 and also a specialist in things occult generally.[23] Before very long he was undertaking an investigation to verify Huysmans's claim that devil worship still persisted in Parisian society of the day.[24]

The Deeper Levels

The resurgence of religious feeling in late-nineteenth-century France at first took merely superficial forms, as we have seen. Esthetic Roman Catholicism and satanism both emerged from a background of diffuse religious unease as essentially no more than literary fashions. External aspects of Roman Catholic worship were exploited to provide a spicing of picturesque originality. Feelings of moral guilt, in conjunction with the generally pessimistic decadent state of mind, found expression in the theme of evil associated with the image of Satan. These feelings also provided a new stimulus to the erotic imagination, although the resulting association of sensuality with religious elements revealed not so much a sincere religious unease as "a kind of conscious delight in depravation."[25] As the years passed, however, this unease began to acquire a deeper dimension. First, we find the emotions and the power of the imagination, linked to the sphere of the supernatural, which is the domain of religious feeling, begin increasingly regarded by artists as a fertile source of material. Second, the 1890s were to see the appearance of a whole series of works in the field of moral philosophy that display a much more precise and genuinely thoughtful approach to the problems of religious life: the existence of a supernatural universe and a life beyond death, the meaning of human life, the necessity for a viable morality.

The development of this deeper religious current was certainly not uninfluenced by the discovery of the Russian novel, which occurred in France between about 1884 and 1889.[26] This discovery was accelerated by the efforts of the Vicomte de Vogüé, whose essays on the subject were collected into book form in 1886.[27] Called *Le Roman russe,* this book soon acquired the status of a literary manifesto. The author did not remain content with merely providing an account of the major works by contemporary Russian novelists, such as Tolstoy and Dostoevski; he presented them as models that French novelists might be well advised to imitate, since the Russian novel, while avoiding the flatness of French naturalism, had succeeded in reconciling a realist depiction of society with a sense of the mystery and depths of the human soul. It also brought a message of hope capable of counterbalancing the pessimism that had so ravaged the minds of recent generations. For, Vogüe attempted to show, the Russian novel also offered its French readers, gnawed by skepticism or foundering in indifference, a new ideal of the religious life. By presenting them with human beings who, even in the abyss of a sinful and corrupt existence, still retained a profound sense of religion, thanks to their humility and the intensity of their faith, such novels would deflect the consciousness of the younger generation from despair and rebellion. In Tolstoy particularly, Vogüé felt, there was apparent a feeling of profound humanity and social compassion that would satisfy the vague social aspirations of French intellectuals.

The influence of Vogüé's book was in fact considerable. "One is glad to acknowledge the date of publication of *Le Roman russe* as a memorable one," Charbonnel wrote, "a date marking the beginning of the neomystical era" (*Les Mystiques*, p. 12). Despite criticizing Vogüé for the imprecision of his thinking, Charbonnel nevertheless acknowledges that his work, which abounds with "exclamations and bravura arias on 'the invisible,' 'the unknown,' 'the universal mystery,' 'that limitless distance that calls to him,' 'compassion, evangelical compassion for the humble, the deprived, and the suffering,' " was the source of "a resurrection of the soul" (pp. 12, 20). It is certainly a fact that from this point on, aided by an increasing number of translations and by laudatory articles from such perceptive critics as Wyzewa—himself deeply read in Russian literature—and Hennequin, the works of the great modern Russian writers were to have a profound effect upon contemporary French sensibility as a whole, and prepare the ground for a whole series of thinkers and essayists who, each in his own fashion, attempted to provide a solution for the increasingly evident religious unease of their contemporaries.

The first of these was Edouard Schuré, with the work he published in 1889 under the title *Les Grands Initiés*,[28] a book animated above all by its author's desire to find some way of healing the rift between science and religion that was tearing contemporary French consciousness apart. Schuré was also concerned to demonstrate that, beyond the diversity and contradictions of the dogmas professed by the various established religions, there existed a common spiritual message, which he saw as constituting the essence of religious faith, an essence upon which all men of good will could come to agree. His method of establishing this common message consisted in systematically applying a distinction between the official doctrines of various churches—always a source of confusion and conflicts among their followers—and a secret, immutable, and universal doctrine, handed down since the beginning of time from initiate to initiate, along the unbroken chain formed by the great sages, the great prophets and founders of religions. The work thus consists fundamentally—if we leave aside the writer's adherence to certain eastern teachings such as metempsychosis—in an attempt to establish a religious syncretism capable of reducing the meanings of the various religions of man to a common denominator, a simple spiritual doctrine buttressed by moral considerations: primacy of spirit over matter; immortality of the soul; man's capacity for perpetual moral improvement. Analyzing Schuré's work eight years after its publication, Charbonnel first gives a very detailed account of its contents, criticizes the basic principle of a syncretism based on the historically fragile hypothesis of a common doctrine—the difficulty of recognizing which in the various religions is compounded by the fact that it supposedly remained secret—but then acknowledges the importance of the book, and does not hesitate to salute its author as "one of the great writers of our time" (*Les Mystiques*, p. 149).

We find Schuré's line of thought taken further in François Paulhan's *Le Nouveau Mysticisme* of 1891.[29] In this work the author attempts to list, then synthesize, the various influences that had combined to produce the new spiritual movement, and then to establish its effects: a sense of mystery, the need for a world beyond, the spiritual significance of the symbolist doctrine, and the influence of Tolstoyism. The next year, 1892, saw the publication of *Le Devoir présent* by Paul Desjardins.[30] Sharing the spiritualist beliefs of Schuré and Paulhan, refusing as they did to give his allegiance to any of the established religions, but above all concerned to provide his contemporaries with a new practical ideal. Desjardins advocated what was in practice an extremely reactionary brand of moral rearmament: acceptance of their lot by the poor as the price of social peace; censorship of the press and of literature, both regarded as responsible for the present demoralized state of the nation; and increased colonization to provide an outlet for the energies of the nation's youth. Finally, as a further link in this chain, we can also include the series of essays by Maeterlinck, beginning with *Le Trésor des humbles* in 1896, that were eventually to earn their author worldwide fame.

A parallel development was also taking place in certain sections of the art world, where a similar fashion for the purely decorative aspects of Roman Catholicism was later succeeded by a rediscovery of true religious art that accelerated a return to Roman Catholicism, with the group that called themselves the Nabis in particular, that was to occur in the literary world only some years later. It began with a rejection of both the conformism of official academic art and the inspiration of the school that had recently stormed its way to the forefront of the artistic scene during the years between 1880 and 1885—impressionism. This double rejection can be discerned clearly in the work of two artists whose genius was to come to its full flowering between 1885 and 1890: Gauguin and Van Gogh. Moreover, at this same time, even apart from the isolated figures of Moreau and Redon, there were two further artists who were to direct the course of painting toward a renewal of spiritual inspiration: Puvis de Chavannes, through the grave symbolism and consciously simplified manner with which he treated his subjects, a style that led him to stress the essential meaning of his figures' postures and faces; and Eugène Carrière, who employed subtle chiaroscuro to bathe his portraits in spiritual mystery. Then, with the formation of the Nabi group in the nineties, this trend became even more pronounced. This history of this movement is well enough known:[31] between 1886 and 1890, already anxious to remove himself as far as possible from life in the capital, Paul Gauguin had taken to spending long periods in the heart of rural Brittany, in the district around Pont-Aven; deeply affected by the harsh yet picturesque life of the peasants there, he began to use their daily life as the subject matter of his work, with the result that the intense faith of the Breton community led quite naturally to the introduction of religious subjects into his painting.[32] Then Paul Sérusier, a young painter who had met Gauguin in late summer 1888, confided in his friends, on his return to Paris, the admiration he had conceived for what Gauguin was doing. During 1889 and 1890 a group of painters gathered around Sérusier himself and his friend Maurice Denis, who felt themselves bound together both by their shared admiration for Gauguin and by their desire for a spiritually inspired direction in art. Moreover, although this spiritual leaning was at the outset more or less identical with the somewhat vague mystical yearnings characteristic of the prevalent sensibility at that time, the personal influence wielded by Maurice Denis, who had been a fervent Roman Catholic ever since childhood, soon led the movement in the direction of an often exclusively Roman Catholic art, as the subjects of many of Denis's own paintings clearly show.[33] What we find in his work, as in that of his friend Filiger, is no longer the mixture of sensuality and religious estheticism that had characterized the previous period, but an art imbued with authentic religious inspiration. Albert Aurier, the art critic of the *Mercure de France* and one of the first to pay any great attention to the Nabis, had clearly perceived this shift in inspiration when he wrote, in an article entitled *Les Peintres symbolistes* in the *Revue encyclopédique* of 1 April 1892:

In the work of the painters I have just mentioned [Gauguin, Van Gogh, Redon], from Gauguin on to Bernard, one could already observe this tendency toward mysticity, but toward an as it were surreptitious mysticity, deviating from its historical characteristics and still slightly pagan. The two painters I must mention now, on the contrary, display a more orthodox mysticity, and one moreover so evidently sincere, so far from the intolerable religious dilettantism current today, that they seem less like artists of the nineteenth century than inspired and naïve picture makers of the thirteenth. They are Charles Filiger... and Maurice Denis.[34]

It should also be remembered that 1892 was the year of the first Salon de la Rose-Croix catholique, an exhibition in which Péladan, having more or less succeeded in reconciling his own Christian beliefs with his occultist stance, tried to group together all those artists of the day whose inspiration was in some way religious. Lastly, it is worth noting that in 1894 Rouault, then still a student in Gustave Moreau's studio, began painting religious subjects such as his *Infant Jesus among the Learned Men* that earned him the Prix Chenavard.[35]

This return to religious themes proper, and to a clearly expressed belief in Roman Catholicism, also became apparent, albeit slightly later, among a number of writers. Edouard Rod, the author of *La Course à la mort,* one of the most significant expressions of decadent pessimism, displayed clear signs of a similar development in his thinking in a work entitled *Les Idées morales du temps présent.* "Only religion," he wrote in it, for example, "can regulate both thought and action at the same time.... One must take part in practical religion, to which the Church has given its definitive, fixed, immutable form in this [Roman] Catholic religion."[36] And although his attitude was still, in 1891 or 1892, an isolated reaction, that ceased to be the case as the end of the century approached, and its last five years were to bring a whole wave of conversions, the most spectacular of which was that of Huysmans, recorded in *En Route.*

However, with this return to traditional religious belief and orthodox doctrine, this particular movement ceased to have any direct bearing upon the history of the literature of imagination. Caught between a diffuse nostalgia for the supernatural and a rejection of orthodox forms of worship, many writers of the time were led to express not so much a genuine religious belief as a sort of emotional and mythical reverie that produced what were often rather bizarre imaginative developments: search for new sensations derived from hitherto unknown mixtures of erotic elements with religious themes or "props"; stimulation of their sensuality by an awareness of doing evil; curiosity with regard to sexual aberrations, leading to the first signs that an awareness of the unconscious, till then excluded from artistic expression, was about to surface in literature; abandonment to mythicoreligious reveries in which, as in Flaubert's *Tentation*, all the heterodox religious speculations accumulated by western culture since Greco-Roman antiquity were regurgitated pell-mell in a great maelstrom of recapitulation. Among these deviant forms of religious feeling, however, there is one, the occultist movement, that was to achieve considerable importance during the last decade of the century, and consequently merits separate examination.

Occultism

The foundations of the occultist fashion that was to become so widespread in the last twenty years of the nineteenth century had been laid down gradually over previous decades by a number of slowly maturing ideas and influences. At the head of these we must, naturally, place the work of Swedenborg, which exerted a major influence on the thought of such writers as Balzac, Baudelaire, and fairly clearly Gautier. Under the Second Empire the occultist movement had manifested itself in three principal forms: first, magnetism, the fashion for which, after its immense vogue in the romantic era, had been partially maintained thanks to the works and personal influence of Henri Delage;[37] second, spiritualism (in the sense of spiritism) which had first appeared in Anglo-Saxon countries about 1845, subsequently spread to France, and became enormously popular there during the first ten years of the Second Empire, thanks in particular to the activities of Allan Kardec; third, a movement represented principally by Eliphas Lévi, whose two major works, *Dogme et rituel de haute magie* and *Histoire de la magie*, published in 1856 and 1869, respectively, were the bibles of the French occultist movement during the decadent period.[38] Certainly we find in Lévi's thought a number of the basic themes that were to bear such fruit in the occultism of the '80s and '90s: first, the assertion, upon which French occultists were to rely in their struggle against the increasingly pervasive influence of Anglo-Saxon theosophy, that there exists a secret and unbroken tradition in western thought that goes right back to its earliest origins; second, the theory, borrowed from Swedenborg, and indeed the basis of all hermetic thought, of a universal analogy to which the doctrine of correspondences provides the key; third, the desire for a reconciliation, under the auspices of occultism, between the two hostile forces, as they were then viewed, of religion and science; last, the concern for practical application, manifest in Lévi's work by his development and description of the necessary rituals for the practice of white magic.

There is little doubt, however, that the years between 1870 and 1880 brought a slackening in this occultist current. The two figures who had dominated occultism under the Second Empire, Allan Kardec and Eliphas Lévi, disappeared from the scene in 1869 and 1875, respectively, and the spiritualist vogue undoubtedly ran out of steam during the first years of the Third Republic. The *Revue Spirite*, which had continued to appear up until 1875, finally ceased publication that year in somewhat mortifying circumstances. Its editor, Leymarie, became codefendant with a photographer in a fraud case, and was eventually sentenced to a year in prison for having published pictures of manifestations that turned out to have been faked. After that, curiosity about occult phenomena rather died down among the public at large, and became restricted to a few literary and society circles.[39] Spiritualist séances were still organized here and there, as for example at the house of Camille Flammarion,[40] and attracted writers such as the playwright Sardou, Charles Cros, Charles de Sivry—Verlaine's brother-in-law and author of stories published in various periodicals of the day[41]—or the critic Saint-René Taillandier,[42] all figures whom one also finds, practically to a man, attending the salon of Augusta Holmès,[43] or swelling the groups centered on Nina Vaillard or Judith Gautier and her husband, Catulle Mendès. In the case of most of these writers who frequented such predecadent circles and who, like Catulle Mendès, Villiers de l'Isle-Adam, Charles Cros, and even Mallarmé, always kept aloof from the Parnassian esthetic and the official poetic doctrine of that time, there was certainly no genuine adherence to occultist theories involved, but rather a mild interest, a skeptical curiosity in phenomena that might possibly provide fresh material for their imaginations.

One has to wait for another ten years or so, until approximately 1886–88, before the occultist movement begins to shake off this quasi-clandestinity and reemerge upon the scene with renewed force. This resurgence was undoubtedly fostered by the influence of researches carried out in the scientific field, or on its fringes, and which in many cases had the effect of drawing attention once again to certain of the phenomena exploited by earlier magnetizers or spiritualists, and occasionally of endorsing their authenticity and providing scientific explanations of them. It is to this category that we must assign, in particular, the work carried out by the two major French psychiatric schools, that in Paris under Charcot and Luys, and that in Nancy under Bernheim and Liebault. In the course of investigating certain mental illnesses, these psychiatrists were in fact led to make a scientific study of the paranormal phenomena upon which spiritualists had based the majority of their beliefs in the possibility of communication with life beyond the grave. Among spiritualists, this communication is achieved in practice via mediums, meaning persons regarded as being particularly receptive to the beyond, and whose behavior during séances bore a striking resemblance to that observed during magnetic and hypnotic trances. The work of Charcot on hypnosis, as well as Bernheim's on suggestion,[44] shed fresh light on such psychophysiological phenomena, and although it cannot be said that they actually provided verification of the spiritualists' hypotheses, they certainly did a great deal to draw public attention to these "secondary states."

It was in very much the same deliberately scientific and positivist spirit that a new learned society was founded in England at this time. Counting both scientists and artists among its members—including Tennyson, Ruskin, and the painter Watts—the Society for Psychical Research set itself the task of studying all paranormal phenomena in a strictly objective fashion. Its activities continued until the end of the century, and one of the first results of those activities was the publication, in 1886, of a book entitled *Phantasms of the Living*.[45] It must be said, however, that this work provided very little in the way of affirmative conclusions with regard to the reality of supranormal phenomena, and indeed acknowledged that the majority of so-called mediums were charlatans and fakers who employed illusionist's tricks to deceive those they had duped. Several years later a similar body saw the light of day even in France, when the Société de Psycho-physiologie set up its own Commission pour l'étude des Phénomènes occultes, which was presided over by the poet Sully-Prudhomme and included a number of eminent men of medicine among its members.

Although the attitude of most specialists and scientists was extremely reserved with regard to so-called occult phenomena, the credulity of the public was nevertheless increased by the attitude of a few genuine scientists, bearers of sometimes very prestigious official titles, who, having been duped by mediums or drawn into making fallacious hypotheses, claimed that they were in a position to confirm even some of the occultists' most bizarre notions, as for example the existence of what they termed the "astral plane." The most notorious example of this was provided by the English scientist William Crookes, a scientist of international reputation, and actually president of the highly respected Royal Society. Crookes undertook a series of experiments between 1870 and 1874 with a young medium called Florence Cook, who successfully convinced him of the reality of certain paranormal phenomena, such as telekinesis and telepathy. In order to explain these phenomena, the credulous scientist eventually developed a theory that posited the existence of a fourth state of matter, which he called the "radiant state." The results of his work, published in 1874 under the title *Research in the Phenomena of Spiritualism,*[46] succeeded in impressing a number of other scientists, and also, of course, the general public. By positing a specific state of matter intermediate between matter and mind, or rather by accepting that mind is merely a more subtle form of matter, Crookes, followed by many occultists of the day, claimed to have made possible a reconciliation between spiritualism and materialism.

Such aberrations of the scientific mind were not confined to Britain. In France, a whole series of men with scientific or medical training allowed themselves to be similarly led astray. There was Lieutenant Colonel de Rochas, for example, a former student at the Ecole Polytechnique and a member of that institution's board of administration at the time, who published a series of works in which he claimed to have proved that a hypnotized subject's powers of touch, far from being limited to the surface of the skin, extended outward from his body, in a series of concentric layers, to a distance of several meters, thus providing a scientific basis for telekinesis.[47] Several years later, in 1895, he undertook a further series of experiments, this time in collaboration with a number of other eminent men—Dr. Dariex, editor of the *Annales de sciences psychiques,* a publication founded with the aim of recording all work being carried out in that field at the time; Count Armand de Grammont, who held a doctorate in physics; and Dr. Sabatier, professor of zoology and comparative anatomy at Montpellier. This second set of experiments, conducted with another medium, Eusapia Palladino, caused quite a stir outside scientific circles. Later still, Professor Charles Richet likewise claimed to have established scientific confirmation of the occultists' basic assertions, and became the prime mover in founding a new science, that of metapsychics.

The first broad consequence of this proliferation of experiments and hypotheses relating to such phenomena as hypnotism, suggestion, telepathy, communication with the dead, telekinesis, levitation, and so on, was a growing inclination among the general public to reconsider the very foundations of scientific positivism, thus providing a boost to the resurgence of the spiritualist movement in the various forms noted earlier. "Whatever the truth of this matter," Georges Vitoux wrote in 1901, "while we wait for the frontiers of this unknown realm to be fully explored, a certain disarray has been brought into the very heart of the positivist camp, whose beliefs still enjoyed unanimous acceptance only a short while ago, and every passing day sees a heightening of this particular uncertainty apparent in the science of the day."[48] At the same time, however, this confusion, which continued right up until the end of the century, between genuine scientific research and wild hypotheses, provided the French occultist movement of the late nineteenth century with one of its most salient traits: the claim of occultists at that time to be working in harmony with contemporary science, their strong desire to reconcile science with religion, and their attempt to exploit the prestige attaching to both as a means of attracting an ever wider public.

History of the French Occultist Movement

As with spiritualism thirty years before, it was from Britain and the United States that the French occultist movement received its initial impetus during the 1890s. Already, some years before, a new cult called theosophy had appeared in the United States under the aegis of the visionary Mme. Blavatsky who in 1875, with the aid of a former spiritualist, Colonel Olcott, had founded her Theosophical Society, membership of which entailed initiation.[49] The foundation stone of theosophy, whose teaching otherwise was often nebulous but consisted mainly in a sort of spiritualism tinged with far eastern mysticism, was the notion that a secret religious tradition, depository of the only true religion and wisdom, had been maintained unbroken since the very earliest antiquity in the east, particularly in India, where it had been jealously preserved in monasteries and religious centers. Having achieved rapid success in the United States, which was a fertile breeding ground for all new sects, the Theosophical Society moved in 1878 to India, where it established its headquarters first in Bombay, then in Adyar. Later still, probably just after 1880, Blavatsky and Olcott traveled to Europe and attempted to propagate their movement in its various capitals. It was in this way, presumably as the result of a visit to Paris by the two founders, that in 1884 the French branch of the Theosophical Society was founded, headed by a certain L. Dramard, who at about that time published a work entitled *La Science occulte: Étude sur la doctrine ésotérique.*[50] This first attempt, which one must assume met with little success, was repeated three years later with a relaunch of this French branch and the appearance of a magazine, *Le Lotus,* edited by Félix-Krishna Gaboriau, the first number of which appeared in March 1887.

Meanwhile, however, a variety of indigenous movements had also appeared, one of whose aims was to wrest control of French occultism from the theosophists by establishing the existence of a specifically western tradition with which they hoped to trump the theosophists' eastern version. There are abundant indications of this increasing interest in occultism during the years 1884–88. First, 1884 was in fact the publication date of the first novel in which occultist themes are quite clearly apparent. This was Joséphin Péladan's *Le Vice suprême,* which appeared with a lauda-tory preface by Barbey d'Aurevilly. Concerning a femme fatale, the Prin-cess d'Este, subjugated to the will of a magus, Mérodack, who instructs her in a doctrine that includes a theory of astral light, the power of the will and the word, it was probably directly inspired in most of its details by the work of Eliphas Lévi. That same year also saw the publication of Saint-Yves d'Alveydre's two most important works, *Mission des Juifs,* and *Mission des souverains,* both of which combine esoteric theories with utopian political doctrines. At the same time, too, René Caillé, son of a famous French explorer and a former student at the Ecole Centrale, hav-ing been initiated into spiritualism and collaborated in the work of Kar-dec's successors, launched one of the first French occultist magazines, *L'Antimatérialiste,* in which he combined expositions of theosophical theory with advocacy of an aggressive form of spiritualism.[51] Last, it should be noted that 1884 also saw the founding of the first bookshop and publishing house to specialize in occultist literature, the Librairie générale des Sciences Occultes, run by Henri Chacornac.

The most important initiatives in this rising current of occultism, how-ever, were to be taken by Stanislas de Guaïta and Papus. The former first came to Paris either at the end of 1882 or early in 1883.[52] Having at first set out on a career as a decadent mystical poet with *La Muse noire* and *Rosa mystica,* both dealing in macabre themes much influenced by Baudelaire and Rollinat, in about 1885, under the influence of Catulle Mendès,[53] he discovered the work of Eliphas Lévi. From then on, since his family fortune spared him the necessity of working for a living, he shut himself away in his ground-floor apartment on the avenue Trudaine—soon to become a meeting place for all followers of occultism—and settled down to assimilate the essential works of modern occultism. His first doctrinal work, *Au Seuil du mystère* published in 1886, was in fact an attempt to provide a historical survey of all the previous specialized literature, with the accent on the existence of an original western tradition as opposed to the purely eastern references of theosophy. Two further works were to follow, collected with the first under the general title *Essais de sciences maudites: Le Temple de Satan* of 1891 and *La Clef de la magie noire* of 1897. From then until his death in 1897 he remained in close contact not only with the principal leaders of the occultist movement, whom he en-tertained regularly on Thursday evenings, but also with the numerous writers who were attracted by the aura of mystery he had gradually created around himself. As a result, and also because his personal wealth guaranteed him against any suspicion of charlatanism, he came to be regarded as the eminence grise, the profoundest thinker, the most erudite exponent of the occultist movement during those years, even though his three theoretical works were in fact no more than somewhat unoriginal compilations of material from earlier occultist treatises or demonological writings.

As for Gérard Encausse—who was to achieve prominence under the pseudonym Papus, derived from a work by Apollonius of Tyana—although still only twenty, and just embarking of his medical studies, when he first entered Parisian occultist circles, he was very quickly to become the kingpin of the movement.[54] Having first joined the French branch of the Theosophical Society, he began his career with the publication of *L'Occultisme contemporaine,* the first in a long series of books aimed at popularizing the subject and the foundation stone of his reputation. For the most part deficient in original ideas, endowed with only a limited philosophical and literary education, he was nevertheless to play a major role, thanks to his dynamic and attractive personality. An active organizer, in 1888 he started the most important, and the most durable, of the occultist magazines, *L'Initiation,* and in 1890 founded the Groupe indépendant d'Études ésotériques. A founder member, with Guaïta and Péladan, of the Ordre de la Rose-Croix, he also simultaneously ran most of the other esoteric sects that flourished at this period, such as the Martinist order. A man of natural affability, a genial and engaging conversationalist, skilled at maintaining both curiosity and also a certain air of mystery around the movement's theories,[55] he also contrived to remain on good terms with the young avant-garde writers of the day, and did everything he could to ensure that artistic circles in general adopted an attitude of benevolent interest in occultism. While Péladan was to play the role of a somewhat flashy, and frequently lampooned, standard-bearer for quasi-Roman Catholic occultism, and Guaïta that of the movement's leading thinker, Papus, the third and last of its representative figures, was to establish himself as the traveling salesman of the beyond.

Between 1887 and 1890, taking every advantage of the intellectual stir and mounting wave of curiosity created by occultism, these three men did everything possible to ensure that their ideas reaped the benefit of that tide of religious unease which the American-based theosophical movement had so successfully harnessed earlier. Preeminent among those ideas was the notion that it was not necessary to base occultism, as the theosophists did, upon any form of eastern doctrine. As Guaïta had tried to show, there was already an autochthonous tradition in Europe itself that stretched back unbroken to the most ancient times. Needless to say, this ideological battle between theosophists and western occultists was largely a cover for personal rivalries. In 1887, when the French branch of the Theosophical Society was relaunched—under the name Société Isis—Papus became a member. The very next year, however, Guaïta himself, Péladan, and a few others—for example, the writer Paul Adam—founded the Ordre de la Rose-Croix, which claimed to have revived the spiritual heritage and traditions of that extremely ancient and legendary secret order. At the same time, all three were extending their activities in other directions. Every Sunday morning Papus played host to a group of faithful disciples, including the young poet Victor-Emile Michelet and the bookseller Chamuel. Indeed, it was at Papus's instigation that the latter opened his Librairie du Merveilleux in the rue de Trévise, an establishment that was to remain one of the major centers for the dissemination of occultism until the very end of the century. In October 1888, Papus also founded L'Hermès, a rival society to L'Isis, and claimed that he too had received endorsement from the international movement's leaders. Finally, *L'Initiation,* launched at the same period, became the French movement's official organ.

During the next few years the movement was to increase both in scope and in popularity. 1889 saw the republication of an earlier work by Adolphe Franck, a member of the Institut de France, on the Kabbala, the time-honored Jewish hermetic tradition, as well as Schuré's *Les Grands Initiés* and *Le Tarot des Bohémiens* by Papus. From 9 September to 16 September 1889, a Congrès spirite et spiritualiste international was held with a view to achieving some sort of unity among the various spiritualist movements, and the French occultists seized this opportunity to intensify their propaganda. Finally, in 1890, the latent conflict between occultists and theosophists—whose ideas were still being promoted by, for example, the magazine *L'Aurore* run by Lady Caithness, duchesse de Pomar—erupted into open and irreconcilable antagonism. Papus formed the Groupe indépendant d'Études ésotériques and a weekly called *Le Voile d'Isis,* publication of which continued from June 1890 till November 1898. At the same time, Péladan, who was determined to remain within the framework of Roman Catholic orthodoxy, founded his dissident Ordre de la Rose-Croix Catholique, which was to be joined, for varying degrees of time and with varying degrees of seriousness, by eminent society figures infatuated with literature, such as the duc de La Rochefoucauld, Léonce de Larmandie, or Gary de Lacroze, as well as writers such as Elémir Bourges and Saint-Pol-Roux, and the composer Erik Satie.

Occultist ideas were also beginning to take hold among the general public, setting a fashion that was to reach its peak between 1890 and 1895, as numerous contemporary accounts bear witness. In the preface he contributed to Papus's *Traité élémentaire de sciences occultes* of 1888, for instance, Anatole France had no hesitation in writing: "A certain knowledge of the occult sciences is becoming necessary in order to understand a great number of present-day literary works. Magic occupies a large place in the imagination of our poets and novelists. They have been caught in the dizzying pull of the invisible, are haunted by the idea of the unknown."[56] Similarly, in his preface to *Les Grands Initiés* of 1889, Schuré remarks, with reference to the arts at that time: "An immense wave of unconscious esotericism is surging through them. Never has aspiration toward the spiritual life, toward the invisible world repressed by the materialist theories of scientists and worldly opinion, been more serious or more real."[57] The novelist Jules Lermina, another convert to the movement after having been a dyed-in-the-wool materialist, draws attention in his book *La Science occulte,* published in 1890, to the resurgence of interest by then surrounding these esoteric theories: "For some time now there has been widespread discussion of subjects that, it must be admitted, had for a long while been relegated to a position among the most deplorable fantasies of the human mind, subjects never mentioned except as fit objects of mistrust, if not of contempt, on the part of sensible people!"[58]

I shall now try to paint a general picture of the occultist movement's activities during the five years between 1890 and 1895 when it was at the very height of its popularity.

First, the movement had at its disposal the three centers of influence constituted by the three recently founded publishing outlets already mentioned. The first of these was the Librairie générale des Sciences occultes started in 1884 by Henri Chacornac at 11, quai Saint-Michel, very close, in other words, to the establishment of the celebrated "bibliopole" Vanier, who was to publish the great majority of symbolist poetry. Over the next few years, Chacornac was to publish both many modern occultist works and also reprints of occultist classics by writers such as Paracelsus, Albertus Magnus, Roger Bacon, and Raymond Lully. In 1887, Lucien Mauchel, known as Chamuel, started the Librairie du Merveilleux, which began operations in the rue de Trévise but later, between 1894 and 1898, used premises in the rue de Savoie. This was above all the house that published the works of Papus and his friends, and later, after 1890, supported the Groupe indépendant d'Études ésotériques. Finally, there was the Libraire de l'Art indépendant, which had its premises in the rue de la Chaussée d'Antin. Run by Edmond Bailly, it began by publishing theosophical writings, such as René Caillé's *Revue des hautes Etudes,* then gradually took on the function of providing a meeting place for writers attracted by mystery and fantasy.[59] "A number of symbolist poets," André Fontainas tells us, writing of Edmond Bailly, "owed him, if not their first successes, at least the fact of having met and made common cause."[60] Among the frequent visitors to Bailly's establishment at this time, Fontainas cites Mallarmé, Huysmans, Villiers de l'Isle-Adam,

Henri de Régnier, Pierre Quillard, Louis-Ferdinand Hérold and, at a slightly later period, Gide, Pierre Louys, Claudel, and Paul Fort.

Then there were the magazines, the most important of which was *L'Initiation*, which appeared from October 1888 until 1912 and was edited by Papus with the assistance of Chamuel himself and a number of other "initiates" such as Barlet, Lejay, and Sédir. Since the intention behind *L'Initiation* was to unify all the various strains of hermetic thought, it promoted itself by proclaiming an extreme eclecticism. "The idea presiding over the foundation of *L'Initiation*," we read in the "Declaration to Our Readers and Subscribers" that prefaced one of the early numbers, "is absolute toleration. . . . It was our desire to demonstrate to members of the Theosophical Society, western Kabbalists, followers of spiritualism, magnetism, or any other branches of occultism, that they are bound together in pursuit of a common aim by an underlying doctrine that provides them all with a common ground."[61] And each of the collaborators making up the "initiated party" of the magazine does in fact seem to have been free to express his personal beliefs quite freely. In successive issues of *L'Initiation* we find some rather wild theories about psychosomatic medicine from Papus, an attempt by a young man named Doinel to revive the gnostic doctrine, excerpts from Guaïta's historical works, reports of experiments in alchemy, and so on. The "common ground" of all these theories consists solely in the affirmation on principle of a vague spiritualism, and a rejection of both positivist materialism and the claims of the Roman Catholic Church. "It is our wish above all," we also read in the declaration quoted above, "to provide reinforcement for the large army of those who are combating the erroneous and already deeply shaken conclusions of materialism. . . . Let us destroy religious hatred by revealing the unity of all forms of worship in a single religion. Let us destroy philosophical hatred by proclaiming the unity of all doctrines within a single science" (p. 101). However, this wish to unite all the spiritual tendencies of the day, including Roman Catholicism, soon incurred the total disapproval of the Roman Church, a disapproval made official in 1891 by the appearance of *L'Initiation* on the Index, along with most of the other occultist literature of the day. However, *L'Initiation* also aimed at achieving a wide literary influence, and was to boast of counting among its contributors such writers as Villiers, Catulle Mendès, Emile Goudeau, and Jules Lermina. From March 1890 on, each issue was to comprise three sectons: initiatory, philosophy and science, and literary. And *L'Initiation* did in fact publish an appreciable number of literary items: poems such as *L'Hespérus* by Catulle Mendès (December 1889, January, February, July 1890), as well as some by Albert Jounet;[62] tales of imagination such as Charles de Sivry's *Le Conte de l'autre monde* (June 1889); Jules

Lermina's *L'Elixir de longue vie* (November 1889, March 1890); as well as fantastical prose pieces by Robert Scheffer (January 1893). Above all, it also provided frequent reviews of contemporary literary works, in particular those of decadent or symbolist writers, to whom it appears in general to have been very well disposed.[63] So how important and how influential was *L'Initiation* in practice? The printings of some numbers might in retrospect seem to have been small; but they were probably just as large as the majority of other avant-garde literary magazines of the time, if we except the *Mercure de France* and the *Revue blanche*.[64] It is therefore not unreasonable to suppose that *L'Initiation*, although it probably did not find many willing converts to occultism in literary circles, since most writers, however well disposed toward it, were not anxious to bow to the authority of Papus and his team, it might well, on the other hand, have helped to some degree in introducing the new literary movements to a wider public.

The work of *L'Initiation* in the occultist field was supplemented by the efforts of a whole series of other magazines, some of them very short-lived, that continued to mushroom right up until the end of the century. Apart from the duchesse de Pomar's *L'Aurore*, which upheld the theosophical point of view, and with which *L'Initiation* engaged in a sporadic polemic, there was also the weekly *Le Voile d'Isis*, also published by Chamuel and edited by Papus, and a host of others. In an article in the *Mercure de France* of June 1896, Jacques Brieu lists some of them: *L'Ame, Demain, L'Humanité intégrale, Résurrection*. Then, in the December issue he was to record the entry of three further contestants into the lists: *L'Isis moderne, La Thérapeutique intégrale*, and *La Revue scientifique et morale du Spiritisme*. In April 1897, still in the *Mercure*, a writer reviewing an article by Papus in *Le Bulletin de la Presse* records the latter's claim that there were then in existence twenty-five "neo-spiritualist" magazines, which Papus had classified as follows: nine occultist, two magnetic, two sociological, two experimental, one literary. These figures, even allowing for some slight exaggeration in the interests of the cause, do nevertheless give some idea of the magnitude of the occultist phenomenon during the last decade of the nineteenth century. It is true that most of these magazines, specializing fairly narrowly as they did in, say, spiritualism, magnetism, magical cures, or alchemy, and often aimed at a popular, credulous public, lacked any artistic content and were of no interest from the literary point of view. But that was not the case with *L'Etoile*, which, as Mercier observes, "was generous in its welcome to the symbolist poets,[65] or with *Psyché*, which during its brief existence during 1891 and 1892, thanks one presumes to the influence of its editor, Victor-Emile Michelet, displayed the highest literary quality of all the occultist magazines, and is rare among them in being less than wholly tedious to read today.[66] *Psyché* was to publish poems by Albert Jounet, Maurice Bouchor, Gabriel Vicaire, Joachim Gasquet, a story by Michelet himself entitled *La Rédemptrice*, and a review of Maeterlinck's play *Pelléas et Mélisande*.

As an adjunct to *L'Initiation* and *Le Voile d'Isis*, in 1890 Papus also founded a publicity and information center called the Groupe indépendant d'Études ésotériques, whose activities were periodically recorded in *L'Initiation*. In one such item, for example (April 1890), we read that the movement's followers were soon to have at their disposal, in premises adjacent to the Librairie du Merveilleux, a library, a reading room, and a lecture hall with 180 seats. By July's issue, the group had already acquired more than three hundred and fifty members; the December issue reported that eighteen study groups had been formed; in June 1891, in a résumé of the group's activities, *L'Initiation* announced that it now had fifty-five local branches, mostly in France but some of them abroad. Gradually, the group succeeded in transforming itself into a University for Higher Studies, which set examinations and conferred degrees and doctorates in Kabbalistic lore.[67] On 11 November 1891, Papus's friends presented him with an honorary diploma signed by Flammarion, Tailhade, Luys, Goudeau, Victor-Emile Michelet, Gary de Lacroze, Lermina, Guaïta, among many others.[68] The following May, Papus and Chamuel traveled to Belgium to deliver a series of lectures to the organization's local branch there.

Not content with all these multifarious activities, and ever the wily impresario, Papus also announced that by virtue of his own past initiation he was now able to revive the defunct Martinist order, and proceeded to do so. However, the revived order, composed of exactly the same members whose names constantly recur in the contents pages of *L'Initiation*, appears to have had little more than a fictitious existence.[69] At the same time, a young man from Orleans, Jules Doinel, was publishing a series of articles in *L'Initiation* aimed at reviving the Gnostic church (November 1889, April 1890, January, June, August 1892). Before long, claiming Simon Magus and Valentinus as his patrons, Doinel anointed himself a bishop, organized meetings at the Librairie du Merveilleux, and consecrated a number of other bishops before finally abjuring his heresy, in 1895, and returning to the bosom of the Roman Church.[70] Albert Poisson, a laboratory assistant working for the Paris Faculty of Medicine, undertook to revive the science of alchemy, and duly published a series of works of the subject before his death in 1894.[71] Then, several months later, interest in alchemy was again revived when Jollivet-Castelot started his magazine *L'Hyperchimie*, to which Strindberg was to contribute on a number of occasions, this being the period of his life when he was living in France and conducting the frenzied alchemical experiments described in his *Inferno*.

It would undoubtedly be naive to take the successive announcements of victory recorded in *L'Initiation* on behalf of these various sects at their face value, or to exaggerate their importance. Apart from the few prime movers, those who might be termed the "standing committee" of occultism and whose names constantly recur at the head of such announcements, the majority of followers must have been recruited from among the eternally gullible, always in search of miracles, or those hoping to communicate with some dear departed. Moreover, after 1894, the affairs of the Papus consortium seem to have run into a period of difficulties. It was at this time that Papus advocated, if the pun is pardonable, an occultation of occultism, as in this statement, for example: "Occultism is fashionable, and that is the greatest danger that could beset it. . . . We have decided to leave the society folk to amuse one another, and to retreat more than ever into the closed groups from which we were obliged to emerge in 1882 only to stop the propagation of doctrines that were leading the nation's intellectual life to destruction" (*L'Initiation*, October 1894). The following year, Chamuel's establishment, and its adjoining center, were transferred to the rue de Savoie, and in October 1896 *L'Initiation* announced: "Our friends know that we have had to suspend activities at our headquarters in order to devote ourselves to intellectual pursuits in closed groups and within the Martinist lodge." In fact, the last years of the century seem to have brought a progressive decline in the stir caused by occultism and the various hermetic groups. 1898 saw the closure of both the Librairie du Merveilleux and that of *Le Voile d'Isis*.

It is nevertheless clear that this movement, even though its involvement with literature and the history of ideas was only a partial one, did have a perceptible effect on the intellectual outlook of literary circles in the last decade of the century. Proof of this is to be found in the journalist Jules Huret's *Enquête sur l'évolution littéraire* of 1891, already referred to earlier. In his survey of the various literary trends of the day, alongside what he calls the psychologists, the naturalists, and the symbolists, Huret devotes a whole chapter to the "magi," which includes interviews with four masters of contemporary literary occultism: Péladan, Jules Bois, Papus, and Paul Adam. In the first of these interviews, Péladan states very firmly that the notion of the symbol, then being exploited by so many young poets, cannot achieve its true meaning except in an esoteric setting: "As for symbolism, it is a hieratic schema. The word has no meaning other than a religious or hermetic one. . . . I therefore fail to understand the use of the term to denote such and such a poet without any metaphysical beliefs." Similarly, commenting on his interview with Paul Adam, Huret sums up that writer's position as follows: "He believes in the reality of the hyperphysical world, in the influence of the planets, he loves the Kabbala, respects chiromancy, graphology, and the systems of Gall and Lavater" (pp. 35–54). Huret's investigation, and the book summing up its results, thus constitute, along with the resulting stir, a sort of official confirmation of occultism as one of the specific currents within the literary movement of the time. Moreover the almost simultaneous appearance of *Là-bas,* and the reactions it provoked from "specialists" like Guaïta and Papus, who accused Huysmans of being a profane dabbler who had distorted the true meaning of the movement, also contributed to maintaining the public's curiosity about occultist matters. Next year, amid tremendous publicity, Péladan organized his first Salon de la Rose-Croix Catholique. Held on the Champ de Mars, and accompanied by a variety of artistic demonstrations, this exhibition also succeeded in arousing enormous public curiosity, despite the attitude of the press, who had for some years past been using Péladan as their favorite aunt sally. The rivalry between the Rose-Croix catholique, which Péladan had founded with himself as its grand master, and the original order founded in 1888, also gave rise over the years to numerous polemics, and these skirmishes, which the popular press promptly dubbed the Wars of the Roses, were assiduously reported.[72] Again in 1888, *La Plume* devoted an entire issue to magic. And the Boullan affair of 1893, together with the two duels it provoked, also scarcely helped to dampen the Parisian public's curiosity with regard to the occultist movement.[73]

Throughout this period, occultist themes were gradually penetrating into literary circles. Apart from the writers already mentioned, such as Paul Adam, Barrès, Anatole France, and Mendès, who all expressed either sympathy with or curiosity about occultist ideas, those ideas were also making a deep impression on the younger generation of writers, those who began to rise to prominence in or just after 1890. Victor-Emile Michelet, who began his career as a journalist in 1883, very quickly came under the influence of both Villiers and Guaïta, and eventually became converted to a form of occultism that was to orient his entire life's work. His first two major personal works appeared in 1890. These were the story *La Rédemptrice,* already alluded to, and a short book entitled *De l'Esotérisme dans l'art,* in which he advocated occultism as a possible means of injecting new blood into the literature of the day. At that time, too, Rémy de Gourmont was being kept abreast of all the latest developments within the movement by his mistress Berthe Courrière.[74] Among the younger poets, Adolphe Retté and Edouard Dubus were undoubtedly the two who felt the pull of occultism most strongly. Later on, Retté was to describe his state of mind at this time: "Inclined to experiment with the murky dangers and delights of occultism . . . utterly without religious upbringing, attracted like most of my generation by anything tinged with mystery and the unexpected; when occultism invaded literature I was caught up in its wake, like many others before me."[75] It is Retté too who recounts how his young friend Edouard Dubus fell under the spell of Guaïta, who introduced him to the drug that led to the young poet's early death in 1894. It is probable, in fact, that Guaïta played host in his ground floor apartment on the avenue Trudaine to a considerable section of the contemporary intelligentsia.[76] That few writers were tempted to range themselves openly among the ranks of the occultists is clear; but it is also true that many of them, particularly among the "decadent" group attracted by mystery and unusual experiences, fell deeply under the spell of occultism, despite being repelled by the obscurity of its writings, or the total lack of literary talent displayed by most of its official supporters.[77] In 1892, in the foreword to his *Récits de l'occulte,* Gilbert-Augustin Thierry says explicitly: "Today, an irresistible momentum is bearing us on toward those mysterious horizons, those clouds whose very shadows glow with light, in which the Great Unknown seems to delight. We are on a voyage of discovery; we need "to know" at last; we question the beyond. . . . We too are driven toward despair by doubt; lies or truth, we feel the need to believe. . . . And there it is, the occult, beckoning us into its fascinating chasms."[78] In the chapter on occultism in his *Entartung,* first published in French in 1894, Max Nordau too comments on this new fascination for the outlandish among a great many writers of the time, and analyzes the works of Péladan and Guaïta in particular. Moreover, while the occultist magazines for their part strove to achieve a literary content, the literary magazines proper, particularly the two most important, the *Mercure de France* and the *Revue blanche,* reciprocated by keeping their readers informed of what was happening within the occultist movement, and often reviewed occultist publications. Between 1890 and 1892, for example, Edouard Dubus was given a column in the *Mercure* specifically devoted to reviews of occultist literature, and in 1895, again in the *Mercure,* we find an article by Jollivet-Castelot drawing attention to the resurgence of alchemy then on the horizon. Then, from June 1896 onward, the same magazine began a regular section, headed *Esotérisme et spiritualisme* and written by a certain Jacques Brieu, that provided fairly detailed news of occultist activities, books, and magazines. It is therefore possible to say, with complete certainty, despite the lack of total interpenetration between the occultist and literary movements of this period, that they did at least have numerous and constant points of contact. The occultists welcomed any approbation they received from the younger generation of writers as an endorsement of their serious intent and intellectual standing; the young writers shared the occultists' fundamental idealism, and were unflaggingly curious with regard to occultism during this period.

Principal Themes of the Occultist Movement

Because the occultist movement comprised so many various chapels, and lacked any truly original intellectual framework, it is scarcely possible to speak of an occultist doctrine. What one can do, however, is isolate a certain number of basic options upon which most adherents of the various movements were in agreement. The first consisted in the adoption of an idealist stance in reaction to the materialism that had underpinned the scientific approach prevalent during the heyday of positivism. In this respect, the occultist movement is of course only one strand in the general current of reemergent spiritualism, in the philosophical sense, whose extent and manifestations we examined earlier. Apart from the passage already quoted from the Déclaration that appeared in the February 1890 issue of *L'Initiation*, there are numerous other texts in which this adherence to a somewhat vague philosophical spiritualism is made clearly apparent. For instance, in reply to Jules Huret's questions, Jules Bois asserted that occultism makes it possible to dispense with "the harsh, material blindness and skepticism of men like Renan" (*Enquête*, p. 49), while Papus observed that "magianism corresponds to a reaction against materialist doctrines in science" (p. 52). This profession of spiritual faith was to be repeated by Papus in a short work dating from 1896, *Le Diable et l'occultisme*, and there is one passage in it that gathers together some of the essential convictions that underlay the entire movement throughout this period. With reference to the new generations being progressively won over to the spiritualist doctrine, he writes:

> Former followers of materialism and atheism, for the most part aware from their own experience of all the forms of despair engendered in the secret recesses of the mind by a pessimism stemming from absence of belief in any kind of ideal, these searchers asked, not from any sectarian faith, not from any particular form of worship, but from all the aspirations of earth toward God and toward the beyond, for rational proofs with which to confront their adversaries. . . . The tradition, thus evoked, answered through the voice of history by offering in occult science the guiding torch, the synthesis they had sought so long; the immortal soul proves its existence by means of facts as strange as

they are unexpected, and, seizing upon this double foundation—the theory provided by hermetism, the experience
provided by fragments of magic known by the name of hypnotism and transcendental psychology—those who were
called occultists sought to lead the intellectual élite of
France back to a belief in the beyond.[79]

This quotation also highlights the second dominant feature of occultism
at that time, which was its ambition to reconcile science and religion—
traditionally seen as opponents—in a new synthesis. The first condition of
such a synthesis, however, was seen to be a rejection of both the hard and
fast dogmas and the discipline demanded by traditional churches, and by
the Roman Church in particular. "There can be no question," Jules Bois
told Huret, "of a simple return to Christianity as it was before, since that,
in our scientific atmosphere, could never be more than a passing fashion"
(*Enquête*, pp. 49–50). Papus constantly adopted this same stance, declar-
ing: "Although we openly affirm our Christian spirituality, that does not
mean that we are subjecting our freedom to any existing church" (*Sciences occultes*, p. 37). In fact, after having continued for a while to expect
benevolent toleration from the Roman hierarchy, a toleration that would
have enabled them to win over a section of Rome's faithful to their own
views, the occultists were eventually disappointed by the official attitude
of the Church, which soon began condemning membership in the initiatory sects with increasing firmness, and in 1891 placed *L'Initiation* on
its Index. After that, the occultists consistently criticized the Church for
its intransigence. In the movement as a whole, however, the extremist
stances taken up by Péladan, who never ceased asserting his orthodoxy,
at least till the end of the century, and by Guaïta, who displayed a constant and very lively hostility toward the Roman Church, seem to have
been the exception rather than the rule. It is historically probable, at all
events, that allegiance to occultism at this period was for some merely a
stage on their return to the fold of orthodox religious practice.

This notion that science and religion could now be reconciled sprang
from the belief, expressed by many occultists of the day, that their researches, which led them to assert the existence of a supernatural universe, were in perfect conformity with the most demanding scientific
method. Thus in his first book, *Au Seuil du mystère*, Guaïta claims that
the theory of astral light makes possible "a rational explanation of the
most disturbing magnetic or spirit phenomena, without having to ask for
help from the shades of our ancestors or from Satanas and his various
legions."[80] Defining the "new mysticism" in 1891, François Paulhan was
to observe that it "is a mysticism that, far from rejecting the scientific
spirit, gladly invokes it."[81] And Guaïta again, introducing an excerpt from

his *Serpent de la Genèse* in the February 1890 number of *L'Initiation,*
addressed contemporary occultists as "bold experimenters, profound
thinkers, who, by applying the very methods of positive science to the
hyperphysical world, have laid down the unshakable foundation of a
monumental synthesis of all human knowledge, and set in place the first
stone of that august temple in which we shall one day celebrate—and not
far hence—the solemn reconciliation of the two warring sisters, science
and faith."

Jules Lermina, in a book that appeared in 1890, went even further, and
maintained that materialism and spiritualism are perfectly compatible,
since the soul is no more than a more refined and subtle form of matter.
Basing his argument partly on Crookes's theory of a fourth state of matter, the radiant state, and partly on the Darwinian theory of evolution, he
claimed that the idea of the soul's survival after the death and annihilation
of the visible body was scientifically acceptable. "The truth is," he
writes, "there is nothing other than materialism, in the sense that any
futures—insofar as they exist—represent nothing but a dilution, a sub-
limation of matter, which will be endowed in other states with properties
that do not exist in the forms of it that we know." If "the supernatural
does not exist, that is because the soul, being a more subtle form of
matter, has a purely natural reality: material and spiritual are no more
than expressions referring to the substance's degree of density or tenu-
ousness." The existence of psychic energy, which corresponds with this
fourth state of matter, thus provides scientific justification, as far as Lermina is concerned, both for the spiritualists' principal hypotheses—
existence of the soul and its survival after death—and for all those previously inexplicable phenomena such as dual personality in mediums,
suggestion, telekinesis, and so forth. The evolution of life as proved by
Darwin does not stop with the human species but continues on upward to
higher beings: "We are ineluctably led to hypothesize the existence of a
stage in nature occurring after humankind, and as far removed from it as
we are from the life of animals."[82]

Clearly this reconciliation between science and religion was dependent
upon the central hypothesis, claimed by the occultists to be a scientific
reality, that between the material and spiritual universes there exists a
third and intermediary level, or what most occultists term the "astral
plane." Different forms of this notion are to be found both in Crookes's
theory of the "radiant state" of matter and in that put forward by the
Austrian Von Reinchenbach based on the existence of a magnetic fluid
called Od, which Colonel de Rochas believed his experiments had confirmed. This theory of an intermediate plane was taken up and enlarged
upon by most late-nineteenth-century occultists in France. In *Au Seuil du*

mystère, for instance, Guaïta uses it for his own purposes when he asserts that in every human being, side by side with the body and the spirit, there exists an intermediate reality or "perispirit," which is a sort of magnetic fluid permitting clairvoyance, telekinesis, and exteriorization of the will. Four years later, in an article in *L'Initiation* (February 1890), he returned to this "faculty inherent in the perispirit, or sidereal double, to project itself out of the physical body, to direct its own movements, to transport itself to the most distant places, while the body remains in a cataleptic state, or at least is no longer animated by anything more than an automatic and as it were vegetative life." During this "astral travel," the astral body, which remains linked to the physical body by a kind of umbilical cord, is drawn into the turbulence of "the fluidic maelstrom," "a vehicle thunderous with all the possible that yearns to be, all the subjective virtualities avid to objectify themselves, all the souls of the various hierarchies impatient for incarnation." Papus too, although he does not go into quite such detail regarding the facts of astral navigation, produced a great deal in the same vein, and claimed that "to know the astral body thoroughly is to possess the most important of the doctrine's keys" (*Sciences occultes,* p. 63). Combining this theory with his own medical knowledge, he also located the physiological seat of this astral body in the sympathetic nervous system. At all events, this picturesque hypothesis of "astral travel" was undoubtedly manna from heaven for contemporary story writers, and echoes of it can be found even in much later work, such as certain pieces by Michaud.

This theory of the astral body had the further advantage that it could be presented as a fresh scientific endorsement of the old, traditional theory of the interdependence of the material and spiritual worlds, in other words the theory of analogy, upon which all occultist doctrines have always been founded. It is this principle that Guaïta is reaffirming, for example, when he writes in his foreword to *Au Seuil du mystère:*

> Magic admits three worlds or spheres of activity: the divine world of causes, the intellectual world of thoughts, and the perceptible world of phenomena. One in its essence, triple in its manifestations, being is logical, and things above are analogous and proportional to those below; with the result that a single cause engenders in each of the three worlds corresponding series of effects that are rigorously determinable by analogical calculations. [P. 8]

Guaïta himself gives an example of this unity and interdependence of all the elements of reality, perceptible and spiritual, when he writes: "It is by virtue of an identical principle that the mollusc secretes its mother of pearl

and the human heart its love; and the same law that governs the communion of the sexes controls the gravitation of suns'' (p. 9). In a slim work
of popularization published in 1890, Papus too bases his argument on
analogy: "What occultism is seeking, what it claims to provide for its
followers, is the link that links all those opposites at war today: might and
right, science and faith, reason and imagination, and so on. . . . This discovery stems from the application of a method of reasoning almost ig-
nored in our day: analogy."[83] The main application of this doctrine of
analogy is in the well-known form of the theory of symbols, whereby, as a
result of vertical correspondences, each object in the perceptible world
becomes the material clue to an invisible reality. And, indeed, as we saw
earlier, it was in an exclusively religious and hermetic sense that Péladan
interpreted this notion of the symbol in his interview with Huret in 1891.

The reason that this "science" and this vision of the world embodied in
the esoteric doctrines are defined as "occult" is that those who professed
them, particularly in the decadent era, asserted the existence of a concealed tradition by means of which this secret knowledge had been
handed on down the centuries from initiate to initiate. At the outset of his
very first book, Guaïta insisted on this secret nature of the doctrine, and
on the dangers threatening incautious or disrespectful dabblers, who
would meet with either death or madness: "The higher science cannot be
the object of a frivolous curiosity; the problem is sacred, one over which
many noble brows have paled in their endeavors, and questioning the
Sphinx upon an idle whim is a sacrilege never left unpunished" (*Au Seuil
du mystère*, p. 14). It was the existence of this tradition that he had set out
to demonstrate, and its history that he was attempting to reconstitute by
studying the works of the greatest initiates in the long chain of the western
tradition, beginning with the "sanctuaries of the ancient world" and the
"occult Christianity of the early Fathers": Albertus Magnus, Raymond
Lully, Nicolas Flamel, Cornelius Agrippa, Paracelsus, Kunrat, Cardan,
Swedenborg, and Saint-Martin; then, in the nineteenth century, Fabre
d'Olivet, Vronski, Louis Lucas, Eliphas Lévi, and Saint-Yves d'Alveydre
(p. 23). Papus likewise asserted that "the path that has led us to our
present concepts . . . is far from being a new one, since it stretches back to
ideas taught in the temples of Egypt as early as 2600 B.C., ideas that later
formed the basis of Platonism and, to a large extent, neoplatonism." He
also claimed to have been personally initiated into Martinism. This theory
of a tradition offered many advantages: it surrounded initiates with an
aura of mystery and dignity, while also making them the privileged de-
positories of immemorial wisdom and knowledge.

However, and this was doubtless an essential element in the prestige
they enjoyed, the occultists, especially those grouped around Papus, also

claimed to be, not miracle workers, since they presented their exploits as being merely the application of scientific knowledge, but experimenters capable of unleashing extraordinary phenomena. In its practical and popular form, occultism presented itself as white magic. Eliphas Lévi had already called his most important work *Dogme et rituel de haute magie;* Lermina gave the subtitle "Practical Magic" to his *La Science occulte* of 1890; Papus in 1893 published a *Traité élémentaire de magie pratique.* Corresponding with this practical magic, which claimed to be purely beneficent and humanitarian in its aims, we also find initiates claiming to have mastered various amazing practices, including "astral travel," which enabled the astral body to leave its earthly body, visit any point on the globe, and talk to spirits and the souls inhabiting the beyond; and exteriorization of the will, which enabled them to perform acts of telekinesis and communicate directly with others. Occult magic also claimed to include all the powers exploited by subsidiary groups: spiritism's communication with the dead; alchemy's transmutation of metals; magic medicine's miraculous cures. Thus, in the last years of the century we find occultism serving as the professed basis for the activities of an astrologer like Ely Star as well as for those of the alchemist Tiffereau, who put out a brochure, advertised several times in *L'Initiation,* that claimed to contain the secret for making gold. In other words, aided by the dubious findings of certain respected scientists, occultism, when directed at a credulous and popular public, was far too often debased from a metaphysical doctrine into mere charlatanism, an exploitation of this period's intense desire for the supernatural remarked upon earlier.

What influence did this resurgence of occultism ultimately have on the development of contemporary literature? Certainly the theory of analogy, as we have seen, was the intellectual foundation of the symbolist doctrine adopted by an appreciable section of the new poetic school, which might lead one to posit a profound symbiosis between the symbolist school and the occultist movement. In fact, however, nothing of the kind occurred, despite the contacts that we know existed between the two movements. The absence of any truly original thought among the majority of the self-styled initiates, their inability to achieve any kind of synthesis, the muddled writing and literary nullity that characterized the occultists' writing—including those of Guaïta, who nevertheless passed for the movement's mastermind—must very quickly have repelled the symbolist poets. Despite Charles Morice's claim that "the occult sciences constitute one of the fundamental angles of art. Every true poet is by instinct an initiate,"[84] the poets themselves showed little eagerness to become involved in the sometimes rather dubious enterprises launched by Papus and his friends, while the 'initiates" for their part were quick to express scorn for the use to which poets were putting "their" symbols. Jules Bois, a mediocre journalist whose main concern with occultism was that it should provide him with sensational copy and a profitable career, provides a good example of this when he takes it upon himself to tell Jules Huret: "Occultism also acts by means of a second element: the symbol. And the symbolist school does not come into that at all. In the occult, the symbol is always linked to a series of religious, psychological, ideal truths; in the symbolist school it is merely the superficial obfuscation of an affected style" (*Enquête,* p. 50).

If occultism, and the doctrines, speculations, and chimerical notions it brought in its train, had any influence during this period, then it was more in the field of prose, where it helped to revive a taste for mystery and fantasy that naturalist literature had suppressed. Practically speaking, occultism resulted in a restoration of the sense of fantasy. "It is not simply a love for the positive fact that has captured people's minds," François Paulhan observed; "there has undoubtedly been a sort of reconquest of those minds by a love of the fantastic."[85] Most commentators during the early years of the twentieth century, when looking back in order to assess the effects of the occultist movement, were likewise to remark on this reemergence of the sense of fantasy. For instance, in his preface to Georges Vitoux's book published in 1901, Emile Gautier was to write: "Never were fantasy and the supernatural so much in vogue as during that unbelieving and frivolous fin de siècle. It reached a positive high tide, to the point of providing material for a whole murky, polyglot, abstruse literature with its own specialized periodicals."[86] We must therefore look for the literary influence of occultism not so much in the field of poetic creation as in the appearance of a whole new wave of fantastic tales that made use of story lines inspired by occultist teachings.

4   THE UNCONSCIOUS AND SEXUALITY

The Decadent Era Is Also the Period When—Even before Freud had developed his fundamental distinction between the conscious and the psychic—the hypothesis of an unconscious, that is, of a mental activity being carried on within the human mind but without the knowledge of the consciousness and independently of it, was to be increasingly posited and adopted by all those involved in the psychological field, whether physicians, psychiatrists, philosophers, or simply writers. However original and revolutionary Freud's theories may have seemed at first, in other words, the fact is that the foundations for them had already been laid down by a succession of earlier thinkers over a long period. Freud did not invent the hypothesis of the unconscious; he simply brought it to final fruition by making it the basic hypothesis of psychoanalysis. The long genesis of the notion of the unconscious throughout the nineteenth century has already been established in a recent book by the American Lancelot L. Whyte, who traces its origins back to the romantic era and points out, for example, that Jean Paul was already displaying foreknowledge of modern theories.[1] Similarly, in the early nineteenth century the philosopher Maine de Biran accepted that the origin of instinctual desires, such as hunger and the sexual drive, is unconscious in nature. In his chapter on Schopenhauer, Whyte is also led to remark that most aspects of the unconscious as we conceive it today are already present in the German philosopher's work. During the next few decades, the theory of the unconscious was to be taken up, simultaneously, by the principal representatives of the British school of psychology, such as Carpenter or Maudsley, and by German philosophers and physiologists. By the 1850s, its dissemination in such specialist fields seems to have been increasing rapidly, and Whyte has found ten or twenty thinkers in every decade from 1850 to 1890 who made at least some minor contribution to it. For example, in his *Principles of Mental Physiology* of 1874, the British psychologist Carpenter devoted an entire chapter to what he called "unconscious cerebration," a term that swiftly became fashionable and was frequently employed by later writers.

119

Clearly, however, it was with Hartmann's *Philosophy of the Unconscious* of 1868 that the notion of the unconscious really came to the forefront.[2] The "unconscious" as defined by Hartmann coincides only partially, it is true, with the meaning ascribed to that term by modern psychology, since he uses it to denote the impersonal and general force that governs the existence of all living things. Hartmann's unconscious has a biological dimension as well as a psychological one; it is that force or energy that obliges individuals to conform with the higher ends of the species, even despite themselves, as when they are controlled by their instinctual mechanisms, for example. In short, it is to some extent a positivist transposition of the religious notion of providence, though in this case a blind providence absurdly driving all living creatures to a futile maintenance and prolongation of life on earth. As far as the influence of this force on human existence is concerned, however, Hartmann did clearly assert that the unconscious plays a determining role in our sexuality. Convinced, like Schopenhauer before him, that sexual activity is in itself obscene and ridiculous, and that man would never subject himself to it unless some unknown and unconscious force were obliging him to bow to the superior desire of the species to ensure its perpetuation, he denounced love as a purely subjective illusion serving to mask the essential mechanism of reproduction. The analysis that Hartmann undertook of love therefore had the considerable merit, and originality, of restating with some force, and in a manner that many of his contemporaries found deeply shocking, the essential role played by sexual elements in the origin and development of an emotion that classical psychology had tended to approach from a too exclusively affective or moral standpoint.

This double tendency—interest in the phenomena of "unconscious cerebration" and recognition of the unconscious but fundamental role of the sexual instinct in love—was to develop still further during the last years of the century. According to Whyte, by the decade between 1870 and 1880 the general idea of an unconscious mind had become a commonplace throughout Europe. Certainly Hartmann's influence, as well as Schopenhauer's, had become widespread in France. Thus the notion of the unconscious forms the very center of a philosophy treatise published in 1880 by Edmond Colsenet, in which, having first analyzed and commented on Hartmann's principal ideas, the writer concludes in favor of the existence of an unconscious psychism: "It is impossible to continue reducing psychic life to mere consciousness of self. Beneath that consciousness, and subordinated to it in ordinary conditions, other consciousnesses, descending on a probably infinite scale, are the terrain of more specialized determinations, albeit analogous in nature to those of which we are directly and consciously aware."[3]

It is true, however, that the notion of the unconscious, or of unconscious mental activity, or unconscious cerebration, which late-
nineteenth-century writers were to use with increasing frequency, remained both ambiguous and ill defined until the end of the century.[4] Some
used the term in the sense that Hartmann had given it, that of a universal
force stubbornly working at the maintenance of life on earth and leading
individuals to sacrifice their personal interest, despite themselves, to the
higher interest of the species. This was very much the case with Laforgue,
who never tired of Hartmann's work and endorsed its principal assertions: the absurdity of an existence prolonged without reason, despite the
suffering and destruction it brings in its wake, on both a general and an
individual level; the illusoriness of love, chaining the individual to the will
of the species; the superiority of the void into which humanity ought
voluntarily to return. It is in this sense that he described himself as
"bowing piously before the unconscious,"[5] and wrote, using the image
already employed by Jean Paul, of "the inner Africa of our unconscious
realm."[6]

For some of Laforgue's contemporaries, however, the notion of the
unconscious was essentially bound up with certain forms of automatic and
involuntary activity in the mental field that could nevertheless lead to
results sometimes quite as positive as willed and methodical conscious
effort. In the field of artistic creation this led to a new way of interpreting
the well-known phenomenon of inspiration. Such was the standpoint
taken by Paul Chabaneix in his work *De l'Inconscient chez les artistes, les
savants et les écrivains,* which appeared in 1897. Having questioned
about forty scientists, painters, and writers, Chabaneix attempted to
demonstrate that the unconscious and involuntary activity of the mind
plays an important role in the genesis of scientific discoveries and artistic
creations, particularly in the form of creative dreams. Pushing the logic of
this thesis to its extreme, he even came to hypothesize the possibility of
an essentially unconscious creative process: "One can very well conceive
of an ideal scientist who, instead of creating his ideas with conscious
reflection, and guiding their progress with his subconscious thought, re-
verses these roles, so that he guides the direction of his activities with his
consciousness but actually accomplishes the work with his subconscious."[7] Here we are clearly already close to the surrealist theory of
inspiration, and to the role that the surrealists were to assign to the unconscious some twenty years later, particularly with their use of automatic writing in artistic creation. Reviewing Chabaneix's work some months
later, Rémy de Gourmont was in enthusiastic agreement: "Consciousness, which is the principle of liberty, is not the principle of art."[8] He was
careful, however, to make a distinction between the unconscious proper,

meaning Hartmann's conception of it, which always remains concealed from the conscious mind, and those phenomena of "automatic cerebration" capable of being more or less clearly perceived by the subject, for which he proposed the term subconscious as a preferable alternative.

For many others, especially among the writers of the time, the term unconscious served to denote the more or less secret activities in the depths of the psyche whose existence could be revealed, or at least sensed, by means of analysis, introspection, or certain exceptional phenomena. If the writers of the period interested themselves in this deeper self, it was precisely because it was in the very nature of the decadent sensibility to explore the most impalpable or most twilit aspects of psychic life. Professing as they did a fundamental idealism that led them to challenge, if not to deny outright, the reality of the external world, the decadents were quite naturally predisposed to turn in upon the self, upon their own consciousness, representing as it did the only reality remaining to them after the shipwreck of the external and illusory world. The decadent is thus quite naturally given to introspection and narcissism. In addition, boredom, and its corollary a passionate desire to escape from the tedium of life at any cost, drive him to search for new and ever more refined sensations, obtained by the aid of more or less artificial means, and themselves worthless unless the consciousness of the subject is used to apprehend them, to concentrate upon their smallest ramifications and developments, to record their first impact and receding repercussions upon the mind. This new form of pleasure can be enjoyed only at the price of hyperesthesia and the hyperacuity of a consciousness that has been transformed into a kind of psychic resonating chamber. It is thus in the nature of the decadent mind to probe the deepest and remotest areas of the human psychic mechanism, or what in those days was still referred to as the soul, in its new psychological sense as opposed to its earlier moral one. There are many texts of the period that offer proof of this hypersensitized concentration upon the inner depths of the soul. In a passage from his *Carnets intimes,* written in about 1887, Albert Samain, for example, recognized the primacy of an inner self over the superficial self that is apparent in daily life: "The more closely I examine myself, the more I find that we do not live in the real, profound, and in some sort absolute sense of life except through the unconscious."[9] It is this same "inner soul" whose mysterious existence and aqueous depths Rodenbach was attempting to capture in his metaphor of a mental aquarium:

> So is my soul alone beyond all influence!
> It is like glass, wrapped round in silence,
> Coiled wholly inward on its hidden shows
> Upon the sort of secret, underwater life
> Where dreams have glimmered in the silvered depths.[10]

To enable consciousness to penetrate the most inaccessible corners of the inner psychic mechanism is also the objective expressed in an anonymous text published in *Le Décadent* late in 1888:

> These emotions once felt, the decadent analyzes them. He cultivates them in the recollection of his reverie, he brings them into focus, molds his thought to them in order to capture their most delicate convolutions. . . . He wishes to know himself, he observes himself, he analyzes and notes everything, down to the most evasive of half-felt emotions, the most tenuous quiver of psychic states scarcely yet formed, barely detectable; and by means of this deep, meticulous, remorselessly pursued investigation, he is constantly pushing back the frontiers of the unconscious.[11]

The same interest in the life of the unconscious is evident in the work of Maeterlinck, as is evident in this sentence from *Le Trésor des humbles,* which Victor Charbonnel used as an epigraph for the first chapter of his book *La Volonté de vivre:* "We live to one side of our true life and we feel that even our most secret and profound thoughts are unconnected with us, for we are something other than our thoughts and dreams." Writing about Maeterlinck's plays, Edouard Schuré takes this same idea even further: "The first observation Maeterlinck made when scrutinizing his own states of soul, and those of people he knew well, was the extremely restricted control that consciousness and reason exercise over our destiny. We are not only slaves of the body that imprisons us, and of the external world that confines us, but we are also surrounded by an invisible world that influences and sometimes determines us." It is true, however, that Schuré interpreted this unconscious area in a way that would confirm his esoteric beliefs: "There is clearly a subconsciousness within us that is in communication with an invisible universe, but one from which we receive only feeble glimmerings and indecipherable signs, because this inner self is asleep, and sunk in densest shadow."[12]

It is clear, then, how during the last twenty years of the nineteenth century, the hypothesis of an unconscious had made sufficient headway to attract the allegiance of a steadily increasing number of writers. Beneath the reassuring appearances of lucid consciousness and the self as described by classical psychology, they divined, darkly apprehended, or struggled to bring into focus a new, secret, mysterious layer of consciousness. But this exploration of the soul's lower depths also led them to discover the importance of sexuality, and to throw new light on some of its forms.

If the decadents discovered sexuality, however, it was only for the most part to reject it, or at least to reject its normal forms. For here we encounter a further aspect of their antinaturalism, one noted earlier, which is a rejection of normal love and sexuality as belonging in the realm of nature. Antinaturalism leads quite naturally to antifeminism, since woman symbolizes nature. This antifeminism was in fact extremely widespread during the decadent era, fostered as it was by the influence of two of the epoch's major thinkers and inspirations, Baudelaire and Schopenhauer.

Baudelaire's antifeminism is well known, since it is expressed time and again in his work, not only in such pieces as *La Soupe et les nuages* or *Le Galant Tireur* from *Le Spleen de Paris,* for example, but above all in his secret diaries, which subsequently became extremely unsecret indeed when Eugène Crepet undertook their publication in 1887. For Baudelaire, woman is necessarily contemptible because she is much closer to nature than man is; she is predominantly animal; and being directly and tyrannically governed by her physical instincts she is incapable of detaching herself from them, so that all her activities are ineluctably directed toward their satisfaction. "Woman is the opposite of the dandy. Therefore she inspires horror. Woman is hungry so she must eat; thirsty, so she must drink. She is in heat so she must be fucked. How admirable! Woman is natural, which is to say abominable."[13] For this very reason she is reduced to her body, and the universe of the spiritual life is absolutely closed to her. Baudelaire even goes on to suppose, in ironic vein, that she has been denied a soul: "Woman cannot separate the soul from the body. She is simplistic, like the brute beasts. A satirist would say this is because she has nothing but a body" (*Oeuvres complètes,* p. 1213). He expresses amazement that women are allowed to attend church (p. 1213). At the same time, however, he is obliged to recognize the demands of his sexuality, and to acknowledge the attraction he feels for woman and her company. In this respect his work is the exemplary statement of a dilemma that was never to cease tormenting the decadent consciousness: the simultaneous recognition of the satanic and perverse nature of love, the contemptible nature of woman, and the impossibility of doing without her. The precarious and painful solution adopted was twofold. First, an acceptance that love and sexuality must be lived and experienced as guilt, that they must be regarded as the foremost expression of satanism, of that fundamental self-abasement constituted by perversion, and expressed in the celebrated passage from *Fusées III:* "I say this: the unique and supreme pleasure of love lies in the certainty of doing evil" (p. 1183). Second, a decision to see and regard the essence of woman as pure animality, to reduce woman to her body, to view stupidity as the best "ornament of beauty" (p. 1260). "Trapped between the hereditary and paternal desire for morality and the tyrannical desire for a woman one must despise," the dandy, the artist, will accept woman in her purely carnal existence and make use of her body alone as a springboard toward the esthetic universe

(p. 1261). And such is indeed the status and the role allotted to woman in a considerable number of the poems in *Les Fleurs du mal*. Hence, too, the corresponding horror that Baudelaire felt for any woman who attempted to escape from this purely physical and sexual status, whether the blue-stocking with her intellectual pretensions, symbolized for Baudelaire by George Sand (pp. 1206–7), or the pure young girl, that "scarecrow, monster, murderess of art" (p. 1216). Nevertheless, the most satisfying solution of all still remained in his eyes an ideal and total rejection of sexuality altogether, an angelic existence elliptically implicit in another sentence from *Fusées:* "The harder a man cultivates the arts the fewer his hard-ons" (p. 1219), and given literary expression in the religious adoration accorded to a purely spiritual female figure symbolized in the Mme. Sabatier cycle of *Les Fleurs du mal*. Thus we already find adumbrated in Baudelaire's work the dissociation of two contradictory and symmetrical female figures, the angel and the sphinx, that recurs throughout the decadent era.

The antifeminism that his contemporaries may have imbibed from Baudelaire's work was to be reinforced by the views on love and woman that Schopenhauer expressed at length in a chapter of *The World as Will and Idea* that was to become extremely well known, and from which Burdeau extracted the most significant passages as early as 1880 in his selection, *Pensées, maximes, et fragments.*[14] Even before Hartmann, who in fact merely reworked his illustrious predecessor's ideas in this field, Schopenhauer reduced love to genetic instinct, and denounced man's attempts to transform it into a purely affective and spiritual experience as the result of a total illusion: "For every tender inclination, no matter what ethereal airs it affects, has all its roots in the natural instinct of the sexes; indeed, it is nothing other than that specialized instinct" (*Pensées, maximes, et fragments*, p. 74). The unique, true, and hidden object of this love that artists and poets vie with one another in celebrating is never anything but procreation and the perpetuation of the species: "That a particular child shall be engendered, that is the only, the true goal of any love story, even though the lovers may be wholly unaware of it" (p. 78). Thus love constitutes a stratagem by means of which the species obliges the individual to sacrifice himself to its superior will, while allowing him to believe that he is following the dictates of his own egotism. Love is a continual hoax: "Every lover, once the great work has been accomplished, is left the victim of a hoax" (p. 85), and a hoax made all the more humiliating for a man, moreover, in that woman does not merit the treasury of passion and poetry that has been expended on her behalf, the worship and idolatry with which lovers always ultimately surround her. For Schopenhauer's picture of the feminine sex is no more flattering than

Baudelaire's. Woman remains eternally a sort of grown-up child, lacking the capacity for any kind of spiritual life, "childish, futile, and blinkered" (p. 118). Ruled by her senses and imprisoned in a purely material view of things, she finds it impossible to think in any true sense: "Since their reason is so weak, everything that is present, visible, and immediate holds them in such thrall that neither abstractions, established maxims, nor energetic resolution can prevail against it" (p. 121). In particular, since they are "created solely for the propagation of the species" (p. 123), women must remain strangers to the domain of esthetic life: they have "neither a feeling for nor an understanding of music, or poetry, or the plastic arts." The logical consequences of this attitude are not hard to draw: the man of sense ought to avoid becoming entangled in the snares and illusions of love; he must reject the "stupid veneration" with which woman has been surrounded by the entire western artistic tradition (p. 127).

Such antifeminism was to become widespread in artistic and literary circles during the decadent era, and, as a result, the image of woman, and the attitude toward her took the form of a twofold myth. Sometimes we find an insistence upon the fundamental futility of woman's essence, the vulgarity of woman's habitual concerns, her purely sensual and animal aspect, and her profound incapacity to achieve access to spiritual and artistic realms. Viewed like this, woman becomes the ball and chain preventing the artist from escaping the triviality of the everyday world. Sometimes, on the other hand, the emphasis is placed upon the destructive nature of passion, the dangerous aspects of a love that delivers man over, bound hand and foot, to a creature who is not only futile, but fundamentally immoral, cruel, and perverse. Hence the myth, destined to achieve such widespread acceptance, of the femme fatale. Moreover these two figures, on the surface so antithetical, are combined in practice to provide any number of intermediate admixtures: if woman leads man to his destruction, then the reason is as often the mere fact of her limited and futile nature as it is her deliberate perversity; the femme fatale is often at the same time a child-woman, doing evil involuntarily and unconsciously.

The first category is particularly in evidence in the works of Huysmans and Laforgue. One of Huysmans's early novels, *En ménage* of 1881, in fact describes precisely the dilemma that Baudelaire had highlighted: the two principal characters, André Jayant and Cyprien Tibaille, a writer and a painter respectively, find themselves confronting the eternal problem, that of reconciling their inevitable sexual needs with the ineluctably disastrous results of feminine company on an artist's productivity. Although both eventually come to terms with their woman problem, one by resuming life with a wife who had deceived him, the other by taking a working class mistress, they both sacrifice their artistic ambitions in the process: Jayant renounces his literary hopes, and Tibaille knuckles down to producing purely bread and butter work. The novel's conclusion drives home the point. After having lost sight of one another for some while, the two friends meet again and exchange disillusioned comments on life: "It comes to the same thing, doesn't it, that's what knocks every known morality on the head in the end. They may go different ways at first, but both roads land you up at the same old place. Ultimately, having a concubine or having a wife, what's the difference, since they've both freed us from artistic worries and the miseries of the flesh. An end of talent and good health instead, what bliss!"[15]

As for the dominant feminine image in Laforgue, one clearly influenced by Hartmann, it is that of a petty and futile creature, the involuntary agent of the unconscious. This is particularly evident in the *Moralités légendaires,* whether in the case of Kate, the young actress addressed by Hamlet, Else in *Lohengrin,* or Andromeda.

The antecedents of the femme fatale in nineteenth-century literature have been studied by Mario Praz in his already much quoted *The Romantic Agony.*[16] Having first appeared during the romantic era in certain of Gautier's works, such as *Une Nuit de Cléopâtre,* this theme continued to evolve during the years of the Second Empire, particularly in the works of Swinburne and Flaubert. The latter borrows the myth and figure of Herodias as we saw in this context earlier. During the last twenty years of the century, illustrations of the same theme become even more abundant, in both the iconographic and literary fields. In literature, for instance, we find the princesse d'Este, portrayed in Péladan's *Le Vice suprême* of 1884.[17] A descendant of the great ducal family of Ferrara, orphaned, then adopted by the Florentine prince Torelli, she has received a literary and artistic upbringing of exceptional breadth. Having accepted one of her admirers, the prince of Malatesta, as her husband, then been raped by him on her marriage night, she decides to take revenge on all men by deliberately inciting them to desire her while remaining totally frigid herself. The first victim of this campaign is Malatesta himself. "My dear husband," she informs him, "were I burned dry with desire, were my continence to be assailed by more temptations than legend attributes to Saint Anthony himself, I swear to you, upon my pride, that I shall never again descend, even if love, that impossibility, should overtake me, to any particular act of the flesh."[18] She holds to this resolve, amusing herself by making mock of a love increasingly inflamed by its impossibility. "Soon," the author adds, "her perversity was not content with merely maddening her husband; it became her habitual vice to exacerbate desire in all those who expressed such feelings for her" (*Le Vice suprême,* p. 50). Once removed to Paris, received by high society, and before long the object of great adulation, she continues to torture all her suitors with her coldness, and glories in her cruelty. "The desire that men express for me insults me," she declares, "and in revenge I fan it higher" (p. 93). The same antifeminism is to be found in Maupassant's work at this time, as when the principal character of his novella *Fou?* says of the woman he loves: "As for her, the woman in all this, the creature of the body, I hate her, I despise her, I execrate her, I have always hated, despised, and execrated her; for she is treacherous, bestial, loathsome, impure; she is the woman of perdition, the sensual and devious animal in whom no soul is, through whom thought never flows like a free and vivifying breeze; she is the human animal."[19]

This type of woman was also to be found depicted in the work of Gustave Moreau, as we noted earlier, and particularly in the vast unfinished painting called *Les Chimères,* which contains a whole series of women endowed with cold and inaccessible beauty.[20] In his own description of this picture, a text often quoted by critics of the day, Moreau distills some of the essential characteristics of the femme fatale myth:

> This island of fantastic dreams embraces all the forms of passion, fantasy, and caprice in woman, in her primal essence, a being without thought, crazed with a desire for the unknown, for mystery, in love with evil in the form of perverse and diabolical seduction. Childish dreams, sensual dreams, monstrous dreams, melancholy dreams, dreams that bear the mind and soul out into the nebulousness of space, into the mystery of shadowy deeps, everything should exude the influence of the seven deadly sins, everything is contained within that satanic ground, within that circle of vices and burning, guilty impulses. . . . They are the theories of queens under a curse, their ears still filled with the serpent's beguiling instruction, they are beings with souls annihilated, waiting by the wayside for that lascivious goat, straddled by lust, whom they will worship as he passes by; lonely beings dark with their dreams of envy and unassuaged pride, in their bestial isolation: women mounting on chimaeras that bear them off into space, then hurtling headlong down again, destroyed by horror and by vertigo.[21]

The triumph of the lustful and cruel woman was also to figure in many of Rops's engravings. For example, *La Femme au pantin,* which depicts a woman holding a tiny puppet in her hand, a man in a suit making helpless gestures. Or in the famous *Pornokratès.* In Wagner, the image of the woman as a sensual siren is embodied in particular by Kundry in *Parsifal.*

Nordau, in his account of Wagner's work, draws attention to the same feminine duality that we have already observed in the work of Baudelaire, where the siren is contrasted with the ideal and spiritual woman: on the one hand, the terrible Astarte of the Semites or the frightful man-eating Kali Bhagawati of the Hindus; and in opposition to this siren figure, the ideal and angelic woman, represented in Wagner's work by a succession of heroines haloed with spirituality, who bring the hero supernatural assistance.[22]

The mythical image of woman presented by the decadents thus clearly mirrors the opposition between angel and sphinx that was to be exploited ad nauseam by contemporary painting, particularly in the case of French and Belgian symbolist painters.[23] In the case of the Nabis—Maurice Denis, Osbert, or Séon—it is the first type, the angel, that predominates. The figure of a woman-angel leading man up toward a paradise of resplendent spirituality was also to recur on several occasions in the work of Jean Delville, in his *L'Amour des âmes*,[24] whose title is adequate indication of its content, and in his *L'Ange des splendeurs*.[25] It is also to be found in *Le Mariage du poète et de la muse* by Carlos Schwabe, which, against a background of high mountains, shows a winged woman drawing the poet up to higher spiritual realms in the sky.[26] The femme fatale, on the other hand, frequently appears in the guise of the sphinx, as in one of Fernand Khnopff's most famous canvases, *L'Art ou les caresses ou le sphinx*,[27] or in *The Sphinx* by the German painter Franz von Stuck, a member of the Munich Secessionist group.[28] Finally, both figures are to be found together in a very strange painting by the Dutch painter Jan Toorop. Entitled *The Three Brides*, it juxtaposes, apparently in some mysterious ceremony, three female figures respectively symbolizing the timid virgin, the triumphant bride in her wedding veils, and the femme fatale with terrifying, predatory eyes.[29]

This dual theme of the angel and the sphinx was to provide the subject and the title for a novel by Edouard Schuré published in 1897. Konrad de Felseneck, the hero of the story, in which the influences of Wagner and Villiers de L'Isle-Adam intermingle, and which is set in a legendary Renaissance Germany, is torn between two female figures. The first, that of an ideal and invisible woman whose features he has created in his own imagination from those of a female ancestor depicted on a stained glass window in the castle chapel, promises him in his dreams a mystical alliance and eternal bliss; the second, embodied in a woman he meets at the court of the Count Palatine, a certain Gertrude von Hohenstein, subjugates him with her all-powerful charms. Having married her, he forgets in her arms the promise he once made to accompany a friend to the Crusades. In his late adolescence, a Nuremburg astrologer, Master

Rupertus, had already given him explicit warning of the alternatives that would later present themselves, and of the vital consequences his choice would have:

> A pale beam from on high will follow you... May you never lose it! Try to grasp it, and when the angel wearing a betrothal crown appears to you... drink in that light! If you glimpse that angel, the voice of silence will speak to you; and if it speaks you will hear the trumpets bray for war.... But beware of the sphinx, who has a woman's face and breasts but a tiger's claws.[30]

A short while after receiving this warning, one day when he chances to fall asleep in the ruins of a neighboring castle while out walking, Konrad does in fact dream that he is being married to the mystic fiancée whose gaze fills his whole being with bliss:

> Her wide, dark, violet eyes, riveted upon me, glowed unwaveringly in their deep sockets, like lamps that guard men's graves. That gaze awoke an answering glow in me, a distant light, a long remembrance of life from long ago.... The voice that seemed to sing those words spread through me like a fall of dew. [*L'Ange et le sphinx*, pp. 127–29]

The celebration of this mystic marriage is interrupted, however, by the intervention of the cruel sphinx:

> There on the bishop's right, between the altar and myself, a terrifying beast had taken up her stand. From the sphinx's leonine body there rose, in shameless arrogance, a woman's torso, morbidly white. The opulent and curving breasts were offering their blood red fruits. The haughty, massive head was that of a Roman empress, commanding of profile, with a powerful and sensual fold beneath the chin, a helmet of tawny hair coiling around the brow. The rosy blood, as it began to flow through that alabaster flesh, caused her skin to quiver, and the golden thicket on her neck to stand on end. With dread, I felt the animal within me encaptivated by the sphinx, as though some writhing monster were drinking at my veins in order to suck life into its own flesh. [P. 134]

This is a fairly plain statement of the insoluble dilemma in which the decadent sensibility found itself with regard to the problem of love and sexuality. Sexual love is condemned, because it debases man to that very state of nature it is the aim of all civilization and culture to abolish. Woman is contemptible, because, being so close to nature, she is a creature of pure instinct to which the spiritual universe is forbidden; because she is the instrument, sometimes innocent and sometimes consciously perverse, by means of which the species achieves a self-perpetuation that, in a world dominated by evil, appears less and less justified. Yet one is forced to recognize that sexual needs subsist, and that they manifest themselves with increasing insistence the more one attempts to ignore them. Love is at once vulgar and attractive, necessary and lethal. The formulation of this problem, as expressed in the art and literature of the period, with its dissociation of two antithetical aspects, that of purely spiritual love represented by the angel, and that of sexuality embodied by the sphinx, is already clearly pathological in character. Let us now examine some of the varying solutions to this dilemma that creative artists of the period offered.

The first, and clearly the most logical, is purely and simply to reject sexuality entirely, to advocate an ideal of total chastity. This, or something very close to it, was the solution offered by Péladan, for example, in *Le Vice suprême*. In her adolescence, the princess d'Este acquired from her tutor a purely manichean conception of sexuality: physical love could be envisaged solely as a degradation. This tutor, the author tells us, "recognized that there was taking place within her that poetic drama of puberty that must end either in the triumph of continued chastity or in the debasement of an accepted animality" (p. 25). In similar vein, her confessor tells her before he dies: "The ideal is continence, chastity" (p. 28). After the trauma of physical violation by a brutish husband on her wedding night, the princess becomes an embodiment of perverse frigidity. The magus Mérodack, for his part, has destroyed the power of his senses to tempt him by a process of gradual immunization that consisted, the author tells us, in reading "all the literature of the Flesh, from Martial to Meursius and de Sade" (p. 124), and has succeeded in triumphing over the sexual monster for good. Henceforward, freed from all illusion, he is able to denounce the mirages of carnal love:

> I have guessed the riddle, and the female sphinx has licked
> my feet; but this spectacle: woman dominating man, has
> always outraged me as an antiphysism. A slave to be pitied
> or a tyrant to be despised, woman quivers at everything,
> reasons in nothing; as oblivious in sublimity as in the mud of
> the gutter, she remains eternally refractory to the idea. [P.
> 210]

On the level of fantasy, this attitude led also to the development of a new myth, a myth of which Péladan was to make himself chief herald, that of the hermaphrodite.[31] This myth signifies the dream of a humanity relieved of its sexuality by the appearance of an ideal being in which both sexes are fused.[32] It was a theme already touched upon by Gautier in *Mademoiselle de Maupin* when he described the fascination exerted upon his central character by the image of the hermaphrodite as depicted in Hellenistic sculpture.

> Thus the hermaphrodite is one of the chimaeras most ardently caressed by idolatrous antiquity.... It is in effect one of the sweetest creations of the pagan genius, this son of Hermes and Aphrodite. Nothing more ravishing could be imagined in this world than those two bodies, both so perfect, harmoniously fused together. [Pp. 224–25]

There still remained a large element of sensuality, however, in this product of Gautier's obsession with pagan beauty, whereas with Péladan, and other artists of his time, the hermaphrodite has become less a being in whom the sexes are combined than a creature without any sexuality at all, an asexual and physically neutral being equally alien to physical love and to the life of the senses generally. Péladan could have found the forerunners of this ideal, in the pictorial field, either in certain equivocal figures depicted by da Vinci, such as his St. John the Baptist, or in certain male figures by English artists such as Burne-Jones or, later on, Simeon Solomon. Certainly he never tired of celebrating the spell it cast on him. In *Le Vice suprême*, as early as 1884, we find this confession: "The hermaphrodite, that nightmare of all decadent eras, pursues me" (p. 99). With *L'Androgyne* of 1891, the hermaphrodite was to become the symbol of the author's moral and esthetic ideal. Indeed, Péladan included in the novel a *Hymne à l'androgyne* that was also printed in *La Plume*.[33] It takes the form a litany in praise of an ideal of frigidity:

> Sex most pure and dying when caressed
> Sex most holy and alone to heaven risen
> Sex most fair and denying its consort...
> Sex negation of all sex...

Rachilde was to adopt a very similar stance in a passage from *Monsieur Vénus*, which Barrès quoted in his preface to the book: "God should have created love on one side and the senses on the other. True love ought to consist in nothing but warm friendship. Let us sacrifice the senses, the animal."[34]

This pure and simple denial of sexuality was not easy to carry out in practice, however. Péladan's not uneventful private life gave the lie to his flawed theories of angelism. Moreover, the myth of the hermaphrodite, far from being totally pure, was more often than not a mask, as with

Gautier earlier, for a homosexuality that was in itself an occasion for guilt. Even Péladan himself came near to lifting that mask, again in his *Hymne à l'androgyne,* when he exclaims: "Intangible Eros, Uranian Eros, to coarse-souled men in times of strict morality you are merely a vile sin; Sodom you are called."

In practice, if we examine the literature and art of the time, we quickly perceive that this rejection of sexuality usually results, somewhat paradoxically, in the emergence of a widespread eroticism rarely seen in previous eras. The paradox is more apparent than real, however: this eroticism appeared precisely because the sexual impulse, having been refused satisfaction in real life, was transposed onto the imaginary plane. So in this period, quite separate from the permanent undercurrent of inferior erotica that exists in any age, we also find a current of erotic literature whose authors were genuine writers, moving in traditional literary circles and with high literary ambitions. Examples of this erotic strain of writing are to be found in the work of such writers as Catulle Mendès, Rachilde, Jean Lorrain, and, somewhat later, Pierre Louys. What is more, most of these writers lived lives in total conformity with the moral standards of the age. The case of Rachilde is particularly significant in this respect. The product of a perfectly respectable background, happily married to Vallette, the editor of the *Mercure de France,* and accustomed to playing hostess in her salon to the élite of France's young writers, her literary career was nevertheless built to a large extent on descriptions of monstrous and deviant sexual behavior, to the great outrage of the public and the astonishment of those who knew her personally. In the same way, many young writers, and particularly Jean Lorrain—modeling themselves somewhat on the "wild romantic" image of an earlier generation—used a great deal of similar material out of a kind of literary bravado.

The sexuality such authors dealt in was also quite often of an abnormal kind, at least according to the moral standards of their day. Decadent literature clearly took delight in describing various types of perversion. And it seems highly likely that the prime cause of this rise to literary prominence of deviant sexuality was the fact that the decadent period coincided with the first systematic investigations into sexual psychopathology. "The last quarter of the century," Patrick Waldberg observes, "was the period when modern sexology first began to take wing, with Krafft-Ebing's inventories, Havelock Ellis's classifications, and the researches into hysteria by Charcot that led to the illuminating intuitions of Sigmund Freud."[35] Apart from this, however, there is the fact that in the eyes of the decadents perversion constituted a means of redeeming at least some part of the sexuality that they condemned in principle while still remaining its victims. Although it was impossible to

reject sex absolutely, condemned though it was by its alliance with nature, at least one could continue to express contempt for nature by indulging in perversions of it. Lastly, it should be said that in favoring the
more reprehensible aspects of sexuality the decadents were to some extent pursuing a deliberately pessimistic policy. Since the artificial alone
has any value on the esthetic plane, and since morality condemns it, then
once "vice" has been chosen why not pursue it to its extremes? By
exalting the abnormal, the decadent sensibility was thus encouraging or
accelerating the self-destruction it more or less secretly longed for. This is
also the reason why this conception of love was so often expressed in a
particularly dubious way, one that sought to aggravate the prevalent feeling of guilt still further by the addition of a sacrilegious intention: hence
the strange mixtures of mysticism and eroticism of which we have already
seen some examples, and the morbid pleasure taken in constantly introducing sexual elements into the supposedly pure and sacred universe
of religion. From this point of view, as we have seen, esthetic Roman
Catholicism sometimes appears to be merely one aspect of a more general
quest for sensual refinements.

The decadents were to seek out the exception rather than the rule in
love, in the name of the esthetic primacy they accorded to the strange or
the artificial, and also as a result of their constant striving to overcome
their boredom and despair at life by discovering new or more refined
sensations. In the field of love these refinements entail an exacerbation of
the senses and ever-increasing complications of the emotions. Ernest
Raynaud, in an article for *Le Décadent,* pointed out that although such
complications had reached their apogee among his contemporaries, they
had already been present in previous literary generations. He observes,
with reference to the Parnassians:

> Our poets are returning to antiquity, but what result could it
> have, this exploitation of the pagan world by souls still hot
> from the romantic fire, by hearts haunted by mystical
> heresies, gnawed by the corrosive joys of alchemy? What
> could the sylvan and lactescent muse of ancient Rome in-
> spire in them, these nervous systems half destroyed by such
> incessant calls to revolution? Nothing natural and chaste
> assuredly. . . . Spurred on to further sophistications, further
> adulterations, by strenuous incursions into foreign litera-
> tures, at a time when devoted and slavish hands were sort-
> ing through the embers of Shakespeare's androphile sonnets
> and Goethe's amazing invocations to Jove's young
> minion—the minds of that time display subtle Sapphic and
> sadistic preoccupations, albeit still timid and as it were
> veiled in shreds of furtive modesty. Gautier insinuates

his equivocal preferences beneath the mask of la Maupin. ... Baudelaire, more honestly, records the dark, disturbing fancies beckoning, yet still fails to open up the question to the extent that was required.[36]

To provide justification for this quest for refinement in sensual pleasure, the myth of the Roman decadence, with its aura of luxury and depravity, was once again invoked, together with another equally mythical and equally decried era, that of Byzantine decadence. Thus we find the authors of *Les Déliquescences* celebrating such periods, in a tone verging on the parodic: "We must do at least this justice to the Roman decadence, that it understood love. By dint of perverse inventions and satanic fancies, it succeeded in making it totally delightful. Oh Decadence, long live Decadence! Love is the flower of an evil spell that grows on graves, a flower bowed down by dark, disturbing scents." We find the corruption of Byzantium depicted by Jean Lombard in his plays *Byzance* and *L'Agonie,* that of Alexandria by Pierre Louÿs in his *Aphrodite,* that of Rome by Jarry in his *Messaline.* In his *Certains* of 1890, Huysmans reprinted a fairly long article on Félicien Rops that is in fact a fascinating study of the relationship between eroticism and the fine arts. In it he demonstrates that eroticism is the fruit of pure and self-sufficient imagination, and that real sexual pleasure destroys it. Seen in this way, decadent eroticism becomes just one of the forms taken by an exacerbated imagination. In the article on Rops, Huysmans points out the coexistence of a profound contempt for woman with a predominant eroticism, particularly in the famous *Sataniques* sequence. In these, Huysmans says, the mind of the artist "goes, mentally, in his waking dream, to the furthest extreme of orgiastic delirium"; he is dealing in "isolated erotic ideas, without material counterpart, without any need for an animal sequel that will assuage them." Huysmans is here expressing one of the principal facts about decadent eroticism: that it was a purely intellectual and cerebral activity. It is these two specific and linked characteristics—interest in perversion and cerebrality—that Waldberg captures so well when he writes:

The disturbing beauty of dying flowers, the traumatic horror of those battlefields and places of torture through which Octave Mirbeau leads the terrified visitors to his *Jardins des supplices,* the incestuous embraces of Giulia and Ulric d'Este recounted by Elémir Bourges in his *Crépuscule des dieux,* those monstrous coupling in the reign of Heliogabalus rendered in such finely chiseled detail by Jean Lombard in his *L'Agonie,* the bitter joys of Lesbos and of Sodom, orgies and rapes, guilty, tortured, torturing loves, these are some of the ingredients that went into the erotic elixir of fin-de-siècle cerebrality.[37]

More or less exhaustive surveys of the various perversions appearing in the literature of the period are already available in the works of Mario Praz and A. E. Carter, so that I shall limit myself here to no more than a few significant and representative examples. First and foremost, of course, fin-de-siècle literature brought out into the open the homosexuality already more or less apparent in the work of Gautier and Baudelaire. We have already seen how the myth of the hermaphrodite was used to disguise homosexual inclinations still regarded at the time as shameful. This process is also to be found in *A Rebours*. In chapter 9, as a result of reading Dickens, Des Esseintes sinks into erotic reveries that display very clearly the simultaneously sacrilegious and cerebral aspects of decadent eroticism, in which religion, with its prohibitions, serves as a spur to sensuality:

> He broke off his reading, and mused, far from prudish, prurient England, on the licentious peccadilloes, the salacious seasonings, that the Church so disapproves; a sudden stirring caught his attention; the anaphrodisia of mind and body he had thought definitive was loosening its grip; solitude was once more working on his disordered nerves; he was again obsessed, not by religion itself, but by the furtive influence of the acts and sins that it condemns. . . . The carnal side of him, in abeyance for so many months, stirred by the nervous irritation of his pious reading, had reawakened, swollen to renewed excitement by all that English cant, had risen up again, and as the stimulation of his senses bore him back in time, so he wallowed in the sewer of past memories. [P. 139]

In other words, Des Esseintes is led to evoke certain amorous experiences from his past. And although these memories are concerned with women, Des Esseintes's sexual choices do without doubt reveal latent homosexual tendencies. The first mistress conjured up, Miss Urania, is in fact an acrobat with a vigorous and athletic body, and the pleasure he experiences in watching her perform is in itself decidedly ambiguous:

> Little by little, as he observed her, strange conceptions stirred; as he admired her suppleness and strength, so he perceived an artificial change of sex occur in her; her graceful tricks, her insipid female posturings receded more and more, and the agile, powerful charms of a male body took their place; in a word, having first of all been a woman, then, after a period of hesitation, of approaching then receding from the androgynous, she seemed to resolve herself, become completely focused, and was a man. [P. 141]

Before long, Des Esseintes becomes disillusioned with Miss Urania, because in bed she displayed "none of those athletic brutalities he simultaneously desired and feared" (p. 142). And what attracts him to his next mistress, a ventriloquist, is again her masculine characteristics: Hair "smoothed flat against her skull as though painted on, and parted like a boy's" (p. 143), and a low, artificial voice, which prompts him to have her recite the dialogue between the Sphinx and the Chimaera from Flaubert's *La Tentation de saint Antoine*.

Such homosexuality, still only latent in Huysmans's work, was to become more and more open during the last decade of the century, with Oscar Wilde in Britain and Jean Lorrain in France. In London, these homosexual tendencies were already apparent in the frequently ambiguous physical characteristics of the young women or men depicted by Pre-Raphaelite painters such as Rossetti and Burne-Jones, and in the work of their immediate successors, particularly that of Simeon Solomon.[38] With the latter, as with Wilde, the bridge was finally crossed, in the sense that both admitted their own homosexuality to themselves, then began increasingly to make it known publicly, with what consequences is only too well known. It is extremely probable that Jean Lorrain likewise indulged in the forbidden loves of Sodom. Certainly his work continued to celebrate an essentially masculine ideal of beauty with increasing openness. Even in his earliest poems, extremely Parnassian in technique, side by side with evocations of the classic female sirens, Helen, Vivian, Melusina, and Salome, we also find him celebrating the charms of the young heroes of Greek mythology, Hylas or Narcissus. In his later work there are certain significant features that recur constantly: a predilection for the company of young thugs; a physical horror of making love to women uneasily combined with furtive heterosexual adventures; and Don Juanism—all indications of homosexuality experienced as a source of guilt, alternately repressed and defiantly proclaimed. In *Monsieur de Phocas*, a novel of 1901, the central character confesses in his secret diary to an obsessive passion for a certain "seagreen gaze," first aroused in him by a contemplation of the Antinous in the Louvre, then later rediscovered in the eyes of certain legendary heroines, like Salome or Astarte, and also in those of the occasional, and nonlegendary, sailor.

Incest too appears in and articulates the plots of an appreciable number of novels and stories of the period. This is the case, for instance, with *Le Crépuscule des dieux* by Elémir Bourges, published in 1884. La Belcredi, a former singer, now official mistress of the duke Charles d'Este, and intent on acquiring undisputed sway over her lover's whole family, makes it her business to inflame the incestuous passion she observes between Hans Ulrich and Christiane, two of the duke's children. She reads them

John Ford's *'Tis Pity She's a Whore,* in which the hero, Giovanni, in-
dulges in a violent and physical relationship with his sister, Annabella; she
has them sing the roles of Siegmund and Sieglinde in Wagner's *Die Wal-
küre.* Finally, having taken his sister sexually, Hans Ulrich kills himself, while Christiane ends her days in a Carmelite nunnery. The same
theme, decked out with a very complicated and novelettish plot, was to
provide the principal subject matter of *Zo'har,* a novel by Catulle Mendés
published in 1886. The debauched Marquis de Roquebrussane has two
children who have never met, Leopold, a bastard recognized by his father
and raised in the family chateau, and Stephana, the daughter of an ad-
venturess who has succeeded, thanks to the intrigues of La Marchisio, a
go-between, in marrying the marquis in his old age. One day Leopold sees
a girl in church and falls in love with her. He later discovers that she is his
sister Stephana. Now forced to live in close proximity with her, he cannot
stifle his guilty passion, and attempts to stop Stephana's marriage to a
local nobleman by causing a scandal. Finally he runs away, and after
numerous adventures becomes a recluse in a small Spanish village. Just as
he is about to marry, Stephana finds him, and they confess their passion
for one another. When La Marchisio lyingly informs them that Stephana
is not in fact the marquis's daughter, they yield to their feelings and go to
live in an isolated house in Norway, where they indulge a passion that
they nevertheless still believe to be criminal. When they finally learn,
from an old friend they chance to meet, that they really are brother and
sister after all, Leopold kills himself and Stephana lies down by his corpse
to die in her turn. *La Faënza,* a novella by Moréas first published in the
November and December numbers of *La Lutèce* in 1883, then reprinted in
Thé chez Miranda, a joint collection with Paul Adam published in 1886, is
similarly based on the theme of incestuous love, in this case that of a
mother for her son.[39] La Faënza, a kept woman, decides at the age of
thirty-four to retire from social life, moves to the country, and concentrates on the education of a son she had given birth to while still very
young. When the son, now nineteen, starts paying court to the daughter of
neighboring friends, she is seized with mad rage. Then, despite having
lived a life of irreproachable virtue for some while, she acknowledges that
she is in love with her son and does everything in her power to seduce
him. Eventually, in order to put a stop to her increasingly pressing advances, the son is forced to stab her to death with a dagger.[40]

The ambiguity of the relationships devised in the decadent era between
men and women, as also the ambiguity of woman's own status, encouraged
the appearance of a sadomasochistic strain in contemporary erotic literature. The decadent imagination, as we have seen, constantly oscillates
between two opposing images of woman: on the one hand the femme
fatale or siren luring those who love her and those she loves to their

deaths, which is the image that occurs most frequently; and on the other, woman as victim.

Siren or victim, these two myths both introduced elements of violence and cruelty into the image of love that on occasion acquire a specifically sadistic dimension—that is to say, taking the term in its precise technical connotation, an association between sexual satisfaction and indulgence in cruelty toward the sexual partner. This manifestation of sadistic tendencies was undoubtedly fostered by a growing dissemination of the divine marquis's own works. Mario Praz, in *The Romantic Agony*, offers a brief survey of the subterranean influence exerted by Sade's work from the romantic era up until the turn of the century. He shows in particular how it influenced and fascinated, not only Jules Janin and Pétrus Borel earlier, but also the two major forerunners of the decadents, Flaubert and Baudelaire. One may justifiably assume that in the later part of the century, without emerging wholly from its earlier quasi-clandestinity, Sade's work had become better known, particularly by an appreciable number of the period's literary figures. Curiosity about his books was undoubtedly maintained by the many references to Sade that inevitably occurred in critical works devoted to Baudelaire. For instance, in a work already mentioned, Maurice Spronck devotes a number of pages to Baudelaire's attitude toward love, and claims to find, following Bourget, "undeniable signs" of sadism in that attitude, which he largely explains away, it should be added, as a by-product of Baudelaire's striving after literary effect. More generally, he also remarks upon an increase in sadistic themes in the literature of the period as a whole:

> It is not that the idea of mingling a painful sensation with a pleasurable one, bleeding wounds with caresses, the sight of death with the fulfillment of the act from which all life flows, is absolutely particular to Baudelaire and our own day. It has fascinated many aging civilizations with its antithetical nature, and we see it hovering over the great decadent eras of Asia or the long orgy of the imperial age of Rome.... Yet one has to leap over the Middle Ages and come to the last few years to find it insinuating itself everywhere, whether in works of imagination, in morals, in the most ordinary actions and thoughts that make up human existence. Although among us it has discarded that terrible aspect of frenzied and murderous fury, accompanied by vast debauches, it makes up for that by the frequency and spread of its incidence.[41]

Nordau claimed to have found this same influence in the work of Barbey d'Aurevilly, whom he accused of having plagiarized Sade, particularly in his *Les Diaboliques*.

It is certainly indisputable that some of the most important writers of the period knew Sade's work, even though the depth of that knowledge may have varied considerably from case to case. Maupassant was certainly no stranger to it. We know that in 1864, while staying at the Chaumière Dolmancé in Etretat, owned by a friend, he made the acquaintance of Swinburne, and that the English poet introduced him to at least some of Sade's works, which he claimed had been the inspiration of some of his own.[42] This fascination with sadism was to surface on several occasions in Maupassant's later work, particularly in the novella *Fou?* which tells the story of a judge drawn first into crime, then into madness, by an irresistible attraction to cruelty. Maupassant observes during the course of his story that killing must be a pleasure, because it closely resembles creation. We also know that in 1882 Huysmans read *La Philosophie dans le boudoir,* which his friend and publisher Kistemaekers had sent him from Brussels. In the letter he wrote to thank Kistemaekers, Huysmans makes it clear that he found the book of no small interest: "Thank you first of all for the *Philosophie* that you were so kind as to send. I've just finished reading this document from la Salpêtrière and Mazas. It is beyond doubt the nadir of debasement, but it is of the greatest interest from the mental point of view . . . "[43]

That curiosity about Sade's works increased steadily during this period is made quite plain by an anonymous article, entitled *Le Marquis de Sade,* that appeared in *La Revue indépendante.* Having first denounced the conspiracy of silence surrounding Sade's work, a conspiracy partly due to "Jules Janin's distasteful tittle-tattle and the sentimental hearsay evidence of the bibliophile Jacob," the author declares his intention of approaching his subject from the strictly objective viewpoint of mental pathology: "And yet what is he ultimately, Sade?" he writes. "A sick man, a historic patient who ought to be observed as doctors observe their patients in a hospital; a patient much more interesting, more complicated, more rare, than the never-ending stream of hysteria cases in the novels of M. X—— or M. Y——." The author also makes the connection between sadism and decadence: "[Sadism] is moreover the privilege of all decadent eras, of all epochs characterized by worn out and overexcited nervous systems, of Rome under the Caesars of the witch-ridden Middle Ages, of Rome at the time of the Borgias, of the present day. . . . What a magnificent history there is to be written of sadism, but the documents are so sparse, destroyed or lost."[44] He then devotes the rest of his article to a brief biography of Sade, based on a few historical documents. Indeed, it may have been the same writer who compiled the biography of Sade that was published by Dentu two years later.[45] At all events it is justifiable to suppose that Sade's work, without being truly accessible, since very few actual copies of his novels could have been in circulation, was much in fashion at this time. In 1886, for example, not only was there the publication of Rachilde's *La Marquise de Sade,* but also, in the review of a novel called *Les Blasées* by a certain Luc Vajernet, the 17 April number of *Le Décadent* quoted this excerpt from the work, which is set in a boarding school for young ladies:

> One day, coming round the corner of the "holy of holies,"
> she heard: Have you read the Marquis de Sade?—It was
> Georgette who had asked the question. No one answered.
> Then Jeanne walked into view, and boldly said: I have.

Despite the schoolgirl bravado presumably involved in this piece of evidence, that does not invalidate it as an indication of the curiosity undoubtedly surrounding Sade's work at the time.

Whatever the extent of real acquaintance with Sade's books at the time, it is certainly the case that descriptions of sadistic behavior began to proliferate in works of the decadent period. For instance, in his collection of critical essays published in 1889 under the title *Certains,* we find Huysmans taking evident pleasure in evoking certain works depicting torture, such as the engravings of Jan Luyken, who "has laid bare in a series of horrible pictorial court records, has simmered and reduced to their bitter essence in these scenes, the meticulous tortures that the theatrical ferocity of the papists inflicted on those tiresome Huguenots" (p. 128), or, later on, Bianchi's depiction of the martyrdom of St. Quentin. This same quirk was to reappear, needless to say, in *Là-bas,* when Huysmans evokes Gilles de Rais and the tortures he inflicted on little children. In *La Muse noire,* Guaïta's first collection of poems, published in 1883, we also find a totally uncompromising description of a sadistic daydream:

> Let my rebellious victim, for a whole day,
> Writhe naked, consumed by a slow fire.
> A woman let it be—and very beautiful.[46]

Laforgue's *Moralités légendaires* also offers frequent examples of such cruelty, although it must be said that there is no overt connection with any sexual impulse. Thus Hamlet, like Flaubert's St. Julien, amuses himself by torturing the animals that cross his path, a canary in a cage, beetles which he impales, butterflies off which he rips the wings, toads whose feet he hacks off. "And finally," Laforgue writes, "that evening, from those victims that had not succeeded in dragging themselves away to die, that he found still there upon his path, a last spasm drove him to exact a pound or so of pierced eyeballs; he washed his hands in them, and rubbed them into all his finger joints" (p. 39). Perseus likewise, not content with having killed the monster guarding Andromeda, must needs hack away at its corpse (p. 241). In Lorrain's collection of long stories, *Buveurs d'âmes* of 1893, the novella *Un Soir qu'il neigeait* tells the story of an extremely rich foreigner who has acquired the habit of taking prostitutes from the Place Maubert back to his home and amusing himself by passing a cutthroat razor to and fro across their throats, for hours on end, until they finally faint. Rachilde's *Les Vendanges de Sodome* recounts how the Sodomites, having driven out their wives, stone one of them to death as a punishment for remaining in the city, then trample on her and crush her in a wine-press.

Naturally, given the predominance of the femme fatale myth, examples of female cruelty also abound in these works. Such cruelty constitutes one of the most frequent themes in Lorrain's tales. In *Sonyeuse* of 1891, for example, the story *L'Inconnue* depicts a high-born sadistic nym-phomaniac who searches out her lovers in the sleaziest parts of Paris in the hope that she will one day be able to witness their executions.[47] In *Les Yeux glauques*, from the same collection, the heroine watches her lover drown. During a boating trip, when a long way from the bank, the lover has undressed and gone in for a swim. The girl then prevents him from getting back into the boat by keeping it tantalizingly just out of his reach as he struggles to catch up. Her pleasure becomes complete as she watches him sink exhausted into the depths. The heroine of *La Princesse aux lys rouges* wanders through the garden of the nunnery where she lives and cuts the lilies that represent the lives of knights who have died for her.[48] This theme of the bloodthirsty woman was to reach its full flowering at the end of the century with Octave Mirbeau's notorious *Jardin des supplices,* in which the young Clara, who presides over the jail of Canton, diverts herself by observing the tortures that are inflicted on the prisoners in the jail's magical garden. This same sadistic strain is also to be found in academically approved paintings of the period, as for example in Roche-grosse's *Les Derniers Jours de Babylone,* finished in 1891, which depicts a sumptuous palace in which groups of naked women are disposed in lan-guorous poses at the feet of their ruler and master. The latter sits on his throne in a meditative pose, his inscrutable mask in stark contrast to the evident terror of a slave girl who is standing with her arms raised in horror as she stares toward the right of the picture, presumably at the invading barbarians about to rush in and slaughter them all.

Homosexuality, sadism or sadomasochism, and incest were the perver-sions in which the art and literature of the period dealt most often; but other, even more aberrant forms of sexual behavior are not totally absent either. There are several examples of bestiality, for example, as in some of the stories in *Thé chez Miranda* or in certain works by Rachilde, such as *La Princesse des ténèbres* or *L'Animale.* Generally speaking, indeed, such perversions appear so frequently that some collections by Jean Lorrain or Rachilde might almost be taken as simply fictional illustrations to some manual of sexual psychopathology. That these authors took great delight in such subjects, and were also deliberately setting out to shock, is beyond doubt. Yet these collections, with all their defects, nevertheless remain valuable evidence both of the guilt feelings that seem more than ever to have accompanied the exercise of sexuality, and of the discovery that had been made, in those pre-Freudian days, of a whole area of the life of the "soul" with which earlier literature had concerned itself only accidentally.

Even when actual sexual perversions were not involved, the pictorial art of the period was still often characterized by an evident erotic content, and this eroticism was all the more insidious in that it attempted to conceal itself behind a mask of middle-class decorum, particularly in the academically approved work of the period. Very often the leading lights of this officially accepted school of painting were in fact indulging, under cover of a respectable academicism, in an eroticism that beneath its superficial distinction was ultimately rather vulgar in its inspiration. This is particularly evident in a great number of mythological or allegorical paintings where the subject is clearly only an excuse for depicting the female nude.[49] This same erotic strain is also very evident in Art Nouveau, where the female form is often used as the basis for a pattern of sensuous arabesques coiling outward from her hair or garments. "A prodigious floral invasion," Patrick Waldberg very justly observes, "sensual, undulating, foaming, bearing nereids and oreads along in its waves, sirens with seaweed hair and virgins in ecstasy, princesses woven round with lilies and convolvulus or hermaphrodites surfacing among water lily pads. There is a whole world of everyday, insinuating sensuality, a whole jungle of sexual symbols whose relentless and suggestive repetitions eventually came to determine the age's modes of love and sexual desire."[50]

Thus, breaking with varying degrees of openness and brutality through the embargoes hitherto placed by convention and decorum on subjects of a sexual nature, the decadent imagination found in eroticism new ways to abandon itself to prohibited or seductive reveries, ways along which it was tempted to venture even further by the fact that it was ultimately only playing a purely cerebral and inward game: a revenge of the imagination against the steadily hardening constraints of bourgeois respectability in fin-de-siècle France and late Victorian England alike.

PART II   FORMS OF
THE DECADENT
IMAGINATION

5 AVATARS OF
THE FANTASTIC

IN PART 1, I ATTEMPTED TO SHOW TWO THINGS: FIRST, THE VARIOUS elements that combined in the first fifteen years of the Third Republic in France, partly through the catalytic effect of fluctuating literary fashion and the work of certain central thinkers such as Bourget, to produce the decadent sensibility; second, the vision of the world underlying that sensibility and esthetic, a vision characterized by both a current of pessimism and a countervailing idealism. Disillusioned with the real life of its time, the decadent generation sought escape in the life of the imagination. It is the various forms that this recourse to imagination took that we now have to examine: the survival and transformation of a fantastic strain in literature with its roots in romanticism; recourse to the artificial, drugs, and dreams; the flowering of a universe of legend or myth; and finally that play of the imagination upon a number of natural elements that I denote by the term elemental reverie. Having established the metaphysical and esthetic foundations of the decadent imagination, we must now survey the principal paths it pursued.

The aim of the fantastic tale (*conte fantastique*), which first appeared in France during the romantic era, mainly under the influence of Hoffmann, was to exploit the elasticity of probability so as to introduce supernatural events into the heart of everyday reality. Originally making use of the demoniac and macabre elements present in the romantic imagination, and above all concerned with arousing the maximum intensity of dread and terror in the reader, it had gradually developed in two different directions, as I tried to show earlier. First, profiting from the advances achieved in the technique of fiction by the realistic novel, it introduced a much greater precision and wealth of detail into the background of reality against which the action was set, thereby endorsing its authenticity, and gave the narrative more rigorous structures in order to direct the reader's sensibility more effectively. Second, an increasing concern for probability led to a progressive interiorization of the supernatural, which came to be depicted as occurring, not on the level of objective reality, but as the consequence of perceptual disturbances. Thus there gradually emerged a psychopathological form of the fantastic, in which phantoms became identified with phantasms, and in which the emphasis was placed less on miraculous distortions of objective reality than upon the human truth of the psychological states involved. Through the accuracy achieved in its evocation of marginal psychological states, such as those related to fear, to morbid obsessional phobias, and to the psychology of crime and madness, the work of Edgar Allan Poe, which became widely disseminated in France from the first years of the Second Empire onward, contributed considerably to this development, which was to reach its apogee during the last two decades of the century with the work of Maupassant and the fantastic elements present in the work of most of the decadent tale writers. These works are characterized in general by an almost total eclipse of the demoniac element, which was now scarcely ever used except in a humorous or parodistic way, by the emphasis placed upon descriptions of abnormal psychological states, and by the desire to renew the setting of fantastic fiction by using everyday modern life as its background.

Maupassant

Originally, Maupassant's fantastic fiction was based upon an absolute negation of the supernatural, linked with positivist beliefs in conformity with the spirit of the age. When, in *Miss Harriett*, he evokes the posthumous fate of the old maid who is the tale's central character, it is from a purely materialist standpoint:

> She was now going to decompose and become part of plant life in her turn. She would flower in the sun, be browsed by cows, carried away by birds as seed, and, having been turned into animal flesh, become human flesh once again. But what is called her soul had been extinguished at the bottom of the black pit. She would suffer no more, she had exchanged her life for those other lives she would now give birth to.[1]

In the same way, every time Maupassant considers the hypothesis of the existence of a God, the only possibility he envisages is that of a sadistic God, savagely bent on creating the human suffering upon which he feeds. The words of the criminal who is the central character of *Moiron*, a novella published in 1887, make this particularly explicit.[2] This being the case, it is hardly surprising to find Maupassant remarking upon the disappearance of a belief in the supernatural, and deploring the demise of the fantastic tradition that is its inevitable consequence, as he does in the person of the stranger encountered by the central character of *La Peur* during a rail journey:

> How disturbing the world must have been in the olden days, when it was so mysterious! The more veils we strip from the unknown the more we depopulate men's imagination. . . . People say to themselves: "No more mystery, no more strange beliefs, everything still unexplained is explicable. The supernatural is disappearing, like a lake being emptied by a new drainage channel; day by day science is eating away at the frontiers of the wonder in things." . . . Yes, Monsieur, by surprising the invisible we have laid waste our imagination. Our world today seems to me a place deserted, empty, bare. The beliefs that gave it poetry have gone.

This attitude was to change perceptibly, however, during the ten lucid years left to Maupassant after the success of *Boule-de-suif*. The first cause of this shift was undoubtedly the hereditary nervous illness that began to affect him. Combined with the delayed effects of the syphilis he had contracted in his youth, this illness, before reducing him to total insanity, was to give rise to a series of increasingly grave symptoms: disturbances of vision, neuralgia, memory lapses, dual personality, and eventually outright hallucinations. There is therefore some justification for supposing that the strange visions caused by some of these phenomena led him to believe in the existence of a mysterious universe beyond that of appearances. In the story *La Peur*, admirer as he was of Turgenev's ability to create an atmosphere of mystery in his fiction, Maupassant accepts the hypothesis of an invisible in which human life as a whole is bathed, and views man as the plaything of mysterious forces whose presence is sometimes revealed, for instance by coincidences:

> With [Turgenev] one can sense it clearly, the vague fear of the invisible, the unknown fear that is behind the wall, behind the door, behind life as it were. With him, sudden flashes of uncertain light flash through us, flashes that give only enough light to increase our dread. Sometimes he seems to show us the meaning of bizarre coincidences, unexpected juxtapositions, circumstances quite fortuitous on the surface, yet guided by a hidden, lurking will. With him, one thinks one can sense an imperceptible thread that is guiding us through life in some mysterious way, as though through a nebulous dream whose meaning perpetually eludes us.

Moreover Maupassant's early faith in positivist science gradually gave way to a much more flexible attitude, one that reveals the influence of certain ideas then in fashion concerning the unknowable. Although the results of science are reliable in themselves, they are able to throw light on one area of reality only: that corresponding to the field of our senses. This theme, first stated briefly in *Un Fou?* of 1884,[3] was to be developed further the following year in *Lettre d'un fou*. After having once more criticized the limited perception of reality provided by our senses, Maupassant now accepts the existence of an irreducible unknown. For the fantastic based on the supernatural he now substitutes a fantastic based on transcendental idealism, a fantastic in which the supernatural becomes the suprasensory or the extrasensory:

> We therefore delude ourselves in our judgment of the known, and we are surrounded by an unexplored unknown. . . . From which I conclude that the mysteries we can but glimpse, such as electricity, hypnotic sleep, the transmission of will, suggestion, and all magnetic phenomena, remain hidden from us only because nature has not provided us with the organ or organs necessary to comprehend them . . . and that the vague terror of the supernatural that has haunted man since the beginning of the world is legitimate, since the supernatural is nothing other than that which remains veiled from us! Then I understood terror!

It should also be pointed out that at this period, which is to say in the years 1884–86, Maupassant's attitude with regard to such phenomena as magnetism or hypnotism, originally one of incredulity, shifted considerably as he studied the work then being done in the field by Charcot and the Nancy school.[4] Thus, as a result of this acceptance of the theory of the unknowable, and his newly aroused interest in the phenomena of paranormal psychology, Maupassant was able to hypothesize the existence of an invisible being, perhaps from another planet, destined to eliminate the human race. This hypothesis, which belongs in the realm of science fiction, was to be developed first in his *Lettre d'un fou* of 1885 and then in the two versions of *Le Horla* that appeared in 1886 and 1887, respectively.

The fantastic element in Maupassant's work nevertheless proved to be very different from that found in previous writers. When the devil appears in one of his tales, *Le Diable,* it is in a laughable and grotesque form, that of a nurse who, anxious to be rid of the old and dying peasant woman she is tending, gets herself up in a grotesque disguise, appears suddenly in front of the old woman, and successfully frightens her to death. The traditional ghost story is also guyed in *Le Noyé:* a sailor's widow, whom her husband used to terrorize and beat up on before he was lost at sea, suddenly hears the dead man's voice shouting insults at her one day. The voice turns out to be that of a parrot. Although the supernatural does not exist, fear, on the other hand, is a very real experience. Of the two aspects of the traditional mystery story, the external one, characterized by intrusions of the beyond into the human world, and the internal one, that of the emotion associated with such intrusions, the second alone remains, and takes over entirely. Fear may have no basis in reason, it may be inexplicable, but it is nevertheless fully experienced, it is as much part of human life as love or the esthetic pleasures. It appears as a more or less cyclic crisis which the human consciousness undergoes in its relations with the real. This is why Maupassant's tales of the fantastic took the form of clinical descriptions of fearful experiences. This also meant that in his case the fantastic ceased to belong to the realm of the imagination and became simply a kind of research into mental pathology, while at the same time ceasing to have any connection with any kind of religious experience. On the other hand, the very precision of his psychological analyses and the total mastery of construction in his stories increased still further the impression of verisimilitude, of real life. We ought first, therefore, to examine the way in which Maupassant talks to us about fear, and how he describes it.

First, he insists on the absence of objective causes for the uneasiness being felt. There is no need for any supernatural or even out of the ordinary event to produce it: the objective world has not changed, and yet the subject's perceptions can still produce a growing dread in him.[5] Certain circumstances can nevertheless help to foster the development of this dread. The victim of fear is generally isolated in some natural setting, preferably at night. Loneliness and darkness still form the two essential ingredients of a situation in which the unexpected may occur. This is the case, for example, with the central character of *Sur l'eau,* who goes out for a row one night on the Seine, drops anchor for a moment to smoke his pipe, then is unable to retrieve the anchor and is forced to spend part of the night marooned in the middle of the river. Similarly, the victim in one of the anecdotes recounted in *La Peur* is a gamekeeper living in an isolated cottage in the middle of a wood; those in *L'Auberge* keep an inn on top of a mountain, which in winter is totally cut off; the setting of *Apparition* is a deserted castle; the central character of *Qui sait* is a man who comes home at dead of night to the isolated house where he lives. These circumstances once established, Maupassant begins introducing unexpected elements, thus triggering the process, referred to earlier, by which, without any change in the outside world itself, the subject's perception of it progressively disintegrates as his anxiety and fear mount. No writer has ever excelled him, in fact, in the analysis and description of the stages through which his victims' nervous sensibilities pass before sinking irrevocably into the black pit of total panic. From this point of view the two novellas *Sur l'eau* and *Le Horla* are exemplary: both present us with a cumulative process during which attacks of steadily increasing anxiety alternate with increasingly less successful attempts to regain a rational equilibrium.

Thus the narrator of *Sur l'eau,* having discovered that his anchor is irretrievably snagged in some unknown obstacle, and reduced as a result to total inaction, to waiting, starts to pay unusually close attention to his surroundings: the slight annoyance he feels turns to uneasiness when he becomes aware of the silence enveloping him, which he feels is abnormal. This uneasiness intensifies as a mist rises and increases his sense of isolation. As they become blurred, melting into the darkness and the mist, the forms of natural objects mislead his perception, or rather, as his perception becomes less certain, it is forced to draw on imagination to complete its data, so that objective elements are increasingly influenced by subjective interpretation. From this point of view one might say that every fantastic adventure begins on the level of perception, that such experiences begin when aberrant perception ceases to achieve an adequate and objective correlation with reality. This atmosphere of perceptual uncertainty, combined with emotional stress, produces a state in which the slightest incident, in this case the sound made by a frog, can trigger the hallucinating mechanism: "Soon the slightest movement of the boat made me uneasy. It seemed to me that it was yawing wildly from bank to bank." A significant detail that clearly reveals the disorder progressively invading the victim's perceptual field: a slight sensation, that of the boat lightly rocking in the current, has been amplified by his general emotive state to hallucinatory proportions. After that, the narrative consists of the alternating attacks of fear and attempts to reason the fear away that constitute the underlying rhythm of any successful fantastic tale:

> I began to reflect on my situation. . . . My mishap had calmed me; I sat down and was at last able to smoke my pipe. . . . A cold sweat froze me from head to foot. . . . I felt myself filled once more with a strange nervous agitation. . . . I felt a horrible uneasiness, there was a pressure at my temples, my heart was beating so hard I felt I was about to suffocate; losing my head, I thought of swimming to safety; then immediately began to shake with terror at the idea. . . . I tried to reason with myself. . . . This stupid and inexplicable feeling of fright was still mounting, turning into panic. . . . How-

ever, by making a violent effort I finally more or less recaptured the reason that was slipping away from me.

Whereas the action of *Sur l'eau* is confined to a few hours, in *Le Horla*
the same process is spread out over several months, and the progress of
the victim's illness, linked to the house haunted by the invisible being, is
broken by two journeys. On the other hand, the description of the various
phases punctuating the central character's gradually mounting fear,
dread, and eventually madness attains an unrivaled clinical precision.
Literally clinical, since it is quite clear that despite the science fiction plot,
which involves an invisible and alien being with the power to impose its
will on human victims by taking over command of their brains, the impression of truth the work as a whole gives is derived largely from the fact
that Maupassant is describing, through the progressive agony of his
character, the psychic disturbances to which he was subject himself. If *Le
Horla* constitutes an exemplary success in the field of the fantastic, it is
because the particular exigencies linked to the historical development of
the genre throughout the nineteenth century happened to coincide with
the personal tragedy of an individual writer progressively obsessed, then
finally taken over, by his own phantasms, and who, in addition, had
achieved technical perfection in narrative construction through assiduous
application to the art of the realistic novella.

Another characteristic of Maupassant's analysis of fear in his stories is
his constant concern to indicate its physiological and psychological aspects simultaneously, and thus to give his narrative the veracity of objective clinical observation. This clinical precision, present in all his most
successful tales, is particularly evident, for example, in the story *Un
Lâche* dating from 1884. The story is that of a man who, on the eve of a
duel, is seized by such dread of the event that he prefers to put a bullet
through his own head rather than face it. On the surface an implausible
story, it is one that perfectly exemplifies Maupassant's conception of fear
as something capable of provoking mental agony so horrible as to force
its victims into suicide. During the hours preceding that fixed for the duel,
we have all the physical symptoms of such fear described to us in minute
detail: uneasiness, insomnia, thirst, breathing difficulties, growing agitation, draining of blood from the face, shaking hands.[6] With Maupassant,
then, fear is no longer just the temporary unpleasantness experienced by
any individual in such unusual circumstances; it becomes a genuine illness, a moral agony of unprecedented intensity. The expressions he employs to describe it are significant in this respect: atrocious sensation;
decomposition of the soul; frightful spasm of the mind and heart; spasms
of the mind in panic; horrible sensation of incomprehensible terror. It

becomes an annihilation of the entire being sucked into the void: "The soul deliquesces; one can no longer feel one's heart; the whole body becomes soft like a sponge; it is as though our entire insides are collapsing" (*La Peur*). In its most acute forms it leads ineluctably to madness, and character after character in Maupassant's novellas does sink ultimately into insanity, whether it be the jealous murderer of *Fou?* or the hospitalized patient of *Lettre d'un fou,* the survivor of *L'Auberge* or the victim in the definitive version of *Le Horla.*

Even when madness is not the final outcome, however, the fear experienced, provided it attains a certain degree of intensity, leaves the victim permanently damaged. By destroying the individual's hitherto stable relations with the objective world, it prolongs its effects long beyond the original incident. This lesson, that the experience of fear scars its victims for life, is found, for example, in *Apparition,* a story whose narrator is still suffering from the consequences of something that happened to him very early in life:

> I too know something strange, so strange that it has been my life's obsession. It is fifty-six years now since this thing happened to me, and yet not a month goes by without my seeing it again in a dream. It has remained with me from that day to this, a scar, an imprint of fear. . . . Yes, for ten short minutes I suffered that appalling horror so acutely that ever since a sort of constant terror has resided always in my soul.

Far from being restricted to certain aspects of everyday experience, fear infects all relations between one's consciousness and the external universe with uncertainty, mistrust, and dread.[7] Even when triggered by a quite anodine and even almost imperceptible incident, fear extends its shadow ever afterward over the whole of its victim's existence.

This analysis of fear in Maupassant's work is combined, moreover, with a whole series of observations and reflections on the phenomena of marginal psychology or mental pathology. Two currents running through the literature of the time intermingle in his work. The first, deriving from Poe, continues the element of theoretical curiosity about and metaphysical reflection on certain states of the human soul found in the American writer's work—anxiety dreams, criminal obsessions, or fantasies of dual personality, for example—and underpinned on the metaphysical level by the theory of perversity. The second current owes its origin to the then-still-recent researches of positivist psychopathologists and psychiatrists, the dissemination of whose discoveries and hypotheses in literary circles we noted earlier. Thus we find Maupassant interesting himself in dreams, and in the waking dream, with its fluidity and often-unexpected free mental associations.[8] On a more clearly pathological level he depicts the psychology of suicide, as in such tales as *Suicide, Promenade,* and *L'Endormeuse*. The psychology of the criminal is magisterially illustrated in *La Petite Roque*, in which, as remorse overtakes the criminal Renardet, the onset and development of an obsessional hallucination are described. Sexual pathology is also well represented, whether it be necrophilia, which is the starting point of *La Tombe*, fetishism as in *La Chevelure*, or incest as in *L'Ermite*. *Un Cas de divorce* offers the secret diary of a man who is at first in love with an extremely beautiful woman, marries her, and after possessing her comes to feel distaste for her and so diverts his sexual instincts onto flowers. Sadism is also implicit in the story *Sur les chats*, whose narrator describes the ambiguous feeling he has for those domestic animals, a desire to stroke them and strangle them at the same time.

An analysis of Maupassant's fantastic tales would remain incomplete, however, if it did not draw attention to the deeper, unconscious level that can be sensed lurking beneath the explicit meanings and plots. His very conception of fear, if my analysis of it is correct, invites us to suppose that the fantastic element in his work is based on what is clearly a pathological state. Thus, the unmotivated character of that fear, on which, as we have seen, he himself so frequently insists, the fact that nothing in objective reality can provide a precise explanation for its occurrence, suggests that its source is wholly internal: the fantastic is not a disintegration of the world but a disintegration of the psyche. Second, the striking contrast between the quasi-anodine nature of the triggering event and the intensity of the emotive reaction, between the ephemeral nature of the original incident and the persistence of its repercussions, forces us to suppose that the event itself is not the source of the psychic disturbance but merely the trigger that releases that disturbance into the consciousness and thus enables it to affect the subject's behavior. In other words, the experience of fear in Maupassant's work should be viewed as merely the symptom of a more general disturbance affecting the deepest levels of the author's psyche.

Without wishing to venture too far into the field of mental pathology, since it lies outside both my competence and our present purpose, I feel that an analysis of the role played by water in Maupassant's work does throw a certain light on the true nature of that psychic disturbance. Several critics, following Bachelard, have commented on the importance of this theme in Maupassant's work, and described the fascination that he clearly felt for water in general.[9] What I now have to say may be viewed as simply an extension of their work.

The most immediately striking thing about the theme of water in Maupassant's work is its profound ambivalence. First, there is water in the form of sea or ocean, agitated by the continuous movement of ripples or waves, at once rocking cradle, heady intoxication, and liberty. A good example of this aspect is the beginning of *Sur l'eau,* where Maupassant describes his famous yacht, the *Bel-Ami,* leaving the harbor at Nice: "It danced on the light, innumerable, low waves, the moving furrows of a boundless plain. It sensed the life of the sea as it emerged from the dead water of the harbor." The sea sets one free, allows one to glide off into blissful self-abandon, intoxicated by the space of unobstructed sky and waves, as in this other passage describing the start of another sea trip just before dawn:

> There we were gliding across the waves toward the open sea.... It is a disturbing and delicious sensation, or emotion: to plunge into that empty darkness, in that silence, on that water, away from everything. It seems to me that one is leaving the world, that one need never arrive anywhere ever again, that there will never be another shore, that day will never come.

This abandonment to the water releases an existential reverie comparable in many ways with Rousseau's on the Ile Saint-Pierre. *Sur l'eau* bears the following epigraph, which sums up the bliss that Maupassant expected when rocked by the sea in contented reverie: "I thought simply, as one thinks when the waves are rocking you, numbing you, and bearing you along with them." In moments of extreme happiness this reverie takes the form of a participation in elemental and cosmic life.[10]

The still water of rivers, of ponds, of marshes is quite different, however. Motionless, or moved by a mysterious and almost silent current, such water is experienced as a murky and disturbing element whose shimmering surface hides mysterious and threatening depths, conceals the slime and mud that symbolize engulfment. This opposition between the shimmering glamour of the surface and the mysterious dangers below is well expressed, for example, in this passage describing the marshy valley of the Argens near Saint Raphaël:

> One senses that everywhere around this deep channel, in all that plain as far as the rising mountains, there lies still more water, the deceptive, dozing, yet living water of the marshes, those great clear sheets in which the sky is mirrored, in which the clouds glide by, dotted with clumps of curious reeds, the limpid, fertile water in which life decays, where death ferments, the water on which fevers and miasmas feed, at once a sap and a poison, water that mantles, seductive and delightful, above mysterious putrefactions.
> [*Sur l'eau*]

The beginning of *Sur l'eau* likewise evokes the theme of the river as a mystery, a simultaneous source of enchantments and of terrors. Indeed, this same story explicitly establishes a significant opposition between sea and river. While the sea is a realm of "vast blue regions," peopled with "strange forests" and "crystal caves," a region of limpid submarine wonder and space, the "silent and treacherous," river is peopled with "dark depths where mud decays." On a first level, then, one can interpret the theme of water as revealing a particular elemental and elementary structure in Maupassant's psyche, one that attributes a positive value to clear, moving water, as in the sea, and a correspondingly negative value to dark and stagnant water, to water seen as concealing terrifying, treacherous, and secret depths.

It is not a great step from this first level, that of elemental reverie, to a second, metaphysical level. Here, the sea would symbolize the pulse of life itself, while stagnant water is associated with the idea of death. This would explain the constant recurrence in Maupassant's work of death by drowning in a river. River water possesses a powerful fascination that induces a confused desire to drown oneself in it. When the narrator of *Sur l'eau* feels his anchor caught by an invisible object, and says he "thought that an invisible being or force was gently tugging at it in the depths of the water," it is no irrelevance that the invisible obstacle is in fact the corpse of an old woman: river water is intimately associated in Maupassant's mind with the idea of death, and he perceives the fascination exerted by such water as a lethal fascination: "It seemed to me that I was being drawn by the feet down into the very depths of that black water." The temptation that drowning represented to him is expressed in one of his very earliest stories, *Le Papa de Simon*, in which the main character, a little boy taunted by his companions because his mother is unmarried, runs away to the river bank and dreams of drowning himself: "The water shone like a mirror. And Simon spent some minutes in beatitude, in that softening of the whole being that follows upon tears."[11] Maupassant also seems to have been obsessed by the theme of the corpse floating with the current, since it even recurs in two slightly different versions of the same story, one entitled *Histoire d'un chien*, the other *Mademoiselle Cocotte*.

At a still deeper level, however, and one that is probably no more than half-conscious, water in Maupassant's work also possesses a value that is both sexual and clearly pathological. The feminine character attributed to water is, of course, one of the commonplaces of mythology and the psychology of dreams; but the feminine nature of water, and the aquatic nature of woman, take on a particularly striking form in Maupassant. There are many passages in his work that provide proof of this unconscious identification of woman with water. In *La Chevelure*, for example, the images used to describe the heroine's hair are revealing in this respect:

> It streamed down, falling in spreading, golden waves to the ground, thick and light, shining and supple as a comet's tail. . . . It flowed through my fingers, tingling against my skin with an extraordinary caressing sensation. . . . In my hand and heart I felt a singular, confused, continual, sensual need to dip my fingers into that spellbinding rivulet of dead hair. . . . I wound it around my face, I drank it, I drowned my eyes in its golden flood.

In *L'Inconnue*, the gaze of the unknown woman passing in the street likewise suggests aquatic images: "And she moved on, having stared me out of countenance . . . with that vague and heavy gaze that seems to leave something behind it on the skin, a sort of glue, as if it were able to coat its object with one of those thick liquids that octopuses use to darken the water and numb their prey."

At this deepest level, then, the fundamental ambiguity of water in Maupassant's psychology coincides fairly closely with the ambiguity of woman herself, viewed either as a mother or, on the other hand, as a lover; the mother, protective and rocking, would thus correspond to the sea experienced as a cradle, the source of all life, a symbol of happiness and emotional expansion. As an example, let us take a passage near the beginning of *Sur l'eau:* "I am floating in a winged home that rocks, bright as a bird, tiny as a nest, gentler than any hammock, and wandering free across the water." The metaphors are not lightly chosen; they represent the emotional and essentially maternal reality of the sea, so that the ship floating upon it becomes in its turn, a nest, a cradle, and a hammock, a place of contentment and security, a kindly home. The simultaneously seductive and frightening water of the river, on the other hand, symbolizes Maupassant's fundamentally ambiguous attitude with regard to woman as a love object, one in which attraction and fear are mixed in equal measure, so that the attraction exerted by river water is a mythical transposition of the author's reaction to sexual love. Again there are numerous texts that provide evidence of this. One thinks first, perhaps, of the story that Maupassant attributes to Turgenev in his own novella *La Peur*, which depicts a huntsman's encounter with the water-woman. This encounter is initially characterized by a feeling of happiness, of pleasurable attraction: "It flowed beneath trees, through trees, filled with floating weeds, deep, cold, and clear," the narrator says of the river that the hunstman chances upon. Then "the huntsman was gripped by an imperious need to plunge himself into that transparent water." And his first contact with the water does in fact result in intense physical elation: "He let himself float gently, his soul at peace, brushed by the water plants and roots, happy to feel their coils slithering lightly over his flesh." But then the other side of the theme begins to appear, those same plants become clutching tendrils; instead of brushing pleasurably against him they are sucking him down, imprisoning him, and the threat concealed by the initial seduction becomes all too plain. At the same time the feminine nature of the water is made explicit, as the nymph hiding in the river's depths rises to pursue the huntsman, a nymph who has assumed the features of a repulsive old woman: "Suddenly a hand fell on his shoulder. He wheeled in shock and saw a terrifying creature eyeing him with avid eyes. It looked like a woman, an old hag." In the phantasmagorical chase that follows there is no doubt that this is a sexual obsession being expressed, agonizing fear of woman as vampire, of woman as a conqueror who envelops the hero in gluey slime, in the yielding mud of her triumphant sexuality: "But the monster swam even faster and was touching his neck, his back, his legs, with little snickerings of joy."

From this same point of view it is also worth rereading the passage in *La Petite Roque* describing Renardet's first encounter with his future victim, an encounter that likewise takes place under the sign of water:

> Thick willows hid that clear pool where the current circles at rest, dozing a little before the next stage of its journey. As he came near, Renardet thought he could hear a slight noise, a gentle splashing that was not quite that of the stream against its banks. Gingerly he parted the leaves and looked. A little girl, quite naked, all white through the transparent stream, was beating at the water with her hands, almost dancing in it, turning round and round with pretty gestures. . . . He had stopped moving, stunned with surprise, with dread, his breath cut off by a strange and poignant emotion. He remained there, heart beating as though one of his sensual dreams had become flesh, as though it was the act of some impure fairy to conjure up before his eyes this troubling and far too youthful creature, this little peasant Venus, born from the eddies of a rivulet just as the other, the great goddess, had risen from the ocean's waves.

The identification here of the adolescent girl with the water, made explicit at the end of the excerpt by the comparison with Venus, is already implicitly suggested from the start: the noise the girl makes as she plays in the water is initially identified with the stream's own splashing, her fresh child's body is inseparable from the transparent water bathing it. Thus in a sense the child has indeed emerged from the water; she is the expression of its perfidious attractions.

Comparison of these two passages, which reveal attitudes superficially so dissimilar with regard to women, since one results in terrified flight and the other in rape and murder, undoubtedly allows us to shed some light on one element in the author's psychological tragedy, which probably consisted in an incomplete transition from childish love, attachment to the mother, to adult sexual love. The resulting behavioral inadequacy in his attitude to women manifests itself as a result in two contrary but equally traumatic ways, either by exaggerated aggressivity (as in *La Petite Roque*) or by anxiety and fear of woman's sexuality (as in *La Peur*). This sexual anxiety probably became acute enough in Maupassant's case to cause impotence, if we are to judge by the evidence of the very revealing story *L'Inconnue*, in which the extremely desirable woman encountered in the street gives herself without the slightest demur to the narrator who, at the moment when he is about to possess her, becomes impotent, his sexuality blocked by fear: "It seemed to me that I was looking at one of those sorceresses from the Arabian Nights, one of those dangerous and treacherous beings whose mission it is to suck men down into unfathomable abysses."

It is therefore probable that the development of the fantastic tale in Maupassant's work is based upon personal experience of an anxiety state clearly linked to his sexuality, and that the mental illness which totally destroyed his lucidity in the last years of his life was incubated, not only by hereditary and physiological factors in his makeup, but also by an inherent emotional instability. This instability, the source of an incapacity to adapt to reality, manifested itself in the form of those causeless fears described too accurately and too frequently in his stories for us to doubt that their author had experienced them personally.

The Fantastic in Decadent Fiction

The trends we have seen emerging in Maupassant's work may also be found in the fantastic writing of most authors of fiction of the decadent era. Here, too, the demoniac element has almost wholly disappeared. When the devil does appear it is in a ludicrous and grotesque form. Edouard Dujardin's *Le Diable helkésipode*, for example, published in a collection entitled *Les Hantises* of 1886, tells the story of a farm girl who has the feeling, every time she climbs into bed, that a devil catches hold of one of her feet. This bizarre variety of devil is baptized by a learned academic who hears the story by the name that gives the story its title. Similarly, here is how Marcel Schwob describes the devil as he appears to the little red riding hood figure who is the heroine of his story:

> An extraordinary creature was crouched beneath a bush, with flaming eyes and a dark purple mouth; on his head two pointed horns stuck up, and he was impaling hazelnuts on them as he picked them with his long tail. He cracked the nuts on his horns, extracted the kernels with his dry, hairy, pink-palmed hands, and ground his teeth as he ate them.[12]

We are a long way here from the devil of the romantic era. The romantics' Satan, a heroic being with an aura of grandeur and beauty, has become in decadent literature a grotesque monkey just about capable of frightening little girls for a moment or two. The difference between these two images is a measure of the degradation the theme had undergone, and of the pressure on writers of fantastic tales to jettison a demoniac supernatural now stripped of all prestige.

This erosion of traditional themes also affected the theme of the ghost, as we find in another of Schwob's tales, *Un Squelette,* a ghost story in which the ghost is turned into a figure of pitiful fun by being presented in a deliberately realistic and everyday setting.[13] The narrator is visited one evening by the skeleton of a former friend, who engages him in a conversation that is in fact a systematic debunking of the macabre. "I thought it might cheer him up a little if I offered him a cigar," the narrator says, "but he declined on account of the terrible state of his teeth, which had been badly affected by the humidity down there." The skeleton itself is amazed at the fear he and his fellow skeletons provoke. "I really cannot see what is so terrifying about us," he cried. "We are hardly men of substance any more. Why, we couldn't buy so much as a single share on the Stock Exchange."

Needless to say, however, a few traces of the macabre do subsist in certain fantastic tales of the time. In *Histoires de tous les diables* by Camille Debans, published in 1882, a story called *Une Nuit chez les morts* recounts how a tourist, after a guided tour of the catacombs in Bordeaux, is accidentally locked in all night with the corpses, which are in a remarkable state of preservation, so that he eventually believes he can hear them moving about, to his increasing terror. Such macabre elements can be found in quite a number of Jean Lorrain's stories also. *Réclamation posthume,* for example, from his *Contes d'un buveur d'éther,* tells how the ghost of a dead woman returns to retrieve her severed head, which the central character has been keeping on a silver salver as an ornament. His *L'Egrégore* presents a new type of ghost, "the corpse of a man or woman insinuating itself into your life and habits, dissolving into your heart, into your admirations, and putting down loathsome roots there, its accursed mouth breathing some fatal passion into you, some madness, an artist's or connoisseur's folly, and stage by stage, by dint of some such hallucinatory and seductive obsession, stretching you out one fine evening in the cold of the grave'' (*Sonyeuse*, pp. 195–209). *Le Mauvais Gîte* is based on the haunted house theme; *Une Nuit trouble* tells how in the deserted wing of a big house, one night of winter storm, a monstrous animal emerges from the fireplace of an isolated bedroom and engages the central character in a terrible struggle. In particular, the macabre in Lorrain is often linked with specific portions of the human body: severed head in *Le Visionnaire*, severed hand in *La Main gantée*, a mask in *Les Trous du masque*.

Although in the case of Jean Lorrain, these macabre elements do contribute to successful tales, in the decadent era generally they nevertheless represent survivals from earlier periods rather than an element capable of paving the way for future developments in the genre. The demoniac supernatural did find a degree of favor again, as we have already seen, with the fashion for satanism that flared up for a few brief years after 1890, as a result of the success of occultism; but that was in fact a merely temporary resurgence that left no deep impression. In fantastic writing of this period such satanic or macabre elements were increasingly to be ousted by a psychopathological form of the fantastic linked with descriptions of marginal and abnormal phenomena. We frequently find authors remarking upon the fact that belief in the supernatural had almost disappeared, and that the fantastic genre can consequently no longer use it as a basis. Thus, in one of his stories, Dujardin puts the following words into the mouth of a positivist physician: "Stories of demonomania, possession, and use of the Kabbala have lost credibility. Today, the supernatural is too far away from us; our minds are no longer preoccupied with the supernatural; we can no longer conceive of people's being obsessed by ideas of magic, witchcraft, or demonology. The occult sciences have lost their interest; the fantastic has had its day; the supernatural is fading into the past; no one will believe that there are still men tormented by the supernatural'' (*Les Hantises*, p. 138). Nor can there be any doubt that a great many of Dujardin's contemporaries would have heartily endorsed those sentiments. Fantasy based on the supernatural needed to be replaced by some new form, as Jules Claretie clearly stated in his preface to Jules Lermina's *Histoires incroyables* of 1885. The suggestion of the supernatural should be replaced by analysis of hitherto insufficiently explored psychological data, following the path opened up by Poe:

In order to write this preface, I have broken off work on a short novel in which I am investigating the phenomena of suggestion from a particular point of view. Hysteria and neurosis attract me, and yet they are mere words. The reality is mental overstimulation or depression. What is happening? What thought processes are taking place inside that malfunctioning apparatus? Is it impossible for us to have any idea at all? No. For since Maury proved that dreams can be tamed, guided by the will, since De Quincey the opium eater and Poe analyzed the sensations of the drug addict and the alcoholic, it has been proved that for any observer sufficiently master of himself to watch himself think there is a deep and inexhaustible mine to be exploited. . . . These infinitely small shifts in cerebral conception are what is interesting to record. That is the true fantastic, because it is the region still uncharted; because in this field the surprises, the antitheses, the absurdities are multiple and recurrent.[14]

Jules Lermina himself was to return to this same idea several times. In *La Peur*, one of his *Histoires incroyables*, he too has a physician who rejects the possibility that earlier fantastic themes might be able to affect the sensibilities of modern readers.

You talk about the fantastic, and think it very ingenious to conjure up ghosts swathed in shrouds, horrible gnomes, so-called spirits of the dead that even ancient Thessalians would have balked at. Enough of such nonsense. Admit it, if one of these ridiculous and grotesque creatures actually appeared through that door now, you'd all laugh like hyenas and see who could send it packing first, with a good thwacking from its own broom, off to this so-called sabbath it's never even set eyes on. [p. 225]

No, this outmoded notion of the fantastic must be replaced with a new and truer kind, one based on fear.

Now fear, I can assure you, is an eminently natural emotion, one that can be excited solely by natural means. It is part of a psychological or physiological order of phenomena so strange that under their influence the human organism will quiver like Ossian's Aeolian harp. The whole being vibrates in that breeze, blowing from we know not where. . . . Then there builds up in us an energy produced by overstimulation whose effect is no longer factitious, as in these cases where you just invent impossibilities.[15]

In practice, it is just such abnormal psychological phenomena, just such anomalies of psychic life, that provide decadent fantastic writing with its essential themes. The first of these, as in Maupassant, is clearly that of fear. As we have just seen, one of Lermina's stories is actually entitled *La Peur*. Inspired by Poe, it tells how a man keeping vigil over the corpse of his beloved is gripped by such panic dread when he thinks he sees the body move that he leaps on it and strangles it. Lorrain, in one of the most famous of his *Contes d'un buveur d'éther, Les Trous du masque*, describes the increasing anxiety and fear of a man attending a strange masked ball peopled with ghostly figures. In Gaston Danville's *Contes d'Au-delà* there is a story entitled *A la dérive* that describes how a young woman goes boating with a man friend one summer night and, as the result of an unmotivated but irrepressible attack of panic terror, kills herself.

Specifically pathological phenomena also motivate the action of a great many stories. Thus Serge Alitoff, the central character in most of Lorrain's *Contes d'un buveur d'éther*, is a neurasthenic, like most of Poe's central characters. The various forms of madness also frequently appear, as in several tales of Dujardin's *Les Hantises*, including *La Future Démence*, the story of a young man who discovers that his mother, whose existence had been concealed from him till now, has just died in a lunatic asylum, whereupon he feels madness overtaking him in his turn. The following story in the same collection, *La Démence passée*, depicts the dilemma of an individual who has just emerged from madness but cannot tell if his memories are true or false. Dual personality, which Poe had used to masterly effect in his *William Wilson*, provides the subject matter for two tales in Danville's *Contes d'au-delà: Le Meurtrier*, which describes how a murder committed during a passing moment of madness leads to a complete split in the murderer's personality, and *La Lampe*, which was dedicated to Ribot. The psychology of the murderer is described in both *L'Assassin* by Debans (*Histoires de tous les diables*) and also Lermina's *Les Fous (Histoires incroyables)*, to cite only two of many possible examples. The phenomena of parapsychology provide material for an equally abundant fund of stories. In *In Anima vili* Danville tells the story of a doctor, a specialist in hypnotism, who, having surprised his wife in the arms of a stranger, has her murdered by a female patient he çan control by means of hypnotic suggestion. *Lisbeth*, by the same writer, presents us with a woman who subjugates her lovers by the magnetic power of her eyes, thereby reducing them to total submissiveness. Finally, in order to rid himself of her tyranny, one of them has no choice but to strangle her.

Another feature of fantastic writing in the decadent era is the increasing use of modern, everyday settings. Whereas the traditional tale of mystery tended to be set in a deserted countryside, underground, or in ruined houses, because such locations favored the appearance of the unexpected and helped to make the reader accept it by destroying his everyday bearings, the decadent tale of mystery, on the contrary, takes place increasingly often against backgrounds taken from everyday modern life, that of the big city. The majority of Lorrains' *Contes d'un buveur d'éther,* for example, take place in Paris. *Les Trous du masque* begins with a cab journey across Paris to a house in the suburbs, and it is in fact the city landscape through which he passes that first begins to excite the narrator's dread:

> We had long since lost sight of the fantastic silhouette of Notre-Dame, outlined beyond the river against a leaden sky. . . . Beside that wan and silent Seine, beneath the spans of its increasingly infrequent bridges, along those embankments planted with tall, emaciated trees whose branches spread out overhead like dead fingers, an irrational fear was taking hold of me.[16]

Similarly, the denouement of *Un Crime inconnu* takes place in a hotel room near the Gare Saint-Lazare; *Le Possédé* is set in a tram; *La Main gantée* in a railroad compartment. Yet again, although in many of his stories Marcel Schwob does indulge his taste for erudite reconstructions by displacing the reader in time back to various past eras, there are others that take place against the very modern setting of the railroad, as with *Le Train 081* and *L'Homme voilé,* both from *Coeur double.*

6 PARADIS ARTIFICIELS

THE REJECTION OF NATURE, WHOSE FIRST MANIFESTATIONS DURING the Second Empire we have already noted in the work of such writers as Gautier or Baudelaire, was to become even more intense during the decadent period. Indeed, one of the specific features of the decadent esthetic is a conscious determination to diverge as far as possible from nature, in an overt repudiation of the classical dogma that the aim of all art is the imitation of nature. For the decadent, art is identified with the artificial, and it is the artificial that must be developed by every available means.

In the first place, this rejection of nature took the form of an antiromantic depreciation of the so-called beauties of natural landscapes. This attitude is to be found clearly expressed in *A Rebours*, for example. "As he said, nature has had her day," Huysmans writes of Des Esseintes; "with the loathsome uniformity of her landscapes and skies she has once and for all worn out the patience of refined minds" (p. 51). And variations of this idea occur in the works of most decadent authors. In his *Moralités légendaires*, for instance, we find Laforgue directing his irony at sunsets: "Another night falling, another sunset about to preen itself; the classic schedule, the more than classic schedule!" (p. 232). In *La Revue indépendante*, reviewing George Moore's *A Mere Accident*, which had clearly been influenced by *A Rebours*, Téodor de Wyzewa expressed the same conviction:

> I know—and I have never understood life in any other way—that what is termed nature, outside us as well as inside us, is hateful, loathsome, and that man's only duty is to free himself from its bonds. . . . The artist, perceiving the futility of that bad dream, must undermine it by every means at his disposal, hate what he sees as natural, and always substitute for it the willed and meditated work of his own soul.

In a similar vein, near the beginning of *Sixtine*, when he is describing the train journey d'Entragues makes back to Paris after a visit at the Château

166

de Rabondages, Rémy de Gourmont defines his character's reactions, as he watches the Normandy landscape unfurling outside, as follows: "The eternal green of meadows being munched by bullocks filled his soul with sadness in the end. The unawareness of the vegetable kingdom is decidedly too depressing a void" (pp. 18, 22). Later still, we find similar sentiments expressed by Péladan.[1]

Depreciating the beauty of natural landscapes was merely one symptom, however, of a more general rejection of nature in all its forms, a rejection expressed at many levels: natural landscapes must be replaced by artificial settings entirely confected by the hand of man; woman as nature made her must be regarded as inferior to a sophisticated woman whose natural ugliness has been concealed by elaborate clothing and cosmetics. Thus Thódore Hannon, reworking Baudelaire's *L'Eloge du maquillage* in one of his *Rimes de joie* of 1879, informs his beloved:

> My soul, as you well know my sweet,
> Loves only what is made by art.

Rachilde, too, in her novel *Les Hors-nature* of 1897, presents us with a character who prefers a length of satin to a woman's skin: "That is an artificial beauty, but it is really and supremely beautiful. All natural beauty has some defect. There is no . . . skin or breast or shoulder whose touch could give me such a sensation."[2] Last, the natural forms of love and sexuality are replaced by sexual perversions, praise of which, varying in its degree of deliberate provocation, became one of the commonplaces of the age, as we saw earlier.

Such, then, was the general attitude adopted by the aesthete, the decadent hero, who was in this respect a continuation of Baudelaire's dandy. The esthete is the man who has become aware of the ultimate ugliness of nature and life, and therefore attempts to abolish life in favor of art. He does not merely strive to make his own existence a work of art; he also attempts to live in a totally artificial world. In its extreme form, this esthetic attitude produced an incapacity to perceive reality at all other than through the medium of works of art, as Bourget observed in the dialogue *Science et poésie* quoted from earlier. One of the two characters proves impervious to the beauty of the flowers massed around them in the florist's shop in which the dialogue is set, and quotes a description of flowers in a Shelley poem which he considers preferable and more moving than the real thing. Bourget's other character thereupon makes this significant reply:

> I must confess that seeing you moved to far greater ecstasy
> by a commentary on reality, a literary expression of it, than
> by the reality itself, I eyed you with an almost melancholy

curiosity. You finally took shape before me as a singular example of our western civilization in all its profound artificiality and its repugnance for any direct embrace of that which is.[3]

Artificial Settings

This consciously willed attribution of value to the artificial was to have a considerable influence on a number of literary themes, and to give a new thrust to the development of the literary imagination. First, purely artificial settings were created, in which machinery of greater or lesser intricacy replaces the elements of the natural landscape. The first manifestation of this trend can be seen in the work of Villiers de l'Isle-Adam, particularly in certain features of *L'Eve future*. Villiers was concerned to provide practical applications of the theory of illusionism whose significance we analyzed earlier. In his eyes, as we saw, the human imagination is capable of creating its own universe, provided its flight can be guided and supplemented by elementary subterfuges. Thus man-made machinery will make it possible to replace a natural landscape, regarded as inherently ugly, with an entirely fictive one. This is the meaning of the description we are given, in the third section of *L'Eve future* entitled *L'Eden sous terre,* of the automaton Hadaly's underground residence, before she becomes Lord Ewald's companion. This residence consists of an immense hall whose vaulted ceiling, lit by a luminous globe at its apex, exactly simulates the vault of the sky: "The concave vault, a uniform black in color, of gargantuan height, overhung the brilliance of that fixed star with the dense darkness of the grave: it was the image of the sky as it appears, somber and black, beyond all planetary atmosphere" (p. 161). The floor is covered with artificial vegetation, waving in the gusts of a factitious breeze, and the two visitors who penetrate this enchanted realm are welcomed by the song of mechanical birds which, the author tells us, "mocked life to the extent of grooming themselves and smoothing down their feathers, with an artificial beak, in some cases, and in others of replacing birdsong with human laughter" (p. 163). Clearly this description—inspired partly by memories of Verne's *Le Voyage au centre de la terre* and partly by the odd inventions created for Ludwig of Bavaria that Catulle Mendès described at about the same time in his *Roi vierge*—is symbolic in intention rather than merely picturesque. When he is imagining this sort of theatrical machinery, one senses that Villiers is wavering between a desire to mock the Creation and nature, now definitively devalued, and that of demonstrating that human ingenuity is perfectly capable, using purely artificial elements, of creating a total illusion of life. It is precisely this same brand of illusion that the automaton Hadaly provides for Lord Ewald, when the worthless singer, the real and thus necessarily disqualified and disappointing woman, is superseded by an artificial woman who can offer both brains and beauty: that Lord Ewald can really fall in love with this automaton is definitive proof that these new possibilities offered to the human imagination by meticulously executed illusion have validity. The moral and esthetic thesis that *L'Eve future* is intended to illustrate is thus that of the superiority of the artificial over the natural.

Huysmans was guided by a similar intention in writing *A Rebours*. When Des Esseintes shuts himself away in his ivory tower at Fontenay, it is in order both to escape from reality and the rest of humanity and also to assert his total faith in the power of imagination. "He felt that imagination could easily supplant the vulgar reality of facts," Huysmans writes of his character. "In his opinion it was possible to satisfy even those desires supposedly most difficult to assuage in normal life, and by the slightest of subterfuges, with the merest approximation of the object toward which those desires are directed" (p. 50). Thus Huysmans comes to advocate a method of systematic and deliberate hallucination aimed in every case at substituting illusion for reality. It is simply a matter of devising practical methods of deceiving the senses: "The whole trick is to know how to go about it, how to concentrate one's mind on a single point, to abstract one's ego sufficiently to bring about the hallucination, and so substitute the dream of reality for the reality itself" (p. 51). In this way the human being will be able to free himself from nature by replacing it with simulacra: "Moreover there is not one of its most reputed and subtle inventions, or its most grandiose, that human genius cannot create for itself; no forest of Fontainebleau, no moonlight, that man-made sets bathed with electric beams cannot reproduce; no waterfall that hydraulics cannot imitate to perfection; no rock that papier-mâché cannot simulate; no flower that plausible silks and delicate painted paper cannot equal" (p. 52).

Thus the diningroom in Des Esseintes's villa at Fontenay, with its special furniture, its dappled light, and its aquarium, enable the dreamer to believe himself in the main saloon of the *Nautilus;* bathing in specially treated water replaces a swim in the sea; and a visit to the English tavern in the rue d'Amsterdam can stand in for a trip to London while avoiding the fatigue and irritations necessarily attendant on a real journey. Here, despite the element of exaggeration, paradox, and, one presumes, humor, Huysmans's almost unlimited faith in the powers of the imagination is nevertheless apparent. No work is therefore more revealing than *A Rebours* of this definitive reversal of esthetic attitudes that was to establish itself during the decadent era, and to pave the way for every succeeding development in modern esthetics. More deliberately than any other artist, with the exception of Wilde, Huysmans asserted the esthetic primacy of artifice, and identified art with the artificial. Speaking of his "natural inclination toward artifice," Des Esseintes repudiates nature once for all, and asserts that "the moment has arrived when we must replace it, as far as we possibly can, by artifice" (p. 123). No chapter is more revealing of this inversion of the traditional roles of nature and art than the one devoted to plants, in which Des Esseintes confesses that at one time he favored artificial flowers over real ones, but that he has now come round to a preference for natural flowers—but only those that give the impression of being artificial (p. 124).

Modernity

This devaluation of nature, this contempt for natural landscapes, was also to bring in its train an increasing exploitation of modernist literary themes, principally those related to the city and the machine. We have already seen how the theme of the city began to appear in the literature of the preceding period, especially in the work of Baudelaire and Gautier. With the former, the city came to symbolize not only the tragedy of modern man sucked willy-nilly into an existence in which he is forced to live on his nerves, but also, through its ever-present resemblance to Babel, the revolt against God. With Gautier, and especially in his travel narratives, it became a place heavy with mystery, a labyrinth. In decadent literature this urban backdrop was to assume an ever-increasing importance.

For there is no doubt that the city, rather than the country, is the normal setting of modern man. It was therefore the city that came to provide the background for most works of the period. In his article on Baudelaire in *Essais de psychologie contemporaine,* Bourget defined the modern mind in terms of three essential elements: "the end of religious faith, life in Paris, and the scientific spirit of the age" (p. 8). And it is true that Paris, the modern Babylon or Byzantium, was to figure as the very symbol of decadence. In Paris, beyond and despite the ugliness still perceived in industrial civilization, poetry and dreams could still infiltrate under cover of darkness. For the majority of writers at this time were concerned to bring out the esthetic possibilities already there in embryo in Baudelaire's *Tableaux parisiens,* and most particularly in *Le Crépuscule du soir:* Paris by night is the city of the human stampede in search of pleasure, whose streets, storefronts, and milling faces are transfigured by the magic of artificial light. It was the "shameless" and "monstrous" city evoked by Bourget, the enormous city "with its hansom cabs, its gaslight, the weariness of overwrought nerves, unassuaged longings, irritations, whores, the thick disgust for this life, a nostalgia for blue or gray countrysides," described by Barrès.[4] To the influence of Baudelaire, moreover, we must also add that of the Goncourts, whose works display a marked partiality for suburban settings, or for those working class areas that ring the capital and crop up again in Huysmans's *Croquis parisiens.* Paris is always there in the background of Laforgue's work too. In 1880, for example, defining the subject of his *Sanglot de la terre,* a verse collection he was then working on, he speaks of "the diary of a Parisian in 1880 who suffers, doubts, and comes face to face with the void, all against the backdrop of Paris itself, its sunsets, the Seine, those greasy cobblestones..."[5]

From this point on, descriptions of Paris by night become ever more numerous: in *Les Demoiselles Goubert* by Paul Adam and Jean Moréas, for example,[6] or in Bernard Lazare's *Les Portes d'ivoire,* in which we find a story whose central character describes his nighttime wanderings through Paris in the hope of meeting his ideal woman:

> And so, companionless, I walked far and wide through a darkened Paris, taking pleasure in the deserted alleyways, peopled with pallid shapes beneath the writhing gas lamp flames, and in secluded, distant, darkened squares. I followed the ghostly army of my own desires. Sometimes I stood motionless for hours on end at the iron-barred gate of some house, far away, over there, near Passy, and waited like an automaton for she-who-was-bound-to-come, dreaming invincibly of the young woman who emerged from the darkness to console and love the Opium eater.[7]

Similarly, in his *Le Soleil des morts,* Camille Mauclair offers us a description of Paris by night as seen from the esplanade of the Sacré-Coeur.[8]

One urban theme was to find very special favor at this time, however, that of the city as a place of labyrinthine canals and alleyways, a city of dread and death that harmonizes perfectly with the dominant, often macabre key of the decadent imagination. The outstanding example in real life was provided by Bruges. It was to an evocation of this city, and the mysterious and dangerous spell it could exert, that Georges Rodenbach, under cover of his highly romantic plot, devoted his famous novel *Bruges-la-morte,* which appeared in 1892. The hero, Hughes Viane, left inconsolable by the death of his adored wife, has come to Bruges to live the life of a recluse, and spends his time in melancholy, interminable walks. One day his path chances to cross that of a woman whose gait, looks, and even voice make her the living portrait of his dead wife. He follows her, discovers that she is an actress in a small theater, makes her his mistress, and soon falls into the delusion that he is reliving a past love. Gradually, however, he discovers that the young woman is domineering and mercenary, then that she is being unfaithful, and he can no longer deceive himself as to the disparities between the living woman and the dead one, whose memory is still alive in his heart. One day, when visiting him, the actress commits an act of sacrilege by snatching up a lock of the dead woman's hair that he keeps on his mantel shelf. He attempts to retrieve the sacred object, and during the brief ensuing struggle, without really meaning to, strangles the actress with the hair. This plot, needless to say, is an echo of the theme of vengeance exacted by the dead from the living much used by Poe, most notably in *Ligeia*.

This story of love and death, of deadly vengeance summoned up by an inexplicable fascination, is orchestrated, however, by the constant presence of its setting. For Bruges is ever-present, truly the dead city of the title, drowned in its own stagnant canals, and in the author's description of it we recognize the fundamentally Poesque identification of water, woman, and death, as for example in the following passage:

> In the prison of its stone embankments, there in Bruges, the stagnant water of the canals where no boats or barges ever move today, in which nothing is reflected but the immobility of gables whose stepped outlines, traced on the still surface, look like funereal stairways leading down into the depths, and up above the lifeless waterways, overhanging balconies, wooden ramps, barred gates leading to decaying gardens, mysterious doors, a long procession of discarded objects, huddled at the water's edge as though begging, clothed in rags of fraying foliage and ivy.[9]

It is at the same time a labyrinth, its indistinguishable alleys and canals forming a maze in which the main character is perpetually in danger of becoming lost: "Anxious, sad, fearing others' eyes, he wandered aimlessly, drifting from one sidewalk to the other, reached the nearby embankments, continued along beside the water, emerged into symmetrical squares, lugubrious with lamenting trees, plunged into the infinite intricacies of the gray streets" (p. 156).

For Bruges to become the very symbol of the city as a source of "spleen," all that is now required is rain:

> It is evening. . . . The drizzle piercing his soul, sometimes as fine as mist, sometimes becoming a light rain, Hughes felt himself reconquered, haunted by that face, impelled toward Jane's home. . . . Briskly, he walked in the opposite direc-

tion, threaded his way through the old neighborhoods, wandered on without knowing where, vague, pitiful, in the mud. The rain fell faster, its drops becoming threads, weaving its stitches ever tighter, thickening, a moist and impalpable net in which Hughes gradually felt himself softening. [Pp. 159–60]

Thus if Hughes is bewitched, it is not only by the strange resemblance that links the living woman with the dead one, but also by the dangerous and lethal spell of this city of water and death. In *Bruges-la-morte,* then, we can see clearly how it was possible for the urban theme to be integrated into the contemporary sensibility by impregnating it with affectivity and mystery.

After the considerable success achieved by Rodenbach's novel, the theme of Bruges, the city of canals and water, the dead city, was to reappear as the setting of Camille Mauclair's novel *L'Ennemie des rêves,*[10] and also in an account of his travels through northern Europe and Germany that Huysmans published in 1902 under the title *De Tout,*[11] in which, prompted by a rereading of Rodenbach's novel, the author offers his own description of the Belgian city. More generally the decadent sensibility was to combine its deep-rooted predilection for urban settings and its morbid obsessions by displaying a marked preference for any city that was both watery and dying. This no doubt explains Henri de Régnier's fascination with Versailles—for the palace at the time was still in a state of almost complete dereliction—and also his preoccupation with Venice, a city that he celebrated, before Proust, on many occasions, much as others did Bruges. Later, when we examine the elemental themes that recur in the decadent imagination, I shall have occasion to return to this profound and very specific conjunction of the aquatic and mineral elements to produce a predominantly macabre effect.

As far as machines were concerned, the attitude of decadent writers, like that of Gautier earlier, remained ultimately ambiguous. On the one hand they abominated the machine as a symbol of modern civilization in all its vulgarity and exclusive preoccupation with profit, yet on the other, as we have seen, they had no qualms about inventing or exploiting ingenious mechanisms to help in freeing their imaginations. In the case of Villiers de l'Isle-Adam, for example, hatred of the modern world and "progress" as symbolized by machinery provides the background for an appreciable number of the *Contes cruels,* such as *La Machine à gloire, L'Affichage céleste,* or *L'Appareil pour l'analyse chimique du dernier soupir,* in all of which the author invents bizarre machines for the sole purpose of deriding science. Yet at the same time, it is by means of a machine, and an extremely advanced form of machine, devised and built by Edison, the sorcerer of Menlo Park, that Lord Ewald is able to console himself for the irremediable inadequacy of real women in *L'Eve future*. Similarly, Huysmans expresses horror at certain creations of modern technology—such as the Eiffel Tower, a constant target of his sarcasm—yet also, in *A Rebours*, celebrates the beauty of a locomotive, or, as we learn from an article devoted to the 1889 Exposition, can be deeply moved by what he sees in the vast Galerie des Machines.

Thus, unlike the modern city, the machine as an element of modernity was not to be completely adopted and accepted during the decadent era. Yet we must recognize that at moments these writers were unable to prevent themselves from being affected by the fascination of the mechanical universe, with its strange new forms and the absolute perfection of its movement. In *Salomé*, one of his *Moralités légendaires*, for instance, it is with undeniable relish that Laforgue describes the observatory of the tetrarch Hérode-Archétypas, with its gigantic cupola. And at the end of this period there are stories by Jarry, such as *Les Gestes et opinions du docteur Faustroll* and *Le Surmâle*, that teem with scientific inventions. Similarly, another novel by Mauclair, *L'Orient vierge* of 1900, celebrates, long before Apollinaire in his *Calligrammes*, the beauty of modern machines devised for mechanized warfare and destruction. Finally, it should be noted that the last years of the nineteenth century saw the beginnings of science fiction, a genre that was not to reach its full flowering until the following century.

Drugs

Until the decadent era the fashion for drug taking had been restricted, as we have seen, to a few groups of writers and artists who, essentially out of curiosity, had investigated the effects of hashish. At the end of the Second Empire, despite the possible influence of Baudelaire's translations of Poe and De Quincey, it is reasonable to assume that the number of genuine addicts in France, and in Europe generally, was very small. All that was to change, however, during the last thirty years of the century, a period during which drug habituation became noticeably more widespread.

This increase in the use of drugs was due in the first place to accidental causes linked with the medical use of morphine, the effects of which are much more powerful than those of hashish or opium in its less refined forms. It was during the Franco-Prussian war of 1870 that morphine was first used on a large scale by German, then French, doctors as an anesthetic to alleviate the distress of severe wound cases or during amputations.

The war over, however, these doctors, still unaware of the risks involved, tended to continue prescribing the drug on a permanent basis to patients suffering from nervous disorders.[12] From then on, as a consequence of such ill-considered prescriptions, the number of addicts throughout Europe was to increase steadily.

A second factor, in France, was the conquest of Indochina during the early years of the Third Republic. The use of opium had been widespread in the far east for a long while. Opium consumption had increased greatly, both in India and China, as a result of the British influence there. Having established its ascendancy in these two areas, and made the opium trade into a state monopoly from which the Crown earned vast revenues, Britain had done everything it could to encourage use of the drug. The French policy in Indochina, although less systematic, was not very different. As a consequence, officers and privates in the French expeditionary forces stationed there often became habitual opium smokers, and then brought the practice back home with them. This tendency was particularly apparent among naval officers, who, having a great deal of time on their hands between ports of call, often became seriously addicted. As a result, more or less clandestine opium dens became progressively more common during the last decades of the century, first in the larger French ports, particularly Marseilles and Bordeaux, then later in the major inland cities. "The colonization of Indochina," Jean-Louis Brau writes in his *Histoire de la drogue*, "encouraged the spread of opium addiction throughout the civil service, the army, and the navy. Early in the [twentieth] century, opium dens in the country as a whole were numbered in their thousands; so much so that in July 1903 the *Petit Journal* supplement devoted a whole color page to the subject headlined: A New Vice. Opium Dens in France."[13]

The combination of these two factors—medical prescription of morphine in the form of injections, and the conquest of Indochina—led to widespread drug taking and lent the phenomenon a truly social dimension. There is abundant evidence of the extent and gravity of this addiction. The use of morphine had by then become frequent, even commonplace, among intellectual and society circles. "Despite early warnings," Brau goes on, "the success of morphine was enormous. Women from the highest society would hold gatherings at which they injected themselves with the drug.... Clubs for morphine addicts began opening more or less everywhere; jewelers were even selling their addict customers special gold-plated syringes in jeweled cases" (p. 84). These observations from a modern specialist in the field are confirmed by contemporary accounts. In 1925, recalling his youth as a medical student, Léon Daudet described vacations spent at Lamalou-les-Bains in those days as follows: "At

Lamalou, around 1885, the use of morphine was as common as that of Vichy water, and a constantly fresh topic of conversation."[14] The epidemic was to continue its spread, despite the alarm sounded by a number of doctors like Dr. Benjamin Ball, who in a pamphlet published in 1885 wrote: "Morphine taking is a vice that has become widespread today in western Europe, and especially France. . . . The abuse of morphine, which in the last few years has reached such proportions, is generally restricted to the upper classes. . . . But very recently this vice has tended to spread even to the workers."[15]

The reason why the habit spread so rapidly was simply that it had become fashionable, first in society circles, then in more and more sections of the population as a whole. In a recent work, E. Carassus has amassed copious evidence of this fashion. Two of his examples are an 1896 article in *Le Figaro* devoted to the phenomenon of "morphinomaniacs"; and an 1890 review in *Le Gaulois* containing this satirical portrait of a fashionable young writer: "25 years old. Poet. Has read *Les Paradis artificiels* and De Quincey. At work on what he believes is a masterpiece. A slim volume celebrating Divine and Subtile Morphine, with hair-raising illustrations, costly paper, de luxe binding, and zero thought content."[16] Moreover a great number of often superficial publications, sometimes combining token disapproval with evident relish for the subject, began to mushroom in the wake of the new fashion. In 1885, for instance, there was *La Comtesse Morphine,* a novel by a certain Marcel Mallat in which the author describes the gradual downfall of an aristocrat, the Countess Iva de Volnay, who after trying the drug as an antidote to boredom, when isolated in the country with only a sick husband for company, gradually becomes an addict and sinks steadily further down the social scale, ending up an old woman at twenty-five, in poverty, living by theft and consorting with criminals. There was also a work by Maurice Talmeyr, *Les Possédés de la morphine,* that claimed to be a meticulously researched account of morphine use among various sections of the Parisian population, and concluded with an interview with a nun employed in the narcotics service of a Parisian hospital.

This fashion does of course tie in with certain profound tendencies of the decadent movement. Given the decadent turn of mind, morphine clearly answers a double need: that of escaping by any possible means from a world where life can be nothing but unhappiness and tedium, and that of discovering new and hitherto unknown sensations by the use of artificial stimuli. Bourget himself had helped to create an identification of modern literature with the use of drugs when he defined the art of the modern poets as "a personal, superacute art, thirsting for the beyond, an art of hashish and opium."[17] And a certain number of writers, partly following the example of De Quincey and Baudelaire, did in fact celebrate the spiritual powers of drugs as abnormal stimuli for the imagination and as remedies for "spleen." Maupassant, who was addicted to ether for the last fifteen years of his life, described its effects in his *Rêve* of 1882:

I understood, I felt, I reasoned with extraordinary clarity, profundity, and power, with a joy, a strange intoxication born of this decoupling of my mental faculties. It was not the dreaming induced by hashish, nor even those slightly morbid visions excited by opium; it was a prodigious activity of the reason, a new way of seeing, judging, evaluating the things of life, and with a certainty, an absolute awareness that this way was the true one.

Jules Giraud devoted two articles, separated by ten years, to an analysis and celebration of the effects of hashish. In the first, he describes the hallucinations induced by the drug in these terms: "What can this simple mortal tell you to compare with the magnificent panoramas that unfold on the screen of your brain, depicting in ever deeper perspective those long arcades in which philosophers wander to and fro in contemplation, those endless avenues of densely leaved trees in whose shade one glimpses groups of laughing lovers at their play ... and those sounding vaults through which there rings the distant echo of a song that has been sung for centuries, and those hanging bridges that span the spaces between stars." In the second, he celebrates the power of hashish "to show the recesses of the unconscious, the laws of caprice, and the mysteries of man's visionary powers, illuminated as on a magic lantern screen."[18] Later, Albert de Pouvourville, an occultist as well as a user of drugs who published some of his writings under the pseudonym Matgioi, likewise asserted that opium has the capacity to reveal the profoundest secrets of the human soul. Like Claude Farrère later, or Louis Lalloy, whose famous *Livre de la fumée* celebrating the practice of opium smoking appeared in 1912, Pouvourville set himself up as a champion of drugs against the threats of intervention and repressive legislation increasingly made by the authorities, during the early nineteen-hundreds.

There were also certain writers in decadent circles who took up the use of drugs with varying degrees of seriousness. Apart from Guaïta and Dubus,[19] there was also the case of Adolphe Retté. Certain of the visionary texts in his *Thulé des brumes,* a collection of prose poems published in 1891, we know to have been written under the influence of hashish.[20] It is also probable that Laurent Tailhade used drugs on occasion. Certainly he published two works containing interesting descriptions and analyses of the effects produced by various drugs, as well as a brief history of the effects of drug taking on literary works, with particular reference to Poe and De Quincey. Here is a passage from his description of the opium user's world:

> In the inferno of these poisons of the intelligence, with [opium] we enter a still narrower circle: as in Dante's forest "the sun falls silent" amid the wan solitudes where the opium poppy sweats a lethe-bringing resin and with its mournful, languid petals rains down dreams or death upon the brows of those who fall into a hopeless sleep beneath its shade. This is the spellbound forest where, blue tinted as an autumn dawn, red as the blood of a slaughtered animal, mauve as the bruised eyes of women in love, the magic plant reveals to those with no more hope the silent gardens that are the vestibules to madness and to death. The stormy twilights coloring a fairyland prospect with unreal flames surround the victim with gold and purple-tinted gauzes, swathe him in clouds that turn to rainbows in the sun, like vapors from some kif or incense burner. But soon, those rainbow mists, those floating veils, curdle to a thicker drapery; the vapors that lately lent the charm of insubstantial outlines to existence now turn to an impenetrable wall, a dungeon, from which its prisoner can no longer find escape except at the cost of abominable tortures.[21]

Whatever the interest displayed in drugs by society and literary circles, however, whatever high hopes many young writers may have entertained that the use of such stimulants would enable them to attain additional imaginative powers, it is an undeniable fact that such use of drugs, far from leading to the appearance of masterpieces on the level of De Quincey's, in fact gave rise to very few genuinely literary texts, mostly of mediocre quality. From this entire body of writing, the only works that deserve salvaging from complete oblivion are probably one novel by Paul Bonnetain, L'Opium of 1886, and a collection of stories by Jules Boissière, Les Fumeurs d'opium, which appeared in 1896. The first of these two works, dedicated to the memory of De Quincey, quotations from whose work are used as epigraphs, tells the story of a young poet, Marcel Deschamps, author of two very decadent-sounding verse collections, Les Chimères and Les Angoisses, who grows weary of life in Paris and decides to go out to Indochina, where he is to perform some vague administrative function. Once there, his distaste for life now exacerbated by an ill-fated shipboard romance, he is naturally persuaded without much difficulty to turn to opium as a means of alleviating his distress. Once again we are given a description of the physical and moral decline that the drug brings in its wake; but certain of the opium dreams described during the descent, all evidently influenced by De Quincey's Confessions, are in fact very well constructed and presented. The following passage, describing a dream in the early stages of his addiction, is a good example:

> At first there was a great silence, an unmurmuring flood in which he floated, without making any effort to swim, drifting like flotsam. Blackness enveloped him utterly, pierced with sparks that soon clustered and flowed together.... He struggled, nausea rising within him, but the water clung, so repugnant that he raised his arms aloft and stretched his neck upward, his revolt past, leaving the water to flow on. It meandered around him with an oily and yet swift tranquility.... and soon the unending flight of that mysterious and unobtrusive current filled him with fear. It slid along without a sound; it was like a death hurtling through darkness. Marcel could see no banks, hear nothing, not even the sound of the current against his flesh. Slowly he felt himself becoming mad with the continuity of that flow, that immobility, that torture without pain.... Days, months, years passed, an eternity of dread.[22]

Les Fumeurs d'opium, Jules Boissière's book, is a collection of stories all set in recently colonized Indochina, with its exotic population, the constant presence of pirates, the mystery of its immense jungle. The theme of opium and the dreams it brings to the characters in some of the tales, as well as the consequences of addiction on their psychology, contribute an original coloring to the book's exoticism.

Although drugs themselves did not directly provoke the appearance of any great literary work in late-nineteenth-century France, the favor in which they were held, and the aura of seduction that surrounded them, were nevertheless indicative of that fundamental need in decadent literature to venture ever further in the quest for new sensations and unexplored pleasures, to follow in the footsteps of the great poets and visionaries who had appeared since the romantic era, and to push the human imagination to its furthest possible limits. This examination of the fashion for drugs thus leads us on quite logically to investigate the subject of oneiric writing generally, of which drug-induced dream narratives constitute only one specific category. For the prime motive behind this interest in drugs, there can be no doubt, was the more general decadent yearning for escape into any dreamworld.

Dreams

During the last twenty years of the nineteenth century, positivist psychophysiological research into mental illness, hallucinations, and all the phenomena of marginal or morbid psychology con-

tinued, as we have seen, amid increasing public interest. Within this research as a whole, the work on dreams still aroused the same lively
interest as it had in the past, and was if anything augmented by the
publication of work by foreign specialists in the field, particularly those by
certain German researchers.[23] Delboeuf, a French specialist, provided a
survey of all such recent work in a series of articles that appeared in the
Revue philosophique during 1879 and 1880.[24] In France itself, on the
psychiatric side, there was also P.-Max Simon, a doctor based in a hospital outside Lyons, who in 1882 published a work entitled *Le Monde des
rêves,* in which one still finds the traditional identification of dream, hallucination, and mental illness; but in addition Simon was particularly
interested in the origin of dream images, in the nature of mental associations, and in the connection between dreams and physiological states.[25]
On the philosophical front, in 1883 there came a French translation of the
Englishman James Sully's *Illusions of the Senses and the Mind,* which
contained many interesting and often original analyses. The author puts
much more emphasis than his predecessors, for example, on the internal
coherence of dream scenarios, thereby anticipating later theories. In
Sully's view, a dream is a composite structure made up of many illusions
contributed by the various senses. Yet this composite structure appears in
some way or another to fuse into a single scene or total sequence of events
which, even though it may appear disjointed or absurd from the waking
standpoint, nevertheless constitutes a coherent whole for the dreamer's
inner vision, and possesses a certain degree of artistic unity. This unity of
the dream scenario is achieved, in Sully's view, by the affective element
present in dreams, and is identical with the basic inspiration of lyric
poetry. Thus, however timidly, we find the notion emerging that dreams
can possess an esthetic dimension.

The number of works on the subject published by physicians, psychiatrists, or psychologists, was to continue increasing until the end of the
century. Even a brief list indicates the intense ferment of ideas surrounding the problem of sleep and dreams during this pre-Freudian period.[26]
Particular mention deserves to be made, however, of the work by Dr. Paul
Chabeneix referred to earlier, *De l'Inconscient chez les artistes, les savants et les écrivains.* In it the author enlarges upon his belief that unconscious processes play an important role in the discoveries or creations of
scientists and artists. He writes, for example, that "from an embryonic
thought right up to the most exciting of discoveries, without forgetting the
wildest images of a disordered imagination, dreams comprehend everything. They are present in every mysterious sabbath orgy, every beatific
vision of paradise. They continue the sleeper's labors, reprocess his preoccupations, turn back to his past, which they distort capriciously, or take

flight into his future."[27] Armed with this conviction, he set about questioning a number of contemporary thinkers and writers about their dream lives and received forty-three replies, some of which, recorded in his book, are not without interest, not only intrinsically, but also because they provide proof, as far as the writers are concerned—those who replied include Rachilde, Retté, and Mauclair—of how topical the question of dreaming and the unconscious was in literary circles at the time. Indeed, one can almost speak of a fashion for dreams in such circles, and a fashion closely linked with the literary ideal of the whole decadent era. For the dream had become the symbol of that escape from the trivialities of the real world that the decadent sensibility yearned for above all else, and we have abundant evidence that it had become one of the period's vogue words. "Dream world, dream world!" we read in Les Déliquescences, that pastiche of decadence published in 1885, "let us take ship to a dream world..."[28] Certain writers, moreover, reminiscing later about this period, in which they had been either participants or observers, refer explicitly to the existence of this fashion. In his preface to L'Art en silence, for example, a collection of critical essays that appeared in 1901, Mauclair notes that "our epoch went as far as it is possible to go along the road of imaginative fantasy worlds, emotional reveries, the vanity of the literary self, and the most ingenious ways of escaping from life."[29] Twenty years later still, he was to refer ironically to what he called "the knights of mist and dreams," observing that "dreams were their cocaine."[30] At the time of the fiftieth anniversary of symbolism, in 1936, Dujardin too was to confess that "on the pretext of attaining our so-called higher reality, we plunged as deep as we could into unreality."[31]

And indeed, if we examine the writings of the decadent period itself, we find allusions to dreams recurring constantly. Poictevin's prose collection of 1884 was actually entitled Songes.[32] In A Rebours, that same year, Des Esseintes praises Gustave Moreau as "the visionary who could abstract himself sufficiently from the world to see the cruel visions and fantastic apotheoses of other ages glow resplendent in the heart of modern Paris," and finds in Redon "the terror of our dreams" (p. 90). In his solitude and melancholy "spleen" he himself experiences "a lethargy haunted by vague daydreams," and watches "a procession of dreams that he experienced passively, without even attempting to escape from them" (p. 108). Similarly, Mallarmé was to display an awareness of and interest in the phenomena of our dream life on several occasions. He wrote of "the antagonism of the dream in man to the fatalities dispensed by misfortune in his life."[33] Questioned by a physician, he defined the poet as a man who "is literally a waking dreamer."[34] In one of his letters he wrote: "You will observe my lack of hesitation in hurling myself into the abyss of the dream that appeared, when I could have remained in the old gardens, among ordinary and reassuring flowers."[35] And finally, he jokingly imagined the formation of a sort of dreamers' club in Paris: "How far civilization is from providing the pleasures attributable to that state! One cannot but be astonished, for example, that an association of dreamers, there resident, does not exist in every large city, so as to support a daily paper that will record events in the light proper to dreams."[36]

If we turn to the verse collections published from 1884 or 1885 on, we find the word, or its synonyms, recurring constantly almost like an underlying pulse. Gustave Kahn's *Palais nomades* of 1887 is typical of many other such examples. In it the poet expresses a wish

> On the soft divans of chance
> To rule his dreams like a Caesar.[37]

Addressing himself, he exclaims: "Oh my half-open dream, rock me toward your mouth" (p. 56); he talks of a "dream so gray" (p. 70), longs to "let his dream wander in the woods" (p. 93). He aspires to

> Sleep as one stretches out wounded
> As one glides away toward mirages
> The mirages of dreams, mirages without hope,
> To sleep beyond the real . . .   [P. 120]

or he confesses: "In the madness of a waking dream my senses walk, in the lethargic logic of an evil waking dream my senses have set sail for the unknown" (p. 122). In Maeterlinck's *Serres chaudes* of 1889, too, one finds expressions such as "dreams' purple snakes" (*Offrande obscure*), "my packs of hunting dreams" (*Chasses lasses*), "the nighttime tedium of dreams" (*Oraison nocturne*), "the voice speaking in my sleep" (*Ronde d'ennui*), "the rising waters of my dreams" (*Reflets*).

The more one becomes aware of the extraordinary inflation to which the concept of the dream was subjected at this period, the more one begins to suspect that it had ceased to have any precise meaning, that "dream" had become merely a synonym for escape from the real. If we attempt to pin down the exact intellectual or affective content it denoted for writers of the time, we do in fact find that it symbolized first and foremost precisely such a flight from everyday reality. That is the meaning with which Bourget endows it, for example, in his 1886 essay on Amiel, when he writes with reference to Des Esseintes:

> This bizarre character is very much a close relation to those
> who write . . . semi-Catholic verses and prose made up en-
> tirely of indefinable nuances, those who proclaim them-
> selves to be followers of Baudelaire or decadents, and who

appear to belong to no real group. It is clear that they have jettisoned any concern to render the truth of life in their art; they have turned their faces to the world of dreams, and sensation for them becomes a tool of fantasy.[38]

Similarly, in an article that appeared in *L'Ermitage* on 15 April 1892, the critic Firmin Roz observes that among contemporary poets the synthesis between "an art of extremes" and "the demands of anxiety-ridden thought" was achieved "outside of life, in dreams, in legends."[39] Slightly later, Retté observed that the symbolists were criticized for "being dreamers more concerned with refinements of form and playing with strange fantasies than with paying attention to the lives and doings of their contemporaries."[40] The world of dreams is indeed the exact opposite both of the reality that the naturalist writers had deliberately restricted themselves to depicting, a visible, concrete, and usually either monotonous or appalling reality, and of the positivist spirit that had been dominating not only scientific research but also artistic creation for the past few decades. The art critic Paul Leprieur was making just this point when he wrote with reference to Gustave Moreau: "Now our positivist and skeptical generation, one so inculcated with a love for facts it has taken realism to excess, and is still doing so, finds itself tormented with regret for things now gone, for a destroyed faith, for lost emotion (for one tires of everything except of feeling) and is now returning, by every possible means, to the dream."[41]

Dreams are also, for certain writers of the time, the sensed presence, beyond the ephemeral world of appearances, of a higher reality, either metaphysical or religious in nature. In this sense, the dream was to be identified with the ideal, even with mysticism, and this was precisely the criticism leveled at young poets by a champion of the naturalists: "Nevertheless, they are all Renées, all rococo aristocrats who refuse to take up their picks and help us in the labors of the age, followers of the absolute, or metaphysics and Christian revelations, of dreams in a word."[42] With Mallarmé and his disciples, who constituted the intellectual wing of the decadent movement, dreams were to be the means, or rather one of the means, of divining that higher and ideal reality whose existence was guaranteed by the theory of symbols. More generally, the dream, as opposed to the external, concrete, palpable world, was to be the domain of man's inner life, of subjective reality. Thus Henri de Régnier was to write in the prologue to his collection *Sites* of his "inner dream,"[43] and the critic Poizat was later to define symbolism in these terms: "It was above all the entry of the dream into literature, it was the turning of man's gaze from the outside to the inside, the contemplation of things as they are reflected within us, as in some still pool."[44] To speak of dreams in this sense is thus to summarize the entire esthetic, intellectual, and affective ideal of the literary generation of 1880.

However, if we may leave aside for the moment this use of the term "dream" as a kind of idealist signpost or guiding light, and examine the literature of that time for evidence of specifically oneiric experiences, we do find that the tide of interest in dreams proper, which had begun to flow as early as the romantic era, was still by no means on the ebb. Quite the contrary, in fact, for there were many writers in the decadent period who published accounts of dreams, either in isolated form or integrated into larger works. Chapter 8 of *A Rebours* contains an account of the nightmare Des Esseintes experiences after having spent some time with strange plants of monstrous form and color. In the course of the dream he is pursued by the horrible specter of syphilis. In *Lutèce* that same year, 1884, Moréas published a piece called *Rêve d'absinthe*, in which he recounts the visions that take over the mind of an "alcoholic and neurotic" writer, Jacques Speers, after he has allowed himself to down too many glasses of the "green fairy."[45] It was also in 1884 that Francis Poictevin published the collection of prose pieces *Songes*, to which I referred earlier. It is true, however, that despite his prefatory statement that "convinced as Shakespeare was that we are such stuff as dreams are made on, I decided to publish these," the work turns out to be less a series of dream narratives than a sequence of impressionist notes evoking the life of a couple. The following year, it was in the form of a dream, and under the title *Cauchemar*, that Huysmans published his review of a new set of Odilon Redon lithographs collectively entitled *Hommage à Goya*, and used each of the plates as a point of departure for fantastic visions of his own.[46]

En rade, published in *La Revue indépendante* during 1886 and 1887, contains three dream narratives. The first, set in a vast and luxurious palace, depicts the presentation of a young girl to a potentate, and ends with an episode of great sensuality; the second recounts an imaginary visit to the moon; the third, and by far the most detailed, prefigures surrealist oneirism in the bizarreness of its images. It was also at this time that Maupassant published *La Nuit, cauchemar*. The narrator of this story, returning to the center of Paris on foot after a nocturnal ramble through the Bois de Boulogne, realizes with growing panic that the city around him is totally silent, deserted, and dead, so that he soon believes he must be the sole survivor of some mysterious catastrophe that has annihilated the rest of mankind. This piece, which is constructed in accordance with the technique usually employed for fantastic tales, whereby one starts from the entirely natural and gradually moves away from it into unreality, provides a particularly successful example of a fusion between dream narrative and tale of fantasy. It also highlights the increasing role played by the theme of the city in the development of oneirism at the time. It was at about this time, for instance, that Verlaine published a piece in *Le Décadent* recording some of his dreams: walks through Paris; a visit to the British Embassy, which he found occupied by strange guards; visits to cemeteries accompanied by his father. Here again we find that the dominant element is the urban setting, which was to become even more predominant during the years that followed:

> I often see Paris. Never as it is. It is an alien city, absurd, and looking always different. I surround it with a narrow and deep banked river between two lines of trees of some sort. Red roofs glisten between very green foliage. It is heavy summer weather, with big, extremely dark clouds, as in the skies of ancient landscapes . . .

We even find a first sketch of the dream Paris, the spellbound city that was to emerge fully in the surrealist period, and, in particular, a description of one of those glazed arcades so dear to Breton and Aragon later on:

> The real Paris can sometimes intervene in these wanderings, but in every case some modifications of my own, some innocent municipal planning on my part, manage to introduce an element of the bizarre and unexpected. Opposite the Bonne-Nouvelle store, for instance, between the boulevard of that name and a street that opens into it, I install a glass-roofed arcade, which consequently makes a right angle. This gallery is very fine, wide and full of commercial bustle, incomparably superior to anything of the kind that exists in reality.[47]

Similarly, in 1887 Paul Hervieu published a strange novel called *L'Inconnu*. Already, in earlier collections of stories, particularly in *Les Yeux verts et les yeux bleus* of the previous year, he had used the theme of madness that was to form the central core of *L'Inconnu,* and also that of dreams. *L'Inconnu* itself consists for the most part of a diary kept by a madman, whose logical and closely reasoned mania takes the form of placing other people in specific situations with the purpose of causing them to adopt particular facial expressions. Above all, however, the plot of the book, consisting of various loosely connected episodes in the diarist's life before his hospitalization, provides the opportunity to narrate events experienced by the madman in a state that wavers between semilucid hallucination, waking dream, and dreaming proper. Thus chapter 4, for instance, which undoubtedly contains echoes of Gérard de Nerval, describes a kind of dream journey through deserted regions, then up to vast mountains, where the narrator encounters an old man—we discover later that he is in fact Adam, and that the journey was one into time past—who tells the story of his life, shows the madman the numberless graves of his offspring, and causes the thousands of generations that have succeeded him to pass before them both in a long procession.[48] Another chapter evokes an opera ball seen through the distortions of the narrator's own hallucinations, which have been exacerbated further by his intake of alcohol, so that the ball is transformed into a bizarre and disturbing phantasmagoria. The novel's final section consists of a commentary on the diary by its editor, a journalist who has been to interview the madman in his asylum and who has come to wonder just how much in his story is dream and how much reality. In other words, L'Inconnu provides us with an example of the way in which oneiric inspiration was sometimes reinforced at this time with material drawn from mental pathology. Undoubtedly influenced by a Hoffmannesque sense of fantasy exacerbated by alcohol, by Poe's analyses of the underlying logic of madness, and by the recent work of psychiatric researchers, the book as a whole consistently presents events as experienced by a hallucinating consciousness whose distorted perceptions take us into a universe identical in many respects to that of dreams.

Further proof of the fashion that existed at this time for dream narratives is provided by a piece published in the May 1887 issue of La Revue indépendante, written by a certain Maurice de Fleury and entitled Hydrargyre. This text, dedicated to Odilon Redon, uses a quotation from Baudelaire's Rêve parisien as an epigraph. The leading character, having pursued his wife through the streets of Paris by night, finds himself being carried along with her on an interminable journey down a Seine that has been transformed into an immense river of mercury:

> On a level with his eyes, like a giant bed, the river stretched out to the horizon, flat, without a ripple, smoother than a mirror, sliding with the smooth unvarying flow of lava; here and there, patches seemed to be powdered with dust, but all the rest, gleaming blue as a new steel blade, glittered with a cold purity and the most absolute clarity; on either side, the black steeps of gigantic embankments, in the center, the disk of the moon, the moon at full . . .

After what seems to the dreamer a journey of infinite duration, the river flows out into an apocalyptic landscape, a lunar landscape suggesting the end of the world or the triumph of some purely mineral form of life:

> Now grayish clouds invaded the sky, casting shadows on the liquid steel surface. A leaden dawn was tarnishing a narrow band of sky over on the horizon: it was a dismal first

light, a daybreak that one sensed to be definitive, without hope that any sun might ever rise; it revealed a distant bend in the river, and on the right bank, silhouetted without perspective against a backdrop of leaden gleams, there appeared strange monuments, burnt out, fantastic in their outlines: frail colonnades sheared off obliquely, facades of decrepit barrack blocks, crumbling at their corners, with thousands of gaping window frames, their friable stone dissolving into slowly trickling screes beneath a deluge of corrosive rain.

Meanwhile, following his *Songes,* Francis Poictevin went on to produce further texts in which the oneiric inspiration was to become even more evident. 1888 saw the appearance of *Paysages* and *Derniers Songes,* followed by *Double* in 1889. These works, varied in their inspiration, combine personal confessions, accounts of travels, impressionist sketches, and also a series of dream narratives: a nightmare in which the narrator is pursued around his apartment by a monstrous bird; a claustrophobia dream; and a labyrinth dream. *Double* ends, in fact, with a genuine dream diary, in which there is an evident concern to recreate the original dream experience as faithfully as literary transcription will allow, and in this respect these pieces, whose literary quality is on occasion slight, acquire a distinctly modern accent.

This fashion for dreams, which began in about 1884, was to continue throughout the last decade of the century. 1891 saw the appearance of Retté's *Thulé des brumes,* in which oneiric inspiration plays a major role: "For certain complex souls of our day," the author writes in his preface, "there are days when life becomes so hostile, its atmosphere so suffocating, that they plunge wildly into the refuge afforded by dreams. Then, sometimes for months on end, the soul lives an abnormal and exaggerated existence, ideas become exacerbated and distorted, feelings take on a fearful intensity." Retté's collection of pieces, composite and chaotic, using the humdrum daily life of a Parisian man addicted to long walks or sitting in cafés as its background, describes a series of visions or hallucinations possibly stimulated by hashish. Beyond the bizarre refinements of his decadent style, many influences can be detected at work: sometimes Shakespearian or Hoffmannesque fantasy, sometimes emotions and a lyrical style inherited from Nerval.[49] In addition, the work abounds in asides during which the author expresses his faith in oneiric imagination, and the positive thirst for dreams that spurs him on. The description of the legendary island of Thule that occurs in the book is used by the author as an opportunity to gather together, as Wilde had done some years earlier, a number of themes drawn from the imaginative world of myth:

> Parsifal worships the Holy Grail there; the melancholy
> Jaques confides his bitterness to the forest trees of Arden,
> and mocks Oberon's horn as it implores the furious Titania;
> Ligeia initiates the student Nathanael into metaphysics;
> leaning on an ivy-twined balustrade, Melusina tears the pet-
> als from camellias, and Astolpho, dismounted from his hip-
> pogriff, collects them with devotion; Sylvia and Aurelia sit
> at the Round Table attentive to an oracle that is being pro-
> nounced by Merlin the great wizard . . . [P. 92]

This work, which caused a sensation in literary circles on its first appearance,[50] was commented on some years later by the author himself in the
following terms: "I wanted to write a work that took place entirely in a
dreamworld, without life playing any role other than as a sort of
springboard that would send me winging toward unknown stars."[51]

In that same year, there also appeared a series of dream pieces by a
certain Robert Scheffer under the title *Sommeil*. As well as descriptions of
visual hallucinations, it includes a number of dream narratives in which
the theme of the city reappears:

> A dead city emerged slowly from the depths of the abyss. It
> was vast in extent, since I wandered through it, as it seemed
> to me, for days on end, without ever passing the same spot
> twice. But an eternal night weighed down on it; the strings
> of perpetually lighted lamps that wound along the embank-
> ments, the arches of the bridges, and the long, long, lifeless
> streets, glittered without giving light. There were tangles of
> steep winding alleyways flanked by towering, gloomy
> houses with leaning walls, pierced by narrow windows; here
> and there, a lantern swung on a chain above the pavement.
> By its wan gleam I could just make out the swaying outline
> of dark pointed roofs, and above them, on occasion, the
> squat dome of a church.[52]

At the same period one also finds many dream narratives contained
within longer fictional works: in Pierre Loti's *Le Livre de la pitié et de la
mort*, which contains a chapter entitled *Pays sans nom* that describes a
flat and deserted landscape seen in a dream; in Camille Mauclair's
Couronne de clarté of 1894; in *L'Aphrodite* by Pierre Louys, in which the
first chapter of book 4 describes the dream of Demetrios; in Gustave
Kahn's *Le conte de l'or et du silence;* and in all of Jarry's work, in which,
with *Les Jours et les nuits* of 1897, the world of dreams, under the specific
influence of De Quincey, makes ever greater incursions into the central
character's real life, so that it eventually takes over his entire existence.
The very frequency of these references is abundant proof that dreams

continued to occupy a favored position in the field of literary inspiration right up until the end of the decadent era.

Simultaneously, we find certain writers beginning to express a clearly stated intention to remove the barrier between dream and reality altogether, by the simple expedient of asserting the identity of the two states. Since, according to the doctrine of subjective idealism, the world is never anything but my idea or representation of it, and since, this being so, it is impossible to discriminate absolutely between hallucinations and dreams, the artist, repelled by the real, will make it his business to undertake a conscious modification of his experience by allowing equal value to real and imaginary worlds that are in any case indistinguishable. Such is the doctrine professed, with greater or lesser degrees of lucidity and daring, by a number of young writers all influenced by Villiers de l'Isle-Adam, such as Rémy de Gourmont, Adolphe Retté, and Camille Mauclair. It is this doctrine, albeit expressed in a somewhat obscure and abstract form, that we find propounded by Gourmont in his *Sixtine* of 1890. Totally disillusioned by reality, d'Entragues finds an escape hatch in the exercise of his imaginary powers. Since "ordinary sensation is no more than a true hallucination" (p. 53), since "the real is what one believes it to be" (p. 80), and since "the only reality is thought,"[53] one must deny the difference between dreams and reality and intervene consciously in one's perceptions by using one's imagination as a "developer." Moreover Gourmont continually restated this rejection of any differentiation between dream and reality in later works. In the story *Le Fantôme* of 1893, the two chief characters, Damas and Hyacinthe, exchange the following lines: "And what difference do you see between the imaginary and the real?—Subjectively, none, Hyacinthe, as you well know."[54] In the *Histoires magiques* of 1894 we find a similar assertion: "Sleep I know, but the unconscious is a stranger to me. My dreams are so much the continuation of my evening thoughts, and in the morning I connect my dreams so logically to the new day's thoughts, that I cannot remember having ceased enjoying full intellectual clarity, even for an hour, during the past thirty years" (*Sur le seuil*). In *Le Château singulier*, the mistress of the château, Princesse Elade, asks the man who has arrived in search of her: "How do you manage to distinguish dream from reality, Vitalis? I dream so vividly that there is no gap between my dreams and my waking life—and I find a certain difficulty in knowing if my sensations are wise or foolish. Being loved pleases me, whether it is a dream or whether it is reality."[55]

Until his conversion early in the next century, Retté likewise continued to assert his determination to identify dream with reality. In the preface to *Thulé des brumes* he claims that the work was inspired by this passage from Poe's *Berenice*, which he presents as a kind of personal artistic manifesto: "The realities of the world affected me as visions, and as visions only, while the wild ideas from the land of dreams became, in turn, not the material of my every-day existence, but in very deed that existence utterly and solely." In the issue of *Hommes d'aujourd'hui* devoted to him in 1894, his esthetic stance was summarized as follows: "He views things in accordance with a particular vision, summed up by his favorite aphorism: Life is a shadow play. His esthetic he has himself often described as being based on the phrase: Art is life seen in a dream."[56] Later, in his *Mémoires de Diogène* of 1903, he was still referring to "this phantasmagoria that many eccentric individuals take to be reality,"[57] and the chief character, after experiencing a dream, cries: "Ouf, I said, wiping my brow, it was just a nightmare—at least I hope it was, for my dreams have taken over my existence to such an extent, ever since my encounter with that strange madwoman, that I can no longer really tell where they begin and where they end" (p. 92).

Camille Mauclair, before the reaction against decadent oneirism that began in 1898 with his two novels *Le Soleil des morts* and *L'Ennemie des rêves*, had also celebrated the magic power of dreams, and indeed used the same sentence from Poe already quoted by Retté as an epigraph for his collection of stories *Les Clefs d'or*. In his letter to Dr. Chabaneix, in *De l'Inconscient chez les artistes, les savants et les écrivains*, he also stressed the importance of dreams in the genesis of his own artistic creation: "I make no distinction between sleeping and waking. I can say that, not only ideas and plans for books, but even their slightest metaphors, are dictated to me in a continual dream."

Thus there is clear evidence that a whole literary generation, the generation that came to the forefront of the French literary scene during the last fifteen years of the nineteenth century, thirsty for escape from reality, assigned a major role in their work to the notion of the artificial that Baudelaire had championed twenty years earlier. Fascination for the modern city, contemplation of an urban landscape metamorphosed by darkness or fog and transmuted by the imagination, use of drugs or abandonment to dreams, the constant factor with these writers was always the desire for a compensatory world that would enable them to bear the ugliness of the real one. The particular use they made of dreams, the faith they placed in their oneiric imaginations, and their determination to look upon reality and their dream lives as "communicating vessels," to employ André Breton's later formulation, make them the essential intermediaries between the romantic oneiric imagination and the flowering of dream literature that was to occur thirty years later with surrealism.

7 THE WORLD
OF LEGEND

MYTHICAL AND LEGENDARY STORIES, WHETHER OF LEARNED OR FOLK origin, handed down by an immemorial oral tradition and gradually recorded by historians whose curiosity was aroused by the poetic intensity they often enshrine, have served throughout the ages as a springboard for the artistic imagination. Writers and poets have constantly turned to such imaginary stories, integrated within a national cultural tradition, to provide them with a framework whose flexibility would enable them to express their personal ideas or images beneath the veil of fiction. It is thus only to be expected that the writers of the decadent generation, thirsting as they did for escape from everyday life, would make liberal use of such legends. And it is in fact the case that no period in the history of French literature has witnessed such a ferment of legendary and mythic references.

This intensive use of legends was fostered by the work of certain more or less specialized folklore experts, some learned but some merely amateurs curious about local traditions, in collecting and recording the various local legends to be found throughout the country. This collecting work continued throughout the last decades of the nineteenth century, as is made clear by the publication of several collections of regional legends: Alsatian legends published in 1884;[1] legends of Savoy collected in 1888 by Charles Buet, a friend of Barbey d'Aurevilly;[2] legends of the Ile-de-France.[3] This work then took on a more systematic and scientific aspect with the launching of a magazine specifically aimed at gathering together and disseminating the researches of such folklore specialists. The first numbers of this publication, entitled *La Tradition,* appeared in 1887.[4] In addition, we also find works aimed at a much wider public, such as Edouard Schuré's *Les Grandes Légendes de France* of 1892, for example.

However, this flowering of the legend in literature also owed a great deal to the existence of a considerable literary and artistic tradition gradually developed throughout the nineteenth century. We should remember, for example, that Victor Hugo, in his *La Légende des siècles,* had attempted to incorporate the whole of human history into his historical and philosophical meditations, and that, in order to illustrate the phases of what he saw as the progressive ascent of the human spirit, he had made use of many legends or myths drawn from the Bible, from Greco-Roman mythology, and from Nordic legend. Contemporaneously, the Parnassians also drew abundantly for their inspiration on Greek or far eastern myths, both for their purely decorative value and as a means of escape from the present. Whereas Leconte de Lisle's *Poèmes antiques* drew its material from Greek myths, his *Poèmes barbares* of 1862 exploited legends from much farther afield, Hindu, Jewish, Egyptian, Scandinavian, and even Polynesian legend. In the same way, after his *Prométhée délivré* of 1842, Louis Ménard had embarked on a passionate investigation of ancient religious myths, which were later to inspire not only his *Poèmes* of 1855 but also that breviary for addicts of ancient civilizations, the *Rêveries d'un païen mystique* of 1876. In short, the whole Parnassian movement, whose influence continued to bear fruit throughout the last third of the century, aroused intense curiosity about ancient Mediterranean or far eastern civilizations with their rich storehouse of recorded myths and legends. The positivist emphasis on a historical understanding of the world, the religious eclecticism of Renan, with his studies of Semitic civilizations in particular, and the vast agglomeration of myths and beliefs embodied in *La Tentation de saint Antoine,* also combined to further this trend. As a result, the French literary world's knowledge and curiosity were gradually extended beyond the western tradition proper, and became increasingly familiar with new mythical complexes deriving from civilizations very distant from it in both time and space.

Lastly, one must also take into account the ever-increasing influence of Wagner, an influence that was to create a fashion, after the rediscovery of his work in France in about 1885,[5] not for mainly Mediterranean or oriental legends as formerly, but for western ones: German in *Die Meistersinger, Tannhäuser,* and *The Ring,* Nordic in *The Flying Dutchman,* Celtic in *Lohengrin, Tristan and Isolde,* and *Parsifal.* Indeed, one might say that the originality of the legendary material in decadent literature is constituted in part by the fact that, following Wagner, the mythologies employed tend to have a much more Nordic coloration, as opposed to the more sunlit southern myths that preoccupied the previous generation. It is not hard to understand why the decadent imagination, with its predilection for mists and mystery, its cultivation of the vague and suggestive rather than the descriptive or picturesque, should find itself in closer harmony with the atmosphere of Nordic legends.

If the world of legend enjoyed such prestige in the literature of this time it was because, on more than one count, it echoed the deepest desires of the fin-de-siècle soul. First, such legendary stories, because they are always located in a distant or long-past world, at once unreal and vague, satisfied the desire for escape experienced so intensely by the collective conscience of the age. The very nature of myths and legendary stories, the frequent elements of improbability they contain, strengthened still further this imaginary dimension so necessary to artists and a public by then weary of excessively dismal depictions of everyday life. Wagner himself, in his *Letter on Music*, had already observed that legend "helps to plunge the spirit into that dream state which swiftly enables it to achieve complete clairvoyance."[6] Faced with the limitations of the positivist and realist conception of the world, the advocates of legend openly asserted the human truth that lay concealed in the stories, a truth that made the question of their historical accuracy quite irrelevant. Such was the attitude adopted on several occasions by Gustave Kahn, for example, a writer who was himself to make copious use of the world of legend. Thus in his *Les Palais nomades*, which appeared in 1887, he asserts that legends from the past possess meaning or value by the very fact that human concerns have remained unchanged over the centuries: "And since all things are alike, all the suns of the years, all the sufferings of the days, listen to the soul of legend that floats and murmurs all about us."[7] Several years later, in his *Conte de l'or et du silence*, he wrote in the same vein:

> Beings, forms, appearances, tales, they are all one. If they never lived, or if someone has thrown around their shoulders the shining mantle of a fancied glamour, what does it matter? The poet who carries these myths and fables in his brain, the race that bears them in its womb, did not invent a single thing that is not possible.[8]

Schuré too, in the preface to his *Grandes Légendes de la France,* invoked the Wagnerian notion that legends are the most faithful expression we have of the soul of the people that conceived them:

> Legend, the lucid dream of a people's soul, is that people's direct manifestation, its living revelation. Like a second and deeper consciousness, it reflects the future in the past. Fantastic figures appear in its magic mirror and speak of those truths that exist outside time.... Until the present, legend among us has been little more than an object of erudite curiosity or mere fancy. Its importance from the standpoint of philosophy and history, or that of individual or transcendent psychology, has not yet been clearly revealed. Romanticism treated legends merely as themes to stimulate the imagination. Since then, we have come to understand

that they are poetry itself, in its most essential form, manifesting itself in an intuitive state of the soul that we term the unconscious, and that sometimes resembles a higher consciousness.[9]

More particularly, for the most intellectual group within the decadent movement—the symbolist poets who were disciples of Mallarmé and who believed, in accordance with the theory of analogy and correspondence, that every material reality possesses a meaning only insofar as it is perceived as the visible counterpart of a spiritual truth—legend became the poet's principal tool in his attempt to capture the presence of these spiritual realities beyond the changing forms of the tangible world. In consequence, most writers working within the symbolist ambit were naturally led to exploit legend in a mythical way: that is to say, to view the succession of anecdotes and events comprised within any legend as a transposition into the concrete and temporal mode of an abstract and nontemporal intellectual message. Such, at all events, was the conception of symbolism that Moréas developed in his celebrated *Manifeste* of 1886, when he defined the objectives of the new poetic school:

> To clothe the idea with a perceptible form which, nevertheless, will not be an end in itself but, while serving to express the idea, will remain subservient. The idea, in its turn, must not allow itself to be stripped of the sumptuous mantle provided by external analogies; for the essential nature of symbolist art consists in never going as far as the conception of the idea in itself. Thus, in this art, the pictures provided by nature, the actions of men, all concrete phenomena, cannot manifest themselves as themselves: they are perceptible appearances intended to represent their esoteric affinities with primordial ideas.[10]

This being so, it is not surprising that, for many witnesses of literary developments at that time, whether external observers or actual participants in the various avant-garde movements, the new literature, and in particular symbolist poetry, was characterized first and foremost by the universal use of legendary themes. In an article printed by *L'Ermitage* in 1894, the writer Henri Mazel, using the pseudonym Saint-Antoine, after having attempted to clarify the meaning of the term symbolism, and carefully demarcated the notions of myth, legend, allegory, and symbol, concluded:

> Ultimately, therefore, symbolism in the correct sense of the term is a literary form characterized by the frequency of works with a double meaning, which is to say mythical and

allegorical works. In a more general sense, this was a period
when, in reaction against a previous period preoccupied
with detail and realism, art plunged back toward the subject
matter of dreams and legend, and attempted to give its
works a more remote meaning by drawing its inspiration
from philosophic and religious ideas.[11]

Similarly, Pierre Quillard declared that in modern poetry the idea had to
be expressed "behind the veil of symbolic legends, which give it, people
believe, a universal value, outside of space and time."[12] At the very end
of the century, the journalist A. Ségard defined the trends prevailing in
literature in terms of the following characteristics: "cerebral excitation, a
taste for wild dreams, passionate predilection for legend and the fantastic."[13] The following year, attempting to sum up the symbolist experience
of which he had been a part, Camille Mauclair wrote: "Use of allegory
and metrical reform, those were the two symbolist postulates."[14]

However, when we glance through the actual literature produced at this
period, there is no avoiding the fact that this desire to exploit the literary
riches afforded by legends and myths suffered in the event from a double
and simultaneous degradation: on the one hand, myth and symbol were
often reduced to soulless allegory; and on the other, the repeated exploitation of the same legendary themes gradually became an ever more
monotonous commonplace, which resulted eventually in the constant use
of stereotyped imagery devoid of both life and any real meaning. Yet most
theoreticians of poetic symbolism had taken the greatest care to make a
distinction between myth or legend on the one hand and allegory on the
other. Although the myth does contain a spiritual meaning of a philosophic, moral or esthetic nature—as with the great Platonic myths, for
example—in order to retain its power of poetic suggestion and its literary
beauty it must also remain fundamentally ambiguous, not immediately
and clearly reducible to an inarguable and single intellectual content. A
narrative of "open-ended" meaning, it must retain an inalienable element
of obscurity and vagueness, that element which is also preserved, beyond
all possible analysis or exegesis, by any work of art. Far from being the
conscious expression of an abstract idea, it must appear primarily as a
venture deeply engaged in the perceptible and concrete world. These are
certainly the requirements formulated by Saint-Antoine in the article
mentioned earlier, when he distinguished between myth and allegory:

> The myth finds its end in itself, whereas the allegory im-
> poses an outside aim on itself. The myth addresses itself to
> the soul more than to the intelligence, it moves rather than
> persuades, eludes us instead of awakening our curiosity; it
> arises as it were spontaneously under the influence of the

religious spirit. The allegory, on the contrary, is always di-
dactic; its double meaning is merely a veil of coquetry; it is
not spontaneous but thought out and willed, the daughter of
reasoning not of inspiration, addressing itself to thought
more than to feeling.[15]

Similarly, Henri de Régnier asserted that the symbol, in order to remain
distinct from allegory, must entail "a certain inevitable obscurity."[16] In
like vein, Albert Mockel described allegorical analogy as "artificial and
extrinsic," as opposed to the "natural and intrinsic" analogy of the symbol. In Maeterlinck's eyes, true symbolism, that of the great universal
works by writers like Aeschylus or Shakespeare, "is unconscious rather,
occurs without the poet's knowledge, often despite him,"[17] a statement
that implicitly condemns any systematic use of symbols, which would
thereby inevitably degenerate into allegory.

Despite these repeated and well-founded warnings, the literary works
of the day too often present us, not with poetic legends or original myths,
but with mere allegories. This is true, for example, in the novel *Les
Demoiselles Goubert* by Paul Adam and Moréas himself, of the passage in
poetic prose entitled *Le Jubilé des esprits illusoires,* in which we are
presented with a number of allegorical characters representing such
legendary and fantastic figures as the Larva, which symbolizes man
bogged down in the world of phenomena; then with a series of classical
heroes each accoutred with a precise meaning, so that Achilles represents
"power relegated to the plebs," Spartacus "the illusion of popular liberty," and Roland "the prejudices of honor."[18] In the address to the
reader that prefaces his *Conte de l'or et du silence,* Gustave Kahn takes
care to forewarn us that "some of the characters represent
ideas. . . . Others represent phenomena of the passions, and behave in
accordance with the customs of legendary life."[19]

Too often, also, in poems of the period, the great myths employed were
stripped of their ambiguity, reduced to a single, conventional, and banal
meaning, so that Orpheus always and inevitably represents the poet of
genius misunderstood by the masses, Narcissus the consciousness turned
in upon itself, and so on. This intellectualist simplification of myths was
particularly apparent in the attempts made to create a symbolist drama
during the '90s. For instance, Pierre Quillard's *La Fille aux mains
coupées,* performed at the Théâtre d'Art on 19 March 1891, presents us in
scene 1 with a girl living alone in a castle keep who proclaims her desire
to leave the world altogether.[20] The author reveals to us that she represents the human soul aspiring toward divine love. Her father, an embodiment of the coarse mass of mankind, makes incestuous advances to her
which she repels. He then cuts off her hands and casts her adrift on the

sea in an open boat. She is washed up on the shore of a fairy-tale land where she is greeted by a hero who is none other than the Poet-King. Whatever the originality and quality of the actual staging, it could scarcely have concealed the grotesque simplemindedness of the plot, which is merely the mechanical transposition of an abstract idea, that of the poet's marriage to man's universal soul. Similarly, the second act of Rachilde's "cerebral drama in three acts," *Madame la Mort,* performed the following day in the same theater, consists of a dialogue in the leading character's mind, as he lies unconscious after taking poison, between two allegorical figures: Life, represented by a young woman, and Death, symbolized by a veiled woman whose appearance is described in the stage directions thus: "a young woman, supple, totally covered by a dust gray veil over a long dress of the same gray. She speaks in an uninflected but clear and decisive voice. She never shows her feet, hands, or face: she is an appearance. She walks, turns, moves quite noiselessly, as a shadow might, but with grace. She does not look like a ghost returned from the dead: she cannot return, she has never been. She is a form, not a being." It is not difficult to imagine how artificial, tedious, and even ridiculous such a plethora of ill-conceived allegories must have appeared when one had to sit and watch them.

However, this disease, which was partly responsible for the almost total failure of the attempts to create a symbolist theater at this time, was also rampant in the field of poetry. Again, the legendary narrative tended too often to become a lifeless frieze of scarcely concealed allegories dressed in vaguely medieval garments, with the Lady in her tower wearing a gold-embroidered gown and representing Woman, the Muse, or the Soul, while her Knight always represented the Poet. As a result, toward the end of the century, when the high noon of the decadent movement and symbolist poetry had passed, there came the inevitable denunciations of the tedium being inflicted upon the reader by this interminable exploitation of the same eternally regurgitated legends, always set against the same eternally mist-swathed fairy-tale backgrounds. By 1899, for example, in an article reprinted in his *Arabesques,* Retté himself was already attacking the commonplaces of symbolist imagery in violent and derisive terms:

> All their efforts were directed at imagining a nebulous and twilit land inhabited solely by melancholy kings, fine talkers dripping with jewelry, heroes in gilded helmets in pursuit of intangible chimaeras, lily-slim knights forever atremble, minstrels singing beneath the balconies of demonic princesses, coiling sirens, cooing shepherds. It was an endless procession of Pale Loiterers, Prince Charmings, Hertulies,

Imogens, and Phenissas: a dusty, raddled, rancid mock-up
of the Middle Ages that made one throw up in disgust.[21]

Camille Mauclair obviously felt much the same:

Born of impressionism, these writers rejected modernity.
That led them to invent a medieval world that was not only
intolerable in itself but in contradiction to their expressed
aversion to romantic emotions. They drowned us in a tedious excess of knights, jewels, springs, roses, and dream
cities. They descended from the sumptuous inventions of
Gustave Moreau into merest pinchbeck; they turned symbols into commonplaces.[22]

The Proliferation of Legends

To list the various mythical or legendary themes that
occur in the literature of the last fifteen years of the century with any
degree of completeness would necessitate an entire volume to itself, and
one that would make tedious reading. I shall therefore attempt no more
than a brief survey of the essential themes, drawing my material as much
from iconography as from literature, since painting and writing at this time
existed very much in a symbiotic relationship, with painters producing
works frequently described as literary and writers often borrowing themes
from painters, as well as writing copious critical appreciations of their
work.[23]

First, there are the legends of biblical origin. In Bernard Lazare's collection of stories *Le Miroir des legendes* of 1891, for example, *L'Eternel
Fugitif* retells the story of the Jewish people abandoning itself to worship
of the Golden Calf while Moses, having climbed Mount Sinai to receive
the Tables of the Law, seems unlikely to return. In Gustave Kahn's *Conte
de l'or et du silence*, mentioned earlier, we are told in the introduction that
the first part takes place in a castle in the legendary country of Sheba." In
Retté's *Cloches dans la nuit* of 1889 we meet the Queen of Sheba again. In
Les Portes d'ivoire, again by Bernard Lazare, the story entitled *Dalila*
offers a new symbolic interpretation of the Samson and Dalila legend.

The biblical story most often used as material, however, is that of
Salome and Herodias, which we touched on earlier with reference to
Flaubert's influence on decadent art. Apart from the works by Gustave
Moreau and Odilon Redon already mentioned, the legend of the young
Jewish princess and her mother was also to appear in numerous poetic
works of the period. In his collection *La Forêt bleue* of 1883, for instance,
Jean Lorrain devotes a poem to Herodias. In Retté's *Cloches dans la nuit*
of 1889 we meet a "perverted and profane Herodias" who "is struck with

terror by the pale head's sudden radiance."[24] And she was also to appear later in the century in a poem by Albert Samain.[25] In the field of prose narrative, Laforgue began work in May of 1885 on his *Salomé*, an ironic work that depicts its heroine making experiments on the Baptist's severed head, then accidentally falling to her death in the sea as she throws it from the palace terrace.[26] In Lazare's *Les Portes d'ivoire*, the story entitled *La Vierge* reinterprets the story of the young princess: in his version she desires the Baptist's death because she has fallen in love with him and does not wish to tarnish that love's perfection by giving herself to him. In the theater, she was to inspire Oscar Wilde's famous play, written in French during his visit to Paris 1892 and corrected at the manuscript stage by Stuart Merrill, Retté, and Pierre Louys.[27] The text was published in Paris in 1893, then the following year in London, in Lord Alfred Douglas's translation, wonderfully illustrated by Aubrey Beardsley, who by the time of his death, in 1898, had become one of the period's most famous artists.[28] *Salomé* was first performed by the Théâtre de l'Oeuvre, on 11 February 1896, as an expression of admiration for its author by French artistic circles on the occasion of his release from jail. Lastly, it was of course the text of Wilde's play that Richard Strauss used as the libretto for his opera of the same name, which was first performed in Dresden in December 1905. Apart from Beardsley's illustrations for the British edition of Wilde's play, the legend of Salome was to inspire many other artists during the final years of the nineteenth century. In particular, there is an engraving by Wilhelm Volz[29] and also a famous painting by Klimt, his *Judith-Salomé*.[30] Philippe Jullian sums up the importance of Salome as a mythical figure in the literature and art of that time as follows: "These three painters [Moreau, Beardsley, and Klimt] also share a common heroine: all awestruck worshipers of Salome, they depict her so often that one may well regard the young Jewish princess, heroine of Laforgue, of Wilde, and of Milosz, as the goddess of Decadence."[31]

Legendary themes and characters borrowed from Greek mythology were even more widespread. It was to Greek mythology that Gustave Moreau turned for the themes of many paintings. Specifically, and in chronological order of their composition or exhibition, we have the water color *Oedipus and the Sphinx*, painted in 1861 and exhibited to great acclaim in the 1864 Salon; *Medea and Jason* (1865); *Thracian Girl Carrying the Head of Orpheus* and *Diomedes Devoured by His Horses* (1866); *Prometheus and Europa* (1869), *Hercules and the Hydra* (1876); *Helen on the Ramparts of Troy* and *Galatea* (1880); and *Jupiter and Semele* (completed in 1896). Each of these works was consciously invested by the artist with a precise symbolic dimension. This is why the critics, and Schuré in particular, attempted to group Moreau's work into a series of cycles, each centered on a great mythic figure or spiritual symbol. First, the "cycle of the poet" centered on Orpheus, who symbolizes the tragedy and anguish of the modern artist. According to Schuré: "The type he generally clothes in a form drawn from mythology or fancy is in fact the driven and wandering poet, tormented by our modern age, a storm-tossed soul at once potent and weak, sublime and wretched, wavering continually from doubt to faith, from splendid ecstasies to black discouragement."[32] Second, the "cycle of woman" illustrated the irresistible and cruel power of woman, represented in particular, apart from the biblical heroines such as Dalila and Salome, by Omphale and Helen. Last, the "cycle of the hero" was analyzed by Schuré as follows:

> Moreau shows us four phases: First, the "cycle of the centaur" represents the struggle between animality and intelligence. Second, the Hercules cycle presents a larger-than-life version of the struggle with the forces of evil. Third, Jason celebrates the conquest of magical secrets or divine truth. Fourth, the "young man and death" provides a foretaste of the supreme revelation awaiting the perfected hero, mown down in the flower of his youth and lying at the threshold of the other world.[33]

Thus, embodied in paintings of an unprecedented strangeness that was bound to strike their imaginations, Moreau's work provided his contemporaries with the example of a systematic use of the great themes of Greek mythology, whose modernized symbolism was adapted to the major preoccupation at the heart of the decadent view of the world: tragedy of the artist confronted with modern life and contemporary society; fear of woman and a terrified obsession with sexuality; dread at the mystery of things represented by the sphinx.

We find this profusion of Greek myths recurring in the poetic works that marked Jean Lorrain's first steps as a writer, to take on apposite example in the field of poetic creation—even though the author was at that time in both inspiration and technique a devotee of the Parnassian school. In his first verse collection, *Le Sang des dieux*, for example, we meet the legendary figures of Eros, Selene, Zeus, Venus, and Helios. Among the mythical elements or beings occurring in literature and art generally at this time, we also find satyrs, depicted in one of Henri de Régnier's *Poèmes anciens et romanesques*, following in the hoofprints of Mallarmé's *L'Après-midi d'un faune*, Bacchus, and Ariadne.[34] The sirens, another symbolic form of the dangerous attraction exerted by woman, also appear, along with tritons, centaurs, Venus, and Prometheus, in many paintings by the Swiss Arnold Boecklin (1827–1901), then very famous in Germany, and whose work Laforgue enjoyed and wrote about during his stay in Berlin.

However, there were three mythical themes of Greek origin that particularly caught the imagination of artists at this period, all three of which were given symbolic meanings to suit contemporary sensibility. The first was that of Orpheus, a favorite, as we have already seen, with Gustave Moreau. What caught the attention of artists in this period was less the theme of the descent into the underworld and the resurrection of Eurydice—which was scarcely compatible with the decadents' fundamental antifeminism—than that of the poet-magician with his power to control the elements, rocks, wild animals, and human beings with the spell of his song, who yet fell victim to the ignorance and fury of the soulless mob, represented by the Thracian women who, according to the legend, murdered him while he was asleep, tore him to shreds, and threw his remains in the river. The journey of Orpheus' head, borne with his lyre to the shore of Lesbos, is the subject of both a painting by Jean Delville[35] and a story by Bernard Lazare, *La Lyre*. The power of Orpheus also provides the theme of a poem by Valéry published in the March 1891 issue of *L'Ermitage* and later reprinted in his *Album de vers anciens*. Later on, the myth of Orpheus inspired Victor Segalen to write a novella published in the August 1907 *Mercure de France*, and also to consider collaborating with Debussy on a musical work using the same theme.

After Orpheus there came the theme of Oedipus and the sphinx, again already used by Moreau. From the decadent standpoint, the sphinx, a hybrid monster with the body of a lioness but the face and breasts of a woman, represented the ideal symbol of woman, a being irremediably different, at once enigmatic and cruel, taking pleasure in slitting the throats of her endless victims, annihilating them, and over whom only the highest hero can emerge triumphant. It is this antifeminist theme that is developed above all in two works by Wilde, *The Sphinx without a Secret*, a story that appeared in 1887, and the poem *The Sphinx*, published in June 1893 by John Lane in a luxury edition with illustrations by Charles Ricketts.[36] It was also the sphinx that inspired a drawing by Jan Toorop in which we see the Egyptian sphinx towering over a crowd of women, some of whom are bowing down in worship while others are making an offering to it: a man and woman lying naked and motionless in death.[37]

The subject that achieved the greatest success, however, to the point of becoming a tedious cliché, was the legend of Narcissus. Narcissus represents the artistic consciousness in its flight from the coarse world of reality, and from the vulgar contact of women, in order to delight in its own subjectivity and its purely internal world. In love with his own reflection, Narcissus thus symbolizes the esthetic attitude, careless of the interdicts of conventional morality or the demands of practical life, shut away inside a purely contemplative existence. This theme, before inspiring *Fragments du Narcisse* in Valéry's *Charmes,* was already present in his *Narcisse parle* from *Album de vers anciens,* first published in *La Conque* of 15 March 1891, and it provided Moréas with the material for a story published in the *Echo de Paris* of 30 January 1891. Mauclair, in his *Eleusis,* offers an intellectual and philosophical interpretation of the myth in terms of the transcendental idealism to which he subscribed at that time; the water mirror in which Narcissus contemplates his own image becomes the mirror of consciousness as it transforms sensation into concept: "In the empty looking glass of his consciousness, man the thinker reflects the beam of sensations projected within him by the prism of his nervous sensibilities....Thus the being, at every moment of its intellectual activity, is contemplating itself in an invisible mirror."[38] Narcissus also became the symbol of the self's permanence as opposed to the endless flux of appearances. In *Le Miroir des légendes,* Bernard Lazare tells the story of a Narcissus punished by the gods for his immoderate beauty. He falls in love with his sister, who rejects his advances, then he dies. One day he thinks he is seeing her again when he perceives his own reflection in a spring. In a story by Jean Lorrain, *Narkiss,* Narcissus becomes a young pharaoh whose superhuman beauty is the cause of endless catastrophes. As a result, the priests who are his guardians confine him to his palace, taking care to remove from it every semblance of a mirror, so that he cannot ever see a reflection of himself. One night, however, he walks out by moonlight into the palace garden, sees his own image in the water of a stream, of course succumbs to the attraction of his own spellbinding beauty, and is drowned in his reflection.[39]

Biblical and Hellenic themes of course possessed the recommendation of a long tradition within French literature; but the same cannot be said for the legendary Celtic universe, which almost completely disappeared from French writing after the late Middle Ages and the romances of chivalry. Despite its expressed desire to rediscover the Middle Ages, the romantic period scarcely went beyond using them as a source of picturesque settings, or moved in the direction of dark fantasies far removed from the spiritual content and affective climate of the magical world inhabited by the Arthurian cycle and the Grail legends. Even in the work of writers such as Chateaubriand, Michelet, or Renan, who because of their origins or personal preoccupations might have been expected to show interest in the world of Breton legend, the occurrence of such myths still remains exceptional. The decadent era, on the other hand, was to witness a revival of this homegrown mythology, in two forms: first, that of the traditional fairy tale, with its wizards, fairies, metamorphoses, knights, and dragons; second, that of the great mythic cycles linked with the themes of the Round Table and the Grail.

Any investigation of this rediscovery of medieval art in France must begin by taking into account not only the work of our own scholars, who were editing, translating, and annotating the great texts of medieval literature, but also the influence of the English Pre-Raphaelites William Morris and Burne-Jones, as well as their immediate successors. Morris, partly influenced by Ruskin and his moral and esthetic rejection of modern civilization, was animated by a nostalgia for the medieval world, which inspired one of his most famous paintings, *Queen Guinevere*,[40] while Burne-Jones used his canvases to create a whole world of legend and myth whose spiritual origin lies essentially in the Middle Ages. In the work of Wagner, too, we find two operas derived from the Celtic Grail legend: first *Lohengrin,* in which Lohengrin reveals in the last act that he is the son of Parsifal (Perceval), king of the Grail, abandons Elsa, and returns to the castle of Montsalvat; second, *Parsifal* itself, for which Wagner drew his inspiration directly from texts by Chrétien de Troyes and Wolfram d'Eschenbach, even though he interpreted their material according to his personal world vision.[41]

"In about 1880," Philippe Jullian writes, "a fairy invasion began."[42] In Lorrain's *La Forêt bleue,* already mentioned earlier, the entire first section of the book, entitled *Le Pays des fées,* is given over to a series of poems devoted to such fairy-tale figures as Vivian, Melusina, and Morgan Le Fay. In *L'Ombre ardente,* he reworks the old French legend of the Sleeping Beauty in a sequence of texts: *Une Belle est dans la forêt, Le Chateau léthargique.* In 1892, the Théâtre de l'Oeuvre presented a version of the Sleeping Beauty written by Henri Bataille and Robert d'Humières with designs by Georges Rochegrosse. For a number of years during the '90s there was a sustained attempt to establish a vein of fairy-tale plays, the principal contributor being Jean Lorrain, with a series of texts, *Brocéliande, Yanthis, La Mandragore,* and *Ennoia,* that were collected and published in 1905.[43]

One of these Breton fairy tales was to achieve particular success, again because of the terrifying image it provided of woman and love: that of Merlin the magician deceived and trapped in a magic circle by Vivian le Fay. Burne-Jones had painted a *Merlin and Vivian* that was exhibited in the 1879 Paris Salon. In Lorrain's work the theme recurs several times. In *La Forêt bleue,* the two poems *Viviane* and *Brocéliande* both retell the old legend, which he also used for the plot of the fairy-tale play *Brocéliande* mentioned above. This story is also frequently alluded to in verse of the time, as for example in this passage from *Syrtes* by Moréas:

> Who will give me back . . . the sacred wood
> Where to the song of lutes fair Vivian appears
> Pouring the philtres of her fleeting lips . . .

Schuré devotes a chapter of his *Grandes Légendes de France* to a detailed account of Merlin's life: his birth and childhood, his initiation into wizardry, his career as adviser to King Arthur, and finally his meeting with Vivian in the forest of Brocéliande. Gustave Kahn, in his *Conte de l'or et du silence,* hybridizes the Vivian legend with that of Lancelot.

In the same way, and largely as a result of Wagnerian influence, the Grail theme was also to become one of the commonplaces of contemporary verse and fiction. In Kahn's *Les Palais nomades,* for instance, we read:

> See how desire is raising to its lips
> The golden trumpets of triumphant dawnings
> Blowing toward the grails in the pale courts of morning.

And in his *Poèmes anciens et romanesques,* Régnier evokes:

> The tall knights of iron and darkness, far
> From the echoes of past jousts, from all the dust and youthful joy
> of tournaments,
> Riding two by two, washed pure by absolution,
> Toward the blood of Grails and hopes of holy wars.

In the preface to his *Miroir des légendes,* Lazare writes of "mysterious Avalons." In the *Conte de l'or et du silence,* Kahn takes the opportunity provided by Joseph of Arimathea's visit to King Balthazar to provide us with a sumptuous description of the mystic vessel that contains the blood of Christ.

More generally, in both verse and prose fiction, Avalon, King Arthur's city, and Montsalvat, the castle of the Grail, were to become, like mistbound Thule, the symbols of legendary and magical lands. Settings and characters were constantly borrowed from the Middle Ages: knights, ladies, castles, swans, greyhounds, horns and fanfares, hawks and palfreys, all elements probably originating to some extent in certain lines of Verlaine's collection *Sagesse,* which appeared in 1880 and contained the famous reference to "the gigantic and delicate Middle Ages." Moreover, it also opened with the very celebrated poem presenting the allegory of the "masked good knight." Thus there developed a "decadent" Middle Ages probably just as artificial as that favored by the romantics, and much more tiresome, in that it never went beyond the allusive use of a few key words that are found repeated to satiety, and beyond, in numberless poems of the time.

Another prime traditional source of fairy-tale subject matter was the work of Shakespeare. During the last years of the nineteenth century we do in fact find a sudden revival of interest in Shakespeare, triggered off no doubt by the state of the theater generally in France at that time. Weary of the photocopies and slices of life still being offered by the naturalist dramatists, to say nothing of the trashy trifles playing in most of the boulevard theaters, many younger writers, desperately seeking for some renewal of theatrical vitality, turned to the great dramatic traditions of other countries, and above all to Shakespeare and the other Elizabethans. Evidence of this return to favor of the great British playwright is in fact abundant. The character of Hamlet, with his disillusion, his inability to act, his teetering on the verge of an almost welcome madness, and his cold irony, the character Laforgue borrowed to make the hero of one of his *Moralités légendaires,* and to whom Mallarmé alluded on so many occasions, was as it were fated to become one of the heroes of decadent mythology. Shakespeare's influence on Maeterlinck's work for the theater has been analyzed too often for me to recapitulate the evidence here.[44] We know, too, that Elémir Bourges was deeply imbued with Shakespeare's plays, and those of the Elizabethan period generally, in which he found appeasement for his yearning after great and noble souls, as potent in their great designs as in their crimes. In 1890, Gustave Kahn was contemplating a production of *Lear.*[45] In *Thulé des brumes,* as we saw earlier, Retté often evokes the Bard's characters. During the years 1891 and 1892 he conducted a running battle with Maurras, in a variety of literary magazines, over the latter's claim that Shakespeare was in fact an artist of essentially Mediterranean temperament.[46] Another indication of this fashion is provided by a humorous article contributed to the literary supplement of the *Echo de Paris* by Maurice Bouchor, and printed in the 24 January 1892 number, entitled "The Shakespearomaniac." Finally, there is the evidence offered by Edmond Jaloux. Reminiscing about the tastes of the group of young writers to which he belonged in Marseilles, during the years 1895 to 1900, he writes:

> Most of us had another god: Shakespeare, that revealer of characters who, the better to depict human nature, had employed the magic mirror of Merlin and the witches, not the pinchbeck item purveyed by the five and dime peddlers of naturalism.... We rated the author of the fairy-tale comedies highest of all.... We didn't see *The Tempest, A Midsummer Night's Dream, As You Like It, Twelfth Night, Much Ado about Nothing, A Winter's Tale, Cymbeline, All's Well That Ends Well,* or *The Two Gentlemen of Verona* as plays. To us, they were exact images of life.[47]

And it is true that these comedies by Shakespeare were to color with their particular atmosphere not only the legend-based plays of writers such as

Jean Lorrain or Robert d'Humières, but also a large proportion of the period's verse and prose stories.

Thus the decadent literary generation, rejecting contemporary reality, desperate for escape and dreams, concerned also to transmit through their poems and stories the metaphysical, moral, or esthetic ideas dear to their hearts, was naturally bound to make intensive use of the world of legends and myths. In consequence, they turned back with ardor to the Greco-Roman mythology bequeathed to them by the classical tradition; they followed Victor Hugo and the Parnassians in attempting to integrate myths and legends from the most distant civilizations, Nordic, exotic, or far eastern, into their work. Under the influence of British painting, they rediscovered the Celtic myths. Deeply imbued with the fairy-tale elements in Shakespeare's comedies, and the great mythic constructions of Wagner, they attempted to interpose the poetic and tinted filter of legend between themselves and reality. However, it must also be said that this use of myth and legend rarely produced wholly persuasive results. In their verse, the essential concern to develop an allusive and suggestive technique, the rejection of narrative and anecdote, led to an elimination of the pictorial element, of the historical and local color essential to imaginative release. In their stories, excessive erudition, or the mannerisms of an excessively technical jargon, spelled death to the simplicity that is indispensable to the world of magic. In both forms, their excessive concern with the idea they were attempting to convey led them into abstraction, thus reducing legends, symbols, and myths to systematic and ultimately uninspiring allegories.

8   ELEMENTAL

REVERIE

ALTHOUGH, AS WE SAW IN THE PREVIOUS CHAPTER, THE DECADENT imagination was ultimately ill served by its use of legendary themes, because those themes were too often depoeticized by allegorical treatment and reduced to incessantly repeated conventional formulas, that imagination was nevertheless employed to greater effect when it made use of certain material elements as a basis for what I have termed elemental reverie. Although the myth of Narcissus, for example, in its aspect as an allegorical narrative, became degraded at this period into a conventional literary cliché that quickly grew wearisome, it did nevertheless entail the use of certain material elements (water, mirror) that gave rise to more original and profounder imaginative developments.

Because they denied themselves description and the picturesque in the name of an ideal based on suggestion, decadent writers deliberately restricted themselves to the evocation of a certain number of details, which were intended to conjure up in the reader's mind, without further aid, either a landscape or an atmosphere. This led them ineluctably to invest certain material realities or objects with an exorbitant metaphorical richness and poetic power, so that these realities or objects usually stand at the center of a very complex constellation of images. It is these constellations that we must now attempt to make explicit, by extending and generalizing the brief analysis made by Guy Michaud of the mirror theme in symbolist poetry,[1] and employing the method so brilliantly pioneered by Gaston Bachelard. It is from this standpoint that we shall now examine the most important constellations of images that emerged during the decadent period in literature, those involving water, the mirror, precious stones, minerals, and vegetation.

Water

We have already seen, in our examination of Maupassant's work, the fascination exerted by water on the imagination of that

207

particular writer. But one might say the same thing about other creative artists of the period. By the very fluidity of its nature, water is particularly well suited to providing the basis for reverie: both are constantly changing, evanescent, subtle. Thus the affective and imaginary meaning of water is modified considerably, indeed, almost totally, according to whether it is live and running or, on the contrary, motionless and stagnant, transparent or murky. Despite the fact that they all consist of the selfsame element, the sea, a stream, or a pond all nevertheless excite very different registers of reverie and imaginative reaction.

Moreover the presence of this key element is in fact constant throughout late-nineteenth-century French literature. It is present at almost every moment in the work of Albert Samain, for instance, as Guy Michaud has observed.[2] It runs throughout the entire work of Henri de Régnier whether we turn to the stories of *La Canne de jaspe* or the poems of *La Cité des eaux*. It is water that supports the imaginary journeyings of Gide's travelers in *Le Voyage d'Urien* and those of Camille Mauclair's *Couronne de clarté*. It was water that most fascinated Jean Lorrain as a child, during his boating trips in the semilegendary park of Valmont.[3] We find passionate evocations of water again and again in Francis Poictevin's *Double*. However, aside from this general fascination, there are also the different specific forms that this theme takes in the world of decadent reverie to be considered.

First, because of its power of reflection water is fundamentally the most natural of mirrors, and it is precisely the mirror that provides us with one of the richest constellation of images in this period's literature. The mirror, according to Guy Michaud, was "one of the key themes of symbolism," "the tool of dreams," "the tool of analogic thought," and even "the symbol par excellence."[4] It is in this mirror that we must now reread, but much more richly and densely perceived than in the previous chapter, the decadents' most favored myth, that of Narcissus. In this case, of course, we have left behind the wave-tossed water of the ocean, the coursing water of quick streams. Here the water must be sufficiently motionless to provide a reflection of the being gazing into it. Such water appears as the seductive surface in which the eternal Narcissus aspires to contemplate himself, primarily, no doubt, in order to enjoy his own beauty, but also in order to pierce the enigma of his own face and gaze. Such is indeed the attraction exerted by water on Laforgue's Andromeda, imprisoned on her island and weary of eternal solitude:

> Right at the end, jutting out to form a promontory, is a strange-looking cliff; Andromeda clambers up it through a labyrinth of natural ramps. From the narrow platform she looks out over her island, and the restless solitude that iso-

lates that island. In the center of this platform the rain has worn a shallow basin. Andromeda has decorated it with pebbles of black ivory, and keeps it filled with pure water. This is her mirror, ever since one springtime, and her sole secret in the world. For the third time today she returns to stare at herself in it. She does not smile at herself, she sulks, she tries to make her eyes look even more serious.[5]

It is this same theme of the natural and spontaneous attraction that the human being experiences for his or her own reflection that was to be illustrated by a number of poems and stories during the decadent period, for example, Jean Lorrain's *Narkiss,* already mentioned, or Camille Mauclair's *Bouclier d'or,* whose hero finds himself similarly forbidden the use of all mirrors, and likewise eventually succeeds in gazing at his own reflection, this time in the burnished surface of a golden shield.

But to contemplate one's reflection in a mirror is also to attempt to discover the truth about oneself, to reach the permanent self behind the multiple flux of the consciousness. This is certainly true of Mauclair's Narcissus in his *Eleusis,* of whom the author writes: "On the ghostly element, on the water more ephemeral than silk, more perverse than the high sheen of hair, on the water as it drew whole worlds along with it, his image stayed" (p. 14). This tête-à-tête can be charged with terror too, as in Régnier's poem *Tel qu'un songe:*

> And on the shore I dug a hole
> In which the clear seawater welled up from below
> And wet my hand. So that, as in a dream
> I leaned above the pool
> And through myself I saw my dream reflected
> Face to face.
> Oh bleeding face, where I appeared before myself
> There in the water mirror in the sand!
> Oh proud and doomed Narcissus,
> May the night
> Fill up that deathly hollow with its monstrous dark[6]

So the mirror reveals man to himself, and this revelation may take on a tragic dimension. That is clearly the implicit lesson of the story that gives its title to Marcel Schwob's collection *Le Roi au masque d'or.* Since childhood, a king has lived his whole life confined to his palace and masked, and all those who enter his presence are masked likewise. One day, however, a blind beggar is brought into the palace, sows doubt in the king's mind, and persuades him that he should attempt to see his own face. While walking in the countryside, the king meets a young girl, who cries out in horror as he removes his mask. He then decides to look at his face reflected in the water of a river:

He ran along the bank, leaned out over the water of the river, and from his lips too there sprang a strangled moan. Just as the sun was vanishing behind the brown and blue hills of the horizon, he had glimpsed a pallid, swollen face, its flaking skin distended by hideous protuberances, and he knew at once, remembering what he had read in books, that he was a leper.[7]

The significance of this story thus derives from the juxtaposition of two themes, that of mirror and that of mask: to look at oneself in a mirror is to accept removal of the mask represented by the social or superficial self in order to recognize one's inner, true self.

In seeking to grasp his own image, Narcissus is therefore committing a sin, and in conformity with the spirit of the classical myth, in which the gods punish Narcissus by turning him into a flower, decadent works also frequently illustrate this theme of punishment. This notion of retribution is expressed with particular clarity in *Le Crapaud,* an autobiographical anecdote to be found in Jean Lorrain's *Sensations et souvenirs* of 1895. The author recounts how, during his childhood rambles through the park at Valmont, he used to spend hour after hour beside a certain spring, and one day, despite having been forbidden to do so by his parents, could not stop himself drinking from it: "Oh, that ferruginous spring in the old park of Valmont, I loved it as passionately, I think, possessed it as voluptuously, as the most adored of mistresses, until the day when I became the object of a cruel revenge, and found in its depths the most foul of punishments" (p. 14). No sooner had he slaked his thirst at the spring—and there is no doubt that drinking from a spring after having gazed at one's reflection in it is the ultimate extension of narcissism—than he noticed on the bottom, in one corner of the pool, the corpse of an enormous toad still oozing blood. Although this is a transcription of an actual childhood memory, it is clear that we are intended to read the text in a symbolic sense. The punishment of the child Narcissus here takes the form of a taint with which he feels himself perpetually and horribly sullied thereafter: "The toad stirred, and I had drunk the water where the monstrous thing had lived, had writhed, and in my mouth, my throat, my whole being, there was a taste of dead flesh as it were, a smell of putrefying water" (p. 15).

More generally, however, the punishment inflicted on Narcissus is drowning: victim of the water's perilous seduction, impelled by a tragic desire to join his own reflection, Narcissus destroys himself. Such is the punishment meted out to the little girl who is the heroine of Gabriel Mourey's story *La Séduction des reflets.*

> She loved to spend her days in the half-light of shuttered
> windows, in the cool calm of that vast Louis XVI drawing-
> room paneled in pale woods.... Its profusion of mirrors
> multiplied her powers of vision to infinity. Their dreaming
> reflections sent the little girl into a trance of ecstasy. At
> sunset, it was her joy to gaze at the rectangles of landscape
> formed by the open windows reflected back from
> them.... She remained motionless for hour after hour,
> transported by the dizzying beauty of their shimmering im-
> ages.[8]

At last, one day when she is watching the sunset in the mirror of a pond,
she falls into the water and is drowned. The same punishment awaits Jean
Lorrain's Narkiss, as we saw earlier. In Rachilde's story *L'Araignée de
cristal*, the penalty paid is madness: one day when he is looking at himself
in a mirror, a tall pier glass in the family apartment, the hero sees his
image shatter.[9] And although the incident has a perfectly rational and
prosaic explanation—a neighbor had been drilling a hole in the party wall,
not stopped in time, and cracked the mirror with his drill from the
back—the hero becomes obsessed with mirrors in general. "My brief
existence," he says "is shot through entirely with their satanic reflection," and eventually he sinks into irreversible insanity.

In another story, by Régnier, the experience of being reflected in mirrors also leads to death, albeit in a different way, since what he describes
is the dissolution of the individual in a series of receding reflections.
Hertulie, the heroine of the story, which has her name as its title, having
finally lost the man she loves, wanders through the long galleries of an
immense palace that is empty of all human presence but filled with innumerable mirrors. Having lost all reason to live, she vanishes in her turn
into the mirror world:

> The rooms through which the fleeing woman passed and
> repassed seemed to her more spacious than before; the
> now-dimmed chandeliers hung in crystalline and pendant
> silence over her; fleeting from room to room, panting and
> weary, in that one where the mirrors were she stopped. Her
> image in them stretched out to infinity. Hertulie was seeing
> Hertulie around her everywhere, beyond and beyond, to the
> far depths of a dream in which she lost all sense of having
> been the starting point of so many ghosts identical to her
> own pallor; she felt herself scattered for ever, and by dint of
> gazing at herself thus, elsewhere on every side of her, she
> became increasingly fragmented till at last, dissolving in her
> own reflections, exorcized from her own being by that

amazing magic in which she imagined her self eternally impersonal, she felt her knees give way and she sank gently to
the floor, inanimate, while in the solitary room, above the
closed eyelids of her bloodless face, the mirrors in their
frames of gold and tortoiseshell and ebony went on ex-
changing the illusory gaze of their reciprocal vacuities.[10]

If Régnier's heroine can fade away into the mirrors, it is because they are
a door that opens into another universe; it is because, like water, mirrors
conceal mysterious depths behind their smooth reflecting surfaces. The
space perceived in mirrors creates a universe that is the twin of the real
universe, but also a different and strange one. This universe is what the
hero of Rachilde's *L'Araignée de cristal* perceives as he gazes into the
great pier glass in his family's apartment:

Beneath the limpid layer of its glass lurked squalid stains.
Water lilies, they could be, buds forming just below the
surface of a stagnant pond, and further back, where the
shadows receded slightly, vague shapes waved, like ghosts
moving through the muddy coils of their own hair. I remembered how once, when looking at myself in it, I had
experienced the strange sensation of sinking into that mirror
up to the neck, as if into some muddy lake."[11]

A little later, the author herself comments on this mystery that the mirror
introduces into reality: "When all is said and done, do we know why that
sheet of glass, once silvered, suddenly acquires the depths of an abyss,
becomes a double of this world?" Then, at the end, she offers an intellectual interpretation that is in total conformity with the vision of the
world prevalent among writers of her day: "The mirror is the problem of
life that man must perpetually face."

This mirror world is naturally full of ghosts, since it was only to be
expected that the decadent period would make use of the traditional belief
that mirrors retain in their depths the trace of every face they have ever
reflected, with the result that it becomes a secret memory, continuously
storing away its simulacra of people and things. Thus the mirror theme
can easily take on a supernatural tinge. In particular, the dead may reappear through mirrors. In Rodenbach's *Bruges-la-morte,* which is
wholly dominated by the combined signs of water, mirror, and death, the
drawingroom of the inconsolable widower retains traces of his dead wife
everywhere: "And in the mirrors, so as not to erase her features sleeping
in their depths, it seemed that their clear surface must be rubbed with a
sponge or cloth only with the utmost caution."[12] When one contemplates
the mirror's mysterious surface, therefore, one is only too likely to re-

ceive the impression of some lurking presence, of hidden eyes looking back at one. This is the feeling expresses by Retté, for example, in a passage from his 1889 verse collection *Cloches dans la nuit:*

> Distant music as he leans above the pond
> The water glinting mirrorlike above deep wells
> And from the depths, aglow with a hermetic
> Radiance, eyes emerging
> Piercing his with ice.[13]

Or by Régnier, in the *Prélude* to his *Poèmes anciens et romanesques:*

> Around our lying mirrors weaves and twists
> A garland frame in which a single rose
> Lives on. And held within that flowering coil
> A crystal lake, once water, dreams and sleeps.
> And in that sea green silence there still prowls
> A gleam, a fleeting dawn, a glint that means
> To wander long in there, lugubrious and lost,
> A flash of ancient eyes still wide in death.[14]

If the mirror, frozen water now immobilized, is the place where living and dead meet, it is because, more generally, there exist profound affinities, a kinship, between water and death. Bachelard established this kinship very clearly in his exploration of two image complexes that recur constantly in poetic texts, those of Charon and of Ophelia. And it is precisely the Ophelia theme, that of the conjunction of water and dead wife, that we find alluded to repeatedly in Rodenbach's *Bruges-la-morte,* already quoted from so many times. Hughes Viane is helped to keep the memory of his dead wife alive not only by the mirrors in his drawingroom but also by his daily contact with the water of the canals:

> In the mute atmosphere of that water and those lifeless streets, Hughes had felt the suffering of his heart less, had thought more gently of the dead woman. He had seen her more clearly, heard her more clearly, recognizing her drifting Ophelia's face as he followed the canals.... It seemed...that a whispering voice rose up from the water—the water coming to him, as Shakespeare's gravedigger suggested it might have done to Ophelia. [Pp. 19, 23]

Some years later, Camille Mauclair's *L'Ennemie des rêves,* a novel whose early pages are also set in Bruges, was to evoke this association between water and death again, this time in order to denounce its fatal influence. He sees the water that flows in the Belgian city's canals as a liquid, female vampire:

Prisoner of moles and sluices, she imprisoned the city in her
turn: she trapped its image and held it jealously. Alert and
never-tiring witness, she dilated her sea green irises and
drank in both its houses and its people, who sank into her
quivering, drained of color by that fierce and ceaseless confrontation. . . . She drained their vitality from the dwellings
whose foundations her caress had been eroding since time
immemorial. . . . She seized the forms of things, she gulped
down half of all existence with a noiseless greed.[15]

It is therefore hardly surprising that the decadent sensibility, saturated as
it was with such macabre obsessions, saw a corpse sleeping in every
spring, as in these lines by Jean Lorrain:

Each spring contains its corpse
Asleep beneath the lily leaves;
Each night, a ghost that breaks the heart,
The drowned man swims up to men's gaze.[16]

Precious Stones

We have seen the mirror portrayed as a form of solid
water, still retaining one of the inherent characteristics of water, the
power to reflect and to suggest the existence of another world, twin to the
real world, but also a world with vague and disturbing depths. The gem,
the precious stone, is also akin in some measure to water, with which it
often shares a like transparency and brilliance. It is a veritable prism of
images, meeting place of the worlds of water, of metal, with which it
shares the quality of hardness, and of fire, whose glow illumines it from
within. And, certainly, in late-nineteenth-century art and literature, the
precious stone enjoyed the most extraordinary prestige.

One of the accidental causes of this prestige was probably the history of
the French crown jewels. Hidden during the war of 1870 in the arsenal at
Brest, then brought back to Paris and stored in the Ministry of Finance
cellars, they were eventually exhibited to the public at the Exposition
Universelle of 1878, and excited great curiosity. Ten years later, as the
result of a new law that forbade the transfer of the majority of the collection to the state, a great public sale of the jewels was held in May of 1887,
an event that brought prospective buyers to Paris from all over the world
and was covered and discussed endlessly in the press.[17] From that moment, jewels were all the rage: they ceased to be merely ornaments for
society figures and were annexed by literature and art.

Gustave Moreau's exotic imagination had already decked the mysterious heroines of his paintings with bizarre and splendid jewels, and when

Huysmans came to describe the master's two most famous works, in *A Rebours,* he attempted in his turn to convey the fiery glamour of those jewels with a matching magnificence of style, as for example in this description of Salome's dance:

> Her breasts rise and fall, and with the rubbing of her whirling necklaces their nipples harden; against the dampness of her skin the diamonds fastened on it glitter; her bracelets, girdles, rings, all spit out sparks; on her triumphant gown, pearl-embroidered, silver-flowered, gold-bespangled, her breastplate of encrusted gold, chain mail with every link a jewel, bursts into flame, twines with little snakes of fire that writhe against the dead white flesh. [Pp. 84–85]

Moreover, chapter 4 also contains what amounts to a short treatise on precious stones, including a listing and descriptions of a great number of gems. The pretext for this insertion is of course one of Des Esseintes's bizarre whims: having covered the shell of a giant tortoise with gold, he has decided to decorate this unusual buckler with a selection of choice stones.

Here, as in so many other areas, *A Rebours* proved a decisive factor in the setting of a fashion. From then on, precious stones were to figure constantly in the verse and prose fiction of the period, constituting one of the fundamental elements of decadent literary imagery. The work of Moréas provides numerous examples. "*Les Syrtes,*" Carassus points out, "abounds in precious stones: beryl, diamond, and chrysoprase."[18] The same is true of Henri de Régnier's first verse collections, particularly of *Poèmes anciens et romanesques,* published in 1890, of which the *Mercure de France* critic Jean Court wrote: "The characters, the things, even the abstractions in which the poet's courtly melancholy delights are all bedecked with an unbelievable profusion of precious stones."[19] The same observation could well have been made about most of the verse collections published during the last fifteen years of the century. "All the symbolists are expert jewelers," André Lebois notes.[20] Among innumerable possible examples, here is Robert de Montesquiou evoking his *Cité mystique:*

> Sardonyx and sard, amethyst and sapphire,
> Chalcedony, jacinth and jasper,
> All ravished with their fire.[21]

Precious stones also found a favorable reception in many prose works. In Gourmont's *Sixtine* we find the heroine receiving d'Entragues in chapter 9 with "her fingers glittering with garnets and opals, with chalcedonies, perhaps, and chelonites" (p. 61), while in a story called *Le*

Fantôme, written in 1891 and published in 1893, several paragraphs are given over to a description of the hyacinth, at once a precious stone (jacinth) and a flower, from which the central character's name is derived. Similarly, Gustave Kahn's *Le Conte de l'or et du silence* contains descriptions of jewels at several points. In chapter 5, for example, during a description of the Passover festivities, the king is described in his ceremonial vestments, wearing "the glittering tiara," and a "necklace of peerless jewels, all incandescent with white fire upon his chest" (p. 150). Lastly, in the slightly later stories of Victor-Emile Michelet, and indeed in all his work generally, gemstones were likewise to play a major role.[22]

Clearly it is possible to criticize decadent writers for having frequently used gemstones as no more than a condiment to their imagery, and one that quickly becomes tedious when they content themselves with merely making lists of precious stones whose names, with their sometimes exotic sonorities, happen to have titillated their taste for rare words and erudite details. However, here again we find that a theme destined to become increasingly hackneyed could also release a more authentic strain of imaginative creativity when associated and confronted with various elemental themes. In its transparency and brightness, the gemstone is akin to water. It is hardly surprising, therefore, that we find jewels and water closely associated in a whole series of images to be found in literature of the period. From this point of view there is probably no text more significant than this passage from Gide's *Voyage d'Urien,* in which, narrating the imaginary travels of Urien and his friends, the author describes how they cross an Arctic ocean bristling with icebergs, and discover a gem set in a block of ice:

> Toward morning, just before dawn, at the hour when the breeze begins to drop, an islet of pure, clear ice came drifting near us; at its center, enclosed like a fruit, like a miraculous egg, there gleamed an immortal gem. Morning star, bright on the waves, we could not tire of gazing into it.[23]

Similarly, in Lorrain's *Monsieur de Phocas,* during a conversation between the narrator and the duc de Fréneuse, the latter establishes a very close relationship between gems and water, particularly the depths of the sea:

> Have you sung its praises enough, that jeweled flora, at once Byzantine, Egyptian, and Renaissance! Have you sufficiently captured the facets of madrepores and underwater gems, yes, underwater, for encrusted as they are with beryls, with peridots, with opals and pale sapphires the

color of waves and seaweed, with a cerulean enamel, almost, they have the look of gems that have lain for long years on the sea bed. Rings of Solomon or goblets of misty Thule's king, they are above all the treasure hoard of sea-drowned towns, and the King of Ys's daughter should have worn such stones, when she handed over the keys of the watergates to the Demon. [Pp. 15–16]

Later in the conversation, the fin-de-siècle aristocrat confesses to the narrator that, suffering as he does from "a morbid attraction to jewels," he is obsessed by the sea green glow that emanates from certain stones, particularly from emeralds, a glow that one also finds in underwater depths, and occasionally in certain eyes:

Gleam of gem or gaze, I am in love, captured, entranced, possessed by a certain sea green transparency; it is like a hunger in me. I search for it, that gleam, but vainly, in the gaze of men and in precious stones, but no human eye possesses it. Sometimes, I find it in the empty socket of a statue's eye, or beneath the painted eyelids of a portrait, but it is always deception; the glow fades as soon as it appears. [Pp. 16–17]

In this passage, despite the evident tics of decadent fashion, the association of gems, water, and the quality of certain looks is almost imperceptible, forming an imaginary complex that is particularly representative of the decadent imagination.

On the other hand, the precious stone is also susceptible of association with vegetable themes. In this case, through the gem as intermediary, mineral and vegetable images achieve a reciprocal exchange of their specific powers. And probably the association of these two themes was strengthened by the fact that jewelers at that time often drew upon the vegetable kingdom for inspiration in their creations.[24] This theme of the jewel flower, associated with that of the artificial and with subterranean depths, is to be found in one of Guaïta's poems from *La Muse noire, Aux Chercheurs de pierreries:*

You scorn, presumptuous miners of the earth,
The radiance of sun in heaven . . .
To jasmines, to carnations, you prefer
Star sapphires; to the brilliance of real flowers
The dazzle of dug crystal blooms.

Several years later, Huysmans was to expand this theme in the first dream of *En rade.* The magical palace that the hero sees in his dream contains a veritable forest of jewelry that gradually comes to life, recalling the visions of *La Tentation de saint Antoine:*

> Around these columns, joined by espaliers of palest copper, a vineyard of precious stones clambered in coiling tumult, twining with steel wires, with convoluted stems whose bronze bark oozed out clearest drops of topaz, shone with the waxy glint of opals. All over it were climbing vine shoots chiseled out of single gems; everywhere there flamed a brazier of slender trunks no fire could touch, a bonfire fueled by the mineral kindling of leaves carved out from varying glints of green, green fire of emeralds, olive of chrysolite, sea green of aquamarine, lime tints of zircon, cerulean clarity of beryl; on every side, on high, on low, at the tips of the supports, at the base of the trunks, the vines were bearing grapes of ruby and of amethyst; bunches of garnets and amaldines, of chrysoprase, of paler olivine and quartz, were darting out fabulous clusters of crimson flashes, purple flashes, yellow flashes, rising in a storming wave of fiery fruits whos sight suggested the too-believable illusion of a wine harvest about to explode beneath the weight of a descending press into a streaming, dazzling must of flames.
> [Pp. 31–33]

If decadent creative artists were so zealous in their cult of precious stones, however, it was also because of a very ancient tradition that associated various gems with a whole symbolic complex in which astrology, magic, medicine, and metaphysics all played a part. This meant that each precious stone was seen as imbued with specific powers, so that it corresponded, in the tangible world, to elements in the spiritual, magical, religious, or occult world. As a consequence, even before Huysmans produced the definitive account of this symbolism of the precious stone in his *La Cathédrale,* many symbolist writers made it their concern to revive the memory of these traditions and to muse on the poetic potentialities they concealed. It was to this branch of symbolism that a young writer of the *Mercure de France* group, Louis Denise, devoted a work called *La Merveilleuse Doxologie des lapidaires,* published in 1893. In his introduction, he wrote: "We delight in the antiquated charm, the anachronistic science—giving off a faint whiff of princely mummies—of the venerable lapidaries such as Epiphanus, Isidore of Seville, and Marbode, whose austere wisdom reveled in these, some would say, sumptuous baubles." He then lists the principal stones, and links each of them, from a Christian standpoint, to a moral symbol and a sacrament. Although this short work is in general too abstract and schematic, it does occasionally display touches that indicate an authentic imagination at work, as for example when Denise associates the opal with the emergence of underground water:

> Sometimes, in the deserts of the Septentrion the earth is shaken by mysterious quiverings, gapes, and disgorges a spurt of boiling water that suddenly erupts heavenward, the violence of its vaporous explosion bringing with it fragments of rock wrenched from the maternal entrails. But, among the lowly and amorphous pebbles that such geysers have thrown up, the greedy eye of man was able to discern the discreet splendors of the opal.[25]

It was from a much narrower occultist viewpoint that Victor-Emile Michelet approached the same subject the following year, when he devoted an article in *L'Initiation* to "the secrets of precious stones." "An essentially symbolic object," he wrote, "the jewel acquires beauty only among races whose art is an expression of the symbol. . . . I believe that the dawning of this young generation of artists, so profoundly beneath the spell of symbolism, will have as its consequence the creation of a revival in the art of the precious stone."[26] He then goes on likewise to consider the principal precious stones and to clarify their precise symbolism and corresponding planetary influences. However, we also find in this text, almost as a by-product, another aspect of elemental reverie: that involving the subterranean world. Before being brought to the light of day by man, every stone has been confined to an obscure existence underground; and by that very fact it acquires links with terrestrial and sometimes even cosmic imagery, as we can detect from the following passage: "In these stones, the slow and mysterious toil of gnomes, of the spirits of earth, has concentrated the splendors with which universal life intoxicates those who have eyes to see. In these multifaceted prisms they have imprisoned the beauty of dawns and dusks, the glow of far horizons, and the glinting of the stars."[27] In the paragraphs he devotes to the diamond, the author takes account of its kinship with light, but views it above all, in a reverie reminiscent of Mallarmé in tone, as a symbol of pure intellect:

> It seems the very sublimity of matter, invisibly pure, impassively serene. Petrified light, concentrated phosphorescence, idealized ice. No material can scratch it, no emotion seems able to penetrate it. It lives in pure intellectuality, dead to all sensibility, dead to all passion, like a heart once plunged into the absolute, now stripped of all tenderness and hate. . . . The alchemists regarded it, of all stones, as having attained the highest summit of nobility and beauty, like gold among the metals, like the sun among all stars.[28]

Minerals and Metals

Having begun from water, we have now been imperceptibly drawn, through the intermediary of crystalline reverie, into the world of minerals and metals. The first aspect in which this imagined presence of metal appears is precisely as a confrontation between metal and water; for it is just such a confrontation that we find in a work that was to haunt writers of the late nineteenth century in France: the operas of Wagner, and in particular *The Ring of the Nibelungs*.

The entire *Ring* could in fact be interpreted from the standpoint of elemental symbolism. The work as a whole both juxtaposes and opposes all the modes of imagined matter: water, represented by the Rhine, from which the gold emerges, and to which, after its cursed stay on land, it is eventually returned; metal, represented by the omnipresent Rhinegold, as well as by the Nibelungs, subterranean demiurges whose task is smelting and working metals—a widespread and traditional association in the mythic imagination which is also frequently found in the work of Gérard de Nerval—and also by Nothung, the sword that Wotan embeds in the ash tree to await Siegmund's arrival, and that Siegfried later reforges with Mime's aid; fire, represented by Loge the god of fire, by the underground forges of the Nibelungs, and also by the climactic funeral pyre, which consumes the bodies of Siegfried and Brünnhilde then destroys Valhalla itself. More specifically, the central argument of the work presents us with the confrontation of gold and water: the entire action, triggered by the Nibelung Alberich's theft of the Rhinegold, tended by the Rhine maidens in the watery depths, is finally resolved only when the Rhine rises, bursts its banks as Valhalla burns, and draws the gold back into itself.

A detailed analysis of *The Ring* from this point of view is obviously outside the scope of the present work. Let me simply observe that Wagner's tetralogy was sufficiently familiar to the educated public of the decadent era, thanks to numerous analyses and translations of the libretti, for the elemental symbolism it contains to have become deeply ingrained in people's minds, however unconsciously.[29] Thus this confrontation between metal and water is made very clear in Schuré's work on Wagner, published in 1875, since he included in it a passage from the libretto of *Rhinegold* that exemplifies it with particular clarity: the opening song of the Rhine maidens as the beams of the rising sun pierce the river's depths and awaken the gold to gleaming splendor. What do these lines convey if not a sort of imagined peak of ecstasy attained by the conjunction, beneath the sign of happiness, of the three primordial elements: metal, water, and fire?

Gold, as a theme, doubtless under Wagner's influence, was also to inspire a number of French writers. In particular it can be said to pervade one episode of Villiers de l'Isle-Adam's *Axël,* the one in which Sara, having gone down into the cellars of the Château d'Auersperg, discovers the treasure. At this point, the memory of the earlier work is made very clear by the fact that in Sara's eyes this treasure takes on the form of a liquid torrent, as is evident from the author's frequent use of metaphors involving water:

> And then, from the arched top of the opening—as it gaped steadily wider—there emerged, first, a glittering shower of precious stones, a rustling rain of diamonds, and then, an instant later, a cascade of gems of every color, washed with light, a myriad of flashing, faceted brilliants, heavy necklaces without number, some of diamonds again, some of jewels like pure flame, some of pearls. This streaming torrent of light seemed, of a sudden, to wash in a great wave over Sara's shoulders and clothes: the precious gems and pearls leapt out around her on every side, clinking on the marble of the tombs and splashing up once more against the white statues in sheaves of dazzling sparks, with a crackling as of some great fire. And as the section of wall moved lower still, half of its height or more by now below the level of the floor, from both sides of the vast recess came thundering, ringing cataracts of liquid gold that flowed out to bathe the feet of the shadowy intruder. Just as the precious stones had done a moment since, now heaving waves of golden coins fell awesomely from the insides of shattered barrels, their hoops now burst by long corrosion and the pressure of their numbers. [Pp. 222–23]

The water metaphors in this passage are clearly more than ingredients in a descriptive process, and undoubtedly have reference to the deeper imaginative levels of the text, which, at the climax of the drama, associates the glamour of water with that of metal. Similarly, if, as it flows out from its hiding place, the stream of jewels and gold covers Sara's body, that is because the chemical betrothal of gold and water is already prefiguring, or transposing onto the level of elemental reverie, her imminent union with Axël.

Although metal is capable of being feminized by contact with water, as we have just seen, it can also take a diametrically opposite imaginative path, one that associates it with images of hardness, coldness, even death, and in doing so identifies it with the mineral world.[30] The image of a universe annihilated by total desiccation, of a purely mineral chaos, was to find a frequent ally in evocations of the moon, the fashion for which doubtless owed a great deal to the works of Camille Flammarion and Jules Verne, and which chimed in only too well with the very decadent notion of mankind's inevitable future doom. The first signs of this use of the moon as the symbol of a petrified universe appear as early as 1885 in Jules Laforgue's *L'Imitation de Notre-Dame de la Lune,* even though the mineralism of that work is still not yet absolutely pure, since it does occasionally offer metaphors associated with water.[31] However, a passage such as the following, from *Climat, faune et flore de la lune,* does undoubtedly reveal the progressive invasion of the lunar landscape by a dryness that makes it a world where the mineral is already almost wholly triumphant:

> This is the fall, spellbindingly, forever,
> Without thermometer, embalming seas and continents,
> Blind meres, ophthalmic lakes, springs
> Of Lethe, ashen breezes, vast ceramic wastes,
> Oases, sulphur springs, extinguished craters,
> Timeworn sierras, cataracts that seem of zinc,
> High chalky plateaus, long-abandoned quarries,
> Grasses older than the graves they grow on,
> Dolmens winding in long caravans.[32]

This process of mineralization reached its ultimate conclusion some months later in the second dream of Huysmans's *En rade,* which describes a dream visit to the lunar landscape, and which has already been analyzed by Gaston Bachelard, in *La Terre et les rêveries de la volonté,* in such detail, and so definitively, that it is hardly necessary to attempt any further comment: a universe of emptiness and nothingness, where everything is immobilized in the ultimate dust, where water no longer occurs except in the form of a thin coating of rime, where the vegetable kingdom itself has become fossilized.

Nor did this theme die out with Huysmans. On the contrary, it was to proliferate in a whole series of later texts. We find an echo of it, for example, in *La Mort d'Odjigh,* one of the stories from Marcel Schwob's *Le Roi au masque d'or.* In this tale Schwob imagines the earth, some time in a legendary and distant past, having become entirely mineralized by the effects of an ever-increasing cold that is gradually extinguishing all life:

> A perpetual winter was making the earth crack open. The mountains that had risen up, vomiting the flaming entrails of the earth into the sky, were gray with frozen lava. These regions were marked with parallel or radiating furrows; these prodigious crevasses, gaping suddenly, destroyed everything above their level by undermining then engulfing them, and one saw long lines of erratic blocks perpetually descending toward them in a long slow slide. The dark air

> was spangled with tiny transparent needles; a sinister
> whiteness covered the countryside; the world seemed
> sterilized by a universal silver radiance. [Pp. 33–34]

One of the last human survivors, Odjigh, a wolf hunter, decides to attempt
to arrest the catastrophe by reaching the North Pole, and the landscapes
he passes through on his way there illustrate the progressive victory, in
this legendary world, of mineral over water:

> He went on his way, and around him life was becoming
> extinct. The rivers had fallen silent long since. The opaque
> air could carry only muffled sounds. The frozen masses,
> blue, white, green, gleaming with frost, seemed the pillars of
> a monumental road. [Pp. 34]

Thus, in this text we find an Arctic reverie associated with lunar reverie, or
taking over from it, in order to illustrate the theme of mineral death. The
latter we also find in Gide's *Voyage d'Urien* of the same year, a work that
can scarcely be understood without reference to this imaginative dialectic
of the elements and the combined influences of Poe and Verne. Here is a
passage which describes the travelers' arrival in a world of cold and ice
that is also that of pure minerality: "Pure gypsums! Salt quarries! White
sepulchral marbles! There is whiteness in the shadows! Light frosts that
would be smiles in sunlight; crystal jewels bedecking darkness; frozen
avalanches!—dunes of moon dust—eider feathers on the spuming
waves—peaks of ice that gleam with hopes unspoken" (p. 59).

Later still, the theme of death by progressive mineralization and the
disappearance of water was to provide the explicit story line of a novella
by Rosny, *La Mort de la terre*. The author imagines a future when mankind is on the verge of ineluctable extinction brought about by the progressive desiccation of the planet. At the same time, there is a new race
evolving destined to succeed us, the ferromagnetals, which are purely
mineral organisms with powers of self-propagation. This scenario provides him with the opportunity to describe the earth when reduced to
desert conditions by the disappearance of all water. It has become "a
sinister landscape of granites, silicas, and metals, a plain of desolation
stretching to the very foot of the bare surrounding mountains, which are
without glaciers, without springs, without a blade of grass or patch of
lichen."[33] The hero of the story, Targ, hoping to achieve the survival of
his species, decides to hunt for water in the depths of the earth, and
having clambered down into a crevasse he enters a subterranean world
that recalls Verne's *Voyage au centre de la terre,* a mineral dungeon: "He
was as it were embedded in the depths of the earth, a prisoner of the

mineral world, a tiny, infinitely weak thing that could be pulverized by a single falling block'' (p. 41). Moreover, his discovery of a cave recalls an adjacent theme, that of precious stones, here wholly identified with the mineral universe:

> He advanced into the cavern. Above him rose an arching vault of rock crystal and gems. At each movement of the lamp, magical, mysterious glints ricocheted around it. The innumerable souls within the crystals awoke at the light: it was a subterranean twilight, a lurking dazzle, an infinitesimal hail of scarlet, orange, jonquil, hyacinthine, or heraldic green gleams. Targ saw it as a reflection of mineral life, of that vast and minuscule, threatening and profound life that was having the last word with mankind. [Pp. 47–48]

Targ does find water, but it almost immediately disappears again, and his heroism wins the human species no more than a brief reprieve from its final annihilation. One of the last landscapes described shows us a world now wholly mineralized, reduced to titanic and frozen geological convulsions:

> An immense tawny wall barred the horizon. The aviator crossed it, and sailed on into the abyss. Gulfs opened up below him, gulfs of darkness, their depths unguessable. On every side were the remaining signs of vast convulsions; entire mountains had crumbled, others were about to topple into the unfathomable void. [P. 94]

Beyond the allegory of the end of the world, the world death that haunted the consciousness of the entire decadent epoch, one senses that this story also conceals the play of an elemental reverie illustrating the triumph of the mineral world.

The Vegetable Kingdom

The theme that was to dominate the decadent epoch more than any other was that of the vegetable kingdom, of plant life. Because plant life is normally linked with the theme of nature, of which it is one of the most important constituent elements, we shall find it treated in a way that manifests with particular clarity the various forms of decadent antinaturalism. Moreover it was to be employed widely by the plastic and decorative arts, particularly by exponents of Art Nouveau, for which, in the form of the arabesque, it was to provide the dominant motif.

What we find in a great number of decadent literary works, in fact, is a vegetable kingdom that has ceased to be stationary, passive, and fragile, and has become, on the contrary, animated, in constant expansion, and aggressive, to the extent that it is threatening to imprison man, to swamp him, to suffocate him with its all-powerful dynamism. Plant life becomes progressively more anthropomorphic, to the point where it takes on the characteristics of a conscious, self-determining entity, and one generally endowed with malevolent intentions as far as man is concerned. This anthropomorphism was not new, of course, since it had already found expression in Greek mythology, which tended to view every tree as concealing a dryad, just as every spring contained a nymph. With the decadent imaginary world, however, this theme was to be revived with a somewhat morbid slant added to it: tree trunks and branches represent human limbs, sap becomes blood, and gnarled trees tend to become tortured bodies. These are very much the images one senses underlying this passage from Maupassant's *Sur l'eau,* for example, in which the author is describing a cork oak forest on the Côte d'Azur:

> They are stripped in this way from the base right up to the first branches, and the denuded trunk turns red, blood red, like a flayed limb. They assume bizarre, contorted shapes, airs as of crippled, epileptic creatures writhing in their affliction, and suddenly I felt that I had been hurled into a forest of torturers' victims, a bloody, hellish place where men had roots, where bodies distorted by pain had come to resemble trees, where life flowed out unendingly, in ceaseless agony, from those bleeding wounds that filled me with the same tension and sudden weakness of the nerves brought on by the sudden sight of blood, the sight of a man unexpectedly run over, or fallen from a roof. And this sensation was so strong that I thought I could hear moans, piercing, distant, numberless shrieks, and when I touched one of the trees, to reassure myself, I thought, as I turned that hand toward my eyes, that as I looked my palm was red.

There is a similar, and equally macabre, imaginary process to be found in *La Princesse aux lys rouges,* the story by Jean Lorrain mentioned earlier, in which a young princess diverts herself by beheading lilies, each flower of which represents the life of a warrior who has died for her:

> But, oh mystery, now there came an exhalation as of sighs and dying gasps, a rain of weeping. The flowers, beneath her fingers, had the elasticity and smooth touch of flesh; at one moment, something warm fell upon her hands, which she took for tears, and the scent of the lilies grew sickening, oddly different now, insipid and heavy. [P. 17]

The flower as martyr occurs less frequently in decadent writing, how-ever, than the flower triumphant, or proliferating, superabundant vegeta-tion endowed with an unbelievable power of growth that has before long covered everything in its path. Then the decadent garden becomes a jungle or a virgin forest, the objectifying image of a nature at once hostile and actively threatening, of a nature that pursues the cycle of its trans-formations, its eternal life, with total imperturbability, utterly indifferent to the human adventure. This theme of the garden as a jungle had already been used with extraordinary power in Zola's *La Faute de l'abbé Mouret* of 1876. For although le Paradou is Paradise, the primitive garden that shelters the loves of the first man and the first woman, it is also an often strangely frightening place. Among the many imaginary themes that are interwoven or juxtaposed in Zola's description of this garden, the first and most important is certainly that of the omnipotence of the vegetable kingdom, this power of propagation that gives the hallucinated spectator the impression of seeing branches and leaves growing before his eyes in a dazzling foreshortening of time:

> The virgin forest was its own construction, a jungle of rosebushes, invading the paths, plunging into unexplored clearings. . . . Creepers covered the earth with frothing car-pets, while climbing roses shot up through other rose bushes, hooked onto them like all-devouring ivies, rocketing upward in green shafts. . . . The clearing was formed of large rosebushes all in tiers, rising with a wild debauch of stems, a thicket of thorny, flexible stalks, so that thick draperies of foliage were hung in mid-air, suspended, like floating canopies between one shrub and the next to form a hovering tent.[34]

All in this garden is metamorphosis. The rose becomes the female body (p. 80). Tree trunks are changed into giants bound by some enchantment (p. 100). Plant life becomes first mineral architecture (p. 91), then running water (p. 95). Often, however, it is its disturbing aspects that dominate: the forest can turn easily into a maze:

> Their tracks vanished as they advanced. The path, having been opened, closed again, and they walked on without di-rection, lost, tricked, at random, leaving nothing in their passing but the swaying of high branches . . . On every side, between living hedges, narrow rides went branching off, twisting around on themselves, intersecting, winding, seeming to end, then capriciously continuing. [P. 100]

Moreover, by its sheer power of expansion, this plant life destroys everything in its way, and transforms all human constructions into ruins.

It does not merely take advantage of ruins in order to colonize them, it creates them:

> Left to itself, free to swell without shame, in the depths of this wilderness shielded by its natural barriers, nature abandoned itself increasingly to every spring, indulged in terrifying revels, delighted in presenting itself at every season with strange bouquets that no human hand would ever pluck. It seemed possessed by a furious desire to destroy anything that man had tried to make; it rebelled, invaded the paths with a wild array of flowers, encircled the necks of all the statues with the coiling ropes of climbing plants, and toppled them; it shattered the flags of pools, of stairs, of terraces, by driving tree roots through them. [Pp. 83–84]

The vegetable kingdom is not only the destroyer of monuments, the creator of ruins, but it can also take on the terrifying shapes of monstrous beasts, and Zola takes advantage of these correspondences between plants and animals to create an entirely new and fantastic flora; then come the poisonous flowers, spreading death with their scent and producing the semblance of a macabre charnel house:

> And Albena led Serge to the right, into a field that was like the garden's graveyard. Dark scabious stood in mourning. Lines of poppies receded in procession, reeking of death, spreading wide the feverish brilliance of their heavy heads. Tragic anemones swarmed in grieving groups, colored like bruises, dusty with some epidemic exhalation. Squat daturas stretched out mouths like purplish cornets in which insects, tired of life, had come to drink a suicidal poison. Marigolds were burying their own flowers beneath their swollen foliage, cadavers of stars in mute death agonies, already breathing out the pestilence of their own decomposition. [P. 86]

This book, with its vast wealth of metaphor, was to prove a germinal influence, as we shall see, on the entire decadent imagination and in fact provided the point of departure for the majority of its vegetal themes. Thus, the theme of the omnipotence of plant life, symbol of the unfeeling play of natural forces which swamp and annihilate all human creations, is found repeated again and again. Also, the theme of plant life is associated in an original way, as it is fleetingly in Zola, with that of ruins: if the abandoned château falls into ruins, it is less from the direct effects of time than as a result of the destructive and corrosive action of the surrounding vegetation in its garden or park, vegetation proliferating in mad profusion so that it not only overruns the walks and paths but dislocates the stonework, however solid, shatters flagstones, topples statues. The formal French garden of the *fêtes galantes* then becomes a pitiless jungle. This is indeed the spectacle presented to us, for example, in the early chapters of Huysmans's *En rade* of 1886, in the course of which the author describes his central character's move to the ruined château of Lourps:

> Low pine branches barred the path, ran along the ground, heaved themselves up again, killing all vegetation beneath them, scattering the earth with brown needles by the thousand, while old vine trunks leapt from one side of the walk to the other across the void, and fastening themselves to the shafts of the pines, coiled around them, snaking up to their very tops.... Great oaks...provided support for parasitic plants that clung around them, branching out into delicate traceries.... It was an inextricable tangle of roots and tendrils, an invading flood of couch grass. [Pp. 55–56]

The same theme appears again in a passage from *Le Voyage d'Urien*. In the course of their journey, the travelers encounter floating islands whose vegetation has covered all the available space. In Gustave Kahn's *Le Conte de l'or et du silence* there is a chapter recounting the dreams of the young hero, Samuel, while he is imprisoned in a tower. One of these dreams, entitled *La Forêt tuée*, extends this theme of all-invading vegetation and introduces us to an enchanted forest in which people become bewitched. In this case, the imagined plant life, apart from being supernatural, is also colored by elements of metamorphosis:

> The plants growing from the earth directly in his path bent down and stretched themselves along the ground. He broke off a branch: there was a sigh of pain. He plunged his knife into a crevice in a tree trunk: blood spurted out, and a human shape hurled itself toward him, showing its gaping breast, then fell back at the foot of the tree with a great cry. [Pp. 252–53]

In *Narkiss,* the Jean Lorrain story already mentioned, the plant life becomes mineralized, and we meet the image of the jewel-flower again:

> In a wild spurt of stems, leaves, and umbels, there came the feverish upwelling of sap, the rage to breed, a writhing lust for life, a ferment of seed, and the unfolding menace of vegetation now excited, overheated, triumphant, gigantic, and hostile.... Flowers huger than clusters of dates, plants higher than palm trees; translucent leaves that seemed swollen with luminous sap; transparencies of aquamarine,

of jade, and snakelike coilings that writhed up to great ex-
plosions of petals and corollas, to falling showers of stars;
whole fields of papyrus plants spattered with star fragments,
calices of unknown shape and color, rigid as metal, others
round and white, buds of magical lotus flowers like ostrich
eggs, haloed by enormous leaves: all of them writhing,
bending, spreading their fronds, interweaving, strangling
one another, joining only to spring apart, parting only to
bend back and coil together once more, frozen in sharp
outline as though carved in bronze against the wan flatness
of dismal marshes, abruptly glimmering like a silver mirror
as the moon appeared. [P. 78]

The element of metamorphosis present in the imaginative processes of
this passage recurs in other texts of the period. There is the theme of the
flower that comes to life, and then, easily superimposed upon it, that of
the flower as monster. The chapter devoted to flowers in *A Rebours*
presents us successively with the flower-organ, which looks like viscera
or purulent wounds, the metal-flower or fabricated flower-object, "a
masterpiece of the artificial," resembling "a stovepipe, a fish slice, a
saber blade," and so on, and lastly the flower as carnivore (pp. 124–28).
Thus vegetal monstrosity becomes ever more pronounced; its faculty for
metamorphosis is given ever freer rein, encouraged no doubt by certain
works of Odilon Redon, as for example the famous flower with a human
head which was the subject, first of a charcoal drawing, then of a litho-
graph published in the *Hommage à Goya* of 1885. This latter Redon work
was to be evoked by both Hennequin and Huysmans, who used it as the
starting point for his story *Cauchemar,* which was discussed earlier. In
this work plant life is the dominant element, but it is associated with either
metallic or organic themes:

From that shadowy water, beneath that opaque sky, there
sprang suddenly the monstrous stem of an impossible
flower. It seemed a rigid rod of steel on which grew hard,
metallic, knife-edged leaves. Then buds emerged, like tad-
poles, like still unformed foetus heads, like pallid fleshy
bubbles, noseless, eyeless, mouthless; at last, one of these
quasi-luminous buds, glowing as though smeared with
phosphorescent oil, burst open, swelled into a pallid head
that rocked in silence on the water.

Then the dangerous aspects of the vegetable kingdom gained predominance. After the carnivorous flower came the flower with a toxic
scent, and it is the macabre elements that are given increasing emphasis.
They had begun to surface already in Bourget's work, specifically in a

passage from his dialogue *Science et poésie* mentioned earlier. The conversation begins in a florist's shop in Cannes:

> This shop, longer than it was wide, was redolent with, as it were, an agony of scents, delicious and intoxicating. . . . The florist wandered here and there through this narrow domain, capitulating to its lethal influence, for her lusterless complexion and too-brilliant eyes . . . bespoke the sure and slow intoxication of that fevered atmosphere. [P. 190]

This macabre strain comes to its ultimate fruition in Mirbeau's *Le Jardin des supplices* which presents us with the spectacle of an oriental prison surrounded by a magnificent garden whose flowers are fed every day with the blood and bodies of executed prisoners; and in a story by Rachilde, *La Peste de Florence,* which describes how Florence is devastated by a plague, abandoned by its inhabitants, and reduced to acres of ruins that are taken over totally by vegetation.[35]

Plant life as a theme was also to be exploited on a large scale in the plastic and decorative arts by a number of schools, culminating, at the end of the century, in what has come to be known as Art Nouveau, which made particularly abundant use of decorative elements derived from plants, and more generally of the arabesque.[36] When the plant kingdom occurs in art, it is used to fulfil the same task as that required of it in literature: to symbolize the blind forces of nature, with its omnipotent dynamism, which overruns and destroys human creations and even imprisons human beings themselves in a proliferating tangle, a plant prison. Similarly, the widespread use of the arabesque corresponds to a desire to saturate perception by drawing it into a maze of curves that submerges and obscures all solid forms. Like baroque art, with which it shares a similar dynamism, as well as a taste for ostentation and superabundance, Art Nouveau aims to provoke an impression of profusion in which the spectator's gaze becomes lost.[37] This cultivation of formal superabundance is evident, for example, in the wrought iron work prevalent at the time, in which the arabesque manifests itself in a particularly pure form. Examples are Gaudi's staircase for the Casa Calvet (1898–1900), the entrance gates of the Palais Guëll, and the Casa Vicens. This same superabundance of curves is also found across the Channel in the works of Beardsley[38] and in the general style of the illustrations for the magazine *The Studio.*[39] In France, where the arabesque proliferated so publicly in posters by artists like Mucha, we find Eugène Grasset expounding the theory behind this fashion, as well as providing classified examples, in his *Méthode de composition ornementale* of 1894, in which he provides clear explanations of the specific function attributed by late-nineteenth-century art to the spiral and the arabesque. What the decadent sensibility required of this profusion of curves and spirals was that it should express the anarchic upsurge of concealed layers of the sensibility, so that there can be no doubt that such art contains a predominantly irrational element. We also find in Grasset's book an expression of the desire for visual saturation, which the author conveys by means of such esthetic concepts as "elegance" or "richness." The ideal art is for him an art that covers every surface totally with a close-knit network of curves:

> Just as it is a fault to decorate plain surfaces if they are of a material very rich in itself, such as certain marbles or woods already displaying great contrasts and variations of color, so it is also a fault to leave long sections empty when the material has no tonal variations of its own. It is not gold, any more than rarity or intrinsic value, that creates richness; it is the method of working even the most poverty-stricken material, and at very little cost, in order, once again, to avoid the visual flatness, coldness, and poverty that even the most costly material can present.... That once grasped, the way is open for the creation of true works of art, works upon which the hand can rest with refined and subtle pleasure, and which will not repel us like the eternally plain and polished glass of mirrors.[40]

In 1901, in a work devoted to the development of contemporary decorative art, Jean Lahor confirms this predominance of the arabesque and plant motifs:

> It was in the work of Horta and Hankar that I first saw such backgrounds, though among other things, especially with them, moderately and very nicely used, backgrounds formed by those flexible lines, waving like strips of seaweed, or broken and serpentine like certain linear caprices of the ancient illuminators, lines that now, among their imitators, lashed into frenzy, have spread from the field of wrought iron work, and a few wall panels, to every kind of furniture, to the entire house, their contortions, dances, delirium of curves becoming an obsession today, and often a torture for the eyes.[41]

Obsession with the arabesque, ornamental delirium, these are indeed terms that one might well apply to the fin-de-siècle decorative style, an obsession and a delirium that are linked to the expression of the concealed self and to the eruption of hitherto-repressed unconscious impulses into the light of day. Anxiety and dread, even perversity and morbidity, the eruption of the unconscious, baroque superabundance of forms expressed

by means of an ever more complex network of arabesques, antinaturalism, violent movement and deliberate visual excess, these are indeed the essential features to be found in the specifically decadent strain
of fin-de-siècle art.

Moreover this vegetable element is also often associated with other
natural elements that lend themselves to the arabesque, and in particular
with the female body. A complex interplay of metaphors and metamorphoses then occurs between the curves of plant elements and certain
feminine features, such as the lines of body and clothing, or the movement
of long hair blowing in the wind. A good example of this is provided by the
cover of La Motte-Fouqué's *Ondine,* executed by Heywood Summer in
England in 1888, where a female body swathed in supple, striated
draperies is seen emerging from an intertwining network of curves that
evoke both the agitation of waves and that of some kind of aquatic vegetation that mingles with the nymph's own hair. Among a thousand other
possible examples of this interplay of arabesques in which the curves of
the female body, hair, and plant life are intermingled, one can also point to
Beardsley's illustration for the List of Pictures page in the first British
edition of Wilde's *Salomé* (1894), in which the heroine is depicted standing surrounded by slender stems erupting into clusters of flowers indistinguishable from her hair. This same procedure occurs in most of
Mucha's posters, particularly the *Saisons* series of 1896 and the *Fleurs*
series of 1897, in Carlos Schwabe's *Fervaal,* many works by Toorop, and
a great many illustrations for *The Studio.*[42] In their use of themes taken
from the vegetable kingdom, then, there is clearly a deep fund of inspiration common to both decadent literature and the art contemporary with it.

Metamorphosis

Our examination of the various elemental themes em-
ployed by the decadent literary imagination has revealed again and again
how easily that imagination was able to move from one element to
another, or to merge them into a single imaginary complex. It is in fact the
case that the whole imaginative life of this period was shot through with a
tendency toward metamorphosis, and that the zones of contact between
the various natural elements provided the most intense stimuli to its poetic imagination. Water becomes mineralized as it turns to ice, as in
Gide's *Voyage d'Urien,* or when, as in so many of the texts we have
encountered, it is viewed as a mirror; the precious stone brings together
the transparency of water and the brilliance of the gem, as well as its
hardness; vegetable and mineral kingdoms fuse their glamours in the
burning bush of jewels described in the first dream of *En rade.* The vege-

table kingdom is also constantly anthropomorphized, as in the case of Redon's human-headed flower and the numberless examples of animated plants, carnivorous plants, and plant-monsters with which texts of the period abound.

In order to grasp the underlying development of the imaginative process during this period, the literature of the time is therefore best read from the standpoint of metamorphosis. Here, for example, from Henri de Régnier's *Poèmes anciens et romanesques,* is a passage in which gems, plants, and water are fused into a single imaginary complex:

> When you took my hands in your pale hands
> And the dead blue
> Of their opals
> My enchanted soul glimpsed lakes of death,
> And in the wood blued by sea green shade with opals
> Of dead water, magical and vegetal water,
> Flowers floated where the silence sleeps ... [P. 97]

Such an approach is also the only means of extracting its true meaning from Pierre Loti's *Le Désert* of 1895, which is an account of how the author set out from Cairo and attempted to reach the Holy Land via the Sinai, Akaba, and the desert around Petra. Beyond the superficial, anecdotal aspect of the work, which is certainly of interest even read simply as a travel book, the desert gradually becomes the theme of an elemental reverie centered on the mineral kingdom. The desert is the triumph of the mineral, of stone, and also a world of death, of total sterility, a lunar universe:

> On the ground there are scatterings of tiny black pebbles, or glittering sheets of mica; but not a plant now, nothing at all. And the landscape begins to become broken and racked, almost mountainous: heaps of gravel and stones, forever useless and unusable, assuming, though why and for what eyes who can say, extremely intricate shapes, which have doubtless been there for centuries, immutable, bathed in this same silence, this perennial effulgence.... And it is an almost terrifying magnificence.... And all is empty, silent, and dead.... It is the splendor of regions that never vary, innocent of those fleeting enticements offered by forests, plants, or grass; it is the splendor of matter in an almost eternal form, freed from all the instability of life.[43]

Around this dominant theme, however, Loti allows his imagination to digress in a number of subsidiary directions. First, the accidental formations of rock and stones occasionally give the impression of obeying some hidden design, of reflecting the influence of an intelligent will. The natural outcrops are then perceived as the ruins of titanic cities: "One feels one is passing amid ruined cities, walking along streets, streets made for giants, between toppled palaces and citadels. The constructions, composed of superimposed layers, are continually rising higher, becoming more superhuman, taking on the shapes of temples, pyramids, colonnades, or huge solitary towers" (p. 85). Or the rocks even seem to be obeying the laws of some astounding natural geometry: "The mountains... assume the strangest shapes, and one is almost prepared to believe that some hand has carefully selected them, grouped them according to more or less similar configurations: for a league or so, there will be sequences of superimposed cones, tiered with an intention of symmetry; then the peaks become flattened, and there follows a series of Cyclopean tables." (pp. 12–20). The desert is also, however, the kingdom of fire, of the marriage between solar energy and stone. Loti describes the plain as "flooded with light, scorched with beams" (p. 26), a place where everything "is picked out with astonishing clarity by an implacable white light" (p. 47). The desert then becomes for him "a region prodigal with its fires, which daily puts on its magical displays of light that no one is there to see" (p. 128). In the full heat of the day it becomes a kind of cosmic oven:

> And, thereupon, there fell sunlight so heavy and so feature-less that it seemed made solely to kill by desiccation!... We had not seen anything so sinister up till then: one was suf-focating in a scorching gloom, through which, as though sinking in search of self-annihilation, there filtered all the light from overhead; to be there is to be in a world that has ended, unpeopled by that fire, a world that no dew will ever come again to fertilize. [P. 90]

And yet, in the gleaming of certain rocks, and through the agency of mirages, the poetic reveries of water can still well up again at moments. For instance, a featureless plain strewn with black pebbles has a tendency to change into a lake: "At first, until burning noon, the solitudes are mere expanses of black pebbles, as though covered with a scattering of coal, and these pebbles gleam, shine in the burning sun, giving an illusion of dampness to the thirsty beings who pass. They stretch for league on league, these black wastes glittering into the distance" (p. 17); while the undulations of the sand call to mind a frozen sea. The desert of Tih, for instance, looks "something like a sea, higher in level than the surrounding regions, and, as it were, frozen by calm weather, leaving it eternally smooth and waveless" (p. 183). Elsewhere "undulations begin to become apparent, like the beginnings of a ground swell as it invades a motionless sea" (p. 199). Elsewhere again, patterns in the stones reintroduce plant imagery: "This morning we are surrounded by flesh-colored sandstones, dendritic like the most precious forms of agate: on every freshly broken surface the most delicate foliage is etched, some like bracken leaves, some like maidenhair fern" (p. 192). Finally, at other moments, ceasing to be angular and geometrical, the rounded shapes of rocks can animalize the stone, so that groups of boulders seem like "piles of petrified animals" (p. 41); certain granites look like "heaps of antediluvian creatures" (p. 80); at times the writer discovers "piled up masses of smooth blocks that to the eye look soft, with strange animallike curves and outlines . . . like great stacks of monsters, piles of pachyderms, salamanders, larvae, or else agglomerations of embryonic limbs" (p. 38).

In this text, then, despite its dominant mineral key, we find the author's imagination running through the entire gamut of elemental reverie by means of incessant metamorphosis. Thus Loti's book, while being a particularly clear and rich example of this play of elemental reveries, is also representative of one of the decadent imagination's essential tendencies.

The Underwater World

This fusion and metamorphosis of natural elements was to find its most favored expression during the decadent era, however, not in the mineral kingdom but in a theme that recurs constantly in the work of many writers, that of the underwater landscape. For those underwater depths conceal an entire world, in which all living forms are represented: plant life in seaweed, animals in the various kinds of fish and shellfish, and even a strange form of life that wavers between the animal and vegetable kingdoms. Moreover its reality is bathed in a particular light, that provided by luminous water, which blurs the forms of things while also making them glow, and gives all realities the appearance of a dream. From this latter point of view it would scarcely be an exaggeration to say that, to the decadent consciousness, the underwater world constitutes a sort of natural and real correspondence with the entirely inner world of dreams. Even as early as *Vingt mille lieues sous les mers,* Jules Verne's descriptions of that still-unexplored world were already impregnated with a natural poetry. Several years later, with the publication of *La Tentation de saint Antoine* in 1874, Flaubert's contemporaries were able to make their first acquaintance with what quickly became a very famous passage, the episode toward the end of the book in which the author evokes the "creatures of the sea." This passage is not only a Darwinian hymn to the glory of the earliest living species, but also a reverie wholly permeated with metamorphosis:

Phosphorescence gleams on the moustaches of the seals, on the fishes' scales. Sea urchins spin like wheels, ammonites unwind like cables, oysters grate their hinges, polyps unfurl their tentacles, jellyfish quiver like crystal balls, sponges float, anemones spit water, mosses and seaweeds have struck root.

And all sorts of plants stretch out their branches, twine into spirals, stretch into points, open into fans. Gourds resemble breasts, lianas coil like snakes. Babylonian Dedaïms, which are trees, have human heads for fruits; mandragoras sing, the root Baaras runs through the grass. Plants are no longer distinct from animals . . . [44]

The combined influences of Verne and Flaubert must undoubtedly be regarded as having provided the initial impetus for the great success this theme was to enjoy from then on. In the 1880 Salon, for example, Moreau exhibited his *Galatée,* which depicts the goddess in an underwater setting, bathed in that dream light that is the particular characteristic of underwater reverie. "In a deep cave such as those loved by Da Vinci," the critic Paul Leprieur wrote, "the nymph is at rest in her unviolated virginity, in her ideal and chaste beauty, half asleep, seated among underwater flowers. . . . Her left arm leans upon a rock, and her long fair locks fall to the sea bed, thick and heavy, like streaming stalactites or falling pearls. Her frail and charming body with its amber pallor . . . stroked by silvered fronds of waving seaweed, seems still half sunk in the vegetable or mineral world around her: red and bleeding corals, sea anemones like flowers, starfish and madrepores, attempts at life, the embryos of souls." [45]

Soon afterward, we find Huysmans's Des Esseintes replacing his diningroom window with an aquarium, through which light must filter before reaching the room. Similarly, Laforgue's *Moralités légendaires* contains, in *Salomé,* a description of an aquarium, with its landscapes, fauna, and flora. A few years later, this underwater reverie is represented on two occasions in Maeterlinck's work: first in *Serres chaudes,* with the poem *La Cloche à plongeur,* which evokes

A whole sea of glass perpetually warm
A whole immobile life of slow green pendulums
And so many curious beings through its walls

and also in the story *Onirologie,* in which, inspired by a poem of Thomas Hood's, he imagines Leander, the legendary swimmer, diving through the underwater depths of the Hellespont, drawn on by a siren unaware that she is killing the being she loves. Verhaeren too published a prose poem entitled *L'Aquarium* in *La Wallonie.*[46] Then, with Georges Rodenbach's *L'Aquarium mental,* the theme of the underwater world becomes clearly identified with that of dreams:

> And his fate was now one with that of the glass:
> To be one sleep shot through with dreams . . .
> All is dream, all is solitude and silence . . .
> The water now is for the pensive plants alone,
> Fronding, floating upward, willing captives
> That are his inner life, embroidering it
> With dreams, his mental canvases . . .[47]

It is this same imaginative strain that we find later on, in certain passages of Gide's *Voyage d'Urien* of 1892, or of Régnier's *Tel qu'un songe,* or in the collection of stories published in 1900 by Edouard Ducoté under the title *Merveilles et moralités,* which contains this description of an aquatic landscape:

> Through the slack surface, one's eyes could freely probe
> into transparent azure liquid and discover the magical
> spectacle offered by the gardens of the deep. On a bed of
> fine sand, all sorts of shells, pearly pink, purple, or violet,
> were scattered, lying motionless, or gently shifting their ca-
> pricious shapes.[48]

Finally let us remember that it was the same underwater world that inspired not only several of the plates in Redon's 1896 album directly inspired by Flaubert's *Tentation,* but also many of the pastels executed between 1902 and the artist's death.

CONCLUSION

THE FINAL YEARS OF THE NINETEENTH CENTURY WITNESSED A RAPID disappearance both of symbolism as a collective movement and of the esthetic upon which decadent literature was based. The disappearance of the symbolist movement has been commented upon and analyzed many times by critics who have studied that movement. In Guy Michaud's view, for instance, symbolism itself crumbled away in a very short space of time and gave way to a multitude of minor rival currents, while the decadent trends that had marked its origins reappeared with renewed force in the work of writers such as Gourmont, Schwob, Montesquiou, and Pierre Louys.[1] William Kenneth Cornell also deals with this swift eclipse in the last chapter of his *The Symbolist Movement*. Similarly, in his thesis, "*La Crise des valeurs symbolistes*," Michel Décaudin has undertaken a detailed analysis of the development of the symbolist movement in poetry, as revealed in the principal magazines and the attitudes adopted in verse collections published during the last years of the century, and shown very clearly how, in France, that movement did in fact continue, but adopted a very different position from that which had prevailed at its outset. Thus although most poets continued to proclaim themselves symbolists during these years, symbolism itself, as an active movement, was clearly dead, as critics of the time acknowledged again and again.[2]

These conclusions are confirmed, moreover, by the evidence of creative writers working at that time, or slightly later, who despite having frequently been active participants in the movement, nevertheless accepted that it had now ceased to exist. The feeling, around the year 1900, that a literary era had come to an end was widespread among writers themselves. Décaudin quotes the statement made by the critic René Doumic, for example, in an article published by the *Revue des Deux Mondes* on 15 July 1900: "The Symbolist School thus appears as a school that has fulfilled its task and had its day."[3] Similarly, in a contemporary article on *Le Symbolisme en France*, reprinted in his collection *L'Art en silence* of 1902, Camille Mauclair both issues the movement's death

238

certificate and also attempts to provide a first summing up of its achievements. With reference to the ideal around which the principal avant-garde writers had grouped themselves, he wrote that "one can regard their movement as having terminated of its own accord" (p. 199). In the next few years other writers were to attempt similar accounts of the movement's achievements, with varying degrees of lucidity and self-congratulation, as for example Gustave Kahn, in *Symbolistes et Décadents* published in 1902, or Retté in his *Le Symbolisme: anecdotes et souvenirs* of 1903.

The observations made by these critics with regard to the history of the purely poetic movement can also be applied, in fact, to the general esthetic ideal and world vision that had characterized literary circles of that time as a whole, an ideal and a vision whose principal feature I have attempted to elucidate in this book, and which I have subsumed under the general concept of decadence. One can go even further, and say that what was collapsing in those final years of the century was less the particular conception of poetry itself than, much more generally, the whole conception of the world and the state of mind that had until that point pervaded the literary world in general. For one does not have to look very hard to perceive that the main technical advances made by symbolist poetry were never in any way challenged during the next few years. One may even say, in fact, that it was during these ensuing years that they achieved definitive acceptance and a widespread influence on the French poetic movement as a whole. Thus poetry became definitively dissociated from those "impure" elements, in the sense Valéry gives that word, constituted by the expression of ideas, decorative description, or the narration of events, all things henceforth relegated, and justifiably so, to the realm of prose. It was this period, too, that saw the clear affirmation, so important for modern poetry, of the distinction between poetry and the use of verse. The same is also true with regard to the great importance henceforth granted, in the poetic use of language, to the musical value of words. One might even say that the symbolist poetic ideal, conceived and progressively clarified during the last two decades of the nineteenth century, but illustrated during those years solely by poets who are today viewed mostly as minor writers, was to reach its true flowering only in the next century, with the work of writers such as Claudel and Valéry, to whom Guy Michaud devotes the final chapters of his book.

What did disappear from view once and for all with the end of the nineteenth century, however, was the entire decadent vision of the world. This vision, as we have seen, was characterized by specific traits: fundamental rejection of the world and a reality regarded as intolerable by man in general and the artist in particular; fundamental pessimism deriving from the conviction that the sum of suffering in human existence is always far in excess of possible happiness; negation, in consequence, of the reality of this despised world and affirmation of an idealism that took a variety of forms—philosophical idealism, subjectivism and solipsism, or mysticism and occultism; resolve on the artist's part to escape reality by all possible means, by creating his own paradise in one way or another, and by resorting to various methods of evasion—refinement of sensations, even taken as far as hallucination, dreams and drugs, exotic imagery and poetic reconstruction of vanished civilizations; rejection of nature in all its forms—natural landscapes, human nature—and a corresponding celebration of artificiality, pursued with the aid of drugs, the artificial aspects of modern life, or sexual perversions; last, a refusal by the artist to participate in the political or social life of his time, in the name of an artistic purity that practical considerations could only sully.

Now these particular traits were to be progressively contested, disparaged, and even condemned in an increasingly radical way, even before the end of the century, by a countermovement whose growing impetus during the 1890s can to some extent be gauged, and which has been largely isolated and identified already thanks to Décaudin's analyses of the developments within the poetic movement. Early signs of it had in fact already begun to appear as early as 1893–95. The phenomenon is particularly noticeable at the level of the refusal to take part in political action, which during these years received a first setback in favor of anarchist agitation, in which a number of writers did in fact become involved. Similarly, as early as 1893 we find a writer like Hugues Rebell contributing an article to *L'Ermitage* in which he attacks certain aspects of the symbolist movement: stylistic complications, horror of the natural, insincerity, abuse of mythological erudition, and legendary embellishments. The following year, 1894, Retté himself, who in his *Thulé des brumes* of 1891 had taken escape to its furthest limits, moved to the country near Lagny, and the resultant contact with nature was to lead him to a total reversal of his previous position: his poetry from that point on was to be directed toward a pantheist celebration of nature and an enthusiastic endorsement of life, as for example in his collection *La Forêt bruissante* of 1896.[4] Simultaneously, he was also to launch a campaign against Mallarmé, whom he viewed as a symbol of the dead end into which literature had been led by the symbolist esthetic. After a first article in January 1895, there came a whole series of pieces, published throughout 1896 in *La Plume* and later in book form under the title *Aspects,* in which he continued his unremitting attack on the decadent vision of the world and his denunciation of Mallarmé's influence. There were also a number of other symptoms of a general reaction against the symbolist esthetic in poetic circles at this time, as Décaudin has shown: development of non-symbolist poetic themes and sentiments in a series of provincial magazines, particularly in the south of France; the influence of Belgian poetry via the works of Verhaeren and Max Elskamp. After 1896 this movement begain to acquire considerable momentum, partly as a result of Retté's conversion, partly because of the new trend in poetry constituted by naturism,[5] and partly because a new poetic generation had begun to emerge with works such as Francis Jammes's *De l'Angélus de l'aube à l'angélus du soir,* Paul Fort's collection of *Ballades,* and, of course, Gide's *Les Nourritures terrestres.*

The decline of symbolism, and of the esthetic upon which fin-de-siècle literature had been based, became precipitous during the last two years of the century. This decline is to be explained, in particular, by the deaths of a number of artists, those whose influence in the movement had in fact been greatest, or whose work had been most representative of it. Verlaine died in 1896. 1898 brought the deaths of Mallarmé and Rodenbach as well as those of Gustave Moreau, Puvis de Chavannes, and Aubrey Beardsley. Moreover, in the space of a few years, and for varying reasons, a number of the movement's most important writers left the Parisian literary scene for good. Huysmans, for example, after his conversion in 1894, chronicled in his *En route* of the following year, was to detach himself increasingly from literature; he ceased to frequent literary circles, and after *La Cathédrale,* published in 1898, withdrew into total silence. Gourmont, totally disfigured by the lupus that attacked him in 1891, was to lead an increasingly isolated existence, even though he continued to play an essential role on the *Mercure de France.* Schwob, whose health had always been delicate, underwent a series of operations in 1895 that failed to restore him to health and forced him to lead the life of a recluse from then on. Mauclair had contracted a chest ailment, and left Paris at the end of the century for a long stay in Marseilles, reflected in his *L'Ennemie des rêves,* and from that time continued to live either in the Midi or at Saint-Leu-la-Forêt outside Paris. In 1901, Lorrain, whose excesses, particularly his use of ether, had gradually undermined his health, likewise took up permanent residence in the Midi before his early death in 1906. Thus, in the space of a few years, the literary establishment was deprived in one way or another of a number of those who had been the avant-garde's most representative writers during the previous few years, those who had given decadent literature its distinctive tone. Finally, it should be noted that 1899 brought the final closure of the Théâtre de l'Oeuvre, which meant the end of symbolist theater. Moreover, as a consequence of Zola's famous article in *L'Aurore* of 13 January 1898, that year and the next were to witness a rising tide of unrest linked with the campaign for a review of the

Dreyfus case. As the whole of French society split into two camps, so its writers were to be drawn increasingly to take sides in this ideological battle, and to repudiate their splendid isolation of previous decades, while one branch of literature, in the work of writers such as Barrès and Maurras, was to concern itself with the open expression of nationalist opinions. The disintegration of the movement was to continue through the first years of the new century with the gradual disappearance of most of the periodicals that had guided and sustained literary life during the previous decade. Very soon, the *Mercure de France* was the only remaining survivor of those original publications.

What is apparent, in fact, in all these developments, is a fundamental questioning of all the principles that had inspired the decadent mentality. First and foremost, the previous generation was sharply criticized for having shut itself away in an unreal dream world. That is certainly the meaning that emerges, for example, from Mauclair's two novels *Le Soleil des morts* and *L'Ennemie des rêves*, published in 1898 and 1899.[6] In the first, a poet named Callixte Armel, who is plainly Mallarmé, himself admits the failure of his life's ideal and the literary dead end into which his esthetic has led him. The second tells the story of Maxime Hersant, a decadent poet living in Bruges who, under the influence of a good woman's love, agrees to return to nature, to reality and joy, by going to live in Marseilles. Mauclair openly uses this plot to declare his disengagement from recent literary fashions. In particular, he denounces the excessive use of imaginary elements, which had become "a means of turning one's back on real life, of avoiding its chores, of reducing the duties it imposes." "It had become a drug," he continues, "a hashish creating the paradise of those who had lost heart." He no longer regards dreams as anything other than "an element of moral decomposition." In more general terms, he expressed a blistering contempt for the attitude of Parisian intellectuals:

> All of them claimed to put their faith in dreams, but none of them truly wrote about them. In their minds it was a sort of murky, undefined principle; their eyes, when they talked about it, became vague.... Glittering above reality, Dreams, the Idea, heralded glowing, artificial dawns that never broke, displayed countries to which there was no access. All the verbose fragments left over from a high-school-level metaphysical education were concentrated in those sonorous terms.... Dream was just the old romantic principle, melancholy, aristocratism, the pessimism of the Werthers and the Renés of this world. [Pp. 252–54]

It was not only the cult of the dream that was denounced, but also the predilection for artificiality, the cultivation of everything rare, the exag-

gerated refinements of sensation that led eventually to a chimerical universe wholly unrelated to life. In his *Essai sur le naturisme* of 1896, we
find the principal theoretician of the naturist trend, Maurice Le Blond,
launching an attack on the two writers who had been the principal masters
of the decadent generation, Baudelaire and Gautier, who, he writes
"scarcely succeeded in doing anything but send the contemporary soul on
a wild goose chase in search of an ideal of appearances and exceptions."[7]
In a chapter headed "Artificial Literature," he also blames them for having directed literature toward the abnormal and the pathological:

> Baudelaire, impotent and neuropathic, and not unaware of
> the fact either, was an extremely baneful ancestor of our
> artificial litterateurs. It is an honor he can claim to share
> with Théophile Gautier and the Goncourts. The morbid, the
> odd, the abnormal, all attracted him. He was a wonderful art
> critic, a passionate analyst of complicated emotions, but he
> understood nothing about nature. . . . He was thus the first to
> initiate our avid minds into sterilizing pleasures.[8]

Similarly, in the preface to *L'Ennemie des rêves,* Mauclair attacks "the
unconscious vanity of professional writers and decadents of today, their
flimsy and factitious vision of existence." In his account of the sudden
crisis which leads Maxime Hersant to desert the decadent ideal, he writes:
"He had a sudden intuition that those people who were rejecting everyday life, seeking out the rare and abnormal at any price, scorning to take
any active role in their times, exhausting themselves with endless
analysis and narcissism, were doomed to intellectual death" (p. 18). For
the decadent writer was now being criticized not only for having shut
himself away in a lofty ivory tower but also, by rejecting life and reality,
for having reached a dead end of solipsism and narcissism. Thus Retté
condemns "the frenzied solitudes in which poets indulge their sterile
ecstasies";[9] Le Blond, attacking Barrès, accuses him of having "devoted
himself in silence to the delicious pastime of analysis";[10] and Mauclair
attacks the cult of the self, which he now regards as a "moral narcotic."
Referring to recent poets, he also writes that "they must learn first not to
analyze themselves so much, and to concern themselves enormously with
others."[11] In 1896, in the preface to his collection of articles *La Crise
morale,* the young Maurice Pujo also singles out solipsism as one of the
causes of that crisis:

> In another phase of the crisis, the man disappointed by the
> external world and the inevitability of its facts renounces all
> attempts at acting upon that world, attempts to live inside
> himself, in the palaces constructed by his own imagination.
> But that is to feed off one's own heart. The source of

dreams, if never replenished or fed by any real act, gradually dries up, along with the life of the man who has given himself up to them. Ludwig II of Bavaria sank into madness and death.[12]

Going even further, and motivated by the violent anticlericalism he professed at this time, Retté denounced in *Aspects* not only the influence of Schopenhauer, whom he described as an "insidious blackguard" (p. 86), but also the various forms assumed by the religious unease of the period, and attacked "those still being poisoned by Christianity in the bastard form of a suspect spiritualism" (p. 167). Equally opposed to all forms of mysticism, he addressed his readers in these terms, for example:

> Do you not realize that Christianity, in its final reincarnation, the mystical rottenness exemplified all around us, constitutes one of the major determining factors of the morbid state of mind you are fighting against? I do not think myself mistaken when I suggest that most of the sado-Christian writers of today must have received a clerical upbringing. Brought into contact with followers of Science, bruised by an environment impervious to their incitements, angered by the hostility of healthy minds, they lose themselves in the most convoluted systems and the most senseless aberrations. [P. 192]

Reacting against the dangerous deviation constituted in their eyes by the decadent state of mind, writers were now beginning to pin their hopes to a new vision of the world characterized by a return to action.[13] These are the three elements I shall now try to isolate and exemplify, with the help of the copious material made available by Michel Décaudin's *La Crise des valeurs symboliques.*

There were in fact a great many writers aspiring to a return to nature, which was of course one of the essential aims of the naturist movement. We find Saint-Georges de Bouhélier stating plainly that "there is nothing admirable outside nature";[14] and Maurice Le Blond summed up the ambition of the new young poets as follows: "We wish to renew our individuality in the universal embrace. We are returning to nature."[15] At that same period, Retté observed with delight that contemporary literature was offering "the spectacle of an admirable renaissance that is growing more pronounced each day ever since it took nature alone as its guiding light" (*Aspects,* p. iii). This return to nature meant, first of all, a rediscovery of the beauty of natural landscapes. And Retté was one of the first to make that rediscovery, which occurred in his case when he moved out to live in the country, in the Guermantes district to the east of Paris, and which he expressed in *La Forêt bruissante,* especially in the "omitted preface" to that collection, which was in fact printed the following year in *Aspects,* and which describes the writer's state of bemused joy at re-discovering mental and physical well-being:

> But I want to express the perfect joy I felt in writing *La Forêt bruissante.* For over a year, wholly surrounded by nature, spurred on by the leafy rustling of the trees, by the scent of flowers, and by the play of light and shade during the summer months, or stimulated by the keening litany of the wind that sobbed through the snow-covered countryside on winter evenings, I watched my heroes take shape, I suf-fered and laughed with them.[16]

It was at this time, too, that Gide was making a similar rediscovery, brought about in his case by the African landscapes encountered during a journey begun at the end of 1894, and expressed in *Les Nourritures ter-restres.*[17] This reappearance of a poetic sensitivity to the beauties of unadorned nature, an attitude that the decadence had striven to abolish, is also perceptible in the very titles of many verse collections published during these years, such as *Les Voix de la montagne* by Michel Abadie, Henri de Régnier's *Les Jeux rustiques et divins,* or Saint-Georges Bouhélier's *Eglé; ou, les concerts champêtres.* Commenting on this new inspiration animating the poetry published during 1896, Retté summed up recent developments in the field in terms that confirm this return to na-ture:

> Despite many hesitations, uncertainties, and momentary weakenings, and despite having been brought up to see things through books rather than their own eyes, the new poets, at last safe from the quags in which they were nearly trapped by those false Pegasuses with bats' wings—the nonsense-mongers, the idlers, the bilious maunderers—are ascending to the light. In all the books we have just looked at there is a tendency to go back to nature, a passionate predilection for the countryside that makes one rejoice. [*Aspects,* pp. 85–86]

In contrast to the Nordic mists and vague landscapes lit by fitful and disturbing gleams that had so often appeared in much recent work, this rediscovery of natural landscapes often tended to take the form of a celebration of specifically Mediterranean nature, with its exuberant veg-etation, its luxuriantly colored flowers, and above all the dazzle of its sunlight that leaves no form in shade. Certainly this was very much the form that Mauclair's return to nature took in *L'Ennemie des rêves.* In persuading Maxime Hersant to leave Bruges, which as we have seen was a symbol of the decadent atmosphere, his mistress, Marthe, "wished to take him with her, like a convalescent, into the violent and sacred sunlight, into a full life lived openly and magnificently, far away from nostalgias and reflections'' (p. 74). And Hersant's convalescence, parallel to Gide's real life convalescence in Africa, is indeed closely linked to the ecstatic discovery of the Mediterranean scene, in which ''the lapidary, clear-cut brilliance of the landscape, the absolute visibility of the tiniest details, banished the possibility of dreams'' (p. 88).

For many writers of the time, this enthusiastic renewal of interest in nature was to lead to a kind of pantheism. In these cases, what is involved is not mere contemplation of nature but a veritable fusion of man with the natural universe, now that the barrier interposed between them by the decadent vision of the world had suddenly been broken down. Attempts at escape into an abstract or religious transcendence produced by decadent anxiety were replaced by adhesion to the immanent wholeness of the cosmos. Hugues Rebell had already professed a pantheist credo as early as 1893, in an article on Moréas's *Le Pèlerin passionné:*

> For the charming soul of the pantheist, the whole world is
> like the garden of the Prince de Ligne, or that of Bel-Oeil, in
> which one glimpses the smiling statue of a goddess or hero
> at every step. The poet cannot imagine dead landscapes.
> Everywhere in nature he discovers life, everywhere he sees
> gods.[18]

This pantheist trend, still permeated in Rebell's case with traditional mythology, was to gain momentum after 1895. In his *Essai,* Maurice Le Blond writes: ''We believe in a titanic and radiant pantheism'' (p. 13). Retté likewise, at that time not uninfluenced by the Hugo of *Chansons des rues et des bois,* exclaimed: ''For hear ye the great news: Great Pan is risen again!'' (*Aspects,* p. 199). This pantheism, professed so openly, was also to lead writers to glory in a parallel return to paganism and barbarity.[19]

Finally, the same movement was to lead to the disappearance of the antifeminism that had been such a marked characteristic of the whole decadent generation. Whereas the decadent hero shrank from woman or, subjugated by her despite himself, regarded her as a source of moral disintegration, creative sterility, and death, Mauclair's Maxime Hersant finds in his mistress, Marthe, a clear-sighted and supportive companion who, by her loving care, helps him back onto the road to life. This is why, in the preface to *L'Ennemie des rêves,* Mauclair felt justified in prophesying a rehabilitation of women: ''We are about to discover the true, the beneficent woman, who has been waiting, patient and unscathed, for the tide of sophisticated lies put out by the novelists to ebb.'' Parallel to the return to nature, we thus find a more general resolve to seek a reconciliation with life. Whereas the decadents, setting dream and life against each other, had decided to turn their backs on the latter and abandon themselves wholly to a universe of dreams, the next generation, inverting this attitude, proclaimed its new love of life from the rooftops. The word life, usually given the benefit of a capital letter, recurs constantly in the poems, manifestoes, novels, or essays that appeared at this time, and may justifiably be regarded in its turn as the key word of postdecadent literature. Michel Décaudin has clearly shown the gradual progress of this rehabilitation of life in the poetry of the time. He points out, for example, the development in Belgian literature, beginning in 1894, of a "poetry wholly imbued with freshness and a confidence in life."[20] He also notes that Vielé-Griffin, in an article published in the October 1895 number of the *Mercure de France,* saw "the glorification of life" or "the worship of life" as the common ground shared by most recently published poetry.[21] Even the titles of two collections published at this time are revealing: Vielé-Griffin's own *La Clarté de la vie* ("The clarity of life") of 1897, and Max Elskamp's *La Louange de la vie* ("The praise of life") of 1898. And one of Maurice Pujo's articles in his collection of essays *La Crise morale* was actually headed "The Return to Life." Mauclair, in *L'Ennemie des rêves,* wrote in similar vein of "a definitive acceptance of life on the ruins of false heavens built from dreams" (p. xxiii) and his central character, summarizing the author's own conversion, proclaims: "I fled the factitious glow of the sun of the dead to seek the natural light of life" (p. 131).

This "life" that such authors were attempting to rediscover, understand, and appreciate again meant, in the first place, daily life, a familiar everyday existence, contact with things and people, as opposed to the abstraction and intellectualism in which the decadent generation had delighted. It also meant, however, a renewal of contact with the life of the people, ordinary people, peasants, workers, or craftsmen, in reaction to the aristocratic individualism of the decadent heroes such as Huysmans's Des Esseintes or Gourmont's d'Entragues. In his *Trésor des humbles* of 1896, Maeterlinck had expressed the wisdom and the mystery concealed by even the most humble existence, the greatness and solemnity that can lie behind the most ordinary activities of everyday life. In the magazine *L'Enclos,* which was published from 1895 until 1898 and in which social and humanitarian concerns were openly and forcefully expressed, we find an assertion of the will to "mingle with the people and with Nature, the principles of all art."[22] The work of Saint-Georges de Bouhélier, Décaudin observes, "celebrates, not without some grandiloquence, the magnificence of everyday actions ... exalts 'village folk' and 'craftsmen.'"[23] Maurice Le Blond, too, was to emphasize the greatness inherent, for any clear-sighted artist, in the work of craftsmen: "Here is a craftsman, his attitude and his function, the landscape that surrounds him, the air that caresses and illuminates him, all that makes him sublime" (*Essai sur le naturisme*, p. 58). And he contrasted the abstractions and allegories that had weighed down so many symbolist works with the sight of "that little Mouquette who presents to any passerby, so ingenuously, the double dawn of her young buttocks" (p. 72). He likewise appreciated the rehabilitation of physical health and the life of the flesh to be found in Verhaeren's *Les Flamandes:* "Since we are so weary of those delusive settings full of wilting and anemic roses, emotional complications, and cerebral sadism, let us love *Les Flamandes* . . . and feel our spirits lift among these fleshly Edens, these red idylls, these joys that may perhaps be coarse but are also wild, untamed, with a soothing and unstinting healthiness" (p. 78). In other words, the fin-de-siècle neurosis was over, and it was time to convalesce, to take the road back to both physical and moral health.

Last, after the deliberate isolation the heroes of the decadence had indulged in, there was a desire to take part once again in collective life, the life of the human community, of work, and of the city. In his *Discours sur la mort de Narcisse,* the funeral oration of a mythical hero who, like Hamlet, had constantly haunted the decadent consciousness, Saint-Georges de Bouhélier adjures his contemporaries to forget their sickly, arrogant, anxiety-ridden introspection: "Ah, let us not stay inside ourselves any longer!"[24] Similarly, in *L'Ennemie des rêves,* Mauclair expressed the exaltation experienced by his two leading characters when they come into contact with the tumultuous life of Marseilles: "But they entered the heart of the violent city with feverish delight in the evenings, to gorge themselves on brutal heroism. They could never have enough of that heady, triumphant sensation of self-annihilation in the crowds" (p. 99).

This new attitude brought in its train, logically enough, a resolve to reexperience the joys and dangers of practical action. Linked to the cult of nature and the cult of life, there was also a cult of energy. And here we must make some mention of the influence of Nietzsche, who, by delivering a message whose practical conclusions were diametrically opposed to those that the previous generation had derived from Schopenhauer, was now to replace the latter as the intellectual authority of this new vision of the world. Indeed, it is worth pointing out, as others have done,[25] that the first complete French translation of any work by Nietzsche, if we except *The Case of Wagner,* was that of *Zarathustra* in 1898, thus coinciding with the first exhaustive study of his work in French, that by Lichtenberger.[26] However, a number of articles or shorter commentaries had begun to appear as early as 1892, so that the educated French public did already have some idea of the German philosopher's ideas. Late in 1892, excerpts from *Zarathustra* appeared in French in *La Revue blanche*. In January of 1893, in a review of the French translation of *The Case of Wagner*, Hugues Rebell insisted on how instructive Frenchmen of the time would find the work of this new German writer, whom he himself regarded above all as a bulwark against the menace of socialism:

> In the tide of vile and hypocritical egotism that is called socialism, in that self-serving ecstasy of the vulgar and weak, one man has arisen to remind this mob, which has forgotten them, of the rights of intelligence, and to raise the head of individual pride against this democracy that praises humility out of envy as well as out of impotence.

However, while interpreting Nietzsche's thought as an aristocratic morality, Rebell also welcomed him as the advocate of energy, of that energy "so necessary to the physician who has set himself the task of curing an extremely sick humanity.... Friedrich Nietzsche is truly the man essential to our society, which is now without direction, without principle, and even without common sense."[27] The following month, again in *L'Ermitage*, Henri Mazel expressed similar ideas. He too asserted that a decadent France could learn a profitable lesson from Nietzsche's work: "If philosophic products, like organic ones, contain an active principle, then Nietzschean philosophy may be one of the most powerful agents of social therapy, at once fearsome and beneficent."

From this point, interest in Nietzsche and his ideas was to increase steadily in literary circles. In late 1894, Henri Albert informed the readers of the *Mercure de France* that he was embarking upon a translation of the German writer's works, and appealed for possible collaborators; further articles also continued to maintain the French public's curiosity.[28] In 1895, a number of excerpts appeared in French in *La Revue blanche*.[29] Finally, in 1898 came two full-length translations, one of *Thus Spake Zarathustra*, the other of *Beyond Good and Evil*, in addition to the study by Lichtenberger.

This latter work, intended as a comprehensive analysis of Nietzsche's thought, contained many observations that the French reading public were able to put to good use. Lichtenberger saw Nietzsche's work as both a denunciation of the decadent world view and also the affirmation of a new morality capable of remedying the ills from which contemporary European civilization was then suffering. And Nietzsche saw the origin of this decadence as lying in the triple influence of Schopenhaurian pessimism; Christianity, which he regarded as the religion of slaves; and the democratic ideal:

> Modern Europe, according to Nietzsche, is profoundly sick. Symptoms of undeniable decadence are visible everywhere. It is as though man today is suffering from an overwhelming fatigue.... Here, egalitarian democracy is trying to turn him into an ugly and contemptible herd animal; there, Christian priests, philosophers, and moralists are all trying to wean him away from this earth and delude him with a chimerical Beyond to which he is supposed to sacrifice his life. The democratic state is a degenerate form of state; the religion of human suffering is a morality of the sick, the art of Wagner, at present triumphant, is an art of decadence. Corruption and pessimism are apparent at every level of modern culture, even the very highest. [*La Philosophie de Nietzsche*, p. 144]

Lichtenberger also demonstrated, with great clarity, how Nietzsche, having followed Schopenhauer in accepting the existence of suffering and its quantitative predominance in human life, then goes on to reject absolutely, in the name of the individual·will and self-affirmation, all the consequences that his predecessor had drawn from that fact, particularly his pessimism and wish for annihilation:

> Instead of concluding, as Schopenhauer did, that the will to live must be negated, Nietzsche, like the Dionysian Greek, admires and reveres this Will that strives eternally for life, and justifies it by every possible means. He is a pessimist, but the conclusion he draws from his pessimism is not the necessity for resignation but the necessity for heroism; he regards asceticism not as an ideal but as a symptom of fatigue, of degeneracy.... And consequently, instead of preaching detachment from life and aspiration to nirvana, as the pessimists do, he regards as "good" everything that contributes to a strengthening of man's will to life, everything that gives existence an added aim or interest, everything that renders it worthy of being lived. [P. 51]

Nietzsche's philosophy thus led to a complete acceptance of life, illustrated by the myth of eternal recurrence, and to a celebration of the superman's will to power. Lichtenberger sums up this attitude as follows: "Given that I live, it is my will that life shall be as exuberant, as prolific, as tropical as possible, within me and outside me. I shall therefore say 'yes' to everything that makes life more beautiful, more worthy of being lived, more intense'' (pp. 103–4). Thus Nietzsche's philosophy was seen, not only in Lichtenberger's book but also in the various articles that had preceded it, as a refutation of Schopenhauer's, as a denunciation of the decadent attitude and an appeal for reconciliation with life and action, a cult of rediscovered human energy and greatness. It is true, of course, that the scarcity of French translations before 1898 meant that direct acquaintance with his work in Parisian literary circles was restricted until that date to those who, like Schuré, Wyzewa, Henri Albert, or Lichtenberger, were able to read him in the original. However, enough articles and commentaries had appeared in the French press for writers to have become aware of his work's originality and general purport, as the conclusion of Lichtenberger's book makes clear: ''In France his ideas have been familiar to us for a long time through numerous magazine or newspaper articles'' (p. 185). The rising tide of curiosity that Nietzsche's work continued to evoke is a clear indication of the general change in the public's mood and state of mind in the last years of the nineteenth century, a change whose principal aspects I have attempted to define.

This return to action and this celebration of energy were soon to raise the problem of the relation between writers and political life. At the outset, both symbolists and decadents had advocated and adopted an attitude of total detachment with regard to the public life of their day. Many influences had contributed to the formation of this attitude: the ancient doctrine of art for art's sake, revived by Gautier; Baudelaire's denunciation of any collusion between poetry and politics; Flaubert's contempt for electoral intrigues expressed in his play *Le Candidat* of 1875; and Renan's skepticism. Although writers had on the whole been in favor of the formation of the Third Republic, they continued to regard the new political establishment with exactly the same contempt they had expressed for officeholders under the Second Empire. Moreover, the savage repression of the Commune had made it quite clear that the price exacted from intellectuals for meddling in public affairs could be a very high one indeed.

The decadent ideology prevalent between 1880 and 1890 could only encourage this total noncommitment on the part of writers. After all, it was a generally accepted fact at the time that the defeat of 1870 had tolled the knell on French national greatness for many long years to come, perhaps forever. Since France, as a human collectivity, was by now enfeebled beyond recovery by the very refinement of its civilization, and therefore doomed to ineluctable decline, any attempt to engage in political activity would have been quite futile. It was this background of general disintegration that was viewed as precisely the precondition for the flowering of vigorous artistic individualities and daring and original works of art. The artist's contempt for the average man, generally referred to as bourgeois or philistine, not only obliged him to turn in upon himself, to cultivate his inner garden and live in a world preserved for works of art; it also made it impossible for him to engage in anything so vulgar and devoid of interest as public debate. The writer viewed himself as belonging to an intellectual aristocracy that had everything to lose by mingling with the mob. Barbey d'Aurevilly's carefully cultivated dandyism and Villiers de l'Isle-Adam's pride in his ancestry inclined them both to follow the same path. Moreover, the very fact that naturalism had advocated a much wider social spread in the novel drove its opponents, as a reaction, to depict only elite circles and exceptional people. It is hardly surprising, therefore, that the works of the period's two most representative writers, Mallarmé in the case of symbolism, and Huysmans in that of decadence, should be almost wholly without political reference. As for Bourget, in his dialogue *Science et poésie,* quoted earlier, we find him condemning the progressive equalization of wealth as "a bad condition for the flowering of certain rare plants" (p. 204), denouncing the establishment of democracy as the triumph of mediocrity "simply because it leads, in politics, to the imbecile sovereignty of the greatest number; in education, to a fruitless dispersal of knowledge; and in economics, to a fruitless dispersal of wealth" (p. 202).

The following decade, on the contrary, was to see a perceptible change in the attitudes and behavior of writers as a whole. In its first stage, this new interest in action became apparent in the varying degrees of support that writers expressed for the anarchist movement. Between 1890 and 1894, there was a wave of anarchist agitation, beginning with demonstrations during the May Day celebrations of 1890 and 1891, then leading to a series of anarchist attacks—that by Vaillant in the Chambre des Députés in December 1893, that by Emile Henry in the Gare Saint-Lazare in February 1894, and lastly the assassination of Sadi Carnot in June 1894. These in turn led to stern repressive measures, such as the *"lois scélérates"* in December 1893, the arrests of January 1894, the executions of Vaillant and Casério, and the trial of the Thirty in August. And during those years an appreciable number of writers belonging to symbolist circles plainly expressed their sympathy with the anarchist movement. As early as 1890 this trend is to be found expressed in the contributions of Paul Adam, Bernard Lazare, and Pierre Quillard to the *Entretiens politiques et littéraires,* the first number of which appeared in April of that year. The following year, Fénéon, Verhaeren, Mirbeau, Mauclair, and Paul Adam all contributed to *L'En Dehors,* the paper founded by Zo d'Axa. In 1893, *La Plume* devoted its May number to a series of articles on the philosophy of anarchy, and from that point on expressed an increasing sympathy with the movement. Lastly, in 1894 Retté was arrested and imprisoned along with a number of other sympathizers or militants, and the same fate befell Fénéon, who was to be one of the accused in the trial of the Thirty, and on whose behalf many writers intervened.

However, we must not exaggerate the extent of this commitment on the part of a few younger writers to the anarchist cause. Retté and Fénéon aside, most writers restricted themselves to an expression of interest merely, without offering any concrete support. As soon as repressive measures began to be taken, the majority of them abandoned the movement entirely in alarm, as Retté was to observe ironically later, in a passage from his *Promenades subversives:*

> Nothing is more curious than the sudden tacks of that bourgeois caste the scribbling breed. Not long ago, since a subversive air was very much the thing, a great many young writers were inclined to advocate anarchism and clamor for a revolution. Before long, however, on account of certain noisy—and justified—incidents, their ardor cooled. It became impolitic to advertise such explosive opinions. Whereupon the fashion for dissidence was abandoned for one of extreme prudence.[30]

Moreover, the reasons for this sympathy with anarchism were much more intellectual than political. If some groups of young writers were favorably inclined to the movement, it was above all because they regarded it as providing a political equivalent of the individualism they were advocating in literature. They saw anarchism not as a popular movement but, on the contrary, as an aristocratic one. This is made plain by the answers to the referendum conducted by *L'Ermitage* in 1893 on the following question: "Which is the better basis for social good, a spontaneous and free organization, or a disciplined and systematic organization?" The results were published in the July number, and despite the great variety of answers, a surprisingly large number began by expressing hostility to any form of authoritarian regime, whether monarchic or socialist in nature.[31] This attitude was summed up by Henri Degron, for instance, when he declared that "what we need, we savages who live in the woods on the fringes of a dream, is solitude, absolute independence, and, above all, no Mister Big."[32] Those who came out openly in favor of anarchy were still very much a minority.[33] But the part played by fashion, and a purely intellectual inclination, in this sympathy for anarchy is most apparent in the reply of Wilde, who wrote: "Once upon a time I was a poet and a tyrant, now I am an artist and an anarchist."[34] Much later, when Mauclair was reminiscing about this period of his youth, and the reasons that may have led him to express interest in anarchism, his conclusions were not so different:

> So I convinced myself that I was an anarchist, because my
> young, hot-headed conscience perceived a host of injustices
> in our society. . . . Added to the various elements contribut-
> ing to my conversion—distaste for degenerate parlia-
> mentarians, artistic distaste for things "bourgeois"—there
> was also the lively sympathy I felt for the defeated com-
> munards (Roussel was my god and Thiers my horror), and
> lastly a lively aversion for the leveling effect of
> socialism. . . . I imagined an aristocratism that would be si-
> multaneously anarchist and yet friendly to the people, and I
> believed in universal pacifist brotherhood while remaining
> mistrustful of internationalism.[35]

That was why he was to denounce—admittedly at a time when he had long
since adopted a much more conservative political position—what he saw
with hindsight as a certain snobbery of anarchism: 'It was very chic to be
implicated, and to receive a visit from a police superintendent was a
coveted honor.''[36]

In fact, after the repression of 1894, the writers who continued to express anarchist sympathies, or even to feel them, were few and far between. One of them was Retté, who continued for several years to launch
increasingly violent attacks upon all forms of authority or oppression,
whether it was the Roman Church, militarism, or colonialism. In his *Promenades subversives,* a series of often vituperative reflections and
maxims published in 1896, we find him berating the judiciary, the army,
and colonialists alike, as well as advocating social revolution and a general strike. Retté's stance, however, perhaps made to appear more spectacular than it really was by the violence of his style, was very much the
exception at that time.

Although anarchy turned out to be no more than a passing temptation
for most writers during the years 1890–94, the same was by no means true
of the Dreyfus affair several years later. It is probable, in fact, that the
politicization of literary circles began to increase gradually from about
1895. There was a widespread rise of nationalist sentiment, perceptible in
the activities of writers like Maurras and Barrès. Gourmont was clearly
aware of these developments when he wrote in the November 1895 issue
of the *Mercure de France:*

> But since the discovery of patriotism, since men have begun
> to slake their thirst with that rancid milk, it is as though the
> tissues of universal life have tightened, folded in upon them-
> selves, imprisoning the essential cells in a strict and jealous
> jail. For a Frenchman, to be French comes before every-
> thing, even genius, even though the French are one of the

most obviously hybridized of all the peoples waving their
guns over the ancient soil of Europe.

As a result, when, after Zola's *J'Accuse* in January 1898, a campaign was
launched to quash the sentence on Dreyfus, and France slowly split into
two camps, the majority of writers also took sides. Long before Zola's
article, another writer, Bernard Lazare, had already played an important
role in challenging the sentence that had destroyed Dreyfus's career. As
early as 1896, in fact, while simultaneously advocating an art of social
inspiration, he had published a pamphlet expounding the thesis that the
sentence was a judicial error.[37] It was in fact Lazare who drew the case to
the attention of the *Revue blanche,* which was to play a major role in the
campaign to have the case reviewed.[38]

In 1898, as result of Zola's intervention, an increasing number of writers were to join in his demand for a pardon. Apart from Lazare and such
contributors to the *Revue blanche* as Lucien Herr and Léon Blum, they
included, for example, Mirbeau, Pierre Quillard, Ferdinand Hérold, Paul
Hervieu, and Jules Renard. At the same time a considerable number
joined the anti-Dreyfus camp. Evidence of how widespread this participation was is still extant in the two lists of names drawn up and published
at the time, the first in the *Hommage des artistes à Picquart,*[39] the second
on the occasion of a subscription organized by the paper *La Libre Parole*
on behalf of the widow of Colonel Henry and published by Pierre Quillard.[40] Of course, all that was required of writers, who mostly came out in
favor of Dreyfus be it said, was to put their names on a list at a newspaper
office. But it is nevertheless true that the Dreyfus affair, which posed the
question not merely of one unjustly condemned individual's rehabilitation, but of the defense of universal moral and political principles, led a
great many writers, particularly among former decadents or symbolists,
to question their previous isolation and to interest themselves more
closely in contemporary political life. With the tremendous stir and agitation it aroused for at least two years, the affair brough a breath of fresh air
into Parisian literary circles, and clearly posed the problem of political
commitment.[41]

Thus, with this simultaneous return to nature, to life, to action, and to
political commitment, it certainly appears that the entire world view on
which the decadent esthetic had been based was crumbling away. Yet it
would be illusory to believe that, once the nineteenth century had ended,
the intense ferment of ideas, curiosity, and experiment in the imaginative
domain that characterized the decadent period vanished without leaving
any repercussions. The decadent imagination, despite a number of trans-
formations, lived on in fact to the middle of the twentieth century, together with its interest in imagination's most anarchic forms, such as the

dream, as well as its predilection for the artificial and the supernatural. It would not be impossible to demonstrate, for example, that in many ways, and despite the clear differences that distinguish them, the surrealist imagination took over and continued the imaginative heritage left by the decadents. Of course, the surrealists were vociferous in their claim to be original, and attempted to give their contemporaries the impression that the movement they were inaugurating represented a radical innovation in the history of French literature. This impression was strengthened by the connection they claimed with the Freudian theory of the unconscious, and the literary consequences they felt they had derived from it: automatic writing; the violent style of their statements; the showmanship of their demonstrations; their refusal to be merely men of letters; and their determination to establish a new conception of life in general that would lead to a simultaneous flowering of love, liberty, and revolution. Further, by nominating Lautréamont and Rimbaud as their precursors, in other words writers whose influence remained minimal during the period of decadence and symbolism, they appeared to be disposing at a stroke of all French literature between 1875 and 1914: in their eyes it was as though between those two great forebears and themselves no work of any importance had seen the light of day, apart from a few references to Apollinaire and Jarry, then later to Raymond Roussel and a few others, such as Saint-Pol-Roux. The silence they maintained with regard to the prose writers of the decadent period could give the impression that they knew nothing of them, or regarded their work as null and void. It is probable, however, that the surrealists were not as ignorant of those writers as their silence might lead one to think, even apart from the fact that the silence was sometimes broken.

We know, for example, that André Breton admitted on several occasions to an admiration for Huysmans. There is the famous passage in *Nadja* in which he confesses his sympathy for both the ideas and the personality of the author of *Là-bas*.[42] Similarly, the preface to *Le Revolver à cheveux blancs* contains an allusion to the first dream of *En rade*. And *Les Vases communicants*, too, contains a laudatory mention of Huysmans's work. This sympathy was confirmed, moreover, by Aragon, who in an article for *Les Lettres françaises* in 1967, reminiscing about his first meeting with Breton in September 1917, tells how they discovered a shared admiration for Mallarmé, Rimbaud, and Jarry, and how Breton also talked to him about Huysmans and Francis Poictevin.[43] It is also known that Breton felt a lifelong fascination for that other great master of the decadent imagination, Gustave Moreau, whose depiction of Dalila he describes at considerable length, for instance, in *Les Vases communicants*. Similarly, Michel Leiris has acknowledged the early influence exerted on him, particularly with regard to the genesis of *Aurora*, by Marcel Schwob's *Le Livre de Monelle*, and also, via Schwob, by the work of De Quincey.[44] The scarcity of documentary evidence presently available, particularly of reminiscences by surrealist writers relating to the intensity of such decadent influences, means that it is probably still too early to elucidate this phenomenon completely. It remains probable, nonetheless, that such an influence was considerable in the movement's early years.

To describe and analyze in any detailed way the gradual transition, over the thirty years from 1895 to 1925, from the imaginative world of decadence to that of surrealism, to isolate the links and affinities that exist between them, would require a whole further book to itself, and certainly goes beyond the aims of this conclusion. However, I should like to sketch a number of guidelines that will indicate the general character of this development. First, it would be possible to demonstrate the continuity of imaginative preoccupations and supernatural themes in the period from the end of symbolism to the outbreak of war in 1914, by investigating the activity of a certain number of personalities, literary groups, or literary trends that form successive links in this history of imaginative life. One would have to begin by taking into account the works of Jarry and Fargue, two writers who, having belonged to the last symbolist generation, that which began to emerge in about 1895, were to remain active beyond the beginning of the twentieth century. In the case of Jarry, who died prematurely in 1907, his prose work, after *Les Jours et les nuits* of 1897 and *Les Gestes et opinions du docteur Faustroll*, written in 1898 and published posthumously, continued after 1900 with, most notably, *Messaline* and *Le Surmâle*, which undoubtedly constitute important events in the history of the French novel's imaginative evolution. Moreover, the influence he exerted on surrealist writers, and the high regard in which they held his work, is known. With Fargue, who remained active for much longer, and whose work was exclusively poetic up till the 1914 war—his *Poèmes* of 1911 being a distillation of his previous work—we find at this period a predilection for both modernity and dreams that was to bear fruit later in a number of prose works. Also of major importance historically was the role played by Apollinaire and his friends, first with the *Festin d'Esope* of 1903–4, then the *Soirées de Paris* of 1912.[45] Similar imaginative preoccupations are also apparent at this time among the group of writers that emerged from the magazine *Méditerranée*, who first came together in Marseilles in 1895 under the leadership of Edmond Jaloux, then reformed again later, after 1905, in the salon of Gilbert de Voisins. The latter had moreover published a fairy-tale novel the year before entitled *Pour l'amour du laurier*. Finally, one would need to take into account the activity and works of a number of Belgian writers, such as Jean de Bosschère and Franz Hellens.[46] The first published a fantasy called *Béâle-Gryne* in 1909 that may be regarded as representative of imaginative developments at the time. As for Hellens, in his series of novels and stories published between 1906 and 1925—*En Ville morte* of 1906, *Le Hors-le-vent* of 1909, *Les Clartés latentes* of 1912, *Nocturnal* of 1919, and *Mélusine* of 1920—he achieved a most original fusion of dream and reality.

It is possible to discern an extension of this imaginative trend in numerous narrative works published between 1920 and 1930. These include *Anicet* by Aragon (1921), *L'Autruche aux yeux clos* (1924) and *Ariane* (1925) by Georges Ribemont-Dessaignes, *Deuil pour deuil* (1924) and *La Liberté ou l'amour!* (1927) by Desnos, the large number of stories written at this same period by Benjamin Péret, in particular *Au 125 du boulevard Saint-Germain* (1923), *Il était une boulangère* (1925), *Et les seins mouraient* (1928), and lastly *Le Point cardinal* (1927) and *Aurora* (1927–28) by Michel Leiris. The majority of these works employ wildly complicated plots, derived partly from the gothic novel and partly from the contemporary novelette serial, to tell the story of the hero's quest for a woman who is at the same time a magical figure and also, quite often, unattainable. The quest moves in an atmosphere of fantasy, improbability, and continual slapstick through a varied series of settings, but with a high incidence of locations in modern day Paris, locations often transfigured by dream and fantasy.

The prime characteristic of all these works is a new treatment of their imaginary content. We find that fantasy, the free play of imagination, is gradually moving closer and closer to reality. For an imaginative content cut off from life, elaborated in a world different from that of reality, a universe of legend, these writers are gradually substituting a fusion between the imaginary and the real, between dream and life, which was to lead to the surrealist type of fantasy in which the strange and wonderful can appear at the very heart of the most familiar and humdrum reality. As early as 1901, in an article in the *Mercure de France,* the critic André Beaunier was already claiming to have observed just such a development in poetry; the role of the symbolist poet, he wrote, consists in "reconstituting in the modern mind a faculty that has been lost: the sense of mystery," and in restoring to the reading public its "faculty of wonder."[47] In other words, for Beaunier the use of symbols in poetry was essentially a means of revealing the mystery concealed in the most everyday realities:

> The separation between the knowable and the unknowable
> is a convenient process useful in facilitating certain lines of

enquiry, because human thought proceeds analytically. But it should be clearly understood that the distinction is no more than a provisory abstraction. For mystery is not external to the real, it is within it. The unknowable is not in juxtaposition to the knowable, it impregnates it. And, to use Littré's comparison, what one should say is not that the dark ocean batters the shores of the tranquil island, but rather that the whole island is impregnated with the ocean's mists. Mystery is not simply something beyond observed facts, mystery is at the very heart of the most rigorous experimental results.[48]

This mystery that André Beaunier, employing an abstract and spiritualist language, was inciting his readers to perceive at the very heart of day to day experience was, as most critics who have studied this period acknowledge, the selfsame mystery that an increasing number of contemporary poets and prose writers were also attempting to reveal in their different ways. Marcel Raymond, for instance, in his now classic work, with reference to such poets writes of "a reconciliation between the real and the imaginary."[49] They were encouraged, he adds, "to perceive strangeness, fantasy, mystery, in reality itself" (p. 233). And it was Raymond again who observed, in the same work, with reference to Apollinaire, that "it is from things themselves, from events, that the wonder should well up" (p. 234). And of André Salmon, whose collection *Féeries* appeared in 1907, he wrote:

André Salmon has successfully forestalled the work of time, the transfiguration brought about by memory, and conjured up elements of poetry or wonder, like so many ultraviolet or infrared rays, in the most historical present. And this wonder is not that of the old poets. It lies at the heart of the world. [Pp. 248–49]

In a similar vein, referring to the work of Jean de Bosschère, Suzanne Bernard was to write of "a search for mystery and wonder not in unreal legends but in life itself,"[50] while Décaudin observes that "Béâle-Gryne moves wonderstruck through a world where the real is constantly transfigured."[51] In 1911, commenting on the recent work of Franz Hellens, Edmond Picard speaks of "the birth of a new talent in which the fantastic and the real are sometimes in balance, sometimes at odds, as in certain Flemish primitives, without either element's ever succeeding in subjugating the other."[52]

These few critical comments on some of the poetry or novels published in the first fifteen years of the twentieth century suggest two observations. First, during those years a fundamental change had taken place in the state of mind of writers generally. Imperceptibly but ineluctably, the barrier that previous generations believed to exist between the universe and human consciousness, between reality and dream, was beginning to disappear. Far from trying to escape from life and reality, these writers see them as the essential nourishment of man's imagination. Thus the contempt for reality that characterized earlier generations was succeeded by the discovery of new dimensions within that reality. What has become important is to know how to reveal the wonder, the unexpected, the poetry, that lies hidden behind the superficial or banal appearances of our familiar world. The second observation is that the apparent isolation of the surrealist experiment from earlier literary trends is largely a distortion and an optical illusion. Far from being an isolated and aberrant phenomenon, the surrealist conception of the inherent magic of the world undoubtedly constitutes the last phase of a long and constantly evolving trend whose roots, as we have seen, reach back as far as the height of the romantic era.

This reconciliation of the real and the imaginary was to become especially apparent in the way that the themes of the artificial and modernity were progressively accepted and enriched, particularly with regard to machines, the imaginative use of science, and the ever more frequent presence of the modern city, which came to be preferred as a setting to the legendary backdrops of the decadent period. This interest in machines is evident, for example, in the work of Jarry, which is permeated with scientific curiosity. As early as 1898, the travels of Faustroll are a transposition of the symbolists' imaginary voyages, as exemplified by Gide's *Le Voyage d'Urien* or Mauclair's *Couronne de clarté,* for instance, but undertaken in a science fiction vehicle whose workings are briefly described, and which employs the physical phenomenon of capillary attraction. Similarly, the island Cyril, in chapter 21, is driven by propellers, partly inspired no doubt by Verne's novel of 1895; and in chapter 31 we are given a description of a microphone. This interest in the imaginative use of science continued throughout all Jarry's later work. The action of *Le Surmâle* is dominated by a titanic contest between a cyclist and a high-speed railroad train. In one of his *Spéculations,* published by *La Plume* in 1903, given over to reviews of a number of contemporary novels, Jarry seizes the occasion to embark upon a historical survey of the science-inspired novel, from *The Arabian Nights* up to Villiers de l'Isle-Adam and H. G. Wells. In a similar vein there is also Apollinaire's *Le Roi Lune,* in which we are transported to a cave in the Tyrol and shown strange inflatable furniture, together with machines that enable one to travel freely through time and enjoy ecstatic nights of love with all the famous heroines of history. One of the stories in Hellens's *Nocturnal* describes a railroad nightmare. In *Mélusine* there are descriptions of a car ride through a modern city and later of a motor boat trip through a cross between the Domaine d'Arnhem and Luna Park. The plot of the novel involves two engineers, Nilrem, a modern scientific transposition of Merlin, and Voltourne, who demonstrates a robot of his own invention to the travelers and also expounds a theory of man as machine.

It would also be possible to show that a number of other essential elements of the decadent imagination continued to appear in some of the most significant works of the first two decades of the new century. The use of dreams as literary material, for example, which had borne such fruit in Jarry's *Les Jours et les nuits* of 1897, was to recur in subsequent works. Early in the century there were Alphonse Séché's *Contes des yeux fermés*, one of which was published in an issue of *Le Festin d'Esope* (March 1904). In 1907 there came Apollinaire's famous *Onirocritique*, which was published in *La Phalange* and can be regarded as heralding not only the surrealists' automatic writing but also their dream narratives. In *Pour l'amour du laurier* by Gilbert de Voisins, published in 1904, the travels that the hero, Sylvius Persane, undertakes with his friend Vincent Lautonne, and which take him into a fairy-tale world where he meets Greek divinities and characters from French folk legend, may be interpreted as so many dream journeys. *Nocturnal* by Hellens, in which the author recounts a number of dreams, was prefaced with this statement: "I have resolved to restore to the night, in these pages, the main incidents of nocturnal existence, and the things I have seen in my dreams."[53] Finally, the foreword to the definitive edition of *Mélusine,* brought out in 1952, makes it plain how near Hellens was at that period to the inspiration of the surrealists who were to follow him:

> *Mélusine* represents a collection of dreams and was literally written in a state of trance, a state in which I was immersed during the whole of that strangely fertile period. Waking one morning, my head still full of a fabulous dream, I rushed to write it down with trembling hand, torn between enthusiasm over my discovery and fear of losing even the slightest precious fragment of it.... I have never dreamed so much as throughout that period of about sixteen months, during which the chapters of my book were transcribed under that mysterious dictation.[54]

The same observation could be made about drugs, evoked by Claude Farrère in his *Fumée d'opium,* a collection of stories published in 1904, and also about the use of occultism in prose narrative works, which occurs not only in stories by Victor-Emile Michelet published during the early years of the twentieth century,[55] but also in two novels by a contributor to *Le Festin d'Esope,* John-Antoine Nau's *Force ennemie*—which was awarded the first Prix Goncourt in 1903—and *La Gennia.*[56]

Lastly, it should be noted that the material employed to fuel the imaginative process in the poetic and narrative works of the decadent period is largely the same as that employed in surrealist narrative and imaginative works. In this respect, Julien Gracq's analysis of the images that occur in Breton's *Poisson soluble* is particularly revealing. Apart from numerous images relating to the vegetable or bird kingdoms, Gracq also points out the frequent occurrence of elements related to the world of light, of whiteness, and crystal (diamonds, aigrettes, necklaces, rings, stars, crystal, eyes, pearls, mirrors, stalactites), which may be taken as a direct continuation of the fascination of decadent writers for mineral and crystalline reverie. "Terms evocative of transparency," Gracq observes, "such as glass, ice, gem, mirror, occur with extraordinary frequency."[57] Later, in an article for *Le Minotaure,* and in much the same vein, Breton was to celebrate the beauty of minerals, precious stones, and, in particular, of crystal.

> It is quite independently of its accidental figurations that I am led to praise the crystal here. No higher learning seems to me capable of being received than that derived from crystal. The work of art, by the same token moreover as any fragment of human life seen from the viewpoint of its profoundest meaning, seems to me without value unless it presents us with the same durability, rigidity, regularity, luster, on every external and internal facet, as a crystal.

Later in the same article he evokes the imaginative metamorphosis that can develop from "the absolute bouquets proffered in the sea depths by alcyonarians, by madrepores," mysterious beings existing at the frontier of the mineral and vegetable kingdoms:

> The inanimate comes so close here to the animate that imagination can allow itself an infinite freedom in playing on these forms, so wholly mineral in their appearance, and make use in dealing with them of that procedure whereby we recognize a nest, a bunch of grapes, withdrawn from some petrifying spring.[58]

Most of the elements in that quotation could easily be found in various surrealist narrative works as well. The imaginative processes of Michel Leiris, for example, are dominated, as Maurice Nadeau has clearly shown, by an obsession with the mineral and with metal, whose metaphysical and erotic significance—obsession with death and horror of flesh with its yielding fragility—is moreover quite evident.[59] Two episodes of *Le Point cardinal* are particularly revealing in this respect. In the first, after a dream journey, the central character arrives in a landscape characterized by a mineral sterility:

> Around me, the new landscape stretched in desolation: no vegetation, but stones, stones and a few clouds. In the distance I could make out abandoned quarries and motionless wagons. All riches here were apparently buried in the very heart of the earth, from which there rose shards of conversation, the noise of arguments and pickaxe blows muffled by the beds of stratified rock interposed between the atmosphere and those stubborn borrowers.[60]

The second is an account of a journey to the pole. To reach it, the traveler is forced to swim through water that steadily increases in density, begins gradually to turn to ice, and finally freezes around him to form a hard, cold shell that traps him completely. Similarly, Damoclès Siriel, the central character of *Aurora*, can eventually experience love only with mineralized women:

> There was almost nothing I liked about women other than their crystalline adornments. When I saw them naked, for my desire to be aroused I was forced to imagine they were statues, cold and rigid beings without viscera, without skin, and not the female variety of those tiny, wriggling bladders full of ill-defined sensations and sobs that call themselves men.[61]

Nor would it be difficult to demonstrate the continuation in these surrealist stories and novels of the underwater theme whose various manifestations during the decadent era we looked at earlier. In chapter 4 of his *La Liberté ou l'amour!* for example, Desnos describes how his hero, Corsaire Sanglot, is shipwrecked, sinks to the seabed, and like Jules Verne's characters discovers all sorts of wonders. This theme is also often transposed in surrealist narrative works into a varietal form that combines it with a modern urban setting: that of the Parisian covered arcade. There are several instances of this in Aragon's work, such as the Passage des Cosmoramas in *Anicet* or the long description of the Passage de l'Opéra in *Le Paysan de Paris,* where the glass roof reproduces the glaucous luminosity of underwater lighting. Moreover, the Passage des Cosmoramas, being a wonderland, enables Aragon to rediscover the fascination of the vegetable kingdom in a hallucination that transforms a grocer's window display into a jungle that soon takes over the whole world with the force of its exuberant vitality:

> Yam roots multiplied, crawled, ran, wound upward, and a whole jungle emerged from the glass egg in which cocoa beans still held the perfumes of the Indies and Americas.

> From the taxidermist's shop, which till then I had failed to
> notice, there sprang the fauna to people these branches and
> lianas, this undergrowth, in all points similar to those num-
> berless animals you see illustrated in expensive
> books.... The vegetation was growing so, the animals be-
> coming so vast in number, that I felt imprisoned, suffocated,
> strangled, as wormy creatures crawled across my face, as
> leggy insects crawled beneath my clothes, as nature took me
> prisoner.[62]

Thus, at the end of this long journey that has led us to contemplate the historical development of various forms adopted by the literary imagination in France, from the romantic era to the dawn of our present century, we find every incitement to regard surrealism as the end result, as far as the imaginative level is concerned, of a long and continuous development. There is little doubt that the writers who claimed allegiance to that movement did everything within their power to exaggerate their originality, both in relation to previous literary trends and to those contemporary with them. Many factors contributed to confirm this apparent isolation: the obvious historical caesura, in both the literary and the political fields, constituted by World War I; the influence during surrealism's gestation period, between 1919 and 1922, of the largely foreign and certainly international Dada movement; the vertigo caused by Freud's discoveries relating to the unconscious, and their possible application in the realm of poetry; the surrealists' own refusal to regard themselves as merely writers, and their widely publicized support later for extreme left-wing political groups, whether Leninist or Trotskyite. However, it is also true that history, including literary history, is not given to abrupt mutations. Although the surrealist vision of the world differs radically from that of the decadents on a number of points, for example in its attitude to woman, it nevertheless remains true that many key themes of the surrealist imagination—the value attributed to dreams and the attention paid to phenomena lurking just below the level of consciousness, celebration of the artificial, discovery of the beauties inherent in modernity, attraction to the bizarre and unusual—were already in gestation during the decadent era.

It would also be desirable to establish, beyond the superficial isolation of the surrealist movement, all the affinities that nevertheless existed between surrealist works and those by other writers of the time similarly fascinated by fantasy and dreams, among whom one would have to include such men as Jaloux, Hellens, Miomandre, and Arnoux. The result of this would be not so much to diminish the relative originality of surrealism as to demonstrate its exemplary and representative character. In this way, now that time enables us to stand back a little from it, we may be able to achieve a new perspective on a movement that undoubtedly remains one of the richest in modern French literature, and one that still continues to fertilize our imagination today.

NOTES

1 The Decadent Era

1. The Trapp dinner occurred on 16 April 1877. Apart from Flaubert, Edmond de Goncourt, and Zola, those present were Huysmans, Mirbeau, Céard, Maupassant, Hennique, Alexis, and several younger writers such as Paul Bourget.

2. Apart from Guy Michaud's key work *Message poétique du symbolisme* (Paris: Nizet, 1961), see also: Kenneth Cornell, *The Symbolist Movement* (New Haven: Yale University Press, 1951); Michel Décaudin, *La Crise des valeurs symbolistes* (Toulouse: Privat, 1960); Noël Richard, *A l'Aube du symbolisme* (Paris: Nizet, 1961).

3. Jean Moréas, *Un Manifeste littéraire, Le Figaro,* 18 September 1886.

4. See Edouard Dujardin, *Mallarmé par un des siens* (Paris: Messein, 1936), p. 211: "Symbolism hardly existed until 1886; the decadents were the precursors of the symbolists; but many symbolists began by being decadents, and decadentism, as I have explained elsewhere, was merely an ephemeral ferment presaging the great poetic movement that was symbolism." See also Michaud, *Message poetique*, p. 234: "Decadence and symbolism were not two schools, as one is generally led to think, but two successive phases of one and the same movement, two stages in the poetic revolution."

5. See Michaud, *Message poetique*, p. 262: "Stemming in all probability from Baudelaire and from Gautier's preface; revived by Verlaine; embodied by Montesquiou; formulated by Huysmans; the decadent attitude, a necessary prelude to the revolution, did not really become a positive force until, having been caricatured by Beauclair and Vicaire and attacked by the national press, it became more than a fashion: a collective phenomenon."

6. Ibid., p. 298, referring to Verhaeren: "Nothing better represents the shift of the decadents toward symbolism perhaps than this transformation of a total pessimism into a promise of life." Cf. also p. 324, where, with reference to an article by Wyzewa, Michaud talks of "the break with the decadent spiritual state and the transition from pessimism to creative optimism."

7. Ibid., p. 234: "'Decadentism' seems to me to have been the stage of lyricism, the outpouring of a disturbed sensibility in a state of crisis, whereas symbolism was the intellectual stage, the phase of reflection upon that lyricism." See also p. 301, where Michaud writes of "plaintive decadent elegies."

8. With reference to Mikhaël, Michaud writes of "the stage of decadent introversion" (p. 282), whereas Samain expresses a "soul closed to the world, afraid of life, taking refuge within itself" (p. 285).

9. Décaudin, *Crise des valeurs symbolistes,* Introduction, p. 15 ff.

10. Michaud, *Message poétique,* p. 393.

11. The reader is referred to Décaudin, *Crise des valeurs symbolistes,* for a more detailed description of the ebbing of symbolism and the emergence of competing trends in this period.

12. See in particular Wyzewa's articles in the February and April 1887 issues of *La Revue indépendante.*

13. Michaud, *Message poétique,* p. 287: "Indifferent to the approaching revolution, he continued, year after year, to cultivate introversion, the lyricism of the subconscious and the elusive emotion, that minor mode in which his brothers in decadence had also delighted, but for a briefer period."

14. A first series of issues appeared from April 1884 through April 1885; the second series, begun in November 1886, continued the same policy, until the point in 1889 when the magazine changed hands and the editorial team was changed.

15. *Revue indépendante,* January and March 1885, January 1887.

16. Tales in January, February, and August 1887; extract from *Axël* in April 1887.

17. *En rade* appeared in serial between November 1886 and April 1887.

18. *Revue indépendante,* April 1887.

19. *Le Mouvement wagnérien en France,* by Adrien Remacle, *Revue indépendante,* May 1884.

20. Translation by Wyzewa of *The Daughter of Lebanon, Revue indépendante,* December 1886.

21. *L'Ecole esthétique anglaise* by Gabriel Sarrazin, *Revue indépendante,* November 1884.

22. *Revue indépendante,* December 1884.

23. From April to August 1887.

24. We refer the reader here to Michel Mansuy's *Paul Bourget* (Paris: Belles-Lettres, 1960), which provides essential information on the writer's role in the formation of the decadent sensibility.

25. *Le Siècle littéraire,* 1 April 1876.

26. Quoted by Mansuy, *Paul Bourget,* p. 240.

27. This novella was to be published in 1801 in the same volume as *L'Irréparable.*

28. *Charles Baudelaire,* in *Nouvelle Revue* of 15 November 1881. Articles on Renan, Stendhal, Taine, and Flaubert followed. *Les Essais de psychologies contemporaine* was published by Lemerre in 1883, the *Nouveaux Essais de psychologie contemporaine* in 1885.

29. Mansuy, *Paul Bourget,* p. 262.

30. Visit to Isle of Wight in August 1880; Scotland and Ireland in July 1881; Oxford in May and June 1883; further visit to England in July–September 1884.

31. Paul Bourget, *Etudes et portraits,* vol. 3, *Etudes anglaises* (Paris: Lemerre, 1889).

32. *Essais de psychologie contemporaine*, 4th ed. (Paris, Lemerre). See Mansuy, *Paul Bourget*, p. 327 ff. whose analyses we follow here.

33. Bourget, *Essais de psychologie contemporaine*, p. 145: "Ah, why is it the common law for all human creatures that pleasure is always disproportionate to the desire? Why is a yearning soul the dupe of a mirage that persuades it that it contains the means for a continuous taste of ecstasy?"

34. Paul Bourget, *Etudes et portraits* (Paris: Lemerre, 1889), vol. 2, *Notes d'esthétique*, p. 202.

35. Bourget, *Essais de psychologie contemporaine*, p. 4: "Temperamentally and rhetorically, Charles Baudelaire surrounds his poems with a vague floating halo of strangeness, convinced as he is, like the writer of that incomparable elegy *To Helen*, Edgar Poe, that there is no beauty not in some degree bizarre, and that astonishment is the precondition of poetic sorcery."

36. Ibid., p. 162, where Bourget notes that Flaubert strives "to paint the images that haunt a mind."

37. See Robert Merle, *Oscar Wilde* (Rennes: 1948), p. 238 ff.

38. Kelver Hartley (*Oscar Wilde: L'Influence française dans son oeuvre* [Paris: Sirey, 1935], p. 228) judges the French influence to be preponderant: "For although his early education, the one imposed on him, had been largely classical, the second, on the other hand, the one acquired by familiarity with books and people of his own choice, was almost entirely French." Robert Merle, on the other hand, reaches more guarded conclusions (*Oscar Wilde*, p. 231 ff.)

39. Letter to the Editor, *Scots Observer*, ?31 July 1890, in *Letters of Oscar Wilde*, ed. Rupert Hart-Davis (London, 1962), p. 268. See also *Pall Mall Gazette*, 24 February 1888.

40. Hartley, *Oscar Wilde*, p. 19; letter to H. C. Marillier, 5 November 1885, *Letters*, p. 180.

41. Letter to Elder, Jan.–Feb. 1885, *Letters*, p. 169; letter to H. C. Marillier, 5 November 1885, *Letters*, p. 185; letter to *Pall Mall Gazette*, February 1886, *Letters*, p. 183, in which Poe is called "this marvellous lord of rhythmic expression." At the end of his life, after two years in prison, Wilde tended to identify his own fate with that of the great American poet as presented by Baudelaire, i.e., as a victim of his compatriots: cf. letter to More Adey, 25 May 1897, *Letters*, p. 567.

42. Letter to W. E. Henley, December 1888. Cf. undated letter to Alfred Nutt, *Letters*, p. 233, n.3; letter to *Scots Observer*, 31 July 1890, *Letters*, p. 268, in which he refers to Flaubert's works in defending *Dorian Gray* against the charge of immorality.

43. See particularly the letter to Arthur Symons, 22 October 1890, *Letters*, p. 276: "I look forward to an evening together, and to a talk about French art, the one art now in Europe that is worth discussing—Verlaine's art especially."

44. Letter to Robert Ross, 6 April 1897, *Letters*, p. 517: "You know the sort of books I want: Flaubert, Stevenson, Baudelaire, Maeterlinck, Dumas *père*, Keats, Marlowe, Chatterton, Coleridge, Anatole France, Gautier, Dante and all Dante literature." In the list of actual works in the postscript the French titles are placed first.

45. The only works of his published in Paris before 1900 were *Salomé*, which

was written in French and appeared in Paris and London simultaneously in 1893, *Le Portrait de Dorian Gray* (Savine, 1895), and *La Ballade de la Geôle de Reading*, Mercure de France, 1898.

46. See Philippe Jullian, *Oscar Wilde* (Paris: Librairie Perrin, 1967), p. 120.

47. Letter from Constance Wilde to Otto Holland Lloyd, 3 June 1884, *Letters*, p. 156.

48. Letter to Robert Ross early in 1889, *Letters*, p. 240.

49. Apart from articles by Bourget, there were also those by Sarrazin: "La Poésie anglaise contemporaine," *Revue littéraire et artistique*, 1 July 1881; "L'Ecole esthétique en Angleterre," *Revue indépendante*, Nov. and Dec. 1884; and a book published in 1885 devoted to *Les Poètes modernes de l'Angleterre*.

50. Th. Bentzon, "La Satire de l'esthéticisme," *Revue des deux Mondes* 80 (1887), pp. 379–98.

51. See Ernest Raynaud, *La Mêlée symboliste*, vol. 2 (Paris, 1920), pp. 125–45; Henri de Régnier, *Figures et caractères* (Paris, 1901); Adolphe Retté, *Le Symbolisme* (Paris: Messein, 1903), pp. 211–13.

52. Oscar Wilde, *Intentions*, in *The Artist as Critic*, ed. Richard Ellmann (London: W. H. Allen, 1970), p. 312.

53. *De Profundis* (London: Methuen, 1949), p. 147.

54. Letter to the Editor of *The Speaker*, December 1891, *Letters*, p. 299.

55. Letter to *Scots Observer*, 9 July 1890, *Letters*, p. 265. See also *Pall Mall Gazette*, 24 October, 9 November 1887; and letter to Mrs. Lathbury, summer 1890, *Letters*, p. 265.

56. P. 360. "What is termed Sin is an essential element of progress.... Through its intensified assertion of individualism it saves us from the monotony of the type."

57. Wilde, *Intentions*, p. 316: "It is style that makes us believe in a thing— nothing but style."

58. See Hartley, *Oscar Wilde*, p. 36, for a discussion of the new renaissance of a sensitivity to wonder in late-nineteenth-century English literature.

59. A. E. Carter, *Baudelaire et la critique française, 1868–1917* (Columbia: University of South Carolina Press, 1963).

60. Charles Baudelaire, *Souvenirs, correspondances, bibliographie, suivis de pièces inédites* (Paris: Pincebourde, 1872).

61. J. K. Huysmans, *A Rebours* (Paris: Fasquelle, 1955), chap. 1, p. 45.

62. See in particular Jacques Petit, *Barbey d'Aurevilly critique* (Paris: Belles Lettres, 1963), pp. 619–25.

63. Maurice Barrès, "Maurice Rollinat," *Jeune France*, 5 November, 5 December 1884.

64. Maurice Barrès, "La Folie de Baudelaire," *Taches d'Encre*, 5 November, 5 December 1884.

65. "A Charles Baudelaire," sonnet, *Revue indépendante*, June 1884, p. 143.

66. Louis Desprez, *L'Evolution naturaliste* (Paris: Tresse, 1884); quoted by Carter, *Baudelaire et la critique française*, p. 65.

67. *Revue contemporaine*, 25 March 1885; quoted by Carter, *Baudelaire et la critique française*, p. 67.

68. Brunetière, "Charles Baudelaire," *Revue des deux Mondes*, 1 June 1887.

69. Charles Baudelaire, *Oeuvres posthumes et correspondance inédite, précédées d'une étude biographique par Eugène Crepet* (Paris: Quantin, 1887).

70. René Ghil, *Traité du verbe*, 2d ed. (Alcan Levy, 1887), p. 19; quoted by Michaud, *Message poétique*, p. 328.

71. Anatole Baju, *L'Ecole décadente* (Paris: Léon Vanier, 1887), p. 2.

72. Rémy de Gourmont, *Le Livre des masques* (Paris: Mercure de France, 1896), p. 57.

73. Maurice Spronck, *Les Artisties littéraires* (Paris: Calmann-Lévy, 1889), pp. 101–9, 127.

74. In 1881, 1884, 1892.

75. In 1879, 1884, 1892.

76. *Contes grotesques d'Edgar Poe et sa vie*, ed. Emile Hennequin (Paris: Ollendorff, 1882).

77. *Oeuvres choisies d'Edgar Poe*, ed. Ernest Guillemot (Paris: Degorce-Cadot, 1884).

78. *Oeuvres choisies d'Edgar Poe*, trans. W. L. Hughes (Paris: Hennuyer, 1885).

79. Edgar Poe, *Derniers Contes*, trans. F. Rabbe (Paris: Savine, 1887).

80. *Aventures d'Arthur Gordon Pym*, trans. Charles Simond (Paris: Lecène et Oudin, 1887). Reprinted in 1888, 1889, 1892.

81. Edgar Poe, *Le Corbeau* ("The Raven"), trans. Stéphane Mallarmé, with illustrations by Manet (Paris: R. Lescide, 1875).

82. *Les Cloches* ("The Bells") trans. Emile Blemont (Paris: Librairie de L'Eau-forte, 1877).

83. *Edgar Allan Poe: A Memorial Volume* (Baltimore: Turnbull Brothers, 1877).

84. For details of Poe's influence on Mallarmé, see Stéphane Mallarmé, *Oeuvres complètes*, ed. Henri Mondor et G. Jean-Aubry (Paris: Pléiade, 1961), pp. 1513–35.

85. *Poèmes d'Edgar Poe*, trans. Stéphane Mallarmé (Brussels: Deman, 1888; Paris: Vanier, 1889).

86. Edgar Poe, *Poésies complètes*, trans. Gabriel Mourey (Paris: C. Dalou, 1889).

87. *Le Constitutionnel*, 19 March 1883.

88. Emile Hennequin, "Edgar Allan Poe," *Revue contemporaine*, no. 1, January 1885, pp. 24–56.

89. Téodor de Wyzewa, *Edgar Poe d'après sa correspondance*, in *Ecrivains étrangers* (Paris: Perrin, 1896), pp. 82–104.

90. Camille Mauclair, *Edgar Poe idéologue*, in *L'Art en silence* (Paris: Ollendorff, 1901), pp. 3–41.

91. Cesare Lombroso, *L'homme de génie* (Paris: Alcan, 1889), pp. xiii–xiv.

92. Arvède Barine, "Edgar Poe," *Revue des deux Mondes*, 15 July, 1 August 1897, and *Névrosés* (Paris: Hachette, 1898).

93. Emile Lauvrière, *Edgar Poe, Sa Vie et son oeuvre* (Paris: Bloud, 1911).

94. Wyzewa, *Ecrivains étrangers*, p. 90.

95. Mauclair, *L'Art en silence*, p. 12.

96. Hennequin, "Edgar Allan Poe," pp. 32–33, 24, 36.

97. Hughes, *Oeuvres choisies d'Edgar Poe*, p. 32.

98. Hennequin, "Edgar Allan Poe," p. 27.

99. Mauclair, *L'Art en silence*, pp. 19–21.

100. Ibid., p. 29.

101. Hughes, *Oeuvre choisies d'Edgar Poe*, Notice, pp. xxx–xxxi: "His work, as has been well said, contains gold, silver, and brass. The gold is to be found in his poetry, the silver in his tales, the brass abounds in his critical works."

102. Guillemot, *Oeuvres choisies d'Edgar Poe*, p. 5.

103. Charles Morice, *La Littérature de tout à l'heure* (Paris: Perrin, 1889), p. 201.

104. Mauclair, *L'Art en silence*, pp. 23, 25, 28.

105. Morice, *La Littérature de tout à l'heure*, p. 200.

106. Gabriel Sarrazin, "Hommage à Redon," *La Vie*, no. 41, 30 November 1912. Further evidence of popularity: in 1882, Redon published an album of lithographs entitled *A Edgar Poe;* in 1889, the Théâtre Libre mounted a play adapted from Poe's *The Tell-Tale Heart* (*Le Coeur révélateur*, one act, by M. E. Laumann, Théâtre Libre, May 1889).

107. See Léon Lemonnier, *Edgar Poe et les poètes français symbolistes et décadents* (Paris: Nouvelle Revue critique, 1932) and *Edgar Poe et les conteurs français* (Paris: Aubier, 1927); Louis Seylaz, *Edgar Poe et les premiers symbolistes français* (Lausanne: Imprimerie La Concorde, 1923); P. F. Quinn, *The French Face of Poe* (Carbondale: Southern Illinois University Press, 1957).

108. Letter to Cazalis, 1864, quoted in Mondor, *Vie de Stéphane Mallarmé* (Paris: Gallimard, 1941), p. 104.

109. Quoted by Lemonnier, *Edgar Poe et les poètes français*, p. 207.

110. *Correspondance André Gide–Paul Valéry* (Paris: Gallimard, 1955), p. 86.

111. Charles Baudelaire, *Les Fleurs du mal* (Paris: Michel Lévy, 1868), pp. 55–70.

112. Chapter 1, where we find the famous phrase "touched with pensiveness," and chapter 3.

113. The novel appeared as a serial in *Le Voltaire*, beginning in November 1881, then in book form in January 1882.

114. Edmond de Goncourt, *La Faustin* (Paris: Charpentier, 1882), chap. xviii, pp. 174–77.

115. Paul Bourget, "Les Lacs anglais," *Nouvelle Revue*, vol. 18 (1882), pp. 857–99; *Etudes et portraits*, vol. 3, *Etudes anglaises* (Paris: Lemerre, 1889), pp. 111–73.

116. *Le Parlement*, 15 February 1883.

117. Barbey d'Aurevilly, *Memoranda* (Paris: Rouveyre, 1883), Préface, p. xxiv.

118. Bourget, *Etudes et Portraits*, vol. 2, *Notes d'esthétique*, pp. 229–44.

119. J. K. Huysmans, "Le Salon officiel de 1884," *Revue indépendante*, June 1884, p. 110.

120. Edouard Rod, *La Course à la mort* (Paris: Frinzine, 1885), p. 114.

121. *Revue indépendante*, December 1886, pp. 284–85.

122. *Revue indépendante*, August 1888; Wyzewa, *Ecrivains étrangers*, pp. 61–74.

123. Thomas De Quincey, *Confessions d'un Anglais mangeur d'opium*, first complete (French) translation by Victor Descreux (Paris: Savine, 1890).

124. Thomas De Quincey, *Jeanne d'Arc*, trans. and with a critical essay by Comte Gérard de Contades (Paris: Champion, 1891): "He was no less profound and mysterious a poet because he wrote in prose, an incurable cherisher of visions. A seer, moreover, rather than a great writer, tracing nervously onto his paper the images he had perceived in the extraordinarily broad field of his inner vision." This preface was later reprinted in the *Revue des deux Mondes*, 15 Feburary 1893.

125. *La Vogue*, n.s., no. 4, April 1899, pp. 12–26; no. 5, May 1899, pp. 88–102; no. 6, June 1899, pp. 161–174.

126. Thomas De Quincey, *De l'Assassinat considéré comme un des Beaux-Arts*, trans. André Fontainas (Paris: Mercure de France, 1901).

127. Thomas De Quincy, *Souvenirs autobiographiques du Mangeur d'opium*, trans. Albert Savine (Paris: Stock, 1903).

128. Albert Samain, *Carnets intimes* (Mercure de France, 1939), p. 237. Quoted by W. A. Raitt, *Villiers de l'Isle-Adam et le mouvement symboliste* (Paris: Corti, 1965), p. 365.

129. Gustave Kahn, *Symbolistes et décadents* (Messein, 1902), p. 313.

130. Edmond Jaloux, *Le Temps*, 27 November 1936.

131. Jules Huret, *Enquête sur l'evolution littéraire* (Paris: Charpentier, 1891), p. xvi.

132. See Pierre-Léon Gauthier, *Jean Lorrain* (Paris: Lesot, 1935), pp. 333–41.

133. Adolphe Retté, *Thulé des brumes* (Paris: Bibliothèque artistique et littéraire, 1891), pp. 23–24.

134. Gustave Flaubert, *La Légende de saint Julien l'Hospitalier* (Paris: A. Ferroud, 1893).

135. Gabriel Mourey, *Monada* (Paris: Ollendorff, 1894), p. 18.

136. Cf. Edmond Jaloux, *Les Saisons littéraires* (Fribourg: L.U.F., 1942), vol. 2, p. 123.

137. Jean Lorrain, *Sensations et souvenirs* (Paris: Charpentier, 1895), pp. 67–68; see also his *Monsieur de Phocas* (Paris: Ollendorff, 1901; then Labin Michel, 1929), pp. 269–71.

138. The charcoal drawing *Apparition* was certainly directly inspired by the Moreau painting of the same name. See Sven Sandström, *L'Oeuvre imaginaire d'Odilon Redon* (Lund, 1955), p. 48; and also Roseline Bacou, *Odilon Redon* (Geneva: Cailler, 1956).

139. Bacou, *Odilon Redon*, p. 76.

140. Hennequin, article for the *Revue littéraire et artistique*, March 1882: Huysmans, *L'Art moderne* (1883), *A Rebours* (1884; Fasquelle, 1955), pp. 95–96; Lorraine, *Un étrange jongleui*, *Sensations et souvenirs*, pp. 213–20.

141. Emile Bergerat, *Théophile Gautier: Entretiens, souvenirs et correspondance* (Paris: Charpentier, 1879).

142. Vicomte de Spoelberch de Lovenjoul, *Histoire des oeuvres de Théophile Gautier*, 2 vols. (Paris: Charpentier, 1887).

143. See Mario Praz, *The Romantic Agony* (Oxford University Press, 1933), p. 340 ff.

144. *Revue des Deux Mondes,* 1 December 1887, pp. 695, 696, 697.

145. Maurice Spronck, *Les Artistes littéraires* (Calmann-Levy, 1889), p. 41.

146. Ibid., pp. 50 and 52.

2 The Spiritual Horizon

1. E. Caro, *Le Pessimisme au XIXe siècle* (Paris: Hachette, 1878). See also Hennequin, "Le Pessimisme des écrivains," *Revue indépendante,* October, November 1884; Brunetière, "La Philosophie de Schopenhauer et les conséquences du pessimisme," *Revue des deux Mondes,* 1 November 1890.

2. J. Burdeau, "Le Bonheur dans le pessimisme," *Revue des deux Mondes,* 15 August 1884, p. 918.

3. Quoted by Michaud, *Message poétique,* p. 257.

4. Quoted by Emilien Carassus, *Le Snobisme et les lettres françaises* (Paris: Armand Colin, 1966), p. 148.

5. Max Nordau, *Entartung* (1892); French translation, *Dégénérescence* (Paris: Alcan, 1894).

6. See also Rod, *Course à la mort,* p. 168: "And a law more inexorable than the threat in the Decalogue makes the sons inheritors of their fathers' defects." This was also the theme of Ibsen's *Ghosts,* produced by the Théâtre Libre d'Antoine in Paris in May 1890.

7. Jules Laforgue, *Moralités légendaires* (Paris: Mercure de France, 1946), p. 28.

8. Jules Laforgue, *Poésies complètes,* ed. Pascal Pia (Paris: Livre de Poche, 1970).

9. Joséphin Péladan, *Le Vice suprême* (Paris: Librairie moderne, 1884), p. 58. Quoted by Mansuy, *Paul Bourget,* p. 347.

10. Jacques Lethève, "Les Thèmes de la décadence dans la littérature française à la fin du XIXe siècle," *Revue d'Histoire littéraire de la France,* January–March 1963, p. 49; Mansuy, *Paul Bourget,* pp. 330–34; Carassus, *Le Snobisme,* p. 154.

11. Emile Zola, *Mes Haines* (A. Fabre, 1866); quoted by Lethève, "Les Thèmes de la décadence," p. 50.

12. Paul Bourget, "Byzance," *Le Parlement,* 5 February 1880; quoted by Mansuy, *Paul Bourget,* p. 332.

13. Barbey d'Aurevilly, *Le Roman contemporain* (Charpentier, 1902), pp. 274–78; quoted by Praz, *Romantic Agony,* p. 291.

14. Cf. Michaud, *Message poétique,* p. 264.

15. Spronck, *Les Artistes littéraires,* p. 55.

16. Arthur Rimbaud, Letter to Paul Demeny, 15 May 1871.

17. Bourget, *Essais de psychologie contemporaine,* p. 8.

18. Quoted in Pierre Maes, *Georges Rodenbach* (Paris: Figuière, 1926), p. 85.

19. Henri Laujol, "Villiers de l'Isle-Adam," *Jeune France,* April 1883.

20. Hennequin, "Le Pessimisme des ècrivains," pp. 64–65.

21. Guy de Maupassant, *Sur l'eau* (Paris: Albin Michel, 1954), pp. 107–9.

22. Hennequin, "Le Pessimisme des écrivains," p. 66.

23. Maupassant, *Sur l'eau*, p. 106.

24. Charles Richet, Preface to Cesare Lombroso, *L'Homme de génie*, trans. F. Colonna d'Istria (Paris: Alcan, 1884), pp. vii–xi: "The man of genius is the man who has been able to do more, better, and differently than other men, his contemporaries. He is therefore an abnormal being, an exception. It is rare, when studying the life of superior men closely, that one does not find in their mental organisms, and in their intellectual processes, something defective, morbid, pathological, in which they may be likened to mad people. . . . One does not depart from the flat and vulgar existence of ordinary men with impunity. Great men have fixed ideas, prejudices, manias, moral perversities, constitutional defects, gaps in their reasoning, sometimes even hallucinations and completely insane ideas. Pride, sensibility, moral irritability, fear, are moral states that with them sometimes acquire diseased proportions."

25. For Schopenhauer's ideas and their dissemination in France, cf. Michaud, *Message poétique*, pp. 210–14; Karl-D. Uitti, *La Passion littéraire de Rémy de Gourmont* (Paris: P.U.F., 1962), p. 63 ff.

26. Schopenhauer, *Le Monde comme volonté et comme représentation*, trans. Cantacuzène (Leipzig, 1886); this translation was followed two years later by that of Burdeau (Paris: Alcan, 1888).

27. Schopenhauer, *Essai sur le libre-arbitre*, trans. Salomon Reinach (Paris: Baillière, 1877); *Le Fondement de la morale*, trans. Burdeau (Paris: Baillière, 1879 [four reprints before end of century]); *Parerga et Paralipomena*, trans. Cantacuzène (Paris: Baillière, 1880); *Pensées, maximes et fragments*, trans. Burdeau (Paris: Baillière, 1880 [reprinted 1881 and 1884]).

28. Edouard de Hartmann (Eduard von Hartmann), *Philosophie de l'Inconscient*, trans. D. Nolen (Paris: Ballière, 1877).

29. Challemel-Lacour, "Un Bouddhiste contemporain en Allemagne," *Revue des deux Mondes*, 15 March 1870.

30. Th. Ribot, *La Philosophie de Schopenhauer* (Paris: Baillière, 1874), p. 49.

31. See for example: Paul Janet, "Schopenhauer et la physiologie française," *Revue des deux Mondes*, 15 May 1880; J. Burdeau, "Le Bonheur dans le pessimisme: Schopenhauer d'après sa correspondance," *Revue des deux Mondes*, 15 August 1884; Brunetière, "La Philosophie de Schopenhauer," *Revue des deux Mondes*, 1 October 1886 and "La Philosophie de Schopenhauer et les conséquences du pessimisme," *Revue des deux Mondes*, 1 November 1890.

32. Paul Bourget, "La Statue de Schopenhauer," *Le Parlement*, 14 June 1883; cf. Mansuy, *Paul Bourget*, pp. 312–14.

33. See Albert-Marie Schmidt, *Maupassant par lui-même* (Paris: Seuil, 1962), pp. 69–72.

34. Guy de Maupassant, *Contes et nouvelles*, ed. Schmidt (Paris: Albin-Michel, 1957).

35. Brunetière, "La Philosophie de Schopenhauer," p. 694.

36. See Gourmont, *Le Livre des masques*, Préface, pp. 11–12.

37. Huysmans, *A Rebours*, p. 35. Cf. also p. 137: "During the last months of his stay in Paris [he was] laid low by hypochondria, crushed by 'spleen' "; p. 99: "He

was overwhelmed by an immense lassitude''; p. 138: ''Once more, deprived of direction, he sank into 'spleen' . . . once again, that solitude so ardently longed for, and finally achieved, had led to an appalling distress of mind.''

38. *Sur l'Eau*, p. 57.

39. Rod, *La Course à la mort*, p. 70: ''Never had I felt so wearied of ordinary sensations. . . . I would have to go through the same streets, meet the same people, carry the same boredom around with me.''

40. Ibid., p. 135: ''I feel too acutely that disgust lies at the heart and root of everything.''

41. Anatole Baju, *L'Ecole décadente* (Paris, 1887), pp. 7–9.

42. Rémy de Gourmont, *Sixtine* (Paris: Mercure de France, 1927), p. 32.

43. Georges Rodenbach, *Bruges-la-morte* (Paris: Flammarion, 1947), p. 20.

44. Maupassant, *L'Endormeuse*, 16 September 1889, *Contes et nouvelles*.

45. Cf. Huysmans, *A Rebours*, pp. 33, 35, 55, 83, 99, 223, and passim.

46. Rémy de Gourmont, *L'Idéalisme* (Paris: Mercure de France, 1895), p. 11.

47. My account follows closely that of Raitt, *Villiers de l'Isle-Adam*, chap. 4, *L'Illusionisme*, pp. 245–64.

48. Villiers de l'Isle-Adam, *Morgane* (Saint-Brieux: Imprimerie Guyon, 1866); quoted by Bornecque, Introduction to Villiers de l'Isle-Adam, *Oeuvres* (Paris, Club Français du Livre, 1957), p. xxxiii.

49. Villiers de l'Isle-Adam, *Tribulat Bonhomet* (Paris, Crès), p. 147.

50. See Raitt, *Villiers de l'Isle-Adam*, pp. 186–216, where Villiers's developing attitude to this problem is analyzed in detail.

51. *Figaro*, Supplément, 1 May 1884; see also Villiers de l'Isle-Adam, *L'Amour suprême* (Paris: De Brunhoff, 1886) and *Oeuvres*, pp. 424–34.

52. Villiers de l'Isle-Adam, *Tribulat Bonhomet*, pp. 142–44: ''Through the mediating idea of Exteriority, which is as it were the weft upon which the eternal becoming of the Cosmos is woven, THE IDEA denies itself in order to prove its being to itself in the form of Nature.''

53. ''Come now, Sir, if others are not dupes of words, I for my part am not to be duped by facts! . . . Since the world has no meaning other than through the power of the words that translate it and the eyes that see it, I am of the opinion that to view all things from a higher level than their reality is the Science of Life, of mankind's only greatness, of happiness, and of contentment.'' Quoted by Bornecque, Introduction, *Oeuvres*, p. xliii.

54. Villiers de l'Isle-Adam, *L'Eve future* (Paris: Pauvert, 1960), p. 117.

55. The meaning and practical implications of illusionism are clearly elucidated in Raitt, *Villiers de l'Isle-Adam*.

56. Published in *La Semaine parisienne*, 7 May 1874.

57. Villiers de l'Isle-Adam, *Contes cruels*, ed. Lebois (Paris: Union générale d'Edition, 1963), p. 128; first published *Revue du Monde nouveau*, 15 February 1874.

58. Villiers de l'Isle-Adam, *Axël* (Paris: La Colombe, 1960), p. 251: ''Oh! the external world! Let us not be dupes of that old slave, chained at our feet, in the light, promising us the keys of an enchanted palace when it hides nothing in its black, clenched hand but a fistful of ashes.''

59. Ibid., p. 202: "Know once and for all that there is no other universe for you than the very conception reflected in the depths of your own thoughts." Cf. also pp. 153 and 197.

60. Villiers de l'Isle-Adam, "Le Succès," 28 May 1885, and "L'Amour suprême."

61. Villiers de l'Isle-Adam, Oeuvres, p. 385.

62. Villiers de l'Isle-Adam, "Propose d'au-delà," Gil Blas, 9 November 1888; Oeuvres complètes (Mercure de France, 1931), p. 10.

63. Quoted by Raymond Pouilliart, Le Romantisme, vol. 3 (Paris: Arthaud, 1968), chap. 3, Le Symbolisme, p. 148.

64. Edouard Dujardin, Les Hantises (Paris: Vanier, 1886), Préface.

65. Revue indépendante, February 1887, quoted by Michaud, Message poétique, p. 355.

66. Edouard Schuré, Les Grands Initiés (Paris: Pettin, 1889), p. xxiii; quoted by Michaud, Message poétique, p. 373.

67. Gourmont, L'Idéalisme, p. 7.

68. Gourmont, Le Livre des masques, Préface, pp. 11–12.

69. Adolphe Retté, Les Mémoires de Diogène (Paris: Fasquelle, 1903), p. 51.

70. Alfred Jarry, Les Jours et les nuits, Oeuvres complètes (Monte Carlo: Edition du Livre, 1949), vol. 5, p. 230.

71. Quoted in R. E. Knowles, Victor-Emile Michelet (Paris: Vrin, 1954), p. 85.

72. Victor-Emile Michelet, "La Rédemptrice," Psyché, no. 1 (November 1891), p. 13.

73. Bourget, Etudes et portraits, vol. 2, p. 222.

74. Préface to the Memoranda of Barbey d'Aurevilly.

75. Michaud, Message poétique, p. 726.

76. André Gide, Traité du Narcisse, quoted by Michaud, Message poétique, p. 731.

77. Camille Mauclair, "Notes sur l'Idée pure," Mercure de France, September 1892, pp. 42–46.

78. Edouard Dujardin, Mallarmé par un des siens (Messein, 1936), pp. 92–93.

3 Religious Unease

1. Victor Charbonnel, Les Mystiques dans la littérature présente (Paris: Mercure de France, 1897).

2. Bourget, Essais de psychologie contemporaine, pp. 8–9.

3. Charles Morice, La Littérature de tout à l'heure (Perrin, 1889), p. 177.

4. Quoted in Henri Mazel, Aux Beaux Temps du symbolisme (Paris: Mercure de France, 1943), p. 12.

5. Rémy de Gourmont, Le Latin mystique (Paris: Mercure de France, 1892), Préface, p. vii.

6. Paul Thévenin, L'Esthétique de Gustave Moreau (Paris: Vanier, 1897), pp. 6–7.

7. Paul Desjardins, Le Devoir présent (Paris: Armand Colin, 1892), p. 23.

8. Victor Charbonnel, *La Volonté de vivre* (Paris: Armand Colin, 1897), pp. 21, 24–25.

9. Gourmont, *Le Latin mystique*, Préface, p. vii.

10. Paul Valéry, *Oeuvres,* vol. 1, ed. Jean Hytier (Paris: Bibliothèque de la Pléiade, 1965), p. 1580.

11. Ibid., p. 1592.

12. Quoted by Charbonnel, *Les Mystiques,* p. 79, and by Carassus, *Le Snobisme,* p. 397.

13. Maurice Barrès, *Oeuvres* (Paris: Club de l'Honnête Homme, 1965), vol. 1, pp. 398–99; see also Carter, *Baudelaire et la critique française,* p. 61.

14. René Doumic, "Les Décadents du christianisme," *Revue des deux Mondes,* 15 March 1895, p. 460.

15. Entitled, respectively, *Satan Scattering the Tares, Rape, Idol, Sacrifice,* and *Calvary;* cf. the description of them in the catalogue of *L'Exposition Félicien Rops* (London: Editions Graphiques Gallery, 1971).

16. Joséphin Péladan, *L'Art ochlocratique* (Paris: Dalou, 1888), p. 50.

17. Stanislas de Guaïta, *La Muse noire* (Paris: Lemerre, 1883) and *Rosa mystica* (Lemerre, 1885).

18. Albert Jhouney, *Les Lys noirs* (Paris, Carré, 1888).

19. J. K. Huysmans, *Certains* (Paris, Tresse et Stock, 1889), pp. 100–108.

20. J. K. Huysmans, *Là-Bas* (Livre de Poche, 1961), pp. 232–33.

21. Stanislas de Guaïta, *Au Seuil du mystère,* 2d ed. (Paris: G. Carré, 1890), pp. 48–49.

22. Stanislas de Guaïta, *Le Temple de Satan* (Paris: Librairie du merveilleux, 1891), pp. 77, 117, 151–61.

23. See Jacques Robichez, *Le Symbolisme au théâtre* (Paris: L'Arche, 1957), p. 137.

24. Jules Bois, *Les Petites Religions de Paris* (Paris: L. Chailley, 1894) and *Le Satanisme et la magie* (Paris: L. Chailley, 1895), with a preface by Huysmans.

25. François Paulhan, *Le Nouveau Mysticisme* (Paris: Alcan, 1891), p. 57; quoted by Michaud, *Message poétique,* p. 466.

26. Charbonnel, *Les Mystiques,* pp. 31–34, lists the major translations made at this time.

27. Vicomte E. M. de Vogüé, *Le Roman russe* (Paris: Plon, 1886); see analysis of this work in Michaud, *Message poétique,* pp. 315–J6.

28. Schuré, *Les Grands Initiés;* cf. Michaud, *Message poétique,* pp. 372–75.

29. Cf. above, note 25.

30. Cf. above, note 7.

31. See in particular Charles Chassé, *Le Mouvement symboliste dans l'art du XIXe siècle* (Paris: Floury, 1947), and catalogue of *Exposition Maurice Denis,* Orangerie des Tuileries, June-August 1970.

32. Cf. in particular *La Vision après le sermon* (1888), *Le Calvaire, Le Christ jaune* (1889).

33. For instance: *Montée au calvaire* (November 1889), *Christ orange* (1889–90), *Mystère catholique* (May 1890; shown at Salon des Indépendants of 1891), *La Messe* (1890), *Mystère de Pâques* (1891), *Lutte de Jacob avec l'ange* (1893).

34. Albert Aurier, *Oeuvres posthumes* (Paris: Mercure de France, 1893), pp. 307–308.

35. See Georges Rouault, *Exposition du Centenaire*, Musée national d'art moderne, May–September 1971, p. 233.

36. Quoted by Desjardins, *Le Devoir présent*, p. 43.

37. Cf. Alain Mercier, *Les Sources ésotériques et occultes de la poésie symboliste* (Paris: Nizet, 1969), pp. 40–42.

38. For an account of his ideas and influence, cf. Pierre-Georges Castex, *Le Conte fantastique en France* (Corti, 1951), pp. 100–102; Mercier, *Les Sources ésoteriques*, pp. 62–71.

39. Mercier, *Les Sources ésotériques*, chap. 3, pp. 79–89.

40. Flammarion was still writing stories inspired by spiritism, such as *Lumen* of 1873.

41. Mercier, *Les Sources ésotériques*, pp. 97–99.

42. See Charles Cros, *Oeuvres complètes* (Paris: Club Français du Livre), p. 550.

43. See Jules Bois, *L'au-delà et les forces inconnues* (Paris: Ollendorff, 1902), p. 18 ff.

44. Bernheim's fundamental work, *De la Suggestion et de ses applications thérapeutiques*, appeared in 1866.

45. *Phantasms of the Living*, by E. Gurney, F. Myers, F. Podmore (London: Society for Psychical Research, 1886; trans. Dr. L. Marillier, Paris, Alcan, 1891 [*Les Hallucinations télépathiques*]).

46. William Crookes, *Research in the Phenomena of Spiritualism* (London: J. Burns, 1874).

47. *L'Extériorisation de la motricité* (Paris: Chamuel, 1896); *Les Forces non définies* (Paris: Masson, 1887); *Les Etats profound de l'hypnose* (Paris: Chamuel, 1892).

48. Georges Vitoux, *Dans les coulisses de l'au-delà* (Paris, 1901), p. 76.

49. For a biography of this extraordinary woman, see Jacques Marcireau, *Une Histoire de l'occultisme* (Poitiers, Société E.L.J.M.). Yelyena Petrovna Hahn, born of German stock in Russia in 1831, was married at sixteen to a much older man, but soon separated from him and set out on an adventurous life. Having traveled through Asia Minor in about 1848, she appeared in London in 1851, where she frequented spiritist circles. She was in Russia from 1858 to 1863; in 1866 in Italy, she knew Garibaldi. From 1871 to 1872 she was in Cairo, where she attempted without much success to found a "miracle club." It was not till 1874, in New York, that fate began to smile on her, when she met a military police officer already won over to spiritist ideas, Colonel Olcott. She died in London in 1891, after having been unmasked as a mere illusionist by the Society for Psychical Research and published the work that became the bible of the theosophical movement, her *The Secret Doctrine*.

50. L. Dramard, *La Science occulte: Etude sur la doctrine ésotérique* 2d ed. (Paris: G. Carré, 1886).

51. For a biography of Caillé, see *L'Initiation*, July 1896. *L'Antimatérialiste*, first number in 1884, became *La Revue des hautes Etudes* (October 1886–February 1887), then *L'Etoile*, which continued until its editor's death in 1896.

52. See Barrès, *Stanislas de Guaïta: Amori et dolori sacrum, Oeuvres complètes*, vol. 7 (Paris: Club de l'Honnête Homme, 1967), pp. 67–75; Oswald Wirth, *Stanislas de Guaïta* (Paris: Editions du Symbolisme, 1935).

53. See James Laver, *The First Decadent* (London: Faber and Faber, 1954), p. 125.

54. For biography of Papus, see Papus, *Comment je devins mystique*, in *L'Initiation*, December 1895, pp. 195–206; *Papus*, biography by Marc-Haven, *Les Hommes d'aujourd'hui*, no. 410, 1893; Wirth, *Stanislas de Guaïta*, chap. 18, pp. 129–33; Philippe Encausse, *Sciences occultes* (Paris: Ocia, 1949), passim. Born in La Coruna, Spain, of a French father and Spanish mother, he was brought to Paris when very young and spent his childhood in Montmartre; his education, begun at the Collège Rollin, was discontinued, probably for financial reasons. Forced to earn his living, he seems to have worked for some years as a laboratory assistant in various Paris hospitals, and we know that in 1890 he was working for Dr. Luys. He continued his studies, nevertheless, and gradually acquired all his official diplomas, becoming a health officer in 1891, a B.S. in 1892, and an M.D. in 1894 (Marc-Haven). A materialist at first, he was won over to occultism by *La Médecine nouvelle*, an alchemical work by Louis Lucas published in 1862. Having become a leader of the occultist movement, he was tireless in his work for it, publishing a large number of works popularizing it from 1887 on. He began practicing medicine in 1894, with a surgery in the rue Jacob. He continued his medical and occultist activities until his death in 1916.

55. See for example the portrait of him drawn by Retté in *Au Pays des lys noirs*, p. 16.

56. Quoted by Michaud, *Message poétique*, p. 372, note 10.

57. Quoted ibid., p. 374.

58. Jules Lermina, *La Science occulte* (Paris: Ernest Kolb, 1890), p. 3.

59. See André Fontainas, *Mes Souvenirs du symbolisme* (Paris, N.R.C., 1928), chap. 16, p. 113 ff.; Victor-Emile Michelet, *Les Compagnons de la hiérophanie* (Paris: Dorbon, 1937), pp. 65–68.

60. Fontainas, *Mes Souvenirs*, p. 117.

61. *L'Initiation*, February 1890, p. 97.

62. On Albert Jounet, see Mercier, *Les Sources ésotériques*, pp. 219–20.

63. See reviews of *Un Caractère* by Léon Hennique (May 1889); *Les Grands Initiés* by Schuré (July 1889); *La Victoire du mari* by Péladan (November 1889); *Les Cahiers d'André Walter* by Gide (April 1891); *Le Culte du moi* by Barrès (January 1891), and so on.

64. Fifteen hundred copies in November 1892, 1,600 in October 1894 and January 1896.

65. Mercier, *Les Sources ésotériques*, p. 233; *L'Etoile*, nos. 1–84, March 1889–December 1895, edited by Albert Jounet with the contributions of Jules Bois, René Caillé, L'Abbé Rocca.

66. *Psyché, revue mensuelle d'art et de littérature*. Chief editor: Emile Michelet; secretary: Augustin Chaboseau. Nine issues between November 1891 and December 1892. On the role of *Psyché*, see E. Raynaud, *La Mêlée symboliste*, 3 vols. (Renaissance du livre, 1918–22), vol. 2, pp. 111–16; Uitti, *La Passion littéraire de Rémy de Gourmont*, p. 158.

67. In March 1894 *L'Initiation* in fact published a thesis, a rather brief one it is true, for a "degree in the Kabbala."

68. See Encausse, *Sciences occultes*, p. 39.

69. See Mercier, *Les Sources ésotériques*, p. 212.

70. See Richard E. Knowles, *Victor Emile Michelet: Poète ésotérique* (Vrin, 1954).

71. *Cinq Traités d'alchimie*, 1890; *Théories et symboles des alchimistes*, 1891.

72. See in *L'Initiation*, August 1891, the sixteen-page supplement on the "Cas Péladan"; see also Vitoux, *Dans les coulisses de l'au-delà*, pp. 177–232.

73. Here is a brief summary of the facts: the Abbé Boullan, after a fairly eventful existence, settled in Lyons, where he revived the Eliac cult started several years earlier by the faith healer Eugène Vintras. Boullan introduced new and dubious elements into the cult, whose religious claims served essentially as a screen for orgies. Informed of all this by a number of indiscrete initiates, including Oswald Wirth, later Guaïta's secretary, the Parisian occultists formally condemned Boullan's activities in 1888. Huysmans, researching initiatory sects for *Là-bas*, made contact with Boullan, who told him that Guaïta and Papus, wanting him dead, were constantly casting spells on him. In an interview with Jules Bois in January 1893, Huysmans passed on these accusations, and the journalist reported them in one of his articles. The result was a double duel, Bois versus Papus and Bois versus Guaïta (April 1893), widely reported in the press.

74. Berthe Courrière was undoubtedly the model for Madame Chantelouve in *Là-bas*.

75. Retté, *Au pays des lys noirs*, p. 12.   ·

76. See R. L. Doyon, *La Douloureuse Aventure de Péladan* (Paris: La Connaissance, 1946), who among the guests or intimates of the "Master" cites Laurent Tailhade and the painter Armand Point.

77. See Raitt, *Villiers de L'Isle-Adam*, p. 185.

78. Gilbert-Augustin Thierry, *Récits de l'occulte* (Paris: Armand Colin, 1892), pp. v–vi.

79. Papus, *Le Diable et l'occultisme* (Paris: Chamuel, 1896), p. 8.

80. Stanislas de Guaïta, *Au Seuil du Mystère*, 2d ed. (Paris: G. Carré, 1890), p. 91.

81. Quoted by J. Grasset in *Le Spiritisme devant la science* (Paris: Masson, 1904), p. 3.

82. Jules Lermina, *La Science occulte: Révélation des mystères de la vie et de la mort* (Paris: Ernest Kolb, 1890), pp. ix, 100, 121–22.

83. Papus, *L'Occultisme* (Paris: Librairie du Magnétisme, 1890), p. 5.

84. Quoted by Raynaud, "Le Symbolisme ésotérique," *Mercure de France*, 1 March 1920, p. 403.

85. Paulhan, *Le Nouveau Mysticisme*, p. 104.

86. Cf. Grasset, *Le Spiritisme devant la science*, pp. 1–2: "All ages are equal before the pull of the supernatural. I do not know whether, as has been said, the epochs with least faith are in reality the most credulous. But it is certain that people accept and love the supernatural with as much fervor today as in the Middle Ages and antiquity."

4 The Unconscious and Sexuality

1. Lancelot L. Whyte, *The Unconscious before Freud* (New York: Barnes and Noble, 1967).

2. See Dennis N. Kennedy Darnoi, *The Unconscious and Eduard von Hartmann* (The Hague, 1967).

3. Edmond Colsenet, *Etudes sur la vie inconsciente de l'esprit* (Paris: Baillière, 1880), p. 144.

4. See in particular A. G. Lehmann, *The Symbolist Aesthetics in France* (Oxford: Blackwell, 1950), pp. 114–25.

5. Jules Laforgue, *Mélanges posthumes* (Paris: Mercure de France, 1903), p. 154; quoted by Lehmann, *Symbolist Aesthetics*, p. 116.

6. Quoted by Lehmann, *Symbolist Aesthetics*, p. 115.

7. Paul Chabaneix, *De l'Inconscient chez les artistes, les savants et les écrivains* (Paris: Baillière, 1897), p. ii.

8. Rémy de Gourmont, *La Création subconsciente*, article reprinted in *La Culture des idées* (Paris: Mercure de France, 1900), pp. 43–66.

9. Albert Samain, *Carnets intimes* (Paris: Mercure de France, 1939), p. 96.

10. Georges Rodenbach, *L'Aquarium mental, Oeuvres* (Paris, Mercure de France), vol. 2, p. 10.

11. *Le Décadent,* 15 December 1888; quoted by Michaud, *Message poétique*, p. 348, note 20.

12. Edouard Schuré, *Maeterlinck et le théâtre de l'âme*, in *Précurseurs et révoltés* (Paris: Perrin, 1926), pp. 228–29.

13. Charles Baudelaire, *Oeuvres complètes* (Paris: Bibliothèque de la Pléiade, 1951), p. 1199.

14. Schopenhauer, *Pensées, maximes et fragments*, trans. Burdeau (Paris: Baillière, 1880).

15. J. K. Huysmans, *En ménage* (Paris: Charpentier, 1881), p. 347.

16. Mario Praz, *The Romantic Agony*, pp. 189–271.

17. Cf. the quotations and commentaries of Praz, *The Romantic Agony*, pp. 244–45.

18. Joséphin Péladan, *Le Vice suprême*, p. 45.

19. Maupassant, *Contes et nouvelles*, vol. 2, p. 785.

20. Paris, Musée Gustave Moreau.

21. Quoted by Paul Flat, *Le Musée Gustave Moreau* (Paris: Société d'édition critique, 1889); Schuré, *Précurseurs et révoltés*, pp. 324–43; Montesquiou, *Altesses sérénissimes* (Paris: F. Juven, 1907), pp. 7–8.

22. See also the analysis of Kundry's character in Catulle Mendès, *Richard Wagner* (Paris: Charpentier, 1886), pp. 255–56.

23. On the iconography of the epoch, see catalogue of exhibition *Peintres de l'imaginaire: Symbolistes et surréalistes belges*, at the Grand Palais, Paris, February–April, 1972.

24. Paris, Bibliothèque d'art et d'archéologie.

25. 1894, *Peintres de l'imaginaire*, no. 19, p. 53.

26. John Milner, *Symbolists and Decadents* (London: Studio Vista, 1971), p. 92.

27. 1896, *Peintres de l'imaginaire*, no. 44, p. 72.

28. Milner, *Symbolists and Decadents*, p. 134.

29. See Renato Barilli, *Il Simbolismo* (Milan: Fabri, 1967), p. 259, and Milner, *Symbolists and Decadents*, p. 120.

30. Edouard Schuré, *L'Ange et la Sphinge* (Paris: Perrin, 1897), pp. 98–99.

31. Cf. Praz, *The Romantic Agony*, pp. 290–330.

32. Carter, *Baudelaire et la critique française*, p. 105.

33. *La Plume*, 1 March 1891, pp. 83–84.

34. Rachilde, *Monsieur Vénus* (Paris: Brossier, 1889), Preface by Maurice Barrès, p. xvii.

35. Patrick Waldberg, *Eros Modern Style* (Paris: Pauvert, 1964).

36. Ernest Raynaud, "Causerie morale," *Le Décadent*, 15 May 1888.

37. Waldberg, *Eros Modern Style*, p. 189.

38. See Milner, *Symbolists and Decadents*, pp. 20–21.

39. Paul Adam and Jean Moréas, *Le Thé chez Miranda* (Paris: Tresse et Stock, 1886).

40. See also R. Jouanny, *Jean Moréas* (Paris: Minard, 1969), p. 311.

41. Spronck, *Les Artistes littéraires*, pp. 121–22; See also p. 123: "Just as he had applied his system of contrasts to sharpen artistic sensations, so he was to employ it as a stimulus for the sensations of love, and to complete his pictures of pleasure with pictures of pain, cruelties, wounds."

42. See Maupassant, *Notes sur Algernon Charles Swinburne*, in Swinburne, *Poèmes et ballades*, ed. Gabriel Mourey (Paris: Savine, 1891). In this preface Maupassant describes the circumstances of their meeting, as well as the fascinating and frightening personality of the English poet, albeit without mentioning Sade.

43. Léon Deffoux, "Trois Lettres inédites de J. K. Huysmans à Henry Kistemaekers à propos de 'A Vau-l'eau' et du Marquis de Sade," *Mercure de France*, 15 January 1925. Cf. also note by Pierre Lambert in J. K. Huysmans, *Lettres inédites à Edmond de Goncourt* (Paris: Nizet, 1956), pp. 74–75.

44. *Revue indépendante*, January 1885.

45. Henry, *La Vérité sur le Marquis de Sade* (Paris: Dentu, 1887).

46. Stanislas de Guaïta, *La Muse noire* (Paris: Lemerre, 1883), p. 48.

47. Jean Lorrain, *Sonyeuse* (Paris: Charpentier, 1891), pp. 141–93.

48. *Echo de Paris*, 11 June 1894, then *Princesses d'ivoire et d'ivresse* (Paris: Ollendorff, 1902).

49. On this point see J.-P. Crespelle, *Les Maîtres de la Belle Epoque* (Paris: Hachette, 1966). Particular examples are: *La Naissance de Vénus*, by Cabanel (p. 32), *La Toilette de Vénus* by Baudry (p. 69), *Rolla* and *La Naissance de Vénus* by Gervex (pp. 72 and 75), *La Jeunesse de l'amour* and *Vénus* by Bouguereau (pp. 89 and 90) and *Byblis changée en source* by Henner.

50. Waldberg, *Eros Modern Style*, Introduction.

5 Avatars of the Fantastic

1. Maupassant, *Contes et nouvelles*, vol. 2, p. 879. First published 9 July 1883.
2. First published 27 September 1887. "God, Sir, is a mass murderer. He has to have deaths every day. He makes sure they happen every day, just so he'll have a good time. He's invented illnesses, accidents, to keep himself quietly amused during all those long months and years; and then, when he gets bored anyway, he has epidemics, the plague, cholera, heart attacks, smallpox; how do I know all the things that monster's managed to think up?"
3. "Everything is a mystery. We communicate with things only with our pitiful, incomplete, infinitesimal senses, which are so weak that they barely have the power to register what is around us."
4. See Castex, *Le Conte fantastique*, p. 382.
5. See also *La Peur*, October 1882: "Fear is a frightful thing, an atrocious sensation, like a disintegration of the soul, a frightful spasm of the mind and heart, the mere memory of which brings on shudders of dread. But it happens, when one is brave, not in the face of an attack, or of a real risk of death, or of any of the known forms of peril: it happens under certain abnormal circumstances, under certain mysterious influences, in the face of nebulous dangers."
6. *Un Lâche*, 27 January 1884: "His hands were shaking a little, with a sort of nervous quiver, when he touched things. His mind was wandering: his thoughts became elusive, abrupt, painful; he felt strangely elated as though he'd been drinking. . . . His whole body was shaken by sudden fits of quivering. . . . His agitation, having ceased momentarily, was now growing again as the minutes passed. All down his arms, all down his legs, and in his chest, he could feel a sort of perpetual shivering or vibration; he couldn't stay in one place, either seated or standing. There was scarcely a drop of saliva left in his mouth."
7. "That is terrible, incurable," the main character of *LUI?* exclaims. "I am afraid of walls, of furniture, of familiar objects that come to life, for me, with a sort of animal life. I am afraid, above all, of the horrible disturbance in my mind, my reason eluding me, muddled, scattered by a mysterious and invisible dread. . . . I speak, and I am afraid of my voice! I walk, and I am afraid of the unknown behind the door, behind the curtain, inside the cupboard, under the bed. And yet I know there's nothing there."
8. For example in *Magnétisme*.
9. See Maupassant, *Sur l'eau*, Préface by Henry Bonnier (Paris: Club Français du Livre, 1964), pp. i–xxxi; Armand Lanoux, *Maupassant dans son élément*, in Guy de Maupassant, *Récits de l'eau et des rives* (Paris: Bibliothèque de culture littéraire, 1965), pp. 6–28.
10. "The joy that fills me, when I feel myself driven on by the wind and carried by the waves, springs from the fact that I am giving myself up to the natural and brutal forces of the universe, that I am going back to a primitive form of life" (*Sur l'eau*).
11. 1 December 1879; *Récits d l'eau et des rives*, p. 40.
12. Marcel Schwob, *Coeur double* (Paris: Ollendorff, 1891), *Le Sabot*.
13. Marcel Schwob, *Coeur double* (Paris: Crès, 1921), pp. 150–59.

14. Jules Lermina, *Histoires incroyables* (Paris: L. Boulanger [1885]), Preface.

15. P. 226. See also Jules Lermina, *Nouvelles Histoires incroyables* (Paris: Savine, 1888), p. 170: "I have, I must admit, an involuntary inclination toward the bizarre and strange; I enjoy finding myself confronted with a special sort of mystery. Ghosts, specters, and the like, all leave me cold. The extranatural, phenomenal, or rather miraculous kind of fantastic neither affects me nor attracts me, since I don't believe in it at all. But where I scent an anomaly, then I am like a hound picking up a scent: I stop dead, I point."

16. Lorraine, *Sensations et souvenirs*, p. 144.

6 Paradis Artificiels

1. Joséphin Péladan, *L'Art idéaliste et mystique* (Paris: Chameul 1894), p. 79: "Nothing that merits the name of art can bear the epithet natural."

2. Quoted by Carter, *Baudelaire et la critique française*, p. 171 ff.

3. Bourget, *Etudes et portraits*, vol. 2, p. 196.

4. *Les Taches d'Encre*, 1884, "La Folie de Baudelaire," quoted by Carter, *Baudelaire et la critique française*, p. 63.

5. Quoted by Michaud, *Message poétique*, p. 301.

6. Paul Adam and Jean Moréas, *Les Demoiselles Goubert* (Paris: Tresse et Stock, 1886), pp. 101–2. Cf. Jouanny, *Jean Moréas*, p. 340.

7. Bernard Lazare, *Les Portes d'ivoire* (Paris: 1897), p. 260.

8. Camille Mauclair, *Le Soleil des morts* (Paris: Ollendorff, 1898), pp. 158–59.

9. Quoted by Pierre Maes, *Georges Rodenbach* (Gembloux: Duculot, 1952), p. 147.

10. Camille Mauclair, *L'Ennemie des rêves* (Paris: Ollendorff, 1900).

11. J.-K. Huysmans, *De Tout* (Paris: Stock, 1902), *Bruges*, pp. 21424.

12. See Jean-Louis Brau, *Histoire de la drogue* (Paris: Tchou, 1968), p. 84 ff.

13. Ibid., p. 29.

14. Léon Daudet, *L'Homme et le poison* (Paris: Nouvelle Librairie nationale, 1925), p. 30.

15. Benjamin Ball, *La Morphinomanie* (Paris: Asselin et Houzeau, 1885), Avant-Propos, and p. 2; see also Dr. Ernest Martin, *L'Opium, ses abus* (Paris: Société d'Editions Scientifiques, 1893).

16. Carassus, *Le Snobisme*, pp. 430–33.

17. Bourget, *Science et Poésie, Etudes et portraits*, vol. 2, pp. 226–27.

18. Jules Giraud, "L'Art de faire varier les effets du haschich," *L'Encéphale*, vol. 1 (1881), pp. 418–25; "Testament d'un haschischéen," *Initiation*, January 1890, pp. 59–70.

19. Cf. Adolphe Retté, *Le Symbolisme* (Paris: Messein, 1903), p. 57.

20. See the evidence of Roland de Marès in *L'Ermitage*, August 1893, quoted by Cornell, *The Symbolist Movement*, p. 46.

21. Laurent Tailhade, *Omar Khayyam et les poisons de l'intelligence* (Paris: Charles Carrington, 1905), pp. 64–65; see also his *La Noire Idole* (Paris: Vanier, 1907).

22. Paul Bonnetain, *L'Opium* (Paris: Charpentier, 1886), pp. 184–85.

23. The most important are Spitta, *Die Schlaff- und Traumzustände* (Tubingen, 1878), and Radestock, *Schlaf und Traum* (Leipzig, 1879).

24. "Le Sommeil et les rêves," *Revue philosophique*, vol. 8 (1879), pp. 329–56; vol. 9 (1880), pp. 129–69, 413–37, 632–49.

25. P.-Max Simon, *Le Monde des rêves* (Paris: Baillière, 1882), p. 13: "At almost every step in the study of dreams we discover resemblances between dreaming and the various phenomena of madness."

26. In particular: Lassègue, *Le Sommeil: Etude médicale* (Paris, 1884); Chaslin, *Du Rôle des rêves*, thesis, Paris, 1887; Sergueyeff, *Physiologie de la veille et du sommeil* (1889); Dr. Paul Tissié, *Les Rêves: physiologie et pathologie* (Paris: Alcan, 1890); Dr. Surbled, *Le Rêve* (Paris, 1898).

27. Chabaneix, *De l'Inconscient*, p. 41.

28. Quoted by Michaud, *Message poétique*, p. 260.

29. Camille Mauclair, *L'Art en silence* (Paris: Ollendorff, 1901), pp. iv–v.

30. Camille Mauclair, *Servitude et grandeur littéraire* (Paris: Ollendorff, 1922), p. 20.

31. Edouard Dujardin, *Mallarmé par un des siens* (Paris: Messein, 1936), p. 99.

32. Francis Poictevin, *Songes* (Brussels: Kiestemaeckers, 1884).

33. Quoted by Henri Mondor, *Vie de Mallarmé* (Paris: Gallimard, 1941), p. 407.

34. Ibid., p. 735.

35. Letter to Rachet, 18 May 1887.

36. Stéphane Mallarmé, *Divagations* (Paris: Fasquelle, 1887), p. 20.

37. Gustave Kahn, *Les Palais nomades* (Paris: Tresse et Stock, 1887), p. 13.

38. Quoted by Robert Baldick, *Vie de Joris-Karl Huysmans* (Paris: Denoël, 1958), pp. 182–83.

39. Quoted by Décaudin, *Crise des valeurs symbolistes*, p. 23.

40. Retté, *Le Symbolisme*, p. 6.

41. Paul Leprieur, *Gustave Moreau et son oeuvre* (Paris: L'Artiste, 1889), p. 53.

42. Louis Desprez, "Les Derniers Romantiques," *Revue indépendante*, July 1884, p. 218.

43. Quoted by Michaud, *Message poétique*, p. 278.

44. E. Poizat, *Le Symbolisme de Baudelaire à Claudel* (Renaissance du Livre, 1919), p. 135; quoted by S. Bernard, *Le Poème en prose* (Nizet, 1959), p. 362.

45. *Lutèce*, 9 February 1884; cf. Jouanny, *Jean Moréas*, pp. 310–11.

46. J. K. Huysmans, "Cauchemar: Le Nouvel Album d'Odilon Redon," *Revue indépendante*, February 1885; article reprinted in *Croquis parisiens* (1886 edition).

47. "Un de mes rêves," *Le Décadent*, 20 November 1886; this text was published simultaneously in *Les Mémoires d'un veuf* (Paris: Vanier, 1886), under the title *Quelques-uns de mes rêves*.

48. Paul Hervieu, *L'Inconnu* (Paris: Lemerre, 1887), pp. 122–48.

49. See William Kenneth Cornell, *Adolphe Retté* (Yale University Press, 1942). One chapter of *Thulé des brumes*, called *Plein rêve*, is headed with Nerval's famous phrase describing dreaming as a "second life." In an article in the 15 March 1903 *Mercure de France*, Retté acknowledged his debt to Nerval.

50. See the reviews by Dubus, *La Plume*, no. 59, October 1891; Maurras,

L'Ermitage, February 1892; Jule Bois, *L'Etoile,* March 1892, which likens Retté's art to that of Jean Paul.

51. *Les Hommes d'aujourd'hui,* no. 417, 1894.

52. Robert Scheffer, *Sommeil* (Librairie des bibliophiles, 1891), p. 13.

53. Rémy de Gourmont, *Le Chemin de velours* (Paris: Mercure de France, 1902), quoted by Raitt, *Villiers de L'Isle-Adam,* p. 264.

54. Rémy de Gourmont, *Le Pèlerin du silence* (Paris: Mercure de France, 1896), p. 66.

55. Rémy de Gourmont, *Le Château singulier* (Paris: Mercure de France, 1894), p. 29.

56. *Les Hommes d'aujourd'hui,* no. 417, 1894.

57. Adolphe Retté, *Mémoires de Diogène* (Paris: Fasquelle, 1903), p. 51.

7 The World of Legend

1. Tuefferd et Ganier, *Récits et légendes d'Alsace,* Berger-Levrault, 1884.

2. Charles Buet, *Légendes des bords du lac,* Tours, 1888.

3. Hervé de Rauville, *Trois Légendes de l'Ile-de-France* (Challamel, 1889).

4. *La Tradition: revue générale des contes, légendes;* afterward *Revue internationale du folklore,* 1st series, April 1887 to April 1897.

5. See Michaud, *Message poétique,* p. 255 ff.

6. Quoted ibid., p. 208.

7. Kahn, *Les Palais nomades,* p. 116.

8. Gustave Kahn, *Le Conte de l'or et du silence* (Paris: Mercure de France, 1898), p. 116.

9. Edouard Schuré, *Les Grandes Légendes de France* (Paris: Perrin, 1892), pp. ii–iv.

10. Jean Moréas, *Les Premières Armes du symbolisme* (Paris: Vanier, 1889), pp. 33–34.

11. Saint-Antoine, "Qu'est-ce que le symbolisme," *L'Ermitage,* June 1894. Article reprinted by Michaud, *Message poétique,* pp. 748–50.

12. Quoted by Pierre Martino, *Parnasse et symbolisme* (Paris: Armand Colin, 1925), p. 162.

13. A. Ségard, *Les Voluptueux et les hommes d'action* (Paris: Ollendorff, 1900), p. 88.

14. Mauclair, *L'Art en silence.*

15. See Michaud, *Message poétique,* p. 749.

16. Ibid., p. 754.

17. Huret, *Enquête sur l'évolution littéraire.*

18. See analysis by Jouanny in *Jean Moréas,* p. 347.

19. Kahn, *Le Conte de l'or et du silence,* Avertissement au lecteur.

20. Dorothy Knowles, *La Réaction idéaliste au théâtre* (Paris: Droz, 1934), p. 138 ff; Robichez, *Le Symbolisme au théâtre,* p. 116.

21. Adolphe Retté, *Arabesques* (Paris: Editions de La Plume, 1899), pp. 19–20. Quoted by Marcel Schneider, *La Littérature fantastique en France* (Paris: Fayard, 1964), pp. 273–74.

22. Mauclair, *L'Art en silence*, p. 203.

23. For a more detailed study of contemporary painting, see Philippe Jullian, *Esthètes et magiciens* (Paris: Perrin, 1969).

24. Adolphe Retté, *Cloches dans la nuit* (Paris, 1889), p. 72.

25. Cf. Jullian, *Esthètes et magiciens*, p. 318.

26. *La Vogue*, June-July 1886, then *Moralités légendaires*.

27. Hartley, *Oscar Wilde*, p. 22.

28. Oscar Wilde, *Salomé, drame en un acte* (Paris: Librairie de l'Art indépendant, 1893); *Salomé* by Oscar Wilde (London: Elkin Mathews and John Lane, 1894). See also the recent republication of the first edition in facsimile by Dover (New York, 1967).

29. Jullian, *Esthètes et magiciens*, p. 319, illustration 97.

30. See *L'Arte Moderna*, vol. 6 *Il Simbolismo*, by Renato Barilli (Milan, Fratelli Fabbri), pp. 281–84, and *Chefs-d'oeuvre de l'art*, no. 99, *Klimt* (Paris: Hachette, 1968).

31. Jullian, *Esthètes et magiciens*, p. 132.

32. Schuré, *Précurseurs et révoltés*, p. 336.

33. Ibid., p. 356.

34. Bernard Lazare, *Le Sacrifice, Miroir des légendes* (Paris: Lemerre, 1892), pp. 39–51 (Bacchus); Régnier, *Poèmes*, p. 54 (Ariadne).

35. *Orphée*, Piccadilly Gallery. See Jullian, *Esthètes et magiciens*, illustration no. 66.

36. Ibid., pp. 52–53.

37. Ibid., illustration no. 86.

38. Camille Mauclair, *Eleusis: Causeries sur la cité intérieure* (Paris: Perrin, 1894), p. 9.

39. Appeared in *Le Journal* of 18 June 1898, then in *Princesses d'ivoire et d'ivresse*.

40. 1858. Cf. Leslie Parris, *The Preraphaelites* (London: Tate Gallery, 1966), no. 32.

41. *Parsifal*, which Wagner worked on for nearly twenty-five years was finished only in 1882, and performed that year.

42. Jullian, *Esthètes et magiciens*, p. 67.

43. Jan Lorrain, *Théâtre* (Paris: Ollendorff, 1905). See also Pierre-Léon Gauthier, "Jean Lorrain," thesis, Paris, 1935, p. 205 ff. This critic sums up the main characteristics of these plays as follows: "Their subjects are fairy land; the settings, a dreamworld; the characters, symbols."

44. See Roger Bodart, *Maeterlinck* (Paris: Seghers, 1962), p. 17; Knowles, *La Reaction idéaliste*, p. 179; Robichez, *Le Symbolisme au théâtre*, pp. 81–82.

45. See biography of Gustave Kahn, published 1890 in *Hommes d'aujourd'hui*.

46. Retté, *Le Symbolisme*, pp. 116–17.

47. Edmond Jaloux, *Les Saisons littéraires*, p. 51.

8 Elemental Reverie

1. Guy Michaud, *Le Thème du miroir dans le symbolisme français*, Cahiers de l'Association internationale des Etudes françaises, no. 2, May 1959, pp. 199–216.

2. Michaud, *Message poétique*, p. 288.

3. Jean Lorrain, *Sensations et souvenirs*, p. 12: "It was already a strange pleasure, given my age, to yield to the fascination of water. Water has always attracted me, led me astray, and its spell over me still remains."

4. Michaud, *Le Thème du miroir*.

5. Laforgue, *Moralités légendaires*, pp. 223–24.

6. Henri de Régnier, *Quelqu'un songe de soir et d'espoir, Poèmes anciens et romanesques, Poèmes* (Paris: Mercure de France, 1895), p 170.

7. Marcel Schwob, *Le Roi au masque d'or* (Paris: Crès, 1917), p. 13.

8. Gabriel Mourey, *Monada* (Paris: Ollendorff, 1894), pp. 65–66.

9. *Mercure de France*, vol. 5, 1892, p. 147.

10. Henri de Régnier, *Hertulie*, 1894, reprinted in *La Canne de jaspe* (Paris: Mercure de France, 1926), pp. 166–67; see Suzanne Bernard, *Le Poème en prose*, p. 521, n. 276, for text and comparison to Mallarmé's *Igitur*.

11. Rachilde, *Le Démon de l'absurde* (Paris: Mercure de France, 1894), p. 22.

12. Rodenbach, *Bruges-la-morte*, p. 8.

13. Retté, *Cloches dans la nuit*, p. 25.

14. Regnier, *Poèmes*, p. 24.

15. Mauclair, *L'Ennemie des rêves*, pp. 44–45.

16. Lorrain, *La Forêt bleue*, p. 59.

17. See Simone Hatem, *L'Empire des perles* (Paris: Plon, 1956), pp. 102–3.

18. Carassus, *Le Snobisme*, p. 159.

19. *Mercure de France*, May 1890, p. 173.

20. André Lebois, *Les tendances du symbolisme à travers l'oeuvre d'Elémir Bourges* (Paris: L'Amitié pour le livre, 1952), pp. 273–74.

21. Quoted by Jullian, *Esthètes et magiciens*, p. 189.

22. See R. E. Knowles, *Victor-Emile Michelet*, pp. 270–76.

23. André Gide, *Romans* (Paris: Bibliothèque de la Pléiade, 1958), p. 54.

24. See E. Jannetaz, *Diamants et pierres précieuses* (Paris: J. Rothschild, 1881), p. 479.

25. Louis Denise, *La Merveilleuse Doxologie des lapidaires* (Paris: Mercure de France, 1893), p. 13.

26. Victor-Emile Michelet, *Les Secrets des pierres précieuses, Initiation*, March 1894, pp. 195–96; *L'Amour et la magie* (Paris: Chacornac, 1936).

27. Ibid., pp. 198–99.

28. Ibid., p. 200.

29. Some of the principal works on Wagner available in French, apart from Schuré's *Le Drame musical* of 1875, were: *Richard Wagner* by Judith Gautier (Paris: Charavay, 1882), and *Richard Wagner* by Catulle Mendès (Paris: Charpentier, 1886), both of which contain detailed synopses of the major operas; and the works of Alfred Ernst (1887), H. S. Chamberlain (1894), and Albert Lavignac (1897). Moreover the libretti of the major works were translated at the same period

more than once. *The Ring* appeared in translation in both 1894 and 1895: *La Tétralogie*, with commentary by L. P. de Brinn Gaubast and E. Barthelemy (Paris: Dentu, 1894); *L'Anneau des Nibelung*, trans. J. d'Offoel (Paris: Fischbacher, 1895).

30. See Gaston Bachelard on the theme he terms "petrifying reverie," in *La Terre et les rêveries de la volonté* (Paris: Corti, 1948), p. 205 ff.

31. See for example, *Petits Mystères*, especially *Mets de la lune dans ton vin* in Laforgue, *Poésies complètes*, p. 164.

32. Ibid., p. 141: this text has already been quoted and commented on by Bachelard, *La Terre et les rêveries*, p. 221.

33. J. H. Rosny, *La Mort de la terre* (Paris: Plon, 1912), pp. 2–3.

34. Emile Zola, *Les Rougon-Macquart*, vol. 2 (Paris: Editions du Seuil, 1970), p. 79. See also pp. 84 and 89.

35. *Mercure de France*, 1899, and *Contes et nouvelles* (Paris: Mercure de France, 1900), pp. 53–69.

36. See Nikolaus Pevsner, *Pioneers of Modern Design* (Penguin, 1964); *The Sources of Modern Architecture and Design* (Praeger, 1968); Maurice Rheims, *L'Art 1900* (Paris, Art et métiers graphiques); Roger-H. Guerrand, *L'Art Nouveau en Europe* (Paris: Plon, 1965). There are a number of useful comments on the definition of Art Nouveau in Philippe Jullian's work as well, and also in the two catalogues for the exhibition *Pionniers du XXe siècle*, at the Musée des Arts Décoratifs.

37. In his famous work on the baroque, Eugenio d'Ors, asserting the existence of a permanent baroque current running throughout the history of world art, explicitly connects late-nineteenth-century art with the baroque esthetic. See Eugenio d'Ors, *Lo Barroco* (Madrid: M. Aguilar [1944?]), pp. 137 and 146.

38. See *The Later Work of Aubrey Beardsley* (New York: Dover 1967).

39. See *Art Nouveau: An Anthology of Design and Illustration from the Studio* (New York: Dover, 1969).

40. Eugène Grasset, *Méthode de composition ornementale* (Paris: Librairie centrale des Beaux-Arts, n.d.) vol. 2, *Eléments courbes*, pp. 160–61.

41. Jean Lahor, *L'Art Nouveau* (Paris: Lemerre, 1901), p. 13.

42. See above, note 39.

43. Pierre Loti, *Le Désert* (Paris: Calmann-Lévy, 1895), pp. 14, 25–26.

44. Gustave Flaubert, *Oeuvres complètes*, vol. 1 (Paris: Editions du Seuil, 1964), p. 571.

45. Leprieur, *Gustave Moreau et son oeuvre*, p. 29.

46. See Suzanne Bernard, *Le Poème en prose*, p. 480.

47. *Mercure de France*, March 1896, then in *Les Vies encloses*. See also Pierre Maes, *Georges Rodenbach* (Gembloud: Duculot, 1952), p. 168 ff.

48. Edouard Ducoté, *Merveilles et moralités* (Paris: Mercure de France, 1900), p. 148.

Conclusion

1. Guy Michaud, *Message poétique*, p. 481: "Thus, in a few writers over-preoccupied with the rare and the refined, symbolism came to an end. With them it was returning to its origins, the decadence."

2. See Decaudin, *Crise des valeurs symbolistes*, p. 86: "One finds a disaffection with regard to symbolism everywhere"; p. 99: "There is constant talk about life, health, social art, and the death of symbolism [in 1899]."

3. Ibid., p. 103.

4. On Retté's development at this time see ibid., pp. 29–33.

5. Ibid., pp. 58–80.

6. Ibid., p. 94.

7. Maurice Le Blond, *Essai sur le naturisme* (Paris: Mercure de France, 1896), p. 20.

8. Ibid., p. 31.

9. Retté, *Aspects*, p. 41.

10. Le Blond, *Essai sur le naturisme*, p. 52.

11. Mauclair, *L'Ennemie des rêves*, p. x.

12. Maurice Pujo, *La Crise morale* (Paris: Perrin, 1898), p. 9.

13. Décaudin, *Crise des valeurs symbolistes*, p. 55: "In 1895 to 1896 one also finds the most various and often unrelated manifestations of a reaction against symbolism and its excesses in the name of life close to nature, of the city, of feelings, of simplicity, and of clarity."

14. Quoted in Adolphe Retté, *Aspects* (Paris: Bibliothèque artistique et littéraire, 1897), p. 194.

15. Le Blond, *Essai sur le naturisme*, p. 14.

16. Retté, *Aspects*, p. 49; text quoted by Cornell, *Adolphe Retté*, p. 76, and by Décaudin, *Crise des valeurs symbolistes*, p. 33, n.32.

17. Décaudin, *Crise des valeurs symbolistes*, pp. 52–53.

18. Hughes Rebell, "La Poésie française," *Ermitage*, October 1893, p. 159.

19. Décaudin, *Crise des valeurs symbolistes*, p. 35.

20. Ibid., p. 41.

21. Ibid., p. 61.

22. Ibid., p. 38.

23. Ibid., p. 60.

24. Quoted ibid., p. 60.

25. Ibid., pp. 46–47.

26. Henri Lichtenberger, *La Philosophie de Nietzsche* (Paris: Alcan, 1898). See also Frédéric Nietzsche, *Le Cas Wagner: Un Problème musical*, trans. D. Halévy and R. Dreyfus (Paris: A. Schulz, 1893).

27. *Ermitage*, January 1893, p. 67.

28. *Mercure de France*, December 1894, p. 392. Other articles, apart from those cited by Décaudin, *Crise des valeurs symbolistes*, p. 46, n.94, are: E. Schuré, "L'Individualisme et l'anarchie en littérature," *Revue des Deux Mondes*, 15 August, 1895; T. de Wyzewa, "La Jeunesse de Frédéric Nietzsche," *Revue des Deux Mondes*, 1 February 1896.

29. *Revue blanche:* April, *La Morale ou la contre-nature;* August, *Nietzsche contre Wagner;* 15 September, *Pensées vagabondes d'un intempestif.*

30. Adolphe Retté, *Promenades subversives,* (Paris: Bibliothèque artistique et littéraire, 1896), pp. 35–36.

31. The organizers summed up the results as follows: 23 in favor of constraint (6 aristocrats, 10 socialists, 7 authoritarians); 24 intermediates (4 wanting constraint and liberty, 3 hesitant, 6 wanting to decide according to individual issues, 11 didn't care); 52 in favor of liberty (14 moderate liberals, 27 liberals, 11 anarchist liberals).

32. *Ermitage,* July 1893, p. 6. See also Victor-Emile Michelet: "As for the preferences of the artist, in my opinion they will always be for liberty without restrictions" (p. 14); Pierre Quillard: "Every political or social hierarchy is necessarily arbitrary, stupid, and harmful" (p. 16).

33. The anarchists included Louis-Ferdinand Hérold, Tristan Klingsor, Roland de Marès, Maurice Pujo, Vielé-Griffin.

34. *Ermitage,* July 1893, p. 21.

35. Mauclair, *Servitude et grandeur littéraires,* pp. 114–15.

36. Ibid., p. 117.

37. Bernard Lazare, *L'Ecrivain et l'art social* (Paris: Bibliothèque de l'art social, [1896]).

38. See A. B. Jackson, *La Revue blanche* (Paris: Minard, 1960), chap. 7, pp. 101–15.

39. *Hommage des artistes à Picquart,* preface by Octave Mirbeau (Paris: Société libre d'Edition des gens de lettres, 1899). Among the signatories were Anatole France, Mirbeau, Saint-Georges de Bouhélier, Ferdinand Hérold, Pierre Quillard, Paul Alexis, Gustave Kahn, Valéry, Robert de Flers, Abel Hermant, Edouard Schuré, and so on.

40. Pierre Quillard, *Le Monument Henry* (Paris: Stock, 1889). Among the names are Gaston Deschamps, Drumont, Gautier-Villars, Jean Lorrain, Pierre Louys, Rochefort, Valéry ("not without reflection").

41. See Jackson, *La Revue blanche,* p. 107: "For pardoning Dreyfus was not enough in itself to soothe the passions the *Affaire* had raised. For many writers the Dreyfus Affair was the crisis of conscience that led them to socialism."

42. André Breton, *Nadja* (Paris: Gallimard, 1928), p. 15: "That is how I find myself with the Huysmans of *En rade* and *Là-bas*—sharing ways of appreciating everything that offers itself, selecting with the partiality of despair from all that is, so that although, unhappily, I have never known him other than through is work, he is still perhaps the least alien of my friends."

43. Louis Aragon, "Lautréamont et nous," *Lettres françaises,* 1 June 1967.

44. See letter to Adrienne Monnier, published in *Les Lettres nouvelles,* June - 1953, p. 510.

45. See Décaudin, *Crise des valeurs symbolistes,* pp. 249–67.

46. See in particular ibid., pp. 306–7, and Suzanne Bernard, *Le Poème en prose,* pp. 583–84.

47. André Beaunier, "Les Parnassiens et les symbolistes," *Mercure de France,* February 1901, p. 387.

48. Ibid., p. 384.

49. Marcel Raymond, *De Baudelaire au Surréalisme* (Paris: Correa, 1933), p. 222.

50. Suzanne Bernard, *Le Poème en prose*, p. 584.

51. Décaudin, *Crise des valeurs symbolistes*, p. 307.

52. *La Chronique*, Brussels, 18 December 1910.

53. Franz Hellens, *Nocturnal, précédé de Quinze Histoires* (Brussels: Les Cahiers indépendants, 1919).

54. Franz Hellen, *Mélusine, Edition définitive* (Paris: Gallimard, 1952), Avant-propos, p. 11.

55. Victor-Emile Michelet, *Contes surhumains* (Paris: Chamuel, 1900); *Les Portes d'airain* (Paris: Figuière, 1919).

56. On John-Antoine Nau, see biography by Jean Royère in *Thérèse Donati* (Paris: Editions françaises illustrées, 1921).

57. Julien Gracq, *Spectre de Poisson soluble*, in *André Breton: Essais et témoignages* (Neufchâtel: La Baconnière, 1949), pp. 184–86.

58. André Breton, *La Beauté sera convulsive, Minotaure*, no. 5, 1939, p. 13.

59. Maurice Nadeau, *Michel Leiris ou la quadrature du cercle* (Dossiers des Lettres nouvelles, Julliard, 1953), pp. 38–39, 56–60.

60. Michel Leiris, *Le Point cardinal* (Editions du Sagittaire, 1927), p. 28.

61. Michel Leiris, *Aurora* (Paris: Gallimard, 1946), p. 81.

62. Louis Aragon, *Anicet* (Gallimard, 1921; Livre de Poche, 1969), pp. 30–31.

INDEX